# Animal Breeding, Welfare and Society

# Animal Breeding, Welfare and Society

Jacky Turner

Hillsborough Community
College LRC

earthscan

publishing for a sustainable future
London • Washington, DC

First published in 2010 by Earthscan

Earthscan Ltd, Dunstan House, 14a St Cross Street, London EC1N 8XA, UK
Earthscan LLC, 1616 P Street, NW, Washington, DC 20036, USA

Earthscan publishes in association with the International Institute for Environment and Development

For more information on Earthscan publications, see www.earthscan.co.uk
or write to earthinfo@earthscan.co.uk

ISBN   978-1-84407-588-1     hardback
       978-1-84407-589-8     paperback

Typeset by MapSet Ltd, Gateshead, UK
Cover design by Susanne Harris

A catalogue record for this book is available from the British Library

Library of Congress Cataloging-in-Publication Data

Turner, Jacky.
Animal breeding, welfare, and society / Jacky Turner.
    p. cm.
  Includes bibliographical references and index.
  ISBN 978-1-84407-588-1 (hardback) — ISBN 978-1-84407-589-8 (pbk.) 1. Animal breeding—Moral and ethical aspects. 2. Animal behavior. 3. Animal welfare. 4. Animal population eugenics.
  I. Title.
  SF105.T87 2010
  636.08'2—dc22

                                                                          2009052603

Mixed Sources
Product group from well-managed
forests and other controlled sources
www.fsc.org  Cert no. SGS-COC-2482
© 1996 Forest Stewardship Council

# Contents

# Acknowledgements

Several organizations and individuals kindly gave permission for the use of images, as acknowledged in the figure legends. I have been much helped by information originally gathered by animal protection organizations, including Compassion in World Farming, Advocates for Animals, Animal Aid, Humane Society of the United States, Royal Society for the Prevention of Cruelty to Animals, National Anti-Vivisection Society, DawnWatch, Farmed Animal Net, and several others as cited in the text. I would like to thank the academic reviewers of various chapters, including Professors Stephen Hall, Clive Phillips and John Webster, and Drs Jack Murphy and David Sargan, for their comments and suggestions, and to thank Professor Peter Goodfellow and other scientists who kindly answered questions. I am very much indebted to Dr Anne Sykes for numerous improvements and corrections to the original text. All remaining errors and inadequacies are mine.

# Introduction

This may be the century when the human interaction with non-human animals on the planet, direct or indirect, moves from management to absolute control. Selective breeding and the application of genetic and reproductive technologies are probably the most important ways in which we exercise this control. The determination of when, how, how often and with whom an animal breeds has moved ever further from natural selection and ever nearer to human purposes and human choices: these include the breeding and use of around 50 billion domestic mammals and birds for food production annually, the breeding of pedigree dogs, cats, racing dogs and horses, and specialized laboratory animal strains. The expansion of human activity to nearly every global environment and every animal habitat means that we find ourselves taking ever greater control over wild animals too, either to preserve or to manage their populations.

Genetic selection of livestock has become an industrial undertaking. The selection of which animals we want to breed from has moved away from assessments made on the basis of appearance and past performance of the animal and its parentage and is increasingly made on the basis of the animal's genes. In some applications, we are increasingly able and willing to manipulate the animal's DNA directly, or at least to collect and store genetic material for future use. Genetically engineered or mutant animals now account for nearly half of all the animals used in laboratory experiments in Britain. Animal genetics is supported by a large professional structure from laboratory and veterinary science to technical services such as artificial insemination and embryo transfer, and by international breeding companies that operate globally.

Reproductive and genetic technology is already used in the breeding of endangered species in zoos and to maintain genetic diversity in small populations of endangered, rare or traditional breeds and species. These technologies are beginning to be used to limit what we judge to be the overpopulation of particular wild species and to control populations of pest and non-native animals when these conflict with human goals.

Often the human control of animal breeding and its ethical basis have been taken for granted. Who would have doubted that breeding a faster-growing chicken, a woollier sheep, a smaller dog or a faster racehorse was a worthwhile enterprise? But how do our efforts impact on the animals themselves, and do they match up to our aspirations about how animal welfare should be respected?

> ## THE METHODS FOR CONTROL OF ANIMAL BREEDING AVAILABLE IN THE 21ST CENTURY
>
> The range of methods for controlling animal breeding includes:
>
> - hormonal control of oestrus;
> - semen collection and storage;
> - fixed-time artificial insemination;
> - embryo transfer;
> - cryopreservation;
> - superovulation;
> - egg harvesting and in vitro fertilization;
> - ovarian and testicular tissue transplants;
> - pregnancy testing and scanning;
> - contraception and sterilization;
> - advancing breeding season;
> - breeding at younger ages;
> - reducing interval to next pregnancy;
> - induction of birth;
> - control of birth environment;
> - pedigree analysis;
> - performance analysis;
> - genomic selection (performance and behavioural traits, health);
> - genome analysis (parentage and relatedness);
> - embryo selection (health, performance traits);
> - genetic engineering and cloning.

## Health and natural behaviour

On the whole, we breed animals for our own benefit, not for theirs. Breeding goals are not always balanced. Some selective breeding has had a range of negative impacts for animals. These include their health, their marketability and their value to humans – and hence their survival prospects and ability to adapt to the conditions we keep them in. Some modern livestock breeds cannot maintain their own health for more than a fraction of their natural lifespans. Too many companion animal breeds carry inherited defects due to inbreeding or to selection for conformations that predispose them to problems of the eye, skin, skeleton, heart and respiratory system.

For many domesticated species, the animals' reproductive lives include some of their most important evolved social behaviour and motivations. Modern mass animal production usually requires that we disrupt or prevent animals' natural reproductive behaviour, including the bonds between mothers and offspring. The dairy industry routinely removed calves from their mothers at one day old. How much does this matter to the animals? Can animals be said to have an interest in following their natural breeding behaviour patterns?

## Assessing benefit and harm

In Britain, the Farm Animal Welfare Council expressed concern ten years ago that 'an attitude may be developing which condones the moulding of animals to humankind's uses, irrespective of their own nature and welfare'.[1] In fact, there is nothing new or modern in the human desire to mould animals to our needs. We have been selectively breeding animals for hundreds, if not thousands, of years. What is new, however, is our ability in this century to do it faster and more effectively and with much greater potential for benefit or harm.

The management of animal populations touches on many aspects of human activity and thinking. It is often based on deep-rooted human assumptions about our place in nature and our right or need to control it, on the pursuit of scientific discovery and economic progress, and also on less noble qualities including, often, indifference to the interests of other species. Ever since humans have consciously used animal breeding as a tool to achieve certain human-defined goals, we have put enormous technical, social and emotional resources into the enterprise. Most often, in history, people's wants and needs have been the first consideration and the impact on the animals has been secondary. But a greater scientific understanding of animals' behaviour, emotions and capacity to suffer in recent decades has led to a questioning and re-evaluation of practices that has a long way still to go. The following chapters look at where we are now in the light of past and potential future practices in animal breeding, what the balance sheet may be from the point of view of animal well-being, and how we could do better in the future.

## Note

1   Farm Animal Welfare Council (1998) *Report on the Implication of Cloning for the Welfare of Farmed Livestock: Part II. Ethical Considerations*, Farm Animal Welfare Council

# 1

# The Industrialization of
# Animal Genetics

During 2007 the world bred an estimated 50 billion chickens, 1.2 billion pigs and 240 million calves born to milking cows.[1] The scale of human effort in food animal breeding – from backyard pig-pen to genetics laboratory – dwarfs that of any of the other ways in which we intervene in the reproduction of animals. This chapter examines how systems of food animal breeding have developed since their roots in 18th-century breed 'improvement' up to the specialist and global commercial companies that offer to supply the best farm animal genetics of today and tomorrow, and outlines some of the implications for animal welfare.

## 1.1 Background and context: From local to global

Humans have been making deliberate breeding decisions in order to change the physical characteristics and often the behaviour of the animals brought under human control since the beginnings of domestication. For these animals, the needs and choices of people have long ago replaced the evolutionary pressure of the environment as the main driver of genetic change, over timescales that range from thousands of years to a few decades. And the theoretical and technical tools at our disposal for doing this are now sufficiently powerful for animal breeding to have transformed from a cottage industry based on the individual breeder's assessment of his, or his neighbours', animals into a globalized science-based industry. Many aspects of food animal breeding may soon be based on animal genome analysis rather than the eye of the breeder, backed by an arsenal of tests, reproductive techniques and hormone treatments. The very term 'animal breeding' is being displaced by 'genetic selection' or 'animal genetics', signalling, or at least intending to signal, the arrival of a truly scientific and technical approach to controlling animal reproduction.

In areas of domestic animal breeding that operate with relatively low numbers of individual animals, such as dog or horse breeding, breeding decisions are still made on the basis of an animal's individual appearance or performance and parentage, and the subjective assessment of the breeder. Genetic tests are used to confirm parentage and increasingly to test for inherited disease, but tradition is still restricting the extent to which science and

> #### BOX 1.1 ANIMAL BREEDING DEFINED
>
> The words 'breeding' and 'reproducing' have essentially the same dictionary meaning and in natural conditions animals breed (or reproduce) without human intervention. The term 'animal breeding' usually has a different meaning and implies the human control of the reproductive processes of animals in order to achieve a particular outcome. 'Animal breeding' usually means that the breeder is making, or attempting to make, a genetic selection of his or her breeding animals in order to achieve genetic change within the animal population.

industry impacts breeding methods. Perhaps we also resist interpreting these animals who we know as individuals in terms of bundles of more or less useful genes. In contrast, the food animal production industry has seen more potential advantage in embracing genetic and reproductive technology to achieve market goals such as high yield, uniformity and predictability, constant supply, and specific production qualities such as body conformation or resistance to economically damaging production-related diseases.

### 1.1.1 Pre-industrial animal breeding

Although people have bred animals for millennia, the concept of the scientific 'improvement' of a breed is a relatively recent one from a historical perspective. It owes much to modern ideas about the desirability and inevitability of continuous scientific, economic and social progress that developed during and since the 18th-century 'Enlightenment'. In earlier times, the aim of animal breeders was often just to maintain their animals' health and productivity rather than lose it, which in itself was difficult enough. There is even evidence that owners may sometimes have bred from their least fit rather than their most fit animals, so the most fit could be sold or otherwise utilized.[2] By the beginning of the 20th century, in contrast, changes in science and society combined to create a series of revolutions in animal breeding that we are still living through. These included the new scientific understanding of evolutionary genetic change and the statistical basis of inheritance; a strong belief in progress towards not only ideal and innovative industrial products but also an ideal genetics (for both people and animals); and rapidly growing and urbanizing world populations and demand for animal-based foods.

Selective breeding simply means that the farmer or breeder identifies certain desired traits for his or her animals and decides which animals should mate with which other animals with the aim of transmitting their desirable traits to the next generation. Animals with less desirable traits are not permitted to breed. Initially, this would not necessarily have entailed any intention to create or maintain a uniform 'breed' in the modern sense. Selective breeding must initially have been done on the basis of a subjective assessment of ability (speed, strength, sense of smell, eyesight) and desired appearance (perceived beauty, shape or size, colour, coat) or food production traits (musculature, milk yield, early maturity). This was done without any of our contemporary knowledge of genetic and statistical methods of studying the inheritance of traits.

By whatever decision-making method, selective breeding has been carried out over millennia of human history. The old dog Argus, who was the only living individual to recognize Odysseus when he returned to his home in Ithaca after the Trojan War, had been bred in Bronze Age Greece for his speed and power in the hunt, as well as, presumably, his loyalty to humans.[3] By 800 BCE the Chinese had already classified dogs by type into hunting dogs, guard dogs and edible dogs.[4] In Thoroughbred horse breeding, the professional breeder's intuition has always had a certain mystique. Hence, the racehorse breeder and trainer Federico Tesio (1869–1954) was known as the 'Wizard of Dormello' (the name of his stud farm) and was said to exhibit 'genius'.[5] According to his memoirs, in his 50 years of breeding he 'never had in mind theories or principles', but worked on the basis of 'his own impressions', guided by his belief that 'Only the best are entitled to reproduce.'[6]

## 1.1.2 Selective breeding by design: 18th- and 19th-century livestock breeds

Robert Bakewell (1725–1795) is normally credited with starting the process of trying to standardize and corner the market in deliberately 'improved' livestock breeds. But the term 'improvement' of livestock, as used by Bakewell's contemporaries onward, and later the term 'genetic progress', are not strictly objective. 'Improvement' and 'progress' mean that animals become more useful for certain human uses – in other words more commercially productive – but self-evidently this does not necessarily mean that the change is an improvement for the animals. As a result, most modern scientists use the term 'genetic change' which is a factual description rather than an evaluation. Genetic change can be either positive or negative from the point of view of animal welfare.

Certain traits that breeders want are not visible in the parents – an obvious example being how a bull transmits milking ability to his daughters – or it is not known how well the traits can be transmitted. Therefore a bull's genetic value has to be judged through the performance and health of his daughters. Bakewell is also credited with the first systematic use of 'progeny testing', in other words assessing the value of a particular animal as a genetic parent by assessing his or her offspring. Bakewell did this by 'letting' his rams to farmers to inseminate as many ewes as possible and recording the productivity of as large as possible number of his offspring.[7] With the addition of modern statistics and computational science, this is still the main method used today in the evaluation of breeding animals.

By 1700 in Britain there were a variety of livestock types, known as 'unimproved' and often regionally based, that had been very little changed for hundreds of years. In the 18th century there was a huge enthusiasm for 'improving' them by both selective breeding and intensive feeding. Farmers started to 'set much store by blood and fashion', as Josiah Twamley wrote in 1784 in his *Dairying Exemplified*,[7] amounting to a national obsession which was recorded in numerous portraits of the individual animals and breeds.[8]

Improvement essentially meant a higher productivity for meat. Bakewell is best known for his 'improvement' or creation of the longhorn cattle and the new Leicester sheep breeds as single-purpose meat-producing animals, or 'butcher's beasts'. He probably did this by like-to-like mating to obtain animals that showed his ideal traits, followed by inbreeding to fix the traits in the breed so that he had males and females who were homozygous for those traits. Animal welfare was probably a low priority. Some believed that 'in-and-in breeding had been carried to a dangerous extent'[7] and Bakewell's inbred pigs were described as 'rickety' or 'fools'. A mid 19th-century livestock show in London was said to exhibit 'panting porkers, asthmatic sheep, and apoplectic oxen'[8] as a result of a fashion for producing animals that were as large and fat and possible.

It was understood that an ideal meat animal should be designed to fatten as fast as possible, and that the maximum possible proportion of the body should be meat rather than inedible parts such as bone. Nineteenth-century livestock portraits show idealized animals with large rectangular or barrel-shaped bodies, bulging with fat and muscle, carrying tiny heads and legs. A mid 19th-century portrait of a new Leicester wether (male sheep) shows the animal's face only just visible within the encircling folds of fat and fleece.[8] The shape of meat animals changed so that they resembled something more like a block rather than a wedge by redistributing muscle from the front to the rear.[7] (Today's breeders also often picture their meat animals from the rear as well as from the side to display their heavily muscled buttocks.)

Selection for milk production also started, and by the end of the 18th century the dairy farmer's main aim was said to be to 'have cows with good bags, or udders; that yield a quantity of milk'.[7] During the 19th century, large-scale zero-grazing urban dairies were set up to supply the towns (where feed was brought to the cows, rather than the cows grazing on pasture). By the end of the century, the selection of cattle into single-purpose (meat or milk) breeds was well under way. Selective breeding had moved the shorthorn, the Scottish beef breeds, the Herefords and the Devon cattle towards meat production and the Ayrshire and Channel Island breeds towards milk production. In the last quarter of the 19th century large numbers of Friesian cattle were imported to Britain from continental Europe and by the mid 20th century were the most used dairy breed.[7]

The primary aims of pre-20th-century livestock breeders were thus essentially the same as those of today: to increase the production and cost effectiveness of the animals for the commercial benefit of the breeder and the farmer, and to increase the food supply to the consumer. Bakewell famously aimed to 'put meat on every table'. An essential and modern aspect of Bakewell's method was that he and his successors were solely pedigree breeders, not meat producers, as were the farmers who rented the 'improved' male animals for mating. In this he can be seen as the precursor of the modern

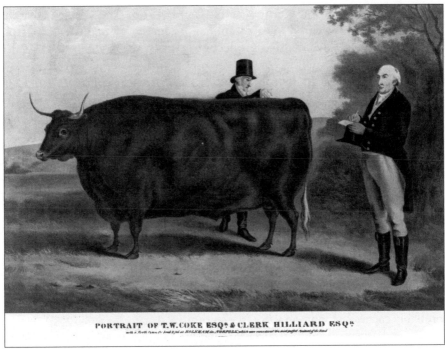

PORTRAIT OF T.W.COKE ESQ⁵ & CLERK HILLIARD ESQ⁵

© Museum of English Rural Life, University of Reading

**Figure 1.1** *The leading livestock 'improver' Thomas Coke (1752–1842) with a Devon ox that he had bred and that was 'considered the most perfect animal of its kind'*[8]

animal genetics industry, professionalized and to a large extent separate from farming. Bakewell's chosen role was to define what was needed (more muscle, smaller bones, faster growth rate), produce animals that had these traits and sell a genetic package in the form of his sheep and bulls to be used as sires. Before this, not only the cattle but the farmers were 'dual-purpose', both breeding and producing meat and milk. The separation of food production and elite animal breeding made it possible for the breeders to cull ruthlessly and never to breed from animals that were not considered a desirable contribution to the next generation.[7] A working farmer, on the other hand, could not afford not to breed from animals that were less than ideal.

Over the last 60 years the practice of animal reproduction has been transformed by reproductive and genetic science, pharmaceuticals such as antibiotics and reproductive hormones, and by the globalization of the market. Animal breeding is now an agri-industrial enterprise whose research and development is funded by corporations and taxpayers alike. Most countries' taxpayers support either state-run animal breeding institutes or research funding, through such bodies as the US Department of Agriculture, the French National Institute for Agricultural Research (INRA), and the Department for

Environment, Food and Rural Affairs (Defra) in the UK. Their research agendas are mainly geared towards animal productivity and disease control within existing, mostly intensive, production systems.

### 1.1.3 From breeds to brands: The global breeding companies

In 2007 a representative of the global poultry breeding company Aviagen described the transformation of breeds into brands over the last quarter century as a process where 'Concentration of breeding into fewer companies has both assisted and driven the development of multiple products within brands and development of the gene pools of different brands to facilitate this.'[9] Pre-modern animal breeders often believed that the traits of a particular animal breed were the result of the geography and climate of its place of origin;[2] but the globalization of animal breeding stands this belief on its head. Today's top animal breeds are global, recruited into the corporate culture and given genetic performance targets to fulfil. They operate in a standardized environment (indoor housing, temperature control, feed composition and quantity) around the world. A modern sow in a modern pig farm in Vietnam is expected to produce the same number of piglets per year as a sow in Iowa. She probably carries the same genetics (see section 1.2.1).

Several aspects of industrialization that are familiar from other consumer products, such as cars and computers, have taken place in animal reproduction. The most important can be listed as:

- the systematic testing and record-keeping of animals' breeding performance, followed by the worldwide dissemination of results to consumers (in this case, farmers);
- assigning a standardized value (in monetary or production terms) of the genetic material of any particular potential breeding animal to the consumer, ranked in relation to others;
- the creation of recognizable brands carrying technical specifications and differentiated for different market sectors;
- globalization of the brands and products.

Of course, many farmers continue to have little contact with the professional breeding companies and their genetic wares. They still obtain breeding animals or semen, in the case of dairy cattle, from other farmers who own pedigree herds. Others still choose their bulls and rams by eye at market. Individual farmers still select their own animals for breeding and employ cross-breeding to maintain hybrid vigour and desired production and health traits, particularly in the less industrialized sheep and extensive beef production. But livestock advisers emphasize the financial benefits of using rams and beef bulls that have a scientifically guaranteed performance in terms of a 'breeding value', even if invisible to the naked eye, rather than those which merely appear attractive. Breeding value is a standard measure of the superiority of an animal, in some commercial respect, compared to the rest of the breed. Advisers point out that you should no more use a ram whose genetics are outdated than use a 1979 tractor.[10]

Increasingly, though, the primary breeding and selection decisions for maximally productive livestock are made at the level of international companies that provide breeding animals and semen, and sometimes embryos. These companies often refer to themselves as providers of animal genetic material (or 'animal genetics'). They seek to provide selectively bred livestock suitable for all customers, from the most intensive and low-cost producers of chickens and pigs, through animals more suited to free-range lives or with particular meat characteristics for a particular market, through to pedigree high-value cattle. In the most commercial sections of food animal breeding, these companies may well be making the decisions that dictate the direction of genetic change.

The global cattle- and pig-breeding company Genus incorporates ABS (dairy and beef cattle) and PIC (pigs). In 2008 the company operated in 30 countries and made sales in 70 countries in Europe, North and South America, Africa, Australia and Asia. In cattle breeding, it operated breeding units (studs) in six countries, with 190 beef and dairy cattle in production testing there and another 2000 'in various stages of product development'. The company tests 400 dairy bulls per year and creates and measures the output of 40,000 of their daughters over five-year programmes. The stud farms yielded 13 million doses of cattle semen annually and the company claimed to have eight bulls in the US top 20 Holstein bull list, including the world's number one bull. The company had 29 per cent of the dairy semen market in Chile and 39 per cent of the imported semen market in Brazil. In pig breeding, the company owned two nucleus herds in the US and Canada that maintain nine purebred pig lines and had 170 subcontracted multiplication units around the world, producing parent pigs. The company had 48 per cent of the pig genetics market in Latin America, operating directly in Mexico and several other countries. In 2008, PIC had an infrastructure of five nucleus herds and ten other sites in China, comprising 3500 great-grandparent and 7000 grandparent breeding pigs. Genus estimates that 100 million meat pigs carrying Genus genetics are slaughtered annually.[11] Another global pig breeder, Topigs, 'stands for rapid genetic progress' and sells almost 1 million breeding pigs in 30 countries per year.[12]

Meat chicken and laying hen genetics and breeding are now concentrated in a small number of global companies such as the Erich Wesjohann (EW) Group, which operates in 100 countries. EW Group incorporates well-known pre-existing companies such as Hi-Line and Lohmann (laying hens) and Aviagen, which in turn owns Arbor Acres, Ross and others (meat chickens). Aviagen has 150 production sites in Europe and North America. Its great-grandparent and grandparent birds and its hatcheries supply day-old chicks to broiler (meat chicken) breeders through an international distribution network.[13] A 2007 industry estimate was that 90 per cent of the world's breeding broilers came from three or four companies.[9]

## 1.1.4 Evaluation: Putting a price on genetic performance

Performance evaluation is an essential aspect of competitive animal breeding. Strains of breeding pigs and poultry are evaluated and marketed by the international breeding companies with a specification of their main performance traits, such as leanness, growth rate, feed consumption, meat yield or number of piglets produced. These specifications can be more or less precise, and can include data as detailed as the expected number of teats on a breeding female pig.[14] For meat chickens, numerical values are given for the expected weight and feed consumption of the offspring at each day of his or her age, and carcase composition.[15]

Cattle and sheep are evaluated as potential parents on the basis of either their own parentage or, more accurately, by the performance of their offspring. In the 20th century the predictions from performance records were modernized by statistical analysis of transmitted traits, typically using the computational method known as best linear unbiased prediction (BLUP), by which the performance of relatives is used to predict the performance of a particular animal. The evaluation of a dairy bull's semen becomes increasingly accurate as the number of his daughters rises into the thousands. Such methods yield evaluations of the animal's breeding value, expressed by various measures such as Profitable Lifetime Index (£PLI) in the UK and the Net Merit Index (NM$) in the US, among others. Typically, these indices give a predicted monetary value to the results of using this animal compared to the average. Other indices in use for meat animals give numerical values for advantages in characteristics such as growth rate. The assessment of the animal's potential to transmit a particular desirable trait to offspring is measured as the animal's predicted transmitting ability (PTA) for a trait, such as for milk production, growth rate or various aspects of health. The final profit index is the weighted sum of all the PTAs that are thought to be relevant. Bulls and rams or their semen are offered with monetary valuations attached, indicating the extra profit to be gained by using this sire rather than another. Their genetic material can thus be priced and marketed.

League tables of the genetic value of animals and breeds at a national and global level are provided by a number of different organizations. The International Committee for Animal Recording has existed for around 50 years and has members in 47 countries in 6 continents, focused on milk production, beef and sheep, and records yearly milk yield for different breeds.[16] The International Bull Evaluation Service (Interbull) is supported by the European Association for Animal Production (EAAP), the International Dairy Federation (IDF) and the United Nations Food and Agriculture Organization (FAO).[17] Dairy cattle evaluations are the most developed, reflecting the high commercial value of the animals. Individual dairy bulls can even have their own individual sales brochures. For pigs and poultry, more mass-produced animals than cattle, the performance advertised by breeding companies is typically in the form of a product specification for the breed or brand rather than an assessment of an individual.

**Table 1.1** *Examples of cattle evaluations*

| Examples of organizations | Data published | Traits assessed |
|---|---|---|
| Interbull[17] An international collaboration of dairy breeders in a number of European countries, the US, Canada, Australia and South Africa | Publishes breeding evaluations of nearly 166,000 bulls of main dairy breeds: • red breeds, Brown Swiss, Jersey, Guernsey, Holstein and Simmental, a dual-purpose breed | Performance of bull's daughter in: • milk production • health and production traits, such as: – productive lifetime (longevity) – fertility – udder health – leg health – easy or difficult calving |
| Industry or governmental organizations: • UK's Dairy Co • US Department of Agriculture (USDA) animal improvement programmes • US Beef Improvement Federation | elite bull lists elite cow lists international top 100 bull lists | |
| Breed societies: • Holstein Association USA • Holstein UK • other dairy or beef cattle breed associations | lists of their own or official evaluations to guide members | |

## 1.2 Technologies and practices: Genes as commodities

### 1.2.1 The world's top breeds

The global spread of the market-leading livestock breeds and brands is so extensive that the FAO is concerned that they are reducing the genetic base of the world's livestock and restricting the choice of breeds that local farmers can make. The top breeds that have disseminated into every corner of the world include the Holstein dairy cow, the Large White, Duroc and Landrace pig breeds, and the Rhode Island Red and Leghorn chickens, all of them originating in Europe and North America.[18] This list does not include the dissemination of the commercial hybrid chickens which now dominate the global market.

The phenomenon is very evident in the dairy cattle breeds. The FAO says that the Holstein ranks as the number one global breed of any livestock species in its dissemination to nearly 130 countries worldwide by 2007.[18] Estimates in 2002 were that Holsteins and related breeds accounted for over 93 per cent of dairy cows in the US and UK and 76.8 per cent in Australia. The proportion was somewhat lower elsewhere, but still large for a single breed (64.6 per cent in France, 48 per cent in Germany and 57 per cent in New Zealand).[19]

The global dissemination of livestock genetics is aided by the large-scale transport of live breeding animals to countries where new breeding and production facilities are being set up. In addition to the presence of PIC in China, the British pig-breeding company ACMC has set up nucleus herds in Thailand, including the company's Meidam great-grandparent line based on

Meishan genetics (branded as '30 years ahead') and using Large White semen. Pig farms in Vietnam may use Large White/Landrace females and Duroc semen and have imported great-grandparent and grandparent pigs produced in Canada from the global pig breeding company Hypor.[20] JSR Genetics, with nucleus herds in 16 countries, has delivered tens of thousands of breeding pigs to Russia, the Ukraine and Romania.[21] Formerly a country of small pig farmers using traditional local breeds, Poland is hosting large-scale production using tens of thousands of new breeding animals supplied by pig genetics companies.[22] Holsteins, sourced from Australia and elsewhere, are the main specialized dairy breed in China and have also been crossed with native cattle.

## 1.2.2 Commercial hybrids in the pig and poultry industry

The genetics of commercial poultry and, to a lesser extent, pigs are increasingly controlled by the international breeding companies who sell the specialized lines of breeding chickens and pigs for the final food production stage (eggs or meat). These companies maintain nucleus stocks of breeding animals, many of them belonging to what were once the commonplace breeds of early 20th-century farming, such as the Landrace, Duroc, Piétrain and Large White pigs, the White Leghorn and Rhode Island Red for egg production, and the White Cornish for chickenmeat production. Selection within these breeds and crossing between different lines and breeds enables the companies to produce a range of breeding animals to fit varied market demand and offer a uniform and predictable product and a 'tailor-made approach to get closer to market requirements'.[23] Cross-breeding both allows traits from different lines to be combined and can benefit from hybrid vigour (heterosis) in the first generation offspring. The parent animals that are supplied to farmers to breed the meat chickens and meat pigs for retail sale are usually crosses of two or three breeds or lines that have different desirable characteristics. The breeding system, termed a 'breeding pyramid', starts with selection within so-called pure lines, test lines and experimental lines at the apex, and expands through great-grandparent lines and grandparent lines to the parent lines and the retail animals at the wide base.[9,18] Globalization and industrial concentration means that there is a tendency for breeding companies to change hands quite frequently and to come under the ownership of multinational food corporations.[24]

The pure lines themselves, and how the final line was created, may be commercially confidential and the FAO says that the chicken companies 'closely guard their pure-line breeding stock'.[18] But the preservation of the pure lines means that the companies can, in principle, react quickly to changing market conditions and bring out a new product. In chicken breeding it takes four to five years from the pedigree selection at the top of the pyramid to the new broiler chicken brand appearing in the supermarkets. Within five years, a pedigree unit of 1 male and 10 females at the top of the pyramid can lead to the production of 150 great-grandparents, 7500 grandparents, 375,000 parent stock birds and 48.75 million broilers for slaughter.[9]

Pig breeding companies sell parent animal genetics in the form of live gilts and boars or their semen to the end-user pig farms who use them to generate meat pigs for slaughter. The male (terminal sire) and female parent lines are typically of different breeds or strains so that both the breeding sows and their offspring meat pigs are first-generation crosses. The companies also sell great-grandparent and grandparent stock to large pig producers to form their own nucleus herds, usually under contract. Breeding lines can be differentiated to produce piglets with particular market specifications: extreme lean for Germany, large hams for Italy or high marbling (intramuscular fat) for Japan. The pig and poultry breeding companies also offer management advice through seminars and courses held internationally on the correct use of their products.

Today's commercial hybrids of the chicken industry were built on the foundations provided by a slower differentiation between egg-laying and meat-producing breeds that took place in the early to mid 20th century. By the 1930s, egg-laying and meat breeds were sufficiently different in performance that males of laying hen breeds were no longer useful for meat and were killed at one day old. In the US, as a result of noting the greatly increased yields obtained from hybrid corn (maize), breeders started crossing the standard laying hen breeds in the hope of achieving similar results. Selected and inbred lines of chickens (sometimes by using mating of full siblings or parents and offspring) from White Leghorn and other breeds such as Rhode Island Red chickens were crossed to obtain hens that laid large numbers of good quality eggs.[25] Faster-growing and heavily muscled meat chickens (broilers) were developed in the US from the White Plymouth Rock (a white strain of the Barred Plymouth Rock) and the White Cornish (originally bred for fighting), a bird with an unusually broad muscular breast. This was encouraged by 'chicken of tomorrow' competitions organized across the country from 1948, recording and publishing the feed intake, mortality, final live weight, carcase quality and breast meat of batches of chickens reared to 12 weeks of age over a three-year period. By the 1960s breeding birds of these new broiler strains were being exported from the US to the UK, Spain, Argentina, Japan and Africa, and leading brands such as Cobb rapidly went global.[25,26]

The specialist primary breeding companies believe that their methods allow a process of continuous innovation and genetic improvement, providing their customers with regular genetic updates. This means that today's genetics become rapidly outdated; stud boars are replaced in a matter of a few months and stud bulls within a few years.

### 1.2.3 Reproductive technologies: How to spread good genes

The main reproductive technologies used for farmed animals are now recognized as having four 'generations' or stages of development[27,28] as the possibilities for the control of reproductive processes have increased (see also sections 2.2.8 and 2.3.2 in Chapter 2):

- First generation: artificial insemination, currently the most widely used and cost effective; in use since the 1930s, more widely from the mid 20th century.
- Second generation: embryo transfer using *in vivo* embryos. Eggs are produced and fertilized in one female animal and subsequently removed for transfer to other females for gestation. Usually involves hormonal treatment to induce the release of more ova than would normally be shed, and then referred to as MOET (multiple ovulation and embryo transfer). Commercial use for cattle since the 1970s.
- Third generation: *in vitro* fertilization (IVF) before embryo transfer. Unfertilized eggs are removed from one animal's ovaries, matured and fertilized in the laboratory before transfer to other females for gestation; allows genetic testing of embryo before implantation. In use since the 1980s.
- Fourth generation: the fourth generation involves manipulating an animal's DNA directly at the stage of egg, sperm or embryo. This can be done by cloning the animal by nuclear transfer (taking the DNA from one animal and putting it into the egg of another animal) or by genetic engineering of the DNA to change, add or disable particular genes. In use since the 1980s (mainly research and development).

To use artificial reproduction methods it is generally also necessary to understand the function of, and sometimes to use, the reproductive hormones that control aspects of the female reproductive cycle: follicle stimulating hormone, luteinizing hormone, progesterone, oestrogen, gonadotrophin-releasing hormone and prostaglandin $F_{2\alpha}$, or their synthetic analogues. These are now widely used in the industry. The methods of artificial reproduction are discussed in more detail in Chapter 2, but the following outlines the size of the industry and the genetic dissemination that it permits.

### 1.2.3.1 Artificial insemination

Artificial insemination (AI) speeds up genetic change because it allows in principle a global choice of semen and a much greater dissemination of the genetics of particular males who have the desired traits. AI is widely used for food animals, especially for dairy cattle, followed by pigs and, more rarely, sheep and goats.

The technology of freezing and thawing cattle semen is now routine, which enables semen to be stored and exported. AI now means that one bull can be made the genetic parent of thousands of calves per year rather than the merely tens of calves per year he would produce by natural mating with the cows in his local area. His semen and hence his genes can be spread internationally and simultaneously. As importantly, the performance of his many daughters can be used to produce statistical accuracy about the performance of his genes and give him 'proven sire' status; thus, the use of AI immensely speeds up selection by the traditional method of progeny testing. In 2009 Picston Shottle, one of the world's top Holstein bulls, had his production traits assessed from 17,725 daughters in nearly 5000 herds[29] and the Canadian Holstein bull Comestar Lheros was assessed from 50,726 daughters in nearly 18,000 herds.[30]

Artificial insemination was estimated to be used on over 110 million breeding cattle (including buffaloes) globally by the turn of the 21st century, with the largest number of AIs (58 million) being carried out in the Far East region (mainly China, India and Pakistan). There were 1600 cattle semen banks globally and the cattle industry produced over 260 million doses of bull semen from a relatively small number of 41,000 bulls at 648 collection centres worldwide. There was an international trade in bull semen (most of it Holstein), with over 19 million semen doses recorded as exported globally. North America was by far the largest exporter, with nearly 14 million doses exported, and Europe both exported and imported about 5 million doses. The proportion of all cattle inseminations that were carried out by AI (rather than natural mating) was 61 per cent in Europe and about 25 per cent in both North America and the Far East.[27] Among Holstein dairy cattle in developed countries, AI has become the most typical method of insemination, with the semen provided by owners of pedigree herds or by specialized breeding companies.

Artificial insemination is now a common method of insemination in large-scale pig production. Globally, 40 million sows were inseminated annually around the turn of the century. Most semen is used fresh, with a shelf life of a few days, because pig semen is much less easy to freeze and thaw successfully than cattle semen, and also because of the integrated nature of most pig industries. A very small minority (fewer than 4 million) of the world's sheep and goats were artificially inseminated annually.[27]

Sexed semen, or 'gender-biased' semen, is available for cattle, produced by technology from companies such as XY Inc and Accelerated Genetics in North America (see section 8.4.3.1 in Chapter 8). Research on the use of sex-sorted Holstein semen is also ongoing in China.[31] Sexed pig semen has also been produced but up to now has had little commercial uptake, although some believe it could increase the efficiency of pigmeat production. Sexed semen has the potential to avoid the production and destruction of unwanted low-value animals such as dairy bull calves that are considered uneconomic for meat production (see section 8.4.2 in Chapter 8). Its widespread use would also represent another step in the human control of animal reproduction.

### 1.2.3.2 Embryo transfer

Embryo transfer (ET), using either MOET or *in vitro*-produced embryos, speeds up the dissemination of female as well as male genes. Instead of giving birth to one calf in a year, a cow with highly valued genes can produce several tens of embryos to be brought to term by recipient cows who are considered to be less genetically valuable.[28] But because of the greater technical complexities and the need for a relatively simple non-surgical procedure for use on farm, embryo and egg swapping are much less used than AI. These technologies are mainly used by primary breeding companies, nucleus pedigree herds or large producers. It is notable that the large majority of the Holstein bulls in the international 100 top sires list were born by embryo transfer.[32]

Records compiled by the International Embryo Transfer Society (IETS) show that cattle breeders transferred over 612,000 *in vivo*-derived embryos and nearly 266,000 *in vitro*-derived embryos during 2005. North America accounted for 45 per cent of the *in vivo*-produced embryos and Brazil, China and Korea accounted for most of the *in vitro*-produced embryos. Nearly 30,000 embryo transfers in pigs and 32,000 in sheep and goats were reported. Korea and Vietnam were experimenting with *in vitro*-produced embryo transfer in pigs.[33]

Embryo transfer in the pig breeding industry is still quite rare because until recently both the processes involved (extracting embryos from the donor pig and re-implanting them in a recipient pig) could only be done by surgery. One of the largest pig-breeding companies believes that future developments in pig embryo transfer would enable a revolution in the way pig genetics are delivered to the end user in the next decades. If embryo freezing and non-surgical embryo implantation became routine, the breeding companies could switch to selling embryos to order and could also provide farmers with strains of suitable sows to use as surrogate mothers.[34]

## 1.2.4 Animal genome projects

The aim of a genome project is to find all the genes on the animal's genome, identify them chemically in terms of the bases of the genetic code, and open up the task of finding their functions. In 1990 (the same year that the Human Genome Project started) the US Farm Bill authorized funding for livestock genome research and the National Animal Genome Research Program was set up.[35] By mid 2008 over 40 animal genome projects were either completed, in progress or planned around the world.[36] Of domestic animals, the genome of the chicken, cow, horse, pig, dog and cat had been either completed or was in the process of refinement and completion.[36,37]

Animal genome projects are multinational, multi-funded projects, involving the animal production industry, academic research institutions and governments. The bovine genome (*Bos taurus*), a first draft completed in 2004, was a US$53 million international collaboration funded by institutions in the US, Canada, Australia and New Zealand.[35] The International Chicken Polymorphism Map Consortium involved more than 20 research funding institutions in the US, Sweden, The Netherlands, the UK, China and Singapore and over 150 scientists worked on the first draft of the genome.[38] The International Swine Genome Consortium, formed in 2003, involves at least 12 partners in the US, Canada and Europe. The US Department of Agriculture (USDA) awarded the project US$10 million with the aim 'to identify and choose genetically superior pigs that resist infectious diseases, yield larger litter sizes and produce leaner cuts of meat for consumers'.[39] The International Sheep Genome Consortium involves scientists and funding agencies from Australia, France,

Kenya, New Zealand, the UK and the US, and aims to provide 'public genomic resources that will help researchers find genes associated with production, quality and disease traits in sheep'.[40] Aquaculture genomic research is being carried out in Japan, the US, India, Chile, China, Canada, Norway, France, Australia, New Zealand and Spain, among others, working on salmonids (such as Atlantic salmon and rainbow trout), cichlids (such as *Tilapia*), catfish, oysters, shrimps and striped bass.[41]

The genome of the domestic dog (an individual of the boxer breed) was published in 2005 by a collaboration of 15 institutions in the US (predominantly), the UK and France.[42] The genome of the domestic cat (an Abyssinian), a collaboration of scientists in 15 institutions in the US (predominantly), Portugal and Singapore, and the genome of the Thoroughbred horse were both published in 2007.[43,44] Among the non-domesticated species where a genome project exists are the honeybee, fruitfly, green anole lizard, painted turtle, opossum, tree shrew, elephant, little brown bat, bush baby, mouse lemur, rhesus macaque, baboon, gibbon, chimpanzee and giant panda.[36]

By 2009 the costs per genome and the speed of sequencing had been reduced to a small fraction of what they once were, so there is no reason why every domestic animal breed and strain should not be genetically analysed. In the long term, the greater understanding of gene function in animals opens the door to greater intervention in animal reproduction for human benefit, for either good or ill. Through genomics the future breeding value of an animal could be evaluated before birth. Research is ongoing that could enable cattle embryos to be tested for traits such as meat tenderness, feed efficiency or genetic diseases before embryo transfer takes place, so only those with desirable market traits would be born.[45]

## 1.2.5 Genomic selection: The Brave New World

One of the first uses to which animal genomes are being put is to attempt to increase the productivity and profitability of livestock breeding. The specialist pig- and poultry-breeding companies already use DNA technology and genomic information in their breeding procedures. Genomics can help them select for traits with low heritability or that are hard to measure on live animals. The European Patent Office has granted around 30 patents on genetic marker-assisted animal breeding.[46]

From 2009, genomics were incorporated into the official predicted transmitting ability (PTA) scores of cattle published by the Holstein Association USA, the UK's DairyCo and the Canadian Dairy Network.[47] The technology behind this is essentially the same as that used in the ongoing analysis of the human genome – that is, the identification of single nucleotide polymorphisms (SNPs). These are expressions of the differences that can exist between individuals at the level of single nucleotides of the DNA molecule; they can be associated with particular diseases or traits. By 2004, 2.8 million chicken SNPs had been found by comparing chickens from different breeds (in comparison,

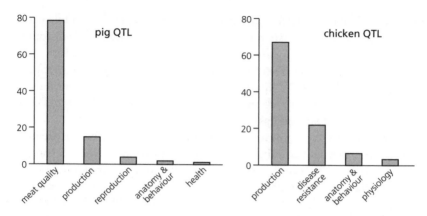

**Figure 1.2** *Percentage of pig and chicken quantitative trait loci (QTL) reported for each main class of trait*

*Source:* PigQTLdb and ChickenQTLdb, 2009[48]

12 million human SNPs had been identified by 2008).[49,50] Genomic breeding values for cattle are not yet intended to stand alone, but they can double the accuracy of performance-based predictions in the case of younger animals who have not yet time to be thoroughly performance tested.[47] Considerable research effort is being put into improving the methodology and accuracy of genomic predictions of breeding value.[51]

Thus genomics potentially allows the identification and targeting of numerous inherited traits much more effectively than selection based on observed performance or phenotype. Based on analysis of the animal's genome, either individual genes or quantitative trait loci (QTL) can be identified and used in selection programmes (see Box 1.2). To systematize current efforts, the USDA has sponsored an 'animal trait ontology' database project where all QTL reported in the scientific literature can be recorded. For pigs, starting with a mere 5 QTL reported in 1994, by 2009 2400 QTL had been reported, of which 78 per cent were related to meat or carcase quality. For chickens, 67 per cent of QTL reported by 2009 were related to production, and 22 per cent to disease resistance.[48]

---

### BOX 1.2 QUANTITATIVE TRAIT LOCI (QTL)

Quantitative trait loci (QTL) are a way of making the connection between an individual animal's genetic make-up and a particular trait (or traits) that the animal displays (such as fast growth). Quantitative genetic traits are those that vary continuously through an animal population, such as weight or litter size. Such traits are probably determined by the effect of several genes. A QTL is a region of DNA in an animal's genome that has been found to be associated with a particular trait or traits as a result of comparing the DNA and the performance of different animals. QTL are not necessarily the actual functional genes that control the trait in question; rather they may be genes that are closely associated with those functional genes.

Those animal geneticists who are concerned with animal welfare argue for the importance of identifying traits that would enable selection for better welfare. But up to now it is evident that productivity has been the main goal of livestock genomic studies. The Eighth World Congress on Genetics Applied to Livestock Production in 2006 included a total of around 840 scientific contributions. A key word search identified fewer than 50 of these papers (around 5 per cent) that mentioned animal welfare, if only in the stock phrase 'health and welfare'. An even smaller minority of contributions focused on the animal welfare implications of breeding goals.[52]

### 1.2.6 The ideal of genetic progress

The concept of continuous improvement, based on continuous scientific discovery and technical innovation, is integral to modern science and therefore has become part of the scientific approach to animal breeding. The modification of farmed animal genetics is a never-ending enterprise, analogous to developments in the auto industry or the computer industry where continuous technical improvement and functionality are expected and needed to fuel the production cycle. In a highly competitive breeding and food production market, there is never a point where food-producing animals will be perfected; the aim is year-on-year 'improvement' in performance. Hy-Line International, a leading breeder of laying hens, has the 'ultimate goal … to produce more efficient birds in each generation'.[53] People may disagree about what the ideal should be, but probably very few commercial farmers want to end 'improvement'. For example, if economic conditions dictate that farmers need to change their practices (indoors to outdoors, a different feed supply, adaptation to climate change or attempts to mitigate the climate impact of livestock), this may open up a new burst of selective breeding.

## 1.3 The impact on animals

### 1.3.1 Animal sentience and animal well-being

Domestic animals are on the one hand the raw materials that selection programmes and genetic research work on, and on the other hand they are sentient individuals. A sentient animal is defined by animal welfare scientists as one that has conscious feelings, and the feelings matter to the animal.[54] A sentient animal has the ability to experience aversive states such as pain, fear and grief as well as pleasurable states such as happiness, to remember the consequences of actions and to assess risk.[55] Although we treat pigs very differently from domestic dogs, there is no scientific reason to think that pigs are less sentient than dogs.

As sentient individuals, animals have an interest in experiencing as little distress or suffering as possible and in enjoying a high quality of life for as long as possible. Many of the detailed questions raised by livestock breeding goals and practices and their welfare implications are dealt with in subsequent chapters. In this section we consider a checklist of how the interests of sentient animals are respected, and to what extent they are harmed, by the advent of industrial genetics in animal breeding.

## 1.3.2 Potential positive impacts

- Understanding of the genes relating to disease and parasite resistance, ease of giving birth and survival of young have the potential to reduce important current sources of animal suffering, as well as improving their productivity (Chapter 3).
- Genetic information about the relationship between animals could be used in combination with QTL-assisted breeding to limit inbreeding (Chapter 3, Chapter 9).
- If the genes controlling qualitative traits could be sufficiently accurately identified, QTL-assisted selection has the potential to reduce animal wastage both during breeding experiments and in commercial breeding. QTL could reduce the number of animals born that are of low value because they do not fulfil market specifications or because their performance is not up to expectations. Animals with a low market value are typically treated with less consideration for their welfare.
- Sex-sorting of sperm or embryos similarly has the potential to reduce the number of unwanted and low-value animals that are born. Unwanted animals may be killed at birth or treated with less consideration for their welfare because of their low market value (Chapter 8).
- Artificial insemination and embryo transfer have the potential to avoid the stress and the risk of disease transmission caused by transporting live animals for breeding purposes.
- Many of the animal-breeding companies and breed societies state that animal health and welfare are important breeding goals.

## 1.3.3 Actual and potential negative impacts

- The industrialization of animal genetics encourages the view that animals are production machines, or packages of useful genes, rather than sentient individuals.
- The industrialization of animal genetics encourages a use-and-dispose approach to breeding animals. The emphasis on continuous genetic progress leads to a high turnover of breeding animals who are disposed of long before their natural reproductive lifetimes would end. This is partly because the animal's genetics have become obsolete in a short time. It is also due to the temptation to over-exploit breeding animals who have valued genetic traits – for example, through high levels of reproduction, milk production or semen production (see Chapters 2, 3 and 8).

- The emphasis on tailoring animals to particular production or market requirements can lead to narrow breeding goals and, in some cases, inbreeding that damage the health of over-selected animals (see Chapter 3, and also Chapter 6 on companion animals).
- The majority of the animal strains produced by the commercial poultry and pig genetics companies are designed for use in intensive production methods. Large-scale intensive production methods tend to reduce the animal's freedom of movement, provide a less complex environment, provide fewer opportunities for natural behaviour or for normal mother–offspring relationships, and are likely to reduce the extent to which the animal is treated as an individual (see Chapters 3 and 4).
- The identification of QTL and the creation of new animal strains by conventional selective breeding both require experimental breeding. Breeding experiments are likely to result in the production of surplus animals, particularly males, and potentially some unhealthy animals. Experiments to assess the behaviour or survival of animals in experimental breeding programmes may themselves cause suffering in some cases – for example, experimental selection against negative outcomes, such as the death of offspring, may involve allowing offspring to die.
- Breeding experiments typically involve more interference with the animal's normal behaviour in terms of handling, weighing and blood testing of animals than would be necessary in routine on-farm breeding. The use of reproductive technology in breeding or experimentation can involve intervention such as administration of hormones, embryo or egg collection from mammals, caesarean sections and electroejaculation of males for semen collection. Handling and invasive procedures such as injections or blood collection can cause discomfort, pain or fear. Most of the procedures involved in breeding are not carried out for the benefit of the animals concerned (see Chapter 2).
- Much of the management of animal breeding, with the aim of maximizing output, fails to respect the natural behaviour of animals and their social and emotional bonds. Early weaning and maternal deprivation are routine in farm animal breeding. Artificial breeding technology (artificial insemination and embryo transfer) deny animals their natural sexual behaviour (see Chapter 4).
- A breeding culture of continuous genetic change will create the need for continuous experimental breeding, probably including genetic engineering and cloning. The techniques used in genetic engineering and cloning increase the risk of abnormal pregnancies and abnormal offspring, involving suffering to both mothers and offspring (see Chapter 2).

There is a growing consensus that the pursuit of productivity has led to the breeding of animals that have become less sustainable because of their genetics and the over-exploitation of their genetic potential. Essentially this means that in many cases animal breeding has increased animal suffering in spite of the potential of modern veterinary knowledge to reduce it. Chapters 2 and 3 discuss the causes and extent of breeding-related welfare problems, how effectively they are being addressed by breeders, and possible solutions.

## 1.3.4 Animal professionals and animal well-being

Animal breeding companies are operating in a competitive global environment where they are under pressure to increase the cost effectiveness of livestock. They are widely viewed in the animal protection movement as putting cost considerations before the health and well-being of animals and in encouraging factory farming. On the other hand, they are responsive to changes in consumer demand and offer some differentiation of products for those who are seeking more robust animals or better animal welfare. Increased consumer demand for a 'good life' for farmed animals[56] could change these companies' breeding goals and encourage them to breed more animals suited to non-intensive husbandry systems.

Large number of geneticists, animal scientists and veterinarians are involved in animal breeding. These professionals are not always able to be in a neutral position between the animal production industry and the interests of animals, because they are employed to further the industry's goals. In some cases, depending on funding arrangements, this may apply also to animal welfare scientists, although in many cases animal welfare scientists are able to be more independent of the industry and have been prominent in bringing poor welfare to public attention and in advocating changes in breeding and husbandry practices. Animal geneticists may have little training or interest in animal welfare, and the welfare implications of genetic research programmes may be missed.

'Animal welfare' is defined by a range of people, professionals, farmers and the public from differing points of view.[54–57] An 'animal production' viewpoint on welfare tends to place high value on the animal's biological functioning and on disease prevention. The absence of disease is an important aspect of quality of life, when disease causes suffering, but it does not guarantee what most people would consider a high quality of life. Animal welfare includes both the physical and the mental state,[58] and the mental state includes how the animal feels about his or her life, including social relationships and the ability to perform natural behaviour. To use a human analogy, it would be possible to be physically healthy in a prison cell without having a good quality of life. In addition, intensive animal production systems themselves can promote stress, disease[59] and injury that cause suffering. It should perhaps be a matter for discussion whether it is appropriate for animal breeding research to carry the label 'animal health and welfare' when the animals concerned are intended to be reared in intensive conditions.

## Notes

1   United Nations Food and Agriculture Organization (2007) ProdSTAT online database, http://faostat.fao.org/
2   Russell, N. (1986) *Like Engend'ring Like: Heredity and Animal Breeding in Early Modern England*, Cambridge University Press
3   Homer *The Odyssey*, Book 17, lines 290–320
4   Serpell, J. (1996) *In the Company of Animals: A Study of Human–Animal Relationships*, Cambridge University Press
5   Hislop, J. (1958) 'Foreword', in F. Tesio *Breeding the Racehorse*, translated and edited by E. Spinola, J. A. Allen
6   Tesio, F. (1958) *Breeding the Racehorse* (including Introduction by E. Spinola), J. A. Allen
7   Trow-Smith, R. (1959) *A History of British Livestock Husbandry, Vol 2: 1700–1900*, Routledge and Kegan Paul
8   Moncrieff, E. (1996) *Farm Animal Portraits*, Antique Collector's Club
9   Laughlin, K. (2007) *The Evolution of Genetics, Breeding and Production*, Temperton Fellowship Report No 15, Harper Adams University College
10  EBLEX (2004) *Better Returns Programme No 2: Target Ram Selection for Better Returns*, EBLEX
11  Genus plc (2008) *Annual Report and Financial Statements 2008*, Genus plc; Genus plc (2008) *Preliminary Results Year Ended 30 June 2008*, 16 September 2008, Genus plc; *The PigSite* (2008) 'Genus advances its porcine strategy for China', *The PigSite*, 19 September 2008
12  Topigs website, http://topigs.websdesign.nl/index2.php?pid=1151&taalkeuze=20, accessed 27 April 2009
13  Aviagen website, www.aviagen.com/output.aspx?sec=10&con=334&siteId=1, accessed December 2009
14  See, for example, Hermitage Pedigree Pigs (2008) Sales brochure, www.hermitage.ie
15  See, for example, Aviagen (2007) *Ross 308 Broiler Performance Objectives*, June 2007
16  International Committee for Animal Recording (2009) *ICAR Country Member Milk Records*, www.waap.it/enquiry/index.htm
17  Interbull (2009) Website information, www-interbull.slu.se/framesida-home.htm; www-interbull.slu.se/eval/framesida-prod.htm, bull data as at August 2009
18  FAO (2007) *State of the World's Animal Genetic Resources for Food and Agriculture*, FAO
19  Defra (UK Department for Environment, Food and Rural Affairs) (2002–2003) *Final Report, Longevity and Lifetime Efficiency of Pure and Crossbred Dairy Cows*, Project number IS0213, UK
20  Lumb, S. (2007) 'British genes making their way into Thailand', *Pig Progress*, vol 23, no 4, pp30–31; Lumb, S. and ter Beek, V. (2008) 'Vietnam's fight to upgrade its health status', *Pig Progress*, vol 24, no 8, pp15–16; *Pig Progress* (2009) 'Hypor ships first GGP and GP pigs to Vietnam', *Pig Progress* online, 22 September, www.pigprogress.net/
21  JSR International, www.jsr.co.uk/international.php, accessed November 2009; *The PigSite* (2009) 'Romanian deal tops landmark year for JSR', *The PigSite*, 11 November
22  Caldier, P. and ter Beek, V. (2008) 'Focus on Poland breed to meat', *Pig Progress*, vol 24, no 10, pp28–29
23  Hypor Inc (2009) Website information, www.hypor.com/, accessed 13 April 2009

24 Gura, S. (2008) 'Concentration in the livestock genetics industry', presentation at the NCCR Workshop on Animal Breeding, Innovation, Trade and Proprietary Rights, World Trade Institute, Berne, 27–28 November 2008 ; Gura, S. (2008) *Industrial Livestock Production and Its Impact on Smallholders in Developing Countries*, League for Pastoral Peoples and Endogenous Livestock Development

25 Whittle, T. E. (2000) *A Triumph of Science: A 70 Year History of the UK Poultry Industry*, Poultry World Publications

26 Cobb-Vantress (2009) 'Company history', www.cobb-vantress.com, accessed 8 April 2009

27 Thibier, M. (2004) 'Role of reproductive biotechnologies: Global perspective, current methods and success rates', in G. Simm et al (eds) *Farm Animal Genetic Resources*, BSAS Publication 30, Nottingham University Press, pp171–190

28 Gordon, I. (2004) *Reproductive Technologies in Farm Animals*, CABI Publishing, Wallingford, UK

29 Genus Breeding (2009) 'Dairy bull search online', www.genusbreeding.co.uk, accessed 15 April 2009

30 Semex (2009) 'Dairy bull search online', www.semex.com, accessed 15 April 2009

31 Xu, J. et al (2006) 'Developmental potential of vitrified Holstein cattle embryos fertilized in vitro with sex-sorted sperm', *Journal of Dairy Science*, vol 89, pp2510–2518

32 US Holstein Association (2009) *Top International TPI Bulls*, April 2009

33 Thibier, M. (2006) 'Transfers of both *in vivo* derived and *in vitro* produced embryos in cattle still on the rise and contrasted trends in other species in 2005', *Data Retrieval Committee Annual Report*, December, International Embryo Transfer Society www.iets.org/pdf/data_retrieval/december2006.pdf

34 van Haandel B. and Charagu, P. (2006) 'Gene transfer and genetic improvement', *International Pig Topics*, vol 21, no 2, pp23–27; Ducro-Steverink, D. W. B. (2004) 'Reproduction results and offspring performance after non-surgical embryo transfer in pigs', *Theriogenology*, vol 62, no 3–4, pp522–531

35 USDA National Animal Genome Research Program (NAGRP), www.csrees.usda.gov/nea/animals/in_focus/an_breeding_if_nagrp.html; www.animalgenome.org/, accessed 15 April 2009

36 'Top billing for platypus at end of evolution tree,' *Nature*, vol 453, 8 May, pp138–139; Li, R. et al (2010) 'The sequence and *de novo* assembly of the giant panda genome', Nature, vol 463, pp311–317

37 GOLD Genomes online database v 2.0, www.genomesonline.org/gold.cgi, accessed 20 April 2009

38 International Chicken Genome Sequencing Consortium (2004) 'Sequence and comparative analysis of the chicken genome provide unique perspectives on vertebrate evolution', *Nature*, vol 432, pp695–777

39 International Swine Genome Sequencing Consortium, www.piggenome.org/, accessed 21 April 2009

40 International Sheep Genomics Consortium, www.sheephapmap.org/, accessed 21 April 2009

41 National Aquaculture Genome Projects, www.animalgenome.org/aquaculture/, accessed 21 April 2009

42 Lindblad-Toh, K. et al (2005) 'Genome sequence, comparative analysis and haplotype structure of the domestic dog', *Nature*, vol 438, pp803–819

43 Pontius, J. U. et al (2007) 'Initial sequence and comparative analysis of the cat genome', *Genome Re*search, vol 17, pp1675–1689

44 Horse Genome Project, www.uky.edu/Ag/Horsemap/, accessed 21 April 2009

45 Iowa State University (2009) 'ISU researchers working to develop, market embryonic test for bovine genetics', news release, 17 September 2009

46  Peter, L. (2009) 'Germans protest over pig patent', BBC News online, 16 April 2009, http://news.bbc.co.uk

47  For one example, see US Holstein Association (2009) *Understanding Genomic Predictions*, www.holsteinusa.com, accessed April 2009

48  Pig QTL database, PigQTLdb, www.animalgenome.org/bioinfo/projects/ATO/; Chicken QTL database ChickenQTLdb, www.animalgenome.org/cgi-bin/QTLdb/ GG/summary, accessed June 2008 and September 2009

49  International Chicken Polymorphism Map Consortium (2004) 'A genetic variation map for chicken with 2.8 million single-nucleotide polymorphisms', *Nature*, vol 432, pp717–722

50  Pearson, T. A. and Manolio, T. A. (2008) 'How to interpret a genome-wide association study', *JAMA*, vol 299, no 11, pp1335–1344

51  For example, Calus, M. P. L., de Roos, S. P. W. and Veerkamp, R. F. (2009) 'Estimating genomic breeding values from the QTL–MAS workshop data using a single SNP and haplotype/IBD approach', *BMC Proceedings*, vol 3, supplement 1, pS10; Macciotta, N. P. P. et al (2009) 'Pre-selection of most significant SNPS for the estimation of genomic breeding values', *BMC Proceedings*, vol 3, supplement 1, pS14

52  *Eighth World Congress on Genetics Applied to Livestock Production*, 13–18 August 2006, Belo Horizonte, Brazil, www.wcgalp8.org.br

53  Arango, J. (2009) 'Improving feed intake and efficiency: Can layer breeders maintain the current rate of improvements in the coming years?', *Poultry World*, June 2009, p30

54  Webster, J. (2005) *Animal Welfare: Limping towards Eden*, Blackwell Publishing, Oxford, UK

55  Broom, D. M. and Fraser, A. F. (2007) *Domestic Animal Behaviour and Welfare*, fourth edition, CABI Publishing, Wallingford, UK

56  See discussion in Farm Animal Welfare Council (2009) *Farm Animal Welfare in Great Britain: Past, Present and Future*, Farm Animal Welfare Council

57  Fraser, D. (2004) 'Applying science to animal welfare standards', paper presented to the OIE Global Conference on Animal Welfare: Applying Science to Animal Welfare, Conference papers downloadable at www.oie.int/eng/Welfare_2004/ speakers.htm; Phillips, C. J. C. (2009) *The Welfare of Animals: The Silent Majority*, Springer, Dordrecht, The Netherlands

58  Farm Animal Welfare Council (2009) *Five Freedoms*, www.fawc.org.uk/ freedoms.htm, accessed August 2009

59  Pew Commission on Industrial Farm Animal Production (2008) *Putting Meat on the Table: Industrial Farm Animal Production in America*, The Pew Charitable Trusts and Johns Hopkins Bloomberg School of Public Health

# 2

# Breeding for Productivity

## 2.1 Background and context: More and faster

### 2.1.1 The primacy of productivity

A representative of a global poultry-breeding company explained in 2000: 'All breeding plans for commercial breeding companies have one major objective in common: to increase the genetic potential of the stock to produce a maximum of saleable high-quality products at minimum cost in a given production system.'[1] Thus, commercial suppliers of livestock genetics promise that their animals are designed for traits that will strengthen the bottom line of the purchaser's business. The Holstein Association USA, which represents the elite of dairy cow breeders, more simply promises 'US Registered Holsteins, for maximum profit'.[2] The second half of the 20th century was a time of unheard-of increases in the yields obtained from agricultural plant crops, through a combination of selective breeding, hybridization and agrichemicals, with average wheat and rice yields doubling or tripling.[3] Livestock breeders took these successes as a model and aimed for similar year-on-year increases in yield from livestock. Overall, they succeeded. This has meant streamlining and specializing animals' bodies for their allotted function and restricting their behaviour in order to maximize their genetic potential.

### 2.1.2 Breeding goals: How to improve productivity and market traits

Every step in an animal's life, from its conception to its final transport for slaughter, affects its productivity and its potential to yield profit or loss. For this reason, the ideal breeding goal is to maximize the animal's performance at every step of the way to achieve greater yield per animal and per unit time. The focus of breeders' efforts is in two broad areas, both of which are designed to cut production costs to the farmer and hence lower prices to the consumer. One is to increase the rate of reproduction. Depending on the species involved, this essentially means increasing the number of surviving offspring and minimizing the time between successive cycles of reproduction. The second area covers all the ways in which the animal's body can increase its productivity in terms of meat, milk or egg production. Together these include:

- faster growth of meat animals to slaughter weight;
- lower feed consumption per unit product;
- better conformity of product to market requirements, such as composition, colour, size, shape, flavour and texture;
- greater uniformity of product;
- decreased interval between births;
- earlier reproductive maturity;
- greater fertility;
- better 'maternal traits' (ability to produce milk and feed young to weaning);
- greater robustness, better health and resistance to stress;
- lower mortality rate of offspring;
- longer productive lifetime of breeding females;
- faster rate of genetic change to achieve the objectives above.

Modern breeders often categorize the desired objectives as production traits (a high yield of the primary product) and functional traits of the animal. Livestock geneticists define functional traits as 'those traits of an animal that increase its biological and economic efficiency not by higher outputs of products but by reduced costs of production'.[4] Overall functioning is an important part of the productivity of an animal; there is a limited advantage in getting a high yield from an animal who is too lame to walk into the milking parlour or to the feeders and drinkers or into the truck for transport to the slaughterhouse, or who collapses from stress during the journey.

By the late 20th century it became clear to animal breeders and farmers that the rapid development of a single aspect of an animal's biology, such as growth rate or milk production, was unbalancing the animal as a whole (see Chapter 3).[5] Breeders then started adding items to their selection criteria to take account of the ever-increasing aspects of its biological functioning that needed to be adjusted. 'Balance' was promised as well as productivity. This has meant more selection, rather than less, and more genetic research. Selection criteria for broiler chickens have changed from essentially one item (growth rate) in 1960, to around ten items in 2007.[6] For dairy cows, by 2008 selection criteria as described by the Total Performance Index had changed from milk production alone to an equation with 11 variable terms whose weights can be mixed and matched by breeders and statisticians in the search for the ideally efficient animal.[7]

Typical functional traits are those that contribute to:

- decreasing the number of young who die early or are born dead;
- increasing the longevity of breeding pigs, dairy cows and ewes;
- improving health by breeding for better resistance to parasites, to infections and to production and genetics-related diseases such as lameness.

There may also be selection for behaviour. This can include animals that are more tractable or that show less aggression or stress in the crowded conditions typical of intensive animal production, or selection for ewes or sows who have more effective maternal behaviour in either extensive or intensive conditions, as required.

Functional traits are sometimes labelled as 'health and welfare' traits. Selecting for functional traits can reduce animal suffering and lengthen animals' lifespans. But this is not principally why such selection is undertaken: cost effectiveness is the main motivation. Ironically, selection for higher yield and the use of intensive management systems are themselves the cause of many of the problems that the selection for functional traits now aims to solve.

### 2.1.3 The rate of genetic change during the 20th century

Selective breeding based on performance and progeny-testing can be expected to produce genetic change in the selected production traits of around 1 to 3 per cent per year increase on the mean for the population.[8,9] Thus in principle a chicken or pig from a selected strain could grow more than one third faster at the end of ten years.

Selective breeding and crossing transmuted the dual-purpose beef and dairy Friesian of the 1950s into the high-yielding Holstein dairy cow capable of producing three to four times the milk yield,[10] with intensive feeding and management. Between 1975 and 2007 the average milk yield that farmers reported per dairy cow (total milk divided by total cows) nearly doubled in the US and increased by 85 per cent in Denmark and 74 per cent in the UK.[11] At least 50 per cent of the increase in yield from dairy cows is estimated to be due to selective breeding.[12]

Traits in poultry and pigs can be changed more rapidly than cattle and sheep because of their faster rate of reproduction. The change in the rate of weight gain of meat (broiler) chickens has been the greatest of all. At eight weeks old, a typical commercial broiler of 2007 was 4.8 times heavier than a typical broiler of 1957 at the same age.[9,13] Around 85 per cent of this change has been due to selective breeding for fast growth, the rest being due to using more nutritious feed.[14] The number of days taken to reach a typical British slaughter weight of 2kg was cut from 63 days in 1976 to 36 days in 1999 and to 34 days (for male chickens) in 2007.[13,15] One of the major breeders of laying hens increased the number of eggs per hen by 3.6 eggs per generation over the 25 years up to 2009, while at the same time reducing the quantity of feed needed per unit output.[16]

Reported data on pig productivity include the following: European pig breeding programmes since 1990 have increased the growth rate of meat pigs by 2.4 per cent per year and the number of piglets per litter by 1.6 per cent per year; litter size has been increasing by up to 3 per cent per year in the US; between 1930 and 1990 the daily weight gain of Dutch Landrace and Yorkshire pigs increased by over 50 per cent, their backfat thickness (a measure of leanness) approximately halved and their feed efficiency increased by 20 per cent.[8,17]

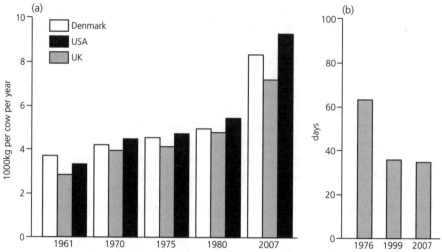

**Figure 2.1** *Historical increases in production reported:*
*(a) Average kilograms of milk obtained per dairy cow kept;*[11]
*(b) number of days to reach 2kg for commercial meat chickens*[13,15]

*Note:* In (b), for 2007 the average performance was 35 days for mixed sexes and 33–34 days for males.[13]

## 2.2 Technologies and practices

### 2.2.1 Specialization for efficiency

The increases in yield from modern livestock have been obtained by specializing their bodies for production of the desired commodity, such as milk, meat or eggs. This has led to large physical differences between specialized strains of chicken and cattle. It has also led to animals whose bodies prioritize production over other physiological functions. The most economically efficient animals are those that direct the largest part of their feed intake to production and have the lowest residual feed intake. As a result, they direct less of their feed to the development of internal organs, bone or fat or to bodily maintenance.[18]

The male and female parents of meat-producing pigs have different tasks and specialization has also taken account of this in order to increase efficiency. An effective male parent is designed to transmit growth rate, muscle weight and leanness. A female parent is designed for fertility and milk production, while also retaining adequate meat-type traits. Modern breeding programmes aim to create the most cost-effective combination of traits for both male and female breeding lines.

### 2.2.2 Selection of meat pigs, sows and boars

A pig has been well described as a 'highly mutable animal, readily bent to the whims of a breeder and, financially, the easiest of all farm mammals to manipulate in step with the market'.[19] One reason for this is that pigs breed so rapidly – at least twice a year, and producing at least ten weaned piglets from each litter to select from. In the mid 18th century British pig breeders imported large numbers of exotic pigs from China, the former Siam and Naples, among other places, which were small and round and had been bred to mature early and to have large litters. These were crossed with the larger, heavier-boned and slower-maturing Old English pigs that utilized feed less efficiently. Historically, pigs were used as a source of animal fat and 19th-century pig breeders aimed at producing ever fatter pigs. These pigs were depicted as almost globular in shape, labouring under mounds of fat. Some of those considered prize specimens had difficulty in standing, walking and sometimes in breathing and were at risk of suffocating while they were sleeping.[20,21]

The fashion for fat pigs ended and in most modern markets lean pigmeat is preferred. Meat pigs are now selected to grow rapidly and produce more muscle from their carcase, in particular from the *longissimus dorsi* muscle (the long back muscle) and the hams. This means a longer back, more muscle depth and less fat; both muscle and fat depth on live potential breeding pigs can be ascertained by ultrasound or CT scans. Lines of female breeding pigs are selected for their ability to produce high numbers of weaned piglets per year, preferably piglets of uniform size and shape. For this the sow or gilt needs need a high ovulation rate, a greater capacity of uterus, a large number of functioning teats and sufficient body reserves to produce milk, while retaining enough body condition to come into oestrus and conceive again shortly after the piglets are removed from her.

While the average number of piglets weaned per sow per year in commercial systems remains in the low 20s, some breeding companies and their customers have increased this to up to 30. The increase is international; in 2008/2009 the average in Denmark was 26.6 and customers in Brazil using sows from Topigs reached 28.6 in 2008.[22] A constraint is that one functioning teat is needed per piglet if every piglet is to survive to weaning, unless artificial feeding is used, so a sow needs at least 12 functioning teats to earn her keep and commonly has between 14 and 16.[23] Geneticists are currently searching for genes associated with higher numbers of teats in pigs.

The companies who produce breeding sows and boars emphasize the productivity and cost effectiveness of their products in their brand names, such as the Genepacker range of female lines and the Geneconverter and Titan sire lines. Geneconverter700 has the 'lowest feed conversion rates achieved by any pig, anywhere in the world' and 'goes to war on feed costs'. He promises an extra profitability of nearly UK£10,000 compared to the average pig herd, per 100 sows, and has an 'extremely high libido'. Hypor's superior sires are 'designed for a purpose'. Other companies offer the Fertilis 'hyperprolific' sows with 'excellent maternal abilities', or sire lines of 'extreme high muscularity', 'extreme conformation' and 'extreme high meat percentage'.[24]

## 2.2.3 The piglet production line

The largest pig-breeding farms often operate a batch system in order to deliver a set number of piglets of the same age to the market per week. This means that on a predetermined schedule a batch of females is inseminated and starts gestation, while at the other end of the reproduction chain another batch of sows has their piglets removed and is returned to the pool for re-insemination. Hormonal treatment with a progesterone such as Regumate and induction may be used to synchronize inseminations and farrowings. Commercial female pigs in intensive systems reach puberty at around five to six months of age and are inseminated, in the majority of cases by artificial insemination (AI), about a month after this. The young female pigs (gilts) are selected for piglet production if they come into oestrus promptly and have the correct weight, shape and at least 12 to 14 teats. Gonadotrophins are sometimes used to bring gilts into oestrus, but they are usually encouraged into their first oestrus by being placed near a boar for a short time daily ('puberty stimulation'). From their first insemination onward, female breeding pigs go into successive cycles of factory reproduction.

In the most intensive commercial systems internationally the pregnant female pigs are confined in a narrow gestation crate (also known as a 'sow stall'). This confinement can be either for the entire pregnancy of $16\frac{1}{2}$ weeks, as is still the case in much of North American pig production, or for the first month after insemination. From 2013 in the European Union (EU), gestation crates will not be legal except during the first month, and are already banned in Sweden and the UK. The gestation crate is essentially an open-topped rectangular metal cage with food and water provided at one end, usually with a concrete or metal slatted floor for excreta to fall through, and is only just wider and longer than the sow's body. She has just enough space to either lie down or stand up, but she cannot move either forwards, backwards or sideways, or turn around. When lying down, her rear may protrude from the end of the crate. Gestating sheds in large intensive operations may contain several long rows of these crated sows. Alternatively, pregnant sows are kept loose-housed in groups. Normally group-housed sows are kept indoors, often on bare concrete or slatted floors or, as typically in the UK, on straw bedding. For maximum efficiency in farrowing and lactation, efforts are made to prevent a sow from getting fat during gestation and her feed may be restricted to as little as one third of what she would choose to eat.[25]

A few days before she is due to farrow, an indoor sow is typically moved to a farrowing crate. The farrowing crate prevents the sow from moving around during the period she is suckling her piglets on the argument that this reduces the likelihood that she will lie on piglets and crush them. It is essentially the same as a gestation crate, normally with a slatted floor and no bedding, but is placed within a slightly larger pen that is separated by bars from the sow. This area is for the piglets to lie in, usually under a heat lamp, and they can approach the sow sufficiently closely to get to her nipples as she lies on her side inside her crate. As in the gestation crate, the sow's choices are limited to standing up or lying down, often with difficulty. Some designs of farrowing crates allow the sow to leave the crate or to have additional space later in the suckling period (see sections 4.2.2 and 4.4.1 in Chapter 4). Free-range pig-breeding farms, which are a significant minority of the industry in some regions and countries, such as the UK, do not use farrowing crates. A high-yielding sow can produce up to 14 litres of milk for her piglets per day and her physiological effort is comparable to that of a high-yielding dairy cow.[25] Some farmers maximize the number of piglets that can be reared per litter by removing some of the strongest piglets from the sow at seven days old and putting them in an automated rearing unit where a milk replacer is dispensed every hour.[26]

At three or four weeks old (or earlier in some systems, mainly in North America), the piglets are removed to be fed up to market weight. The sow is re-inseminated at her next oestrus that should occur around one week later and the cycle of reproduction begins again, giving an ideal turnaround time of about five months per litter. The time it takes to produce one litter can be reduced by weaning the piglets as early as possible and by minimizing the 'wean-to-oestrus' interval. Productivity could in principle be increased further by inducing gilts to reproduce at younger ages, and experiments have achieved reproduction at half the normal age of puberty. This is not normal commercial practice because gilts are not very fertile at this early age.[27]

There is a high turnover of sows, typically 40 per cent each year or more (see section 3.2.2 in Chapter 3). On average, a sow will have between four and six litters before she dies or is discarded from the breeding herd on account of failing health, fertility or lactation. If she fails to become pregnant again after her piglets are removed, she may not be given a second chance. A significant number of sows go before or immediately after their fourth farrowing – in other words after two years of breeding life – although the natural lifespan of a pig is over 15 years.[25,28,29] The 'cull sows' are typically fattened and sold for lower-grade meat.

## 2.2.4 Selection of cattle for meat or milk production

Selection for production purposes has created striking visual differences between the Holstein, a breed selected for milk production and a breed such as the Charolais or the Limousin, selected for beef production. The Holstein cow is tall with slender legs and very little visible muscling; she is often very bony around the rump and tail head, indicating that she is not designed for meat. She needs a large body that allows a high feed intake to maintain milk production. Her most striking feature is the very large udder which resembles a balloon blown up between her legs and protruding between them at the rear. It can become pendulous with use, hanging to below her hocks. The Holstein bull is also lightly muscled, with close to a right angle between his straight back and his hind legs. In comparison, the pedigree Charolais bull, one of the most popular global breeds used for beef, is a hulk of flesh. He is compact, thick legged and stocky, with bulging muscles on his neck, legs, shoulders, back and rounded rump. The Charolais suckler cow is likewise markedly stocky in build and thick legged, although less heavily muscled than the bull. She has a relatively small inconspicuous udder, even when suckling a calf. While pedigree suckler herds of Charolais cows are common in France, their country of origin, in many other regions the Charolais or Limousin bull is used as a terminal sire to transmit fast growth and substantial muscling to cross-bred calves. The Charolais is a global brand used in at least 64 countries.[30] By 2009 Limousin bulls were chosen to sire 22 per cent of all the calves bred in Britain.[31]

Dairy breed selection has been driven by the goal of maximum milk production. In 2003 it could still be said of dairy breed selection that 'Just about every [selection] index formulated for the United States gives yield more emphasis than any other trait.'[32] The average yield of Holstein herds in production-testing in the US is 10,400kg of milk containing 230kg of butterfat and 320kg of protein a year.[33] She thus yields more than her own weight in product per year. Elite high-yielding Holsteins in the US and the UK produce up to 13,000kg per lactation, and the very highest yielding can produce over 30,800kg of milk in a 12-month lactation.[2,12] This is an average of 84kg produced in the udder per day over a year.

By the end of the 20th century it was clear that production demands were taking their toll on the Holstein's overworked body[34] and more terms related to functional health have been added to the selection criteria (see section

© Tim Scrivener

**Figure 2.2** *Premium dairy cows on display at the 2009 Dairy Event, Stoneleigh Park, England*

**Table 2.1** *Examples of dairy cattle selection criteria, 2008*

| Trait in selection index | Holstein Association USA 2008 TPI[7] | DairyCo (UK) 2008 PLI[35] |
|---|---|---|
| Milk production | 47% | 45.2% |
| Lifespan | | 21.1% |
| Early reproduction/fertility | 19% | 18.5% |
| Udder health | 20% | 11% (udder and somatic cell count) |
| Ease of calving and number of stillbirths | 3% | |
| Mobility/locomotion | 8% | 4.1% |
| Body size | 3% | |

1.1.4). By 2008, the Holstein Association USA's Total Performance Index (TPI) and the UK's Profitable Lifetime Index (PLI) included multiple measures of pregnancy rate, milking lifetime, difficult births and stillbirths, the udder's depth and attachment, and the position of udder and teats, feet and legs, body conformation and somatic cell count (the quantity of white cells, indicating udder infection, in milk).[7,35] In 2009, across developed countries the proportion of the total index devoted to milk, protein and fat production ranged from 75 per cent in Japan to 69 per cent in Australia to 30 per cent in Scandinavia.[35]

As dairy breeds have been increasingly specialized for milk, beef breeds have been increasingly specialized for muscle. Over 30 years the average beef cattle carcase has become heavier, by around 2.3kg per year in the UK,[12] and leaner. The heavily muscled breeds such as the Limousin, Belgian (or 'British') blue and Charolais have become the most popular for inseminating dairy cows to produce beef calves, to compensate for the lack of muscle in the dairy breeds. The Belgian blue breed and some lines in the Charolais and other breeds have 'double-muscling'. This is caused by a mutation in the myostatin gene that normally controls muscle growth and has the effect of increasing muscle and reducing subcutaneous fat in the animal, as well as other physiological effects (see section 3.2.4 in Chapter 3). Some pure beef breed cows become so muscle bound that they are unsuited to breeding and suckling calves. Most beef production therefore relies on cross-breeding to get a desired mix of the exaggerated traits that the last half century has created in cattle breeds.

## 2.2.5 The dairy production cycle

For the owner of a commercial dairy cow, one of her most important attributes is her ability to get pregnant when required and infertility is one of the main reasons for cows being culled by their owners. After puberty, cows come into oestrus every 21 days until they conceive. Dairy heifers are generally inseminated by AI from the age of 15 months upward in order to have their first calf at 22 to 28 months of age, after 9 months' gestation. In order to maintain a 12-month interval between calvings, ideally a cow should become pregnant again three months after her calf is born. In practice the calving interval is often longer (sometimes as long as 15 months) and much research is being devoted to reducing it (see also section 3.2.3).

Depending on the rate of replacement of milking cows, up to 30 per cent or more of all the calves born in UK dairy herds are needed to become dairy cows in their turn. Unless sexed semen is used (see section 8.4.3.1 in Chapter 8), this means that up to two-thirds of the dairy herd will be inseminated with dairy bull semen.[31,36] The remainder are inseminated with semen from beef bulls in order to produce suitably muscled beef cross calves to be sold on either for rearing for beef, or to be used to breed beef cattle. Commercial suppliers offer dairy farmers a choice of semen from a range of proven beef bulls, from the relatively modestly muscled Hereford to the double-muscled Belgian Blue. The 'Fertility Plus' and the ominously named 'Fertility Plus Last Chance' products offered by Genus Breeding combined semen from three bulls of the same or different breeds in one straw; the rate of capacitation of sperm varies between different bulls, giving a longer window within which fertilization can occur.[37]

Dairy bulls are on offer to transmit a variety of desirable traits to their daughters and commercial semen companies provide statistical details on the breeding values of their sires for production, reproduction and health traits. Semex has offered a 'Power Line' of bulls chosen to deliver Health Power, Udder Power, Life[span] Power, Production Power, Foot and Leg Power, and Conformation Power. Udder Power bulls 'keep your cows' udders producing volumes of milk lactation after lactation'. Health Power bulls emphasize fertility and durability over milk production. The daughters of Foot and Leg Power sires 'have the feet & legs to get up and down with ease, walk through the [milking] parlor and get to their feed and water'.[38]

The use of artificial insemination rather than a live bull means that the cow's owner is left with the problem of determining when she has come into heat. The cow's oestrus typically lasts on average under 24 hours, and is followed by ovulation several hours later. In practice, many cows may be inseminated when they are not in fact in oestrus. When they turn out not to be pregnant, or not to maintain the pregnancy, they have to be inseminated again. Modern large-scale production systems make it less easy for a stockperson to detect the signs of increased activity and mounting behaviour that indicate a cow is in oestrus. Breeders and farmers can use various aids to heat detection, from the low-tech (tail-paint, to record mounting behaviour) to pressure-activated mounting detectors, vaginal probes, hormone level testing, closed-circuit television and pedometers.

It would be convenient for milk producers to be able to control the entire oestrous cycle of their dairy cows so they know when to carry out AI and can minimize the time the cow is 'empty'. When it is known that the cow is cycling, she can be administered progesterone from a controlled internal drug release (CIDR) device inserted in the vagina. Progesterone inhibits ovulation, and the cow can then be inseminated a couple of days after the device is removed, allowing the producer to synchronize the insemination and calving of a batch of cows. More complex protocols using timed administration of hormonal drugs, such as gonadotrophin-releasing hormone (GnRH) or progesterone and prostaglandin $F_{2\alpha}$ ($PGF_{2\alpha}$), by CIDR and injection to synchronize AI across a herd are under continuing development.[27] Fixed-time AI is a service that breeding companies can offer to farmers and is promoted as an attractive strategy that will 'put you in control'.[39]

Once a dairy cow has calved, the calf is removed almost immediately after birth to be reared separately and the cow is milked for a lactation period of around 10 months (or often 12 months in the US). She then has a two-month 'dry' period before the next calf is born. Much research has been carried out into how to increase the peak yield of her lactation and how to reduce the fall-off in yield after the peak. An artificial aid to increase milk production is the synthetic growth hormone bovine somatotrophin (bST), which can be injected into dairy cows every two weeks. In 2007 nearly 43 per cent of large dairy operations (those milking over 500 cows) used bST in the US but it has been banned in the EU on grounds of animal welfare.[40]

Genetic change in dairy cows has also changed the way they are fed and housed. Cows traditionally produced milk from grazing on pasture in the summer and from conserved grass in the winter, but for 'high genetic merit' cows this is no longer the case. With bodies designed for very high milk production, they can no longer get enough nutrition from grass and need additional sources of energy and protein such as cereals and soya (or, in the 1980s, the ground-up meat and bones of other cows). The largest and highest-yielding herds in the US and Europe are increasingly kept indoors for longer periods, or kept permanently indoors in 'zero-grazing' systems, so that their nutritional intake can be controlled and maximized. Reducing their movement also reduces the proportion of feed they need to consume for body maintenance and temperature control. Increase in genetic merit has thus gone hand in hand with intensification and concentration in the industry, and cows are increasingly likely to be kept in large herds.

If a dairy cow fails to get pregnant too often, or has any other health problems that prevent her from keeping up the reproduction/lactation cycle, she will be culled from the milking herd and sold to produce lower-grade beef. Dairy cows are discarded early in their lives. Studies in the US, Australia, Sweden and the UK show that on average dairy cows have been lasting between 2.5 and 3.5 lactations, and suggest that the replacement rate has been

**Table 2.2** *US milking herd sizes*

| Size of herd (number of cows) | Percentage of total milk cow population (US) |
| --- | --- |
| Under 100 | 24% |
| 500 or more | 50% |
| 1000 or more | 38% |
| 2500 or more | 21% |

*Source:* USDA (2008, vol 1, Chapter 1)[41]

higher in the larger farms.[42] Thus in modern dairy production a cow spends over two years growing up and gestating her first calf and is slaughtered three or four years later. The natural lifetime of a cow could be 20 years (see section 8.3 in Chapter 8).

## 2.2.6 Selection of meat chickens and laying hens

All commercial breeds of chicken are now specialized either for egg production or for meat production and their physical characteristics have moved in opposite directions. Laying hens are typically light bodied, active and inquisitive, spending much of their days foraging and able to run fast across an outdoor range. In appearance an adult laying hen resembles what we think of as a typical chicken, but the males of laying breeds no longer have enough muscle on their breasts to make them marketable for eating. In comparison, the physical proportions of the meat chicken (broiler) have changed markedly. The broiler has been specialized for fast growth and large amounts of breast meat and at six weeks old is about the same weight as an adult laying hen. Viewed from the front, the modern broiler is broad, with short thick legs set far apart and a bulging breast. Continuous genetic selection for breast meat has moved the broiler's centre of gravity forward. Broilers have to walk more slowly, with their feet further apart and their toes pointing outwards, and keep their feet in contact with the ground as much as they can.[43] Compared to a laying hen, they are very inactive (see section 3.2.1 in Chapter 3).

## 2.2.7 The egg and chicken production line

Specialized laying hens are immensely productive. They have been genetically selected to continue laying during winter and to lack the motivation to incubate their eggs. Compared favourably to 'Olympic athletes', they produce their own bodyweight in eggs every 30 days. Even active free-range hens use more than half of their feed intake for egg production and very little for body maintenance. For cost efficiency, breeders have genetically selected for lighter and smaller hens in order to reduce the maintenance feed requirement still further.[44]

Chicks of either meat or egg-laying strains are shipped at one day old from the hatchery to the farm where they are to be reared. Chicks of laying hen strains are sexed immediately after hatching and the male chicks are destroyed (see section 8.4.1 in Chapter 8). A young hen starts laying at around 16–20 weeks of age and continues for around 12 to 14 months at an average rate not far from one egg per day, so that she would be capable of laying 300 eggs in a year. By 14 months the hen's rate of laying drops below economically acceptable levels. In Europe, hens are then considered 'spent' and are sent to slaughter at typically around the age of 70–80 weeks. In the US and many other countries, the hens are often 'force moulted' as a group and then used for one or two shorter cycles of laying. This can take the hen to over two years old before she is culled. Forced moulting involves some shock treatment, such as the sudden reduction or complete removal of the hens' feed (complete feed withdrawal would be illegal in Europe and from 2006 is no longer allowed by the US United Egg Producers welfare guidelines[45]).

Selection of broiler chickens has focused on growth rate, percentage of breast meat and feed conversion efficiency. The speed of growth is critical to the economics of broiler production operations because it determines how many crops of broilers can be sold per year and the profit per bird is minimal. Typically between six and eight batches of fast-growing broilers go through a broiler shed per year, grown from one day to slaughter weight, in a shed containing 10,000 to 20,000 chicks, sometimes more. Breast meat is the most important product and now accounts for about 18–20 per cent of the live weight of the bird.[13,46] Selection reduced the quantity of feed needed to produce 1kg of breast meat from 20kg in 1976 to around 7kg by 2007.[15]

In 2007, a typical Ross 308 male chicken weighed 42g at hatching, when he was delivered to the broiler shed he would be reared in. After 34 days his weight had increased nearly 50-fold, to 2.1kg. In the UK, he is typically slaughtered at this weight. In a further three weeks his weight would have doubled again to 4.2kg. The females grew marginally less rapidly, taking four more days to reach 2.1kg. In the last week of his life a Ross 308 male gained more than 0.5kg, or more than a quarter of his final weight.[13] The heritability of growth rate is still high (around 30 per cent), which means that the breeding companies could continue to select for even faster growth rate.[9]

The parent chickens who produce the meat chicks for rearing are known as 'broiler breeders'. They are selected for rapid growth and muscle development, while the female breeders are also required to have adequate egg-laying and fertility traits. Unlike the majority of the world's commercial laying hens, broiler breeder hens are kept with males in open sheds rather than in cages so that they can mate regularly (female chickens retain sperm for several days). Typically one breeder male will be kept for every seven to ten breeder females. The females produce about 150 chicks during a 40-week laying period[47] and then are sent to slaughter in the same way as commercial egg laying hens. Their eggs are incubated in a hatchery and the chicks supplied to a broiler production farm.

Modern broilers are selected to have a growth rate that assumes that their life will be no more than a few weeks in duration – if their lifespan is longer, the fast growth rate causes problems. A fast-growing broiler chicken has a large appetite and eats more than a slower-growing chicken would do at the same age.[18] These characteristics create a problem for rearing the broiler breeders. The breeding birds have great difficulty in reaching adulthood in good health if they are allowed to eat as much as they want, and death rates can be as high as 20 per cent.[48] To be effective breeders, they are required to reach somewhat less than 3–4kg when they are mature at around 24 weeks of age. If the females were allowed to eat their fill, by 24 weeks they would weigh over 6kg and could become fat and lame with reduced fertility.[49] They might not even survive to that age. Numerous studies have shown that restricting the quality or quantity of the feed given to broilers is the quickest way to reduce the incidence of the most common metabolic diseases that they suffer from (see section 3.2.1 in Chapter 3). For this reason, broiler breeders are fed very restrictively (especially the males) during their rearing period and sometimes during adulthood. Their feed allowance is reduced by half or more and they may be allowed only one quarter of the amount they would choose to eat.[48–50]

## 2.2.8 The uses of reproductive biotechnology

Artificial insemination (AI) and embryo transfer (ET) are more efficient ways of utilizing an animal's reproductive capacity than natural breeding and make it possible to spread desirable genes more rapidly. A single semen collection from a bull is sufficient to inseminate 400–600 cows; from a ram, 30–40 ewes; and from a boar, 20–30 sows.[27] The theoretical potential progeny per year of a bull, ram and boar through AI have been estimated as in the region of 66,000, 13,000 and 22,000, respectively.[51] Already the majority of the top Holstein cattle are born by ET. The technology exists for immature eggs to be removed from a pre-pubertal heifer as young as two to four months old, which would enable her in principle to produce several calves by surrogates before she herself reached puberty.[52] If the time comes when genome testing for desired traits is reliable, animals could be selected while they were still in the uterus or shortly after birth. When the method of nuclear transfer produced Dolly the sheep[53] and other clones in the late 1990s, some animal scientists predicted that cloning opened a new era in the rapid generation of animals optimized for food production. An Australian genetics company envisaged frozen 'families' of thousands of cloned cattle embryos, delivered to farmers at a price competitive with semen.[54]

By the turn of the 21st century cattle clones, sheep clones, pig clones and goat clones were being produced in universities, research institutes and biotechnology companies around the world.[55,56] Flocks and herds of transgenic sheep, goats and cows had been bred from genetically engineered founder animals. These animals were intended either for use in food production or as a source of biomedical products, such as human proteins or organs suitable for transplants. The European Food Safety Authority (EFSA) estimated in 2007 that there were up to 4000 cattle clones and 500 pig clones living worldwide.[56] Several top-yielding Holstein dairy cows have already been cloned in the US and their offspring sold.

In 2008 the world's two main food regulatory bodies, EFSA and the US Food and Drug Administration (FDA), followed by Japan's Food Safety Commission in 2009, concluded that meat and milk from clones or their offspring were essentially safe to go on sale to consumers.[56,57] In 2009 the FDA issued regulatory guidelines for the commercial production of transgenic animals.[58] Both the FDA and the European Medicines Agency (EMEA) have given drug-use approval to the human protein antithrombin (trade name

Atryn), produced in the milk of transgenic goats.[59] These decisions open the way for the retail use of the fourth generation of biotechnology for livestock.

## 2.3 The impact on animals

Genetic selection, modern breeding procedures and the market's demand for higher productivity have changed food animals' bodies and lives. Chapter 3 looks in detail at some of the effects on animals' health and lifespan, while in this section we note some of the consequences of changes in management and breeding methods.

### 2.3.1 Confinement: Behavioural restriction and health

Selection of animals for maximum cost effectiveness has its counterpart in the restrictive husbandry methods that the animals experience. Restricting animals' movement gets the best performance from their genetics. It reduces feed costs for body maintenance because activity is minimized and answers economic questions such as 'What is the minimal space that can accommodate one sow?'[25] The two husbandry systems that became almost universal in commercial pig breeding and egg production from around 1970 onwards were the battery cage for laying hens and the gestation crate ('sow stall') for pregnant pigs.

Since the 1990s or earlier, quantities of scientific research showed that these confinement systems cause physical and psychological suffering to hens and sows. The evidence was reviewed by the European Union's Scientific Veterinary Committee (SVC) in 1996 for hens and in 1997 for sows. A 2005 assessment of hen housing systems by the scientific Panel on Animal Health and Welfare concluded that battery cages present a 'very high' risk to hens' welfare in six areas of impact, compared to two areas of impact for hens with outdoor access[60] (and no housing system for keeping thousands of hens together is without drawbacks).

The use of the farrowing crates is still almost universal in indoor pig breeding systems. Their effects in restricting behaviour are discussed in section 4.2.2 in Chapter 4; but the confinement also has physical effects. Studies in Denmark, Sweden and Ontario, Canada, have found that a high proportion of sows develop shoulder sores in farrowing crates, caused by pressure from prolonged lying on hard floors, such as concrete or cast iron slats. In Ontario, 34 per cent of the sows studied developed a significant shoulder lesion. In Denmark, in the severest cases the sow arrived at the slaughterhouse with a deep open shoulder ulcer exposing the bone.[61]

## 2.3.2 Breeding procedures

### 2.3.2.1 Artificial insemination (AI) procedures

Artificial insemination of cows can be carried out by a veterinarian, a trained technician or a farmer doing 'DIY-AI'. The procedure involves the operator inserting an arm into the animal's rectum to grasp the cervix and guide the insemination tube through it. This is considered a routine procedure carried out on millions of dairy cows annually, but it is probably not comfortable for the cow and has the potential to cause long-term damage if done inexpertly. It is much more difficult to put a tube through the cervix of a sheep, and laparoscopy is the usual method (which in the UK must be done by a veterinarian): this means that AI is not a common commercial practice for sheep. While attempts have been made to develop methods of AI by putting a tube through the ewe's cervix, sometimes involving treatment with oxytocin, these have led to a 'high incidence of cervical damage and stress'.[27]

AI of pigs is straightforward and is routinely carried out by pig farmers. The female pig will stand for insemination when she is in oestrus and the cervix holds the insemination tube. In the most industrialized operations, breeding females are inseminated standing in a row with their rear end towards the inseminator, who proceeds down the line with a catheter and semen bag. Devices are available to speed up and partially mechanize this process. One incorporates a saddle across the sow's back carrying the semen pack under pressure from rollers, relieving the operator of the task of holding up the semen pack until insemination is complete. An auto sow stimulator is available that can be moved down the line in advance of the inseminator. One device has a concave design that nips the sow's abdomen, mimicking the boar's front legs.

The overuse of highly rated sires using AI has the potential to spread genetic disease rapidly. The very unpleasant condition bovine leucocyte adhesion deficiency (BLAD), which affects the immune system of young calves, appeared increasingly in Holstein dairy cattle worldwide in the later 1980s and early 1990s. It was traced to an individual 'high genetic merit' bull. Even after a genetic test for the disease was in place, some carrier bulls continued to be used because of their superior performance traits.[62-64]

### 2.3.2.2 Embryo transfer procedures

Multiple ovulation and embryo transfer (MOET) involves subjecting cows to potentially stressful and uncomfortable procedures that would not be necessary in natural reproduction. The 'donor' cow is treated with gonadotrophins to induce her to superovulate, followed by artificial insemination and later by 'flushing' of the embryos from the uterus using fluid (this requires epidural anaesthesia). Up to ten, but often fewer, embryos are recovered per flush. Embryo collection can be repeated at intervals of six to eight weeks, providing potentially large quantities of embryos for sale. Dairy heifers can be flushed for embryos from the age of 11 months, several months before she would normally start her first pregnancy. The surrogate cow usually has to be treated with hormones to synchronize her reproductive cycle to receive the embryo and maintain pregnancy. The transfer of the embryo is painful and requires epidural anaesthetic injection and a sedative.[27]

*In vitro*-produced (IVP) embryo transfer involves taking oocytes (egg cells) directly from the 'donor' animal's ovary. One way of obtaining eggs is to collect the whole uterus with the ovaries attached from cattle slaughterhouses. Another method is 'ovum pick-up' (OPU) from live cows. The oocytes are mechanically drawn out ('follicular aspiration') from the ovary using a needle attached to a vacuum pump. The needle is inserted into the vagina and then pierces the vagina wall to reach the ovary, guided by the operator's hand inserted into the animal's rectum. Several oocytes can be taken from the cow between once and three times a week. The oocytes are then matured and fertilized in a laboratory and transferred to the uterus of a surrogate cow. One cow in the US reportedly produced 176 transferable embryos over three years by ovum pick-up.[65] Oocyte extraction from sheep and goats is done by surgery.

According to animal scientists, OPU can be used without damaging the structure or function of the ovaries and the reproductive ability of the 'donor' cow and thus her productivity. The measurements that led to these conclusions included physiological measures of stress, milk production, immune function and examination of the ovaries for damage;[27] but we might want to give greater weight to the subjective experience of the cow in relation to restraint in a crush, injection and invasive handling. The procedure requires epidural anaesthesia, and the UK's Farm Animal Welfare Council raised concerns that frequent injections of anaesthetic into the spine would result in chronic pain at the cow's tail-head.[66] *In vitro* embryo production increases the risk of abortion, abnormal placentas, emergency surgery, difficult births and the death of offspring just before or after birth, often because the calves are oversized (large offspring syndrome).[27]

## 2.3.3 Survival and wastage in biotechnology

In general, increasing the level of artificial reproductive technological intervention increases adverse outcomes.[57] Typically, only a few per cent of cloned embryos or embryos injected with modified DNA develop into viable cloned or transgenic animals. In 2008, EFSA cited the proportion of viable offspring from cloned embryos transferred to surrogate mothers as often under 10 per cent, although success rates can be higher and vary widely.[56] Cloning experiments at the turn of the century typically used tens of surrogate mothers to produce a handful of viable offspring (see Table 2.3). Clones not uncommonly have abnormal or undeveloped skeletons or hearts, lungs, kidneys, livers or immune systems. As in *in vitro* embryo production, large offspring syndrome is a recognized feature of cattle cloning, associated with long and difficult births, caesarean sections and abnormal placentas.[56,57,67,68] EFSA concluded that the 'welfare of both the surrogate dam and a significant proportion of clones has been found to be affected' by the various adverse health outcomes.[56]

**Table 2.3** *Examples of animal use and surviving offspring reported in cloning experiments using nuclear transfer (NT)*

| Species and reference | Embryos transferred after NT | Number of surrogate mothers | Live births | Number born dead | Number of surviving offspring |
|---|---|---|---|---|---|
| Sheep[69] | 120 | 78 | 4 | | 0 |
| Sheep[70] | 80 | 42 | 14 | 5 | 3 |
| Sheep[67] | 93 | 41 | 9 | 3 | 0 |
| Cattle[71] | 20 | 14 | 2 | – | 1 |
| Pigs[72] | 586 | 10 | 5 | – | 5 (at 3 months) |
| Pigs[73] | 3104 | 28 | 13 | – | 4* (at 3 months) |
| Pigs[74] | 1141 | 11 | 15 | 5 | Not stated |

*Note:* * Only one of the surviving offspring was 'normal'. Six other piglets born were due to mating of the surrogate, not from NT embryos.[73]

## 2.4 The professionals, the public and the future

### 2.4.1 Animal health professionals

Professionals in animal physiology, reproduction and health have been at the forefront of the industrialization of animal production and reproduction. Many see no inherent problem in the enterprise and view reproductive technology as valuable 'to improve the genetics of a herd or flock'.[75] In livestock breeding, veterinarians are employed to assist the production aims of the owner rather than the interests of the animals (although, of course, these two may coincide). According to a 2009 UK government report on the future of farm veterinary practice: 'The roles, responsibilities and training of veterinarians in the welfare of farm animals are unclear.'[76]

In practice, veterinarians spend much time assisting farmers to maximize the reproductive success of the animals by tasks such as confirming pregnancy in cattle. In the UK, the number of newly qualified veterinarians choosing to enter large animal (food animal) practice has declined. This may be, at least in part, because young veterinarians do not see these tasks as essentially related to the welfare of individual animals. The 2005 position statement of the American Veterinary Medical Association (AVMA) on the debate on gestation crates for pregnant sows illustrates these dilemmas. The AVMA pointed out that some veterinarians 'are opposed in principle to close confinement of animals, some are opposed in principle to the use of animals for food, and some work with the swine industry to maintain animal health and productivity'.[77]

### 2.4.2 Legislative and voluntary regulation

In the EU, the evidence provided to the public by animal welfare scientists has been an important factor in legislative reform of livestock husbandry systems. As a result of political lobbying by animal protection organizations and the public, the EU legislated to end the use of veal crates from 2007, battery cages from 2012 and gestation crates (sow stalls) from 2013.

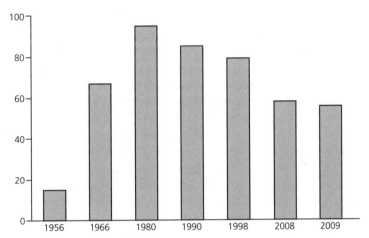

**Figure 2.3** *Changes in the percentage of eggs produced from caged hens in UK as a result of changes in consumer demand*[78]

*Note:* data for 2009 are for the first half of the year.

Political and consumer pressure has already led to increasing numbers of food producers and retailers, restaurant companies and local authorities in Europe and North America taking the decision not to sell or use eggs produced by caged hens. In the UK the proportion of eggs produced in battery cages decreased from a peak of 95 per cent in 1980 to 56 per cent in the first half of 2009.[78] There is now a clear trend towards legislative or voluntary phase-outs of gestation crates internationally. In 2007 Australia agreed a ten-year phase-out. By 2009 seven US states had passed legislation to end the use of gestation crates, and commercial producers accounting for more than 25 per cent of US pigmeat had agreed voluntary phase-outs.[25]

Legislative or voluntary regulation of genetic change has so far made less progress than regulation of husbandry systems, although the EU's Scientific Panel on Animal Health and Welfare reviewed welfare aspects of the genetics of high-yielding dairy cows and of fast-growing meat chickens in 2009–2010 (see section 3.3.4 in Chapter 3 for marketing standards that limit the genetic potential for growth rate of meat chickens).

## 2.4.3 Choices in livestock breeding to 2050

The next half century will be a testing time for food animal production. If the world's human population continues to grow and wishes to consume meat, milk and eggs at the current level and rate of growth, this will probably involve using maximally productive animals, as well as billions of additional animals annually. The world population, 6.7 billion in 2010, is projected to be 9.2 billion by 2050, an increase of 2.5 billion people in 40 years.[79]

If the world chooses to continue along the path of high consumption of meat and milk, the pressure on the animals that deliver it can only increase.

Each animal will be expected to yield more and faster in order to justify the vast global resources of land, crops, water and energy that are devoted to meat and milk production and in attempts to limit the environmental and climate impact of the livestock industry. Greenhouse gas reduction targets need to be met by the animal production industry, which tends to argue that the best way to do this is to increase the output obtained from each animal used, thus obtaining the same output from relatively fewer harder-working animals.

As Chapter 3 shows, genetic selection and management for productivity has already gone too far from the point of view of animal health and well-being. A growing number of animal geneticists and scientists are interested in breeding animals for greater robustness, even if this means somewhat lower production. But the solution to the problem of extreme breeding for productivity may be as much a societal one as a technical one. An alternative view has emerged both among some policy-makers and the public: that scaling down livestock production in the rich countries of the world would be one of the fastest and most effective responses that we could make to reduce the environmental footprint of food production and to free up food crops for the growing world population. A significant reduction in the production and consumption of meat and milk would allow farmers to use slower-growing and hardy animals that require lower inputs of concentrate feed and energy. In terms of global environmental resources, these would be more 'efficient' and more sustainable than the high-input high-output overspecialized livestock that we have been aiming for over the previous decades.

---

### BOX 2.1 DILEMMAS OF SHEEP BREEDING: MULESING

Sheep bred to have large fleeces and long tails are more at risk of flystrike because flies are attracted to faeces caught in the wool of the sheep's backside. The flies lay eggs in the wool and the maggots then eat the sheep's flesh. During the 20th century in Australia, Merino sheep were introduced in order to increase the yield of high-value fine wool. Merino sheep have been selectively bred to carry folds of wool-bearing skin on their bodies and, in particular, woolly folds around the tail and perineal region, which increases the risk of flystrike. To deal with this, from the 1930s the 'mulesing' procedure was developed. Mulesing involved cutting off the folds of skin around the breech and tail to create an area of flat scar tissue on which wool does not grow, either by clamping the skin and cutting off the surplus with a knife, or by using secateurs or shears, without anaesthetic or pain relief. Sheep farmers could alternatively have opted to selectively breed sheep with plain breeches, as the heritability of skin wrinkling and of bare breeches in Merinos are both quite high, but most did not do so.[80]

Mulesing has continued to this day. Public opposition and pressure from retailers internationally led to the Australian sheep industry agreeing a voluntary phase-out of the procedure after 2010; but the industry announced in 2009 that it would not be able to meet this deadline. Best practice currently is to use an anaesthetic/antiseptic spray on the wound immediately after mulesing, providing some short-term pain relief, and sometimes an analgesic injection before mulesing. Retailers and the Australian sheep industry now agree that breeding will be the longer-term solution.

## Notes

1    Preisinger, R. and Flock, D. K. (2000) 'Genetic changes in layer breeding: Historical trends and future prospects', in W. G. Hill et al (eds) *The Challenge of Genetic Change, Occ. Publi. Br. Soc. Anim. Sc. (BSAS)*, vol 27, pp20–28

2    Holstein Association USA (2009) Website home page, www.holsteinusa.com/, accessed 23 April 2009

3    Legg, B. J. (2005) 'Crop improvement technologies for the 21st century', in R. Sylvester-Bradley and J. Wiseman (eds) *Yields of Farmed Species*, Nottingham University Press, Chapter 3

4    Barillet, F., Astruc, J. M. and Lagriffoul, G. (2006) 'Functional traits in small dairy ruminants: Genetic variation and relationships with milk production', paper no 02-01 presented to the Eighth World Congress on Genetics Applied to Livestock Production (WCGALP), Brazil, 13–18 August 2006, Belo Horizonte, Brazil, www.wcgalp8.org.br

5    Hill, W. G. et al (eds) (2000) *The Challenge of Genetic Change in Animal Production*, Occasional Publication of the British Society of Animal Science *(BSAS)* no 27, Edinburgh, http://bsas.org.uk/downloads/genchan/contents.pdf

6    Laughlin, K. (2007) *The Evolution of Genetics, Breeding and Production*, Temperton Fellowship Report No 15, Harper Adams University College, UK

7    Holstein Association USA (2008) *Understanding Genetics and the Sire Summaries*, March 2008, www.holsteinusa.com/

8    Simm, G. (2008) 'Breeding for productivity, efficiency and quality', paper presented to the Scottish Agricultural College Outlook Conference 2008: Food Security in a Climate of Change, Edinburgh, 11 November 2008, www.sac.ac.uk/mainrep/pdfs/breedingoutlook08.pdf, accessed September 2009

9    Simm, G. et al (2005) 'Limits to yield of farm species: Genetic improvement of livestock,' in R. Sylvester-Bradley and J. Wiseman (eds) *Yields of Farmed Species*, Nottingham University Press, Chapter 6

10   Williams, J. (2004) 'The value of genome mapping for the genetic conservation of cattle', in G. Simm et al (eds) *Farm Animal Genetic Resources*, BSAS Publication No 30, Nottingham University Press, pp133–149

11   United Nations Food and Agriculture Organization (2008) ProdSTAT, online database, http://faostat.fao.org/

12   Garnsworthy, P. C. and Thomas, P. C. (2005) 'Yield trends in UK dairy and beef cattle', in R. Sylvester-Bradley and J. Wiseman (eds) *Yields of Farmed Species*, Nottingham University Press, Chapter 20; Shook, G. E. (2006) 'Major advances in determining appropriate selection goals', *Journal of Dairy Science*, vol 89, pp1349–1361

13   Aviagen (2007) *Ross 308 Broiler Objectives*, Aviagen

14   Haley, C. S. and Archibald, A. L. (2005) 'Livestock – genomics and productivity', in R. Sylvester-Bradley and J. Wiseman (eds) *Yields of Farmed Species*, Nottingham University Press, Chapter 19

15   McKay, J. C. et al (2000) 'The challenge of genetic change in the broiler chicken', in W. G. Hill et al (eds) *The Challenge of Genetic Change in Animal Production*, Occasional Publication of the British Society of Animal Science (BSAS) No 27, Edinburgh, pp1–7

16   Arango, J. (2009) 'Improving feed intake and efficiency: Can layer breeders maintain the current rate of improvements in the coming years?', *Poultry World*, June, p30

17   Merks, J. W. M. (2000) 'One century of genetic change in pigs and the future needs', in W. G. Hill et al (eds) *The Challenge of Genetic Change in Animal Production*, Occasional Publication of the British Society of Animal Science

(BSAS) No 27, Edinburgh, pp8–19; Whitney, M. (2009) 'Managing highly prolific sows', *The Pigsite*, May 2009, www.thepigsite.com

18 Emmans, G. C. and Kyriazakis, I. (2000) 'Issues arising from genetic selection for growth and body composition characteristics in poultry and pigs', in W. G. Hill et al (eds) *The Challenge of Genetic Change in Animal Production*, Occasional Publication of the British Society of Animal Science (BSAS) No 27, Edinburgh, pp39–52

19 Trow-Smith, R. (1959) *A History of British Livestock Husbandry, Vol 2: 1700–1900*, Routledge and Kegan Paul, London

20 Moncrieff, E. (1996) *Farm Animal Portraits*, Antique Collectors' Club

21 Wiseman, J. (2001) *The Pig: A British History*, Duckbacks, London

22 Genesus Genetics, website information, www.genesus.net/commentaries/feb-19-07.htm, accessed 22 April 2009; Trickett, S. (2009) 'Putting pig research into practice', *Farmers Weekly*, 9 October 2009, p30; *The Pigsite* (2009) 'Topigs achieves over 27 weaned piglets per sow per year,' *The Pigsite* online, 21 April, www.thepigsite.com/; *Pig Progress* (2009) 'Topigs reach 28.6 piglets per sow in Brazil', *Pig Progress*, online news, 10 July, www.pigprogress.net/

23 Tarrés, J. et al (2006) 'Analysis of longevity and exterior traits on Large White sows in Switzerland,' *Journal of Animal Science*, vol 84, pp2914–2924

24 JSR Genetics (2008) *Latest News: New World Beating Boar Goes to War on Feed Costs*, 15 April 15; Geneconverter sales leaflet, www.jsr.co.uk/contents/17188_Geneconverter_Leaflet.pdf; Génétiporc, website information, www.genetiporc.com/expertise/genetics/, all accessed June 2008; Hypor Inc, Hypor website boar lines, www.hypor.com/; www.hypor.com/dynamic.php?first=46c852241f3f8&second=46c8d94291fe3&third=46c8e2aabb7f9, accessed September 2009; Hypor (2009) Advertisement, *The PigSite*, newsletter, 30 November

25 Council for Agricultural Science and Technology (2009) *Scientific Assessment of the Welfare of Dry Sows Kept in Individual Accommodations*, no 42, March 2009

26 Trickett, S. (2009) 'Pre-weaning systems lowers mortality rate', *Farmers Weekly*, 3 July, pp41–43

27 Gordon, I. (2004) *Reproductive Technologies in Farm Animals*, CABI Publishing, Wallingford, UK

28 Gadd, J. (2008) 'Weaning capacity', *Pig Progress* online, 4 November 2008, www.pigprogress.net

29 Meat and Livestock Commission (2003) *The British Red Meat Industry*, Meat and Livestock Commission

30 FAO (2007) *The State of the World's Animal Genetic Resources for Food and Agriculture*, B. Rischkowsky and D. Pilling (eds), FAO, Rome

31 Long, J. (2009) 'Beef calf registrations in decline according to EBLEX', *Farmers Weekly Interactive (FWi)*, 3 November; see table giving inseminations by beef bulls and by dairy bulls 2008/2009

32 Wilcox, C. J., Webb, D. W. and DeLorenza, M. A. (1992, 2003) *Genetic Improvement of Dairy Cattle*, Animal Science Department, University of Florida

33 Holstein Association USA (2009) *Holstein Breed Characteristics*, www.holsteinusa.com/holstein_breed/breedhistory.html, accessed April 2009

34 McGuirk, B. (2000) 'Genetic changes in ruminants: Historic trends and future prospects', in W. G. Hill et al (eds) *The Challenge of Genetic Change in Animal Production*, Occasional Publication of the British Society of Animal Science (BSAS) No 27, Edinburgh, pp29–38

35 DairyCo (2008) *Breeding Briefs: A Quick Guide to Genetic Indexes in Dairy Cattle*, DairyCo Breeding +, May 2008; Bluhm, W. (2009) *The Role of Crossbreeding in UK Dairy Breeding*, International Agri-Technology Centre for Morrisons/Arla

36  Roberts, D. J. et al (2008) *Beyond Calf Exports: The Efficacy, Economics and Practicalities of Sexed-Semen as a Welfare-Friendly Herd Replacement Tool in the Dairy Industry*, Scottish Agricultural College, Compassion in World Farming and the RSPCA

37  Genus Breeding (2009) *Genus Beef Sires 2009* and *Fertility Plus*®, Online sales leaflets, www.genusbreeding.co.uk

38  Semex (2008) 'Power line', www.semex.com/semex.cgi?lang=en&power=view&sid=1211273761GQ, accessed 29 April 2009

39  Genus Breeding (undated) *Information on the Benefits of Synchronised AI for the Suckler Herd*, Leaflet, www.genusbreeding.co.uk

40  US Department of Agriculture (2007) *Dairy 2007 Part I: Reference of Dairy Cattle Health and Management Practices in the United States, 2007*, Animal and Plant Health Inspection Service; RSPCA (2008) *Farm Animals Information: Bovine Somatotrophin (BST)*, RSPCA; Brinckman, D. (2000) 'The regulation of rBST: The European case', *AgBioForum*, vol 3, no 2/3, pp164–172

41  US Department of Agriculture (2008) *The Census of Agriculture 2007*, USDA, Chapter 1

42  US Environmental Protection Agency (2005) *Ag 101: Lifecycle Production Phases*, www.epa.gov/agriculture/ag101/dairyphases.html, accessed 6 May 2009; Smith, J. W, Ely, L. O. and Chapa, A. M. (2000) 'Effect of region, herd size, and milk production on reasons cows leave the herd', *Journal of Dairy Science*, vol 83, pp2980–2987; Haworth, G. M. et al (2009) 'Relationships between age at first calving and first lactation milk yield, and lifetime productivity and longevity in dairy cows', *Veterinary Record*, vol 162, pp643–647; Hultgren, J. and Svensson, C. (2009) 'Heifer rearing conditions affect length of productive life in Swedish dairy cows', *Preventive Veterinary Medicine*, vol 89, no 3–4, pp255–264; Defra Science Directorate (2008) *Research Project Final Report, AC0205: Developing Technologies to Improve the Fertility of Dairy Cows*, www.defra.gov.uk, accessed June 2009; Trickett, S. (2009) 'Why some cows never turn a profit', *Farmers Weekly*, 25 September 2009, p36; Farm Animal Welfare Council (2009) *Opinion on the Welfare of the Dairy Cow*, FAWC, October 2009

43  Scientific Committee on Animal Health and Animal Welfare (2000) *The Welfare of Chickens Kept for Meat Production (Broilers)*, European Commission; Corr, S. A. et al (2003) 'The effect of morphology on walking ability in the modern broiler: A gait analysis study', *Animal Welfare*, vol 12, pp159–171; Corr, S. A. et al (2003) 'The effect of morphology on the musculoskeletal system of the modern broiler', *Animal Welfare*, vol 12, pp145–157; Skinner-Noble, D. L. and Teeter, R. G. (2009) 'An examination of anatomic, physiologic, and metabolic factors associated with well-being of broilers differing in field gait score', *Poultry Science*, vol 88, no 1, pp2–9

44  Knowles, L. (2008) 'Disease prevention policy success on vets' own unit', *Poultry World*, November, pp36–37; Marangos, T. (2008) 'Is the lower-spec diet the best way to economise?', *Poultry World*, November, p31

45  United Egg Producers (undated) *Animal Husbandry Guidelines for UEP Certified 2007–2008*

46  Aviagen (2007) *Ross 708 Broiler Objectives 2007*

47  Aviagen (2007) *Ross 308 Parent Objectives 2007*

48  Savory, C. J., Maros, K. and Rutter, S. M. (1993) 'Assessment of hunger in growing broiler breeders in relation to a commercial restricted feeding programme', *Animal Welfare*, vol 2, pp131–152

49  Scientific Committee on Animal Health and Animal Welfare (2000) *The Welfare of Chickens Kept for Meat Production (Broilers)*, European Commission

50  Stevenson, P. (2003) *Witness Statement in the High Court of Justice, Queen's Bench Division, Administrative Court, August 2003*, Compassion in World Farming. This statement cites the scientific evidence relating to feed restriction and hunger in broiler breeders.

51  Legates, J. E. and Warwick, E. J. (1990) *Breeding and Improvement of Farm Animals*, eighth edition, McGraw Hill Publishing Company, New York

52  Rudolph, N. S. (1999) 'Biopharmaceutical production in transgenic livestock', *Trends in Biotechnology*, vol 17, no 9, pp367–374

53  Wilmut, I. et al (1997) 'Viable offspring derived from fetal and adult mammalian cells', *Nature*, vol 385, pp810–813

54  McClintock, A. E. (1998) 'Impact of cloning on cattle breeding systems', *Reproduction, Fertility and Development*, vol 10, no 7–8, pp667–669; Lewis, I. M., Peura, T. T. and Trounson, A. O. (1998) 'Large-scale applications of cloning technologies in agriculture: An industry perspective', *Reproduction, Fertility and Development*, vol 10, no 7–8, pp677–681

55  Pennisi, E. and Vogel, G. (2000) 'Clones: A hard act to follow', *Science*, vol 288, pp1722–1727

56  European Food Safety Authority (2008) 'Food safety, animal health and welfare and environmental impact of animals derived from cloning by somatic cell nucleus transfer (SCNT) and their offspring and products obtained from those animals', *The EFSA Journal*, vol 767, pp1–49

57  US Food and Drug Administration (2008) *Animal Cloning – A Risk Assessment*, www.fda.gov/AnimalVeterinary/SafetyHealth/AnimalCloning/ucm055489.htm, accessed November 2009. For a discussion and comparison of outcomes, see Chapter V and Appendix C.

58  US Food and Drug Administration (2009) *Guidance for Industry: Regulation of Genetically Engineered Animals Containing Heritable Recombinant DNA Constructs*, FDA, January

59  *Nature* (2009) 'Transgenic drug gets green light from the United States', *Nature*, vol 457, 11 February, p775

60  Scientific Veterinary Committee (1997) *Report on the Welfare of Intensively Kept Pigs*, European Commission; Scientific Veterinary Committee (1996) *Report on the Welfare of Laying Hens*, European Commission; Panel on Animal Health and Welfare, European Food Safety Authority (2005) 'The welfare aspects of various systems of keeping laying hens,' Annex to *The EFSA Journal*, vol 197, pp1–23

61  Jensen, H. E. (2009) 'Investigation into the pathology of shoulder ulcerations in sows', *Veterinary Record*, vol 165, pp171–174; *Pig Progress* (2009) 'Danish sows face shoulder ulcer problems', *Pig Progress* news online, 21 January, www.pigprogress.net; Rolandsdotter, E., Westin, R. and Algers, B. (2009) 'Maximum lying bout duration affects the occurrence of shoulder lesions in sows', *Acta Veterinaria Scandinavica*, vol 51, p44; Zurbrigg, K. (2009) 'Sow shoulder lesions: Risk factors and treatment effects on an Ontario farm', *Journal of Animal Science*, vol 84, pp2509–2514

62  Nagahata, H. (2004) 'Bovine leukocyte adhesion deficiency (BLAD): A review', *Journal of Veterinary Medical Science*, vol 66, no 12, pp1475–1482

63  Powell, R. L., Norman, H. D. and Cowan, C. M. (1996) 'Relationship of bovine leukocyte adhesion deficiency with genetic merit for performance traits', *Journal of Dairy Science*, vol 79, pp895–899

64  Williams, J. (2004) 'The value of genome mapping for the genetic conservation of cattle', in G. Simm et al (eds) *Farm Animal Genetic Resources*, BSAS Publication 30, Nottingham University Press, pp133–149

65  Gordon, I. (2003) *Laboratory Production of Cattle Embryos*, second edition, CABI Publishing

66  Farm Animal Welfare Council (1997) *Report on the Welfare of Dairy Cows*, FAWC

67  Loi, P. et al (2006) 'Placental abnormalities associated with post-natal mortality in sheep somatic cell clones', *Theriogenology*, vol 65, pp1110–1121

68  D'Silva, J. (2005) 'Farm animal cloning from an animal welfare perspective', paper presented to Ethical and Legal Aspects of Farm Animal Cloning: Cloning in Public Project Workshop, Prague, 24–25 November 2005, www.sl.kvl.dk/cloninginpublic/index-filer/Joycedsilvalecture.pdf, accessed 5 May 2009

69  Denning, C. et al (2001) 'Deletion of the α(1,3) galactosyl transferase (GGTA1) gene and the prion protein (PrP) gene in sheep', *Nature Biotechnology*, vol 19, pp559–562

70  McCreath, K. J. et al (2000) 'Production of gene-targeted sheep by nuclear transfer from cultured somatic cells', *Nature*, vol 405, pp1066–1069

71  Zakhartchenko, V. et al (1999) 'Adult cloning in cattle: Potential of nuclei from a permanent cell line and from primary cultures', *Molecular Reproduction and Development*, vol 54, no 3, pp264–272

72  Polejaeva, I. A. et al (2000) 'Cloned pigs produced by nuclear transfer from adult somatic cells', *Nature*, vol 407, pp86–90

73  Lai, L. et al (2002) 'Production of alpha-1,3-galactosyltransferase knockout pigs by nuclear transfer cloning', *Science*, vol 295, pp1089–1092

74  Kurome, M. et al (2008) 'Production of transgenic and non-transgenic clones in miniature pigs by somatic cell nuclear transfer', *Journal of Reproduction and Development*, vol 54, no 3, pp156–163

75  Thibier, M. (2004) 'Role of reproductive biotechnologies: Global perspective, current methods and success rates', in G. Simm et al (eds) *Farm Animal Genetic Resources*, BSAS Publication 30, Nottingham University Press, pp171–190

76  Lowe P. (2009) *Unlocking Potential: A Report on Veterinary Expertise in Food Animal Production*, Department for Environment, Food and Rural Affairs, UK

77  American Veterinary Medical Association (2005) *AVMA Policy: Pregnant Sow Housing*, AVMA, June 2005

78  Farm Animal Welfare Council (1997) *Report on the Welfare of Laying Hens*, FAWC; Department of Environment, Food and Rural Affairs (2009) *UK Egg Packing Stations Throughput and Prices*, Defra, UK, 6 May 2009

79  Population Division of the Department of Economic and Social Affairs of the United Nations Secretariat (2006) *World Population Prospects: The 2006 Revision and World Urbanization Prospects*, United Nations

80  Phillips, C. J. C. (2009) 'A review of mulesing and other methods to control flystrike', *Animal Welfare*, vol 18, no 2, pp113–121

# 3

# Productivity and Animal Health

## 3.1 Background and context: Unintended consequences

By the beginning of the 21st century, the unintended consequences of the drive to higher livestock productivity had become a matter of public and professional concern, debate and sometimes outrage. During the previous several decades the most important trend in food animal breeding had been genetic selection for a greater yield from one particular body part or function at the expense of the rest of the animal's anatomy and physiology, to the extent that some animal scientists predicted that 'the end point of such selection will be disaster'.[1] The results are sometimes expressed in genetic terms – unfavourable genetic associations between production and health traits – or in terms of genetic selection that has unbalanced or overworked the animal's body. In any event, the result has often made animals less viable and less healthy and reduced the quality of their lives. At the beginning of the 21st century efforts are being made to reverse the damage and this story is far from over. We cannot as yet be sure what the future outcome will be from the point of view of the quality of life experienced by farmed animals.

Some argue that while there may have been problems in the past, the damaging trends have now been halted or reversed, or shortly will be. Researchers believe they are identifying many of the functional and health traits that will enable animals to cope better with the high demands of modern animal production. But few disagree that selection for the goal of increased yield has harmed animals.[2–4] Some see the undesirable consequences as a technical problem in breeding, genetics and husbandry that can and will be solved with a cleverer application of science to animal productivity. Others will see them as an entirely predictable consequence of an excessively instrumental approach to animals, in which we take control of their genetics and reproduction for our own goals without sufficient consideration of their interests.

One underlying problem is that very highly productive animals live too close to a biological knife-edge. As specialized meat, milk, egg or piglet production machines, they need more care and monitoring of their nutritional intake, body condition and environmental temperature than low-input, low-output animals. While the most competent farmers may provide the necessary care, others will not. As discussed in Chapter 2, obtaining maximum feed efficiency often involves keeping the animals indoors for life in order to realize their genetic potential for productivity. This chapter looks at how some of the following aspects of breeding for high productivity have impacted on the health and quality of life of chickens, pigs, cattle and sheep:

- extreme conformation;
- excessive growth rates;
- large litters and large offspring;
- excessive production of milk per lactation or of eggs per year;
- excessive physiological demands on breeding females;
- inbreeding;
- effects on general robustness and adaptability to environmental and disease challenge.

Well-documented examples show that selection and management for increased production have led to animals experiencing more pain, a higher death rate or shorter breeding lives than they could have if they were less highly selected for production. Death rate and longevity can be measured directly so long as reporting is complete, but pain is a subjective experience and harder to confirm scientifically. Scientists use both physiological measurements (such as levels of stress hormones and heart rate) and changes in the behaviour of the animals to assess pain, such as how they walk, stand or lie.[5] None of these indicators of pain is perfect or unambiguous to interpret, and many species avoid giving overt signs of pain. But a sheep that shows 'extreme' and lasting fear of the stockperson who carried out mulesing is probably indicating that the procedure was very painful[6] and has a lasting memory of that pain.

## 3.2 The impact on animals

### 3.2.1 Meat chickens (broilers)

Most of the health and welfare problems that have affected intensively reared broiler chickens can be attributed to selection for excessive growth rate, heavy weight and high proportion of breast muscle (see Chapter 2). The main welfare impacts most clearly related to growth rate that have been documented in the last two decades are:

- lameness and skeletal problems;
- heart failure;
- high mortality;
- restrictive feeding of broiler breeder birds.

In the view of poultry experts writing in 2003, the underlying problem is that 'Since the early 1950s, poultry breeding has focused on increasing profitability, with little regard for the effect on the skeletal, respiratory or cardiovascular systems or the well-being of the bird.'[7]

Other impacts where the effects of growth rate and a crowded indoor environment interact include:

- inactivity;
- breast, leg and foot sores;
- heat stress.

### 3.2.1.1 Growth rate and health

The death rate of fast-growing meat chickens (broilers) can be seven times that of young laying hens of the same age. Normal and accepted death rates of broilers over their short rearing period are between 2.5 and 5 per cent.[8] A death rate of 5 per cent in a shed of 20,000 broilers would amount to 1000 potentially painful deaths within six weeks. Skeletal disorders and heart failure have been common causes of death of fast-growing broilers.

Lameness in meat chickens has been extensively studied and documented. Lameness has a number of immediate causes, but the primary cause is excessive growth rate. According to a 2003 review: 'There is no doubt that the rapid growth rate of birds used for meat production is the fundamental cause of skeletal disorders, nor that this situation has been brought about by the commercial selection programmes used over a period of 40–50 generations.'[7] Essentially, the bird's growth has been intentionally skewed towards muscle rather than the skeleton and internal organs needed to support the growth[1] so that the bird's muscle weight grows faster than its skeletal development can cope with. Skeletal disorders include:[9]

- femoral head necrosis (bacterial chondronecrosis with osteomyelitis), a very painful condition causing chickens to 'vocalize loudly when pressure is applied to the affected region';
- spondylolisthesis (kinky back), which causes partial paralysis, in which the lame broilers sit on their tail with feet extended or fall to one side;
- severely painful ruptures of the gastrocnemius tendon, causing the birds to 'creep' on their hocks using their wings for support;
- twisted legs (valgus-varus deformity);
- tibial dyschondroplasia, a disorder of bone growth which has been found in the past to affect from 30 per cent to over 50 per cent of fast-growing chickens, and can lead to mild or severe chronic pain.

Gait Score (GS) is a widely used measure of the walking ability of chickens, ranging from GS = 0, indicating normal gait, up to GS5, indicating that the bird is so lame that it is unable to walk. GS3 indicates that the bird is having difficulty moving around and prefers to sit whenever possible, probably because standing and walking are painful. A UK survey by the School of Veterinary Science at Bristol University, published in 2008, tested 51,000 chickens in 176 commercial flocks representing 4.8 million birds, owned by large chicken producers who cooperated with the research. At around 40 days

© Compassion in World Farming

**Figure 3.1** *A lame broiler chicken unable to use one leg*

old, only 2.2 per cent of the chickens had no walking abnormality. Nearly 28 per cent of the birds had Gait Scores of 3 or above, in spite of the fact that stockmen remove and cull obviously lame birds from broiler sheds at least once a day.[10] This is about 2 per cent higher than the levels of lameness reported by the same university in 1992.[11] Similar levels of skeletal problems have been found in Scandinavia[12] and are probably worldwide because the same fast-growing strains are used globally.

Chickens scoring less than GS3 for lameness may still find walking difficult and be in some pain. Experiments have found that lame chickens preferentially choose feed laced with carprofen, an analgesic, including chickens scoring GS1.[13] The chickens that are crippled may be suffering from chronic pain and anxiety because they cannot get to food and water, and some lie on the floor until they die from dehydration.[14] In contrast, chickens of egg-laying breeds (not selected for fast growth) choose to spend a lot of their time foraging and walking around their range, when they have one. Fast-growing broilers towards the end of their lives spend between 76 and 86 per cent of their time lying down and even lie down to eat. Chicks of egg-laying breeds spend less than 30 per cent of their time lying down at the same age.[8,15]

Heart failure can affect fast-growing broilers at only a few weeks old. They are at risk of developing heart and lung problems because these organs struggle to supply the oxygen and blood flow demanded by their high metabolism.

Pulmonary hypertension develops, leading to ascites, a form of heart failure in which the abdomen becomes dilated with fluid so that the bird has difficulty breathing and 'is in obvious physical distress'.[16] The number of deaths from ascites has been reported by farmers to be 1.4 per cent in the UK in 1993.[17] Past surveys suggested that from 0.1 to 3 per cent of chickens in Europe died from sudden death syndrome, or 'flip-over'; in this condition apparently healthy birds convulse and fall over dead after ventricular fibrillation, a condition related to their rapid metabolic rate.[8,16]

Slower-growing strains of broiler, such as those used in organic and premium free-range production, are more active and healthier. They spend on average more than twice as much time walking or running compared to fast-growing broilers,[18] and carry out significantly more perching, scratching and ground-pecking.[19] In a Swedish study, at six weeks old over 85 per cent of slower-growing chickens had normal walking ability, while between 65 and 84 per cent of the fast-growing birds had some degree of walking abnormality when both groups were fed *ad libitum*.[20] Fewer slow-growing broilers develop tendon degeneration, heart abnormalities and curvature of the spine.[19] A US study in the early 1990s found the death rate of modern broilers was more than twice that of chickens from an unselected strain dating from 1957, mostly due to ascites and 'flip-overs'.[21]

As discussed in section 2.2.7 in Chapter 2, the breeding birds of broiler strains ('broiler breeders') are severely feed restricted to keep them viable and fertile up to adulthood. In some countries, but not permitted in the UK, 'skip-a-day' feeding is used, where these birds, who have evolved to spend most of their days foraging and eating, are not fed at all one day in two. Studies of feed-restricted broiler breeders have shown they are 'chronically hungry, frustrated and stressed'.[22,23]

### 3.2.1.2 Interaction of environment and breed type

When intensively reared broilers reach a typical weight of around 2kg there can be 15–20 birds per square metre in a broiler shed (depending on regulations and local practice), and this level of crowding makes it harder for the chickens to move around easily. Overcrowding tends to increase the build-up of wet chicken faeces in the floor litter and this in turn increases 'ammonia burns' or sores on the chickens' breasts, legs and feet where they are in contact with the litter. Because they spend most of their time lying down, especially if they are lame, they are more at risk of hock and breast burns. A Cambridge University survey in 2005 found that 82 per cent of broiler carcases in UK supermarkets had evidence of hock burns.[24]

Overheating and high humidity are other consequences of fast growth and a crowded indoor environment. Faster-growing chickens generate more heat and need a cooler ambient temperature than their ancestors. In poorly regulated sheds, chickens are observed to start deep panting in the last two weeks of their lives.[25] If the ventilation fails in hot weather there can be high mortality.

---

**BOX 3.1 COMPASSION IN WORLD FARMING'S CHALLENGE TO THE LEGALITY OF FAST-GROWING BROILER CHICKENS**

*adapted from a text by Stevenson (2003)*[26]

In 2003 the British farm animal protection organization Compassion in World Farming (CIWF) brought a case in the High Court in London against the Department for Environment, Food and Rural Affairs (Defra). This took the form of a judicial review, a process for challenging the lawfulness of the government's policies or actions. CIWF argued that under European Union (EU) and UK law the use of fast-growing broiler genotypes should be ended because these lead to chronic hunger for feed-restricted breeding chickens and also to painful lameness and heart disease for the meat chickens. CIWF's legal arguments were that:

- The EU's 1998 General Farm Animals Directive stipulates that animals must be given a sufficient quantity of food to maintain them in good health and satisfy their nutritional needs. In addition, UK law requires animals to be given sufficient food to promote a positive state of well-being. CIWF argued that restrictive feeding breaches these laws.
- The Annex to the same EU Directive states that 'No animal shall be kept for farming purposes unless it can reasonably be expected, on the basis of its genotype or phenotype, that it can be kept without detrimental effect on its health or welfare.' CIWF argued that there is abundant scientific evidence to show that fast-growing broiler genotypes cannot be kept without many of the birds suffering from painful leg disorders and heart problems, and that therefore the use of these fast-growing genotypes should be ended.

Defra argued that today's broilers have been bred to grow so quickly that if the breeders were not put on restricted rations their growth would be so fast that many would suffer from leg, heart and other health problems. Therefore the broiler industry is entitled to strike a balance between the competing welfare problems of hunger and of the need to restrict the bird's feed to prevent suffering from serious health problems. CIWF argued that it is not necessary to find such a balance because scientific research clearly shows that the slower-growing strains of chicken can be given sufficient to eat to prevent hunger without being at risk of health problems.

Although CIWF lost the case, the judge said that it had highlighted an important aspect of the standards of humanity in a civilized society. The judge required CIWF to pay only two-thirds of Defra's costs, which indicated that he recognized the seriousness of the issues that CIWF had raised.

---

## 3.2.2 Pigs

Selection for fast growth and leanness and for larger and frequent litters has also begun to affect the health of both breeding pigs and growing pigs (reared for meat). The effect on the survival of piglets is discussed in section 3.2.5. The main areas of impact are:

- physical exhaustion of sows;
- lameness and heart problems;
- in some strains, susceptibility to stress;
- possibly increased susceptibility to infectious disease.

We saw in Chapter 2 that breeding sows on average have a very short reproductive lifetime, often two years or fewer, before they are sold for slaughter or die on farm. Over the last decade as the number of piglets produced per sow per year has increased, the average lifetime of a breeding sow has decreased. By 2007, in the US the turnover of sows was nearly 60 per cent per year (culling 51 per cent, deaths 8 per cent), and around 52, 45 and 38 per cent in Canada, Britain and Japan, respectively.[27] Sows are most often discarded and culled because of reproductive failure and lameness.[28-30] Culling and death often happen around the time of farrowing and after weaning, when ill health and reproductive failure take their toll.

Breeders and the pig industry are aware that the high culling and death rate of sows is linked to a number of interrelated factors involving workload, environment and breeding. Sows could in principle be bred with the ability to be productive for longer; some defects in leg conformation have a moderate heritability[31] and sows with a larger number of functioning teats are less likely to be culled.[28] On the other hand, modern sows are bred to have large bodies and to have relatively slender legs so that a smaller proportion of the animal's feed goes into producing bone. The sow's weight, which increases as she gets older, encourages lameness. Large litters increase the demands on the sow's body reserves and on her legs. The breeding of pig strains for leanness can mean that the sow does not have enough fat to maintain lactation and so 'milks off her back', loses condition and thus the ability to re-conceive. Breeding for leanness also has the effect of reducing the sow's appetite during lactation, so she may not effectively replenish her reserves. Her failure to match her food intake to her output can be compounded if she eats less because of heat stress or because lameness prevents her from reaching food and water. In aiming for 'hyper-prolificacy' and as many as 25–30 weaned piglets per sow per year, the pig breeding industry may have forced the pace beyond the physical capacity of the females, creating what one industry adviser has described as 'shattered sow syndrome'.[32]

The evidence is that many sows are lame. US studies have found that 99.8 per cent of cull sows had some degree of leg problem.[33] In Denmark, degenerative arthritis, which causes joint swelling and pain, was found in 88 per cent of culled sows and 93 per cent of the sows who died on farm.[30] A study of pig farms in England found that 16.9 per cent of gestating sows had an abnormal gait,[34] and lameness accounts for the majority of deaths of sows on UK farms.[35] Results from the UK industry body BPEX in 2009 suggest that deaths are more likely when sows are managed more intensively, in particular when:[35]

- they are housed indoors rather than outdoors (nearly twice as likely to die);
- they are housed (indoors) on slatted flooring rather than on straw;
- they are managed in batch reproduction rather than the less rigid schedule of the continuous flow system.

---

### BOX 3.2 MODERN PIG GENOTYPES, STRESS AND DISEASE

During the 1960s and 1970s it was found that a recessive gene (the 'halothane gene') associated with extremely lean and muscular pigs also caused unusual levels of stress, leading to high mortality and poor meat quality. Such pigs were found in the high-lean Piétrain breed and others. Most lines of lean pigs have by now had the halothane gene bred out, but some breeding lines have perpetuated it. Heterozygous offspring have somewhat reduced meat quality[36] and are 4.5 times more likely to collapse and die in stressful situations, such as transport and handling, than normal pigs.[37]

Some research suggests that selection of pigs for growth and leanness may have reduced their capacity to resist disease, because their bodily resources are over-directed to production. The use of modern pig breeds may have a role in the global spread of serious viral production diseases such as porcine reproductive and respiratory syndrome (PRRS, or 'blue ear'); studies in China found that pigs in large pig farms, more likely to use modern breeds, were more than twice as likely to be infected with PRRS than small farms using local breeds. The use of infected semen and buying in pigs from outside may also have been factors in infecting the large farms.[38]

---

In analogy to what has happened to fast-growing broiler chickens, selection has probably forced the pig's body to allocate too many resources to growth and musculature, leaving insufficient resource to other organs that are needed to cope with the pig production environment. By the late 1980s the weight of a commercial pig was 2.8 times that of a wild boar of similar age, but the relative size of the heart (as a proportion of body weight) was 45 per cent lower.[37] The Scientific Panel on Animal Health and Welfare of the European Food Safety Authority (EFSA) concluded in 2007 that: 'The genetic selection of pigs for rapid growth and lean meat without enough consideration of other factors has led to some widespread and serious problems, in particular leg disorders, cardiovascular malfunction when high levels of activity are needed or stressful conditions are encountered, and inadequate maternal behaviour.'[37] A study of nearly 90 pig herds in England found that 19.7 per cent of finishing pigs, only a few months old, had abnormal gait indicating some degree of lameness.[34]

### 3.2.3 Dairy cows

There is a high level of agreement that the health and robustness of high-yielding dairy cows has been damaged by excessive genetic selection for milk yield and for physical characteristics such as the large, slender and bony frame of the Holstein cow in particular.[4,39,40] The EFSA Panel on Animal Health and Welfare concluded in 2009 that 'Long-term genetic selection for high milk yield is the major factor causing poor welfare, in particular health problems, in dairy cows.'[40] Her health and quality of life have been damaged in the following areas:

- decreasing fertility;
- lameness;
- mastitis;
- digestive problems;
- difficult births and stillbirths.

**Table 3.1** *Milk yield per lactation of US Holstein dairy cows born in the last two decades of the 20th century (average for the breed)*

| Trait | Year of birth 1980 | Year of birth 2000 |
| --- | --- | --- |
| Milk yield (kg) | 8003 | 11,505 |
| Fat yield (kg) | 290 | 419 |
| Protein yield (kg) | 241 | 345 |

*Source:* Shook (2006)[4]

The most conspicuous adverse effect of selection over the 20th century was a reduction in the cow's productive lifetime. The number of lactations that a cow has in her life can be reduced either because she takes longer to become pregnant again after calving or because she is culled at a younger age because of reproductive failure or ill health. The proportion of Holstein dairy cows in the north-east US still alive at four years of age decreased from 80 per cent in 1957 to 60 per cent in 2002, while their average milk yield more than doubled over the same period.[41] Around half of US dairy cows of all the main dairy breeds (Ayrshire, Brown Swiss, Guernsey, Holstein and Jersey) born in 1999 did not survive to have a third lactation,[42] and a significant proportion of US Holstein heifers may not complete one lactation.[43,44] In Britain there is also concern that the average number of lactations per cow has decreased since 1980, mainly due to a fall in fertility, and National Milk Records data from 2009 show that too many cows do not reach a third lactation and hence never become profitable.[45]

Holsteins tend to be inbred through the national and international use of top-ranking bulls, and inbreeding has been increasing.[40,46] In 2004 the effective population size for US Holsteins (from 3.7 million cows enrolled in milk recording) was calculated to be 60. An analysis of US Department of Agriculture (USDA) records suggests that two bulls born in the 1960s, Elevation and Chief, were related to 30 per cent of recorded US Holsteins of 2005.[46] In August 2009, seven of the ten Holstein bulls ranked highest in the UK's Profitable Lifetime Index (PLI) had the same father, O-Bee Manfred Justice, a top international sire with thousands of daughters worldwide.[47] 'Inbreeding depression' typically results in a reduction in fertility and an overall decrease in health and robustness.

Fertility is a key indicator of dairy cow fitness, but the pregnancy rate for Holsteins was decreasing at around 1 per cent per year in the UK and around 0.5 per cent per year in the US in the last quarter of the 20th century. By the end of the century their conception rate was only 43 per cent in the UK and 34 per cent in the US.[4,41,48,49] It appears that the industry accepted these reductions in fertility at the time because they were associated with large increases in milk yield.

Loss of fertility and fitness seem to be the result of creating a cow who puts her main physiological effort into one function – milk production. This makes cows more fragile and more difficult to feed and look after adequately. Her genetic drive to secrete milk, fat and protein can exceed her capacity to eat enough nutrients to support this output,[50] particularly in early lactation, shortly before she is expected to start another pregnancy. Cows in early lactation (producing perhaps 50kg of milk a day) are therefore in negative energy balance and make up the deficit by using their bodily reserves. They may metabolize functional tissue during negative energy balance, which is technically starvation, and 'This risk is particularly severe in high-producing genetic strains', according to EFSA's 2009 report.[40] Loss of body condition disrupts the cow's oestrous cycle and is believed to be a major factor in fertility failure.

Mastitis and lameness are two painful and debilitating conditions associated with breeding for high milk yield. By 2007, the very painful udder infection mastitis was reported to be at an 'historical high' in the UK and was estimated at a mean of 71 cases per 100 cows per year.[51,52] Numerous studies show high levels of lameness in dairy cows internationally.[53–56] A 2008 study of Danish Holsteins found that 25 per cent of heifers had signs of lameness even before first calving and 81 per cent had abnormal conformation of the feet and legs.[53] In Brazil, Holsteins were 3.8 times more likely to develop foot problems than the lower-yielding Brown Swiss breed, and 4.5 times more likely than girolando cattle (a Holstein–gyr (*Bos indicus*) cross).[56]

High-yielding cows are more likely to be kept indoors in zero grazing conditions, but housing on hard floors is bad for their feet and legs and increases lameness.[57] When cows are in pain they stand and walk differently, arching their backs, bobbing their heads, taking longer for each stride and trying to take their weight on three legs.[58] We are probably asking cows to carry uncomfortably heavy weights of milk in their udders, whether or not they are lame, and studies show that they walk more easily after they have been milked.[59]

Other welfare problems include acidosis of the rumen (from concentrate feed intended to boost nutrient intake), displaced abomasums and stillbirths. In 2006 the US Holstein Association reported that 8 per cent of calves were stillborn or died within 48 hours.[42] The Holstein breed is now much criticized or derided by some, like a sports car that has been found to have serious design faults. Other professionals believe that high-yielding dairy cows, well managed and carefully selected, can avoid welfare problems and are essential for the success of the dairy industry. Dairy scientists see evidence that we passed the nadir of health associated with dairy cow breeding in the 1990s and that the current trend in health is upward, as a result of better selection indices.[4,42] In 2009, Canadian dairy scientists analysed Interbull data up to the start of 2008 and concluded that 'a significant genetic progress for longevity has been achieved worldwide'.[60]

---

**BOX 3.3 THE RESULTS OF INADEQUATE CARE OF DAIRY COWS**

A study of 80 dairy farms by Bristol University Veterinary Department in England was reported in the *Veterinary Record* in 2003. In the 20 per cent of farms judged 'worst' for dairy cow welfare the following range of health outcomes were found:[61]

- 33–61 per cent of the cows were classified as 'thin';
- 25–47 per cent of the cows were observed to have a bloated rumen;
- 5–40 per cent of calvings needed assistance;
- 28–47 per cent of cows conceived to first service;
- 47–120 recorded cases of mastitis per 100 cows per year;
- 30–50 per cent of the cows were observed to be lame;
- 70–97 per cent of cows were observed to have swollen hocks;
- 29–50 per cent were observed to have ulcerated hocks;
- 50–78 per cent of cows were observed to have 'severe difficulty' in standing up, suggesting they were suffering from limb pain.

---

## 3.2.4 Beef cattle

As discussed in Chapter 2, beef cattle during the second half of the 20th century were bred to be faster growing and more muscular, and some pedigree breeders selected their bulls for extreme muscularity. The EU's Scientific Committee on Animal Health and Animal Welfare (SCAHAW) in 2001 concluded that hyper-muscularity could lead to leg disorders, calving difficulties and reduced lifespan of the breeding cows.[62] Fast-growing Limousin bulls can grow at a rate of 2kg per day, faster than their bones, ligaments and tendons can cope with.[63]

Those most extreme conformations are in the 'double-muscled' cattle homozygous for the mutated myostatin gene. During the 20th century, breeders deliberately selected for double-muscling in the Belgian blue and Piedmontese breeds in particular, and to a lesser extent in the Charolais breed. Charolais cows sired by homozygous double-muscled bulls between 1996 and 2006 had around 16 per cent higher muscle scores and around 10 per cent lower skeletal scores than cows that had normal sires.[64] Double-muscled cattle are more susceptible to stress and get tired more easily, according to the SCAHAW. They often have increased difficulty of calving because of the muscularity of both mother and offspring. A survey in 2000 of French pedigree records showed that 88 per cent of Belgian blue cows had a caesarean section for their first calf.[62] Charolais breeders usually avoid breeding from cows who are double-muscled themselves and the number of homozygous double-muscled bulls is only a few per cent of the total breeding bulls.[64] But the mutation is still considered useful and is retained in beef breeds because of its effect on offspring.

## 3.2.5 Reproductive output of pigs and sheep

Genetic selection to increase the number and the size of offspring has had negative results for both mothers and offspring. By 2000, it was becoming clear that the selection of sows to produce larger litters tended to increase the proportion of piglets that were stillborn or died before weaning.[65–67] In France, the average number of piglets born per litter increased from 11.9 in 1996 to 13.8 in 2006, while the death rate of piglets increased by 10 per cent.[66] In the UK, 15–20 per cent of piglets die before weaning, an estimated 2 million piglets per year.[68]

Large litters put higher demands on the sow's placenta to supply oxygen and nutrients to the foetuses. If the placenta's supply is inadequate, some pig foetuses fail to develop properly. Although breeding companies promise that their breeding sires and dams will produce more 'uniform' litters, in reality larger litters tend to have a wider range of piglet sizes, including a higher proportion of small and weak piglets that do not survive. Differences between a piglet's size and the mean size for the litter are one of the primary factors in stillbirth.[69] Modern pig strains are selected for large size, leanness and long backs, to increase their meat yield. While the larger piglets of a litter are most likely to survive, stillborn piglets have been found to be disproportionately long and thin. In general, piglets that are rounder in shape (higher body mass index) are more likely to survive to weaning.[68,70]

Large litters can take up to five hours or more to be born, increasing the risk of death and oxygen deprivation, especially for those born later in the farrowing (oxytocin is often administered to the sow to speed up farrowing). Very large piglets can become obstructed and die during farrowing. Small and weak piglets are less likely to suckle soon enough and are more likely to get chilled, become inactive and die from hypothermia, starvation or from being crushed by the sow. The selection for larger sows also increases the risk that she will crush her piglets. Crushing is more likely still if the sow has poor muscle tone from lack of exercise and has difficulty manoeuvring herself within a narrow farrowing crate (see section 4.2.2 in Chapter 4).[65,71]

In view of these facts, in 2007 the EU's Scientific Panel on Animal Health and Welfare recommended against selection for more than 12 piglets per litter,[72] contrary to what some in the global industry are aiming for. However, selection for large litters may produce more weaned piglets for sale, when the higher number of piglets born outweighs the increase in the death rate.

Selection for ewes who produce more than one lamb per litter can have results that are analogous to increasing the number of piglets per litter. The mortality of young lambs remains globally very high, in spite of the immense advances in veterinary knowledge and medicine during the 20th century.

Lambs are most at risk of dying in their first week of life, from chilling, starvation and infections, and the large majority of ewe deaths also occur around lambing. The sheep industry internationally appears to accept that many lambs will not survive their first weeks. In the UK the lamb death rate is recorded as 10–15 per cent, including those born dead, but it can be much higher[73] and lamb deaths are not always recorded. In New Zealand, two Romney herds studied in 1997–2000 had a lamb mortality rate of 19 per cent.[74] In Australia, cross-bred and Merino herds have a lamb mortality rate of 22–27 per cent.[75]

The sheep industry has at least two economic drivers of their breeding goals, and these can conflict. One is to increase the size and musculature of lambs and to increase the number of lambs per litter. The other is to minimize the labour and cost involved in shepherding, which requires the breed to be hardy in outdoor conditions and to give birth easily ('easy-care' sheep). In conditions such as highland sheep farming in Scotland, which is often not cost effective and survives on public subsidy, hardy Scottish Blackface ewes are used and in harsh hill conditions they are usually not expected to produce more than one lamb each.

Sheep that are kept to be commercially productive are expected to produce closer to an average of two lambs each and this inevitably increases the number of triplet litters that are born. Farmers may even regard triplets as a necessary evil in order to increase the overall lambing percentage for their flock. In New Zealand, an increase in triplet lambs and in pre-weaning mortality has accompanied a 24 per cent increase in lamb output per ewe since 1960.[76] Triplets are born with lower temperatures and lower red blood cell counts than twins and, as in large piglet litters, it appears that the mother's placenta has often not been able to provide enough oxygen and nutrients to all the growing foetuses.[77] British sheep veterinarians have commented that 'In prolific breeds reproductive output has outstripped the digestive ability to maintain such output. This is partly due to abdominal space limitations, but also to sheer nutrient demand (a ewe with triplets has the equal demand of a sow with 30+ piglets).'[78]

In Scottish Blackface lambs, triplets have 3.6 times the risk of being born unviable and are nearly twice as likely to die before weaning compared to twins.[79] In an Australian study of Merinos, 23 per cent of singles, 32 per cent of twins and 45 per cent of triplet (or higher) litters failed to survive.[80] As with large litters of piglets, there is a wide range of weights between triplet lambs and the smallest have less chance of surviving to weaning age. In a New Zealand study, death rates were 56 per cent for the lightest, 40 per cent for the medium and 28 per cent for the heaviest lamb of a triplet.[81] As the ewe normally has only two teats, one of the triplets is often cross-fostered to another ewe, which increases the risk to its survival. Selection for ewes with four functional teats has been attempted in the prolific Lleyn breed.[82]

The drive to achieve more and larger lambs also impacts the health of the ewes. Twin-lamb disease (pregnancy toxaemia) is a metabolic disease caused by insufficient nutrient intake in pregnancy and is known to be more likely in ewes carrying twins and triplets or one very large lamb. Affected ewes cannot stand or eat, tremble, become comatose and often die. A ewe gestating more than one lamb has to put all her resources into the foetuses rather than into other functions such as her immune system, making her more susceptible to problems such as worms that a ewe carrying a single lamb could resist without chemical treatment.[83] Large litters may thus contribute to the wider animal health problem of increasing resistance to anthelmintic drugs.

Prolapse of the vagina and difficult births are also associated with selection for larger litters and for larger lambs. In the large-sized breeds selected for meat yield in the UK, such as the Suffolk, the lambs have been bred to be so large that around half of ewes cannot give birth without assistance and the lambs have to be pulled out routinely.[84] In a British case reported in the *Veterinary Record* in 2008, several Texel-cross ewes who developed ventral rupture before lambing, possibly related to carrying multiple lambs, came from a flock where up to 100 ewes had oversized udders that hung so close to the ground that the lambs struggled to suckle.[85]

### 3.2.6 High-yielding laying hens

During a laying period of 14 months, a modern hen is capable of laying almost 350 eggs,[86] and selection has increased the size of the egg relative to the size of the hen.[87] Her health is impacted both by her genetic potential for production and by commercial conditions where thousands of adult hens are kept together. Scientists at the Clinical Veterinary Science Department of the University of Bristol examined 26 commercial laying hen flocks and found that the hens' physical condition at the end of the laying cycle was a cause for concern in all husbandry systems. The hens tended to be emaciated, to have lost feathers, to have broken bones and to have damage to their vents. Their continuous output of egg shells depletes their bones of calcium, making bones brittle and easily broken (see section 8.3.2 in Chapter 8). A high proportion of hens in the Bristol survey were affected by these health problems, including:[87]

- medium to severe damage to vent or abdominal feathers: 81.2 per cent of hens;
- keel-bone fractures: 55.7 per cent of hens;
- emaciated body condition: 25.5 per cent of hens;
- damage to vent from pecking: 9.4 per cent of hens;
- bloodstained eggs: 1 to 2 per cent of eggs.

The study concluded that 'artificial selection for high productivity in modern layer hens is the primary cause of these welfare problems, which are only marginally influenced by the housing system'.[87]

Feather-pecking, vent-pecking and sometimes cannibalism are very serious problems in modern egg production if hens are kept crowded together and cannot escape from attack. Feather-pecking is related to husbandry methods but it is also known to be heritable and is associated with breeding for high egg production by individual hens; it is also found to increase when hens are stressed by high production or cold weather that increases their nutritional demand.[88] Breeding experiments in the US, in which no intervention was made to save hens who were being pecked, have demonstrated a link between selection for high egg production and deaths from pecking. The USDA has reported that mortality increased tenfold in one experimental line of 'commercial' hens over 20 years of selection for increased production. In one US experiment, hens of a commercial line selected for high production in individual cages were kept in groups without intervention, resulting in a cumulative mortality of 80 per cent by 58 weeks of age. Selection of hens for 'group production' (that is, taking into account the number of hens killed in the group during the production period) reduced the mortality to 20 per cent of the hens. The individual hens in the group were less high yielding but stayed alive longer.[89] In order to reduce injuries from pecking, commercial egg producers usually amputate the sharp end of hens' beaks (usually carried out at the hatchery).

## 3.3 The professionals, the public and the future

### 3.3.1 Breeders, animal scientists and farmers

There are several possible responses to the evidence that managing animal reproduction with the primary aim of increasing yield is bad for animal health and welfare. Ideally we would never have carried out such excessive selection for productivity, but we have done it and the health problems need to be solved. One logical approach would be to stop breeding the worst-affected animal strains, such as fast-growing chickens and high-yielding dairy cows. But most scientists and breeders are confident that they can continue to 'stay good' while they 'play God' in taking on the role of natural selection.[90]

Many animal scientists believe that it is not a change of objective – overall productivity – that is needed, but better attention to detail. They argue that many of the deleterious side effects of selection have been spotted over the last couple of decades and are already being dealt with in breeding programmes. Studies have shown that cows selected for high milk production may have genes that have a negative effect on fertility, which could in principle be bred out.[91] In this view, better selection based on analysis of genetic trends in interacting traits can reconcile the goals of productivity and animal health so effectively that we achieve a 'win–win' situation for farmer and animal alike.[2,92] Most animal ill health and disease causes economic losses either in the short or long term, as well as suffering to the animals. It is thus obviously in the interest of breeding companies and farmers to reduce ill health that is related to past genetic selection when this leads to greater overall cost effectiveness. Because there is genetic variation in traits such as leg health and offspring survival as well as in productivity, it should in principle be possible to breed animals that more cost effective than today because they combine good health with good productivity.

Breeders have already started to change their breeding goals. During the 1990s the major chicken breeding companies started selection to reduce the genetic predisposition to lameness and heart disease.[93] Dairy breeding professionals believe that their broadened breeding goals since the 1990s (see section 2.2.4 in Chapter 2) have made, and will make, major improvements in dairy cow health. The US Lifetime Net Merit indexes introduced in 2003 'have, for the first time, resulted in theoretical selection responses in the desired direction for all traits', according to US dairy scientists.[4,94] A refinement of statistical methods can select for these desirable traits but select against the inbreeding that is blamed for many of the problems of dairy cows (multi-trait and optimized selection).[2,95] The objective is that this would select for dairy cows who have lower milk yields per lactation, but who would be longer lasting and more fertile, and hence more profitable overall.[96]

These changes in thinking and practice among breeders and some farmers have not reversed the genetics of the breeds concerned overnight. In the mid 2000s only 2.2 per cent of meat chickens in a large British survey had a normal walking ability by 40 days old.[10] Many high-yielding dairy cows internationally still do not survive for more than three lactations. The next decade will show whether or not the farming and breeding communities achieve major improvements in the longevity of breeding animals and the health of both parents and offspring. In the absence of regulation, how soon this happens probably depends on how farmers assess the economics of each course of action. There is now a large scientific research effort devoted to elucidating the genetic traits associated with health, long productive life and offspring survival in dairy cows, pigs and sheep. This could lead to the selection of breeding ewes and rams on the basis of the lambs' survival rate and the ewes' ability to care for the lambs, and the selection of breeding pigs on a similar basis, using indicators such as the size, shape and vigour of the offspring and the mothering behaviour of the dams.

Some believe that multi-trait selection is not enough to rescue the Holstein breed, partly because selection for 'better' traits will have to be made within the same narrow gene pool of the existing breed. In this view a better route would be cross-breeding to increase genetic diversity and hybrid vigour, or changing to more robust and less extreme dairy breeds.[44,46,96] By the beginning of the 21st century none of the main dairy cow breeds used in the US, at least, had an impressively long working lifetime.[42] Does this suggest that the tendency to over-exploit dairy cows' productive potential is more fundamental than the 'Holstein problem'? If producers switch to less extreme breeds, economic pressures may force them over time to seek higher yields from these cows too. In that case, within a couple of decades the same problems may re-emerge in breeds that have been less intensively exploited in the past.

## 3.3.2 Neglected problems

Some breeding strategies that would very clearly benefit animals seem to receive little attention from animal scientists, with some exceptions,[39,68,84] possibly because they are less directly related to overall productivity. Sheep, for example, were bred to have woolly fleeces and long woolly tails at a time when wool was a valuable commodity. Today this means that the large majority of lambs are subjected to the painful procedure of tail-docking without anaesthetic in order to reduce the risk of flystrike, and all sheep are subjected to the stress and sometimes injury caused by shearing. Hair sheep and wool-shedding sheep breeds already exist but are rarely used. Sheep that shed their heavy winter coats in summer include the Wiltshire Horn breed, which needs no tail-docking or shearing, and derived from the Wiltshire Horn are the easy care breed and the Katahdin breed in the US, which have additionally been bred to be hornless. Many cattle breeds, including all dairy breeds, are horned and the calves are routinely subjected to disbudding or dehorning for management reasons. These procedures involve stress and discomfort or even extreme pain, depending on the method and the pain relief provided. We have yet to see a well-funded scientific effort put into the project of 'breeding out' the somewhat medieval mutilations that livestock are still subjected to.

## 3.3.3 Changing animals versus changing husbandry

Some current breeding projects aim to select animals that show lower levels of stress or aggressive behaviour in typical farming environments. Farming environments are often designed for management convenience and economic efficiency rather than to be consistent with the natural behaviour of the animals, and they may promote aggression and stress. Fattening pigs, for example, are frequently mixed with unfamiliar pigs for management reasons or when they are sold, which is known to increase stress and fighting, and they are often kept crowded on concrete or slats, without any material to satisfy their natural behaviour of foraging.

Genetic selection for calm behaviour raises an obvious ethical question. Should we be trying to adapt animals for life in intensive husbandry systems, rather than adapting our animal production practices to reduce the very obvious sources of stress and conflict: overcrowding, unnatural social groupings, barren environments, disruption of social bonds, frustration of natural behaviour, boredom, rough handling and live transport? Many geneticists and animal scientists choose to work within the limits set by conventional (often intensive) production rather than looking for more animal-friendly husbandry solutions to behavioural problems.[97]

## 3.3.4 The public and consumers

The public, as consumers of animal products, are often shocked when they become aware of certain aspects of modern food animal breeding. In the UK, the media exposure of the excessive growth rate and levels of lameness in broiler chickens in 2008 led to a 40 per cent increase in retail demand for slower-growing chickens, such as those that conform to the Freedom Food indoor standard, and those used in free-range and organic chickenmeat production. But slower-growing chickens are still only a small percentage (perhaps 10 per cent) of the UK total of 800 million chickens slaughtered per year. British consumers have also been shocked by the revelation that over 100,000 male bull calves of dairy breeds are shot at birth annually because their breeding makes them uneconomic for meat production (see sections 8.4.2 and 8.4.3 in Chapter 8). Animal protection organizations are very critical of these extremes of selection (see Box 3.1) and advocate the use of slower-growing meat chickens, more robust dairy cows whose male calves are suitable for meat production, and in general the use of animals that are well suited to a more extensive and preferably free-range existence. The public, if given the choice, might well prefer to support extensive production rather than to fund, as taxpayers, breeding experiments to design animals suited to living in factory farms.

The public in developed countries globally has, however, got used to the availability of cheap meat, milk and eggs and in large quantities. There is a fundamental contradiction here because large quantities of animal-based foods for the global population can only be produced by using fast-growing and high-yielding animals that are almost certain to suffer as a result. The premium Label Rouge meat chickens of France that live for over 81 days, roost in trees and forage on the woodland floor take very much more time and money to produce. They are not a practical mainstream solution if the world's population wants to eat half a chicken breast each per day. The inescapable conclusion is that if we want to move away from over-selected food production animals, we need to eat less of their products and pay more for them.

### 3.3.5 Sustainable animals for the future

The last 30 years have shown that the drive to increase the productivity of food animals has reduced their ability to sustain health and life, as individuals and as breeds. In future, animal breeders may manage to optimize production and the physical and psychological health of the animal, substantially reducing ill health and pain in our current, mainly intensive, production systems. This would be very desirable but the concern remains that, in a competitive global environment, there will always be a temptation to work these new and better-designed animals to the physiological limit once again. It is not clear yet that we have learned all the lessons. As long as farmed animals are regarded primarily as units of production, it will be very difficult to avoid this outcome.

A genuinely sustainable alternative would be to stop regarding farm animals as units of production and start considering them as sentient individuals, with a right to a good quality of life and health while they are in our custody.[98] We could start by putting voluntary limits on what can be achieved by animal breeding, or taking other steps to encourage producers to change the genotype that they use. These could include limitations on the:

- growth rate of broiler chickens;
- milk yield per lactation or per day of dairy cows;
- number of piglets per litter, the weaning age and growth rate of piglets;
- number of lambs per litter;
- growth rate of beef cattle, including pedigree herds;
- egg output of laying hens as a ratio of body weight.

A limit to the growth rate of broiler chickens is a measurable and achievable goal. Existing EU marketing rules for poultrymeat, legal organic marketing standards and several independent welfare assurance standards already do this by specifying either the minimum age at which broiler chickens can be slaughtered or the maximum daily weight gain, or both. These must apply if the producer wishes to label the meat as 'free-range', 'organic' or conforming to some other specified standard (such as Freedom Food). To reach a typical slaughter weight at 81 days of age in good health, for example, a slower-growing strain of chicken has to be used. It would be entirely feasible to introduce a minimum age of slaughter for all broiler chickens sold in a particular jurisdiction, such as the EU. The switch would be made easier because the slower-growing commercial chickens already exist and are available from at least one of the major meat chicken-breeding companies.[99]

These reforms in animal breeding would require the world's rich countries, at least, to reduce their consumption and production of food animals from the current overconsumption down to sustainable levels. This shift would offer huge benefits in animal welfare. It would enable farmers to use slower-growing and lower-yielding breeds kept in free-range conditions more consistent with the natural behaviour of the animals. Relaxing the pressure for maximum yield would allow farmers to give the animals more freedom of movement, opportunity for natural social and family behaviour, and choice of environment.

Reducing the number of food animals produced would also be a solution to a number of seemingly intractable problems related to the global overproduction of livestock. These problems include: methane and nitrous oxide emissions from animal production; carbon dioxide emissions from deforestation for animal feed production and cattle grazing; water pollution by animal manure; overuse of water and scarcity of cropland; and public health problems related to the overconsumption of animal-based foods that is implicated in the global rise in chronic diseases.[100]

## Notes

1    Emmans, G. C. and Kyriazakis, I. (2000) 'Issues arising from genetic selection for growth and body composition characteristics in poultry and pigs', in W. G. Hill et al (eds) *The Challenge of Genetic Change in Animal Production, Occ. Publi. Br. Soc. Anim. Sc. (BSAS)*, no 27, Edinburgh, pp39–52
2    Simm. G. et al (2005) 'Limits to yield of farm species: Genetic improvement of livestock', in R. Sylvester-Bradley and J. Wiseman (eds) *Yields of Farmed Species*, Nottingham University Press, Chapter 6

3   Hill, W. G. et al (eds) (2000) *The Challenge of Genetic Change in Animal Production, Occ. Publi. Br. Soc. Anim. Sc. (BSAS)*, no 27, BSAS

4   Shook, G. E. (2006) 'Major advances in determining appropriate selection goals', *Journal of Dairy Science*, vol 89, pp1349–1361

5   See discussions in Weary, D. M. et al (2006) 'Identifying and preventing pain in animals', *Applied Animal Behaviour Science*, vol 100, no 1–2, pp64–76; Broom, D. M. and Fraser, A. F. (2007) *Domestic Animal Behaviour and Welfare*, fourth edition, CAB International, Wallingford, UK; Webster, J. (2005) *Animal Welfare: Limping towards Eden*, Blackwell Publishing, Oxford, UK

6   Phillips, C. J. C. (2009) 'A review of mulesing and other methods to control flystrike', *Animal Welfare*, vol 18, no 2, pp113–122

7   Whitehead, C. C. et al (2003) 'Skeletal problems associated with selection for increased production', in W. M. Muir and S. E. Aggrey (eds) *Poultry Genetics, Breeding and Biotechnology*, CAB International, pp29–52

8   Scientific Committee on Animal Health and Animal Welfare (2000) *The Welfare of Chickens Kept for Meat Production (Broilers)*, European Commission; Assured Chicken Production (undated) *Poultry Standards 2009–2010*, Assured Chicken Production

9   McNamee, P. T. and Smyth, J. A. (2000) 'Bacterial chondronecrosis with osteomyelitis ('femoral head necrosis') of broiler chickens: A review', *Avian Pathology*, vol 29, pp253–270; Julian, R. J. (2004) 'Evaluating the impact of metabolic disorders on the welfare of broilers', in C. Weeks and A. Butterworth (eds) *Measuring and Auditing Broiler Welfare*, CAB International, Wallingford, UK, pp51–59; Butterworth, A. (1999) 'Infectious components of broiler lameness: A review', *World's Poultry Science Journal*, vol 55, pp327–352; Sanotra, G. S., Berg, C. and Lund, J. D. (2003) 'A comparison between leg problems in Danish and Swedish broiler production', *Animal Welfare*, vol 12, pp677–683

10  Knowles, T. G. et al (2008) 'Leg disorders in broiler chickens: Prevalence, risk factors and prevention', *PLoS ONE*, vol 3, no 2, p1545

11  Kestin, S. C. et al (1992) 'Prevalence of leg weakness in broiler chickens and its relationship with genotype', *Veterinary Record*, vol 131, pp190–194

12  Sanotra, G. S., Berg, C. and Lund, J. D. (2003) 'A comparison between leg problems in Danish and Swedish broiler production', *Animal Welfare*, vol 12, pp677–683

13  Danbury, T. et al (2000) 'Self selection of the analgesic drug carprofen by lame broiler chickens', *Veterinary Record*, vol 146, pp307–311; Webster, J. (2005) *Animal Welfare: Limping towards Eden*, Blackwell Publishing, see p128

14  Julian, R. J. (1998) 'Rapid growth problems: Ascites and skeletal deformities in broilers', *Poultry Science*, vol 77, pp1773–1780

15  Weeks, C. A. et al (2000) 'The behaviour of broiler chickens and its modification by lameness', *Applied Animal Behaviour Science*, vol 67, pp111–125

16  Julian, R. J. (2004) 'Evaluating the impact of metabolic disorders on the welfare of broilers', in C. Weeks and A. Butterworth (eds) *Measuring and Auditing Broiler Welfare*, CAB International, Wallingford, UK, pp51–59

17  Maxwell, M. H. and Robertson, G. W. (1998) 'UK survey of broiler ascites and sudden death syndromes in 1993', *British Poultry Science*, vol 39, pp203–215

18  Weeks, C. A. (2002) 'Some behavioural differences between fast and slow-growing strains of poultry', *British Poultry Science*, vol 43 (supplement), ppS24–S26

19  Bokkers, E. A. M. and Koene, P. (2003) 'Behaviour of fast- and slow growing broilers to 12 weeks of age and the physical consequences', *Applied Animal Behaviour Science*, vol 81, pp59–72

20  Bassler, A. W., Berg, C. and Elwinger, K. (2005) 'Rearing broilers in floorless pens in pasture: IV. Effects on the conditions of the birds' legs and feet', cited in

A. W. Bassler, *Organic Broilers in Floorless Pens on Pasture*, PhD thesis no 2005:67, Swedish University of Agricultural Sciences, Sweden, Appendix IV

21   Havenstein, G. B. et al (1994) 'Growth, livability, and feed conversion of 1957 vs 1991 broilers when fed typical 1957 and 1991 broiler diets', *Poultry Science*, vol 73, pp1785–1794

22   Savory, C. J., Maros, K. and Rutter, S. M. 1993) 'Assessment of hunger in growing broiler breeders in relation to a commercial restricted feeding programme', *Animal Welfare*, vol 2, pp131–152

23   Scientific Committee on Animal Health and Animal Welfare (2000) *The Welfare of Chickens Kept for Meat Production (Broilers)*, European Commission (see Section 9.1)

24   Broom, D. M. and Reefmann, N. (2005) 'Chicken welfare as indicated by lesions on carcases in supermarkets', *British Poultry Science*, vol 46, pp407–414

25   McLean, J. A., Savory, C. J. and Sparks, J. H. C. (2002) 'Welfare of male and female broiler chickens in relation to stocking density, as indicated by performance, health and behaviour', *Animal Welfare*, vol 11, pp55–73

26   Stevenson, P. (2003) *Compassion in World Farming's Court Case Regarding Factory Farming of Broiler Chickens: Summary of Main Points of Court's Judgment*, Compassion in World Farming, www.ciwf.org.uk

27   Bates, R. O. (2009) 'Sow herd removals', *The Pig Site*, Michigan State University, May, www.thepigsite.com/articles/2/breeding-and-reproduction/2710/sow-herd-removals; Hypor (undated) 'Management for high sow longevity', *The PigSite*, www.thepigsite.com, accessed November 2009

28   Tarrés, J. et al (2006) 'Analysis of longevity and exterior traits on Large White sows in Switzerland', *Journal of Animal Science*, vol 84, pp2914–2924; Serenius, T. and Stalder, K. J. (2004) 'Genetics of length of productive life and lifetime prolificacy in the Finnish Landrace and Large White pig populations', *Journal of Animal Science*, vol 82, pp3111–3117

29   Charagu, P. K. and van Haandel, B. (undated) *Selection for Sow Longevity – Hypor's Approach*, Hypor Inc.

30   Kirk, R. J. et al (2005) 'Locomotive disorders associated with sow mortality in Danish pig herds', *Journal of Veterinary Medicine Series A*, vol 52, no 8, pp423–428

31   Fernàndez de Sevila, X. et al (2009) 'Genetic background and phenotypic characterization over two farrowings of leg conformation defects in Landrace and Large White sows', *Journal of Animal Science*, vol 87, pp1606–1612

32   Gadd, J. (2009) 'Hyperprolificacy and the shattered sow syndrome', *Pig Progress* online, 25 August, www.pigprogress.net

33   Serenius, T. et al (2006) 'Genetic associations of length of productive life with age at first farrowing and leg soundness score in Finnish Landrace population', paper no 06-08 presented to the Eighth World Congress on Genetics Applied to Livestock Production, 13–18 August 2006, Belo Horizonte, Brazil, www.wcgalp8.org.br

34   KilBride, A. L., Gillman, C. E. and Green, L. E. (2009) 'A cross-sectional study of the prevalence of lameness in finishing pigs, gilts and pregnant sows and associations with limb lesions and floor types on commercial farms in England', *Animal Welfare*, vol 18, no 3, pp215–224

35   White, M. (2009) *NADIS BPEX Commentary January 2009*, NADIS and British Pig Executive, www.bpex.org.uk/downloads, accessed May 2009

36   Warriss, P. D. (2000) *Meat Science: An Introductory Text*, CABI Publishing, Chapter 6

37   Scientific Panel on Animal Health and Welfare (2007) 'Scientific report on animal health and welfare in fattening pigs in relation to housing and husbandry', *The*

*EFSA Journal*, vol 564, pp1–100 (see, in particular, section 7.1.2) and 'Scientific opinion on animal health and welfare in fattening pigs in relation to housing and husbandry', *The EFSA Journal*, vol 564, pp1–14

38   Knap, P. W. and Bishop, S. C. (2000) 'Relationships between genetic change and infectious disease in domestic livestock', in W. G. Hill et al (eds) *The Challenge of Genetic Change in Animal Production, Occasional Publication of the British Society of Animal Science (BSAS)*, no 27, pp65–80; Wu, J. et al (2008) 'Relationship between herd size and the prevalence of PRRS in pig herds in China', *Veterinary Record*, vol 163, pp90–91

39   Klopčič, M. et al (eds) (2009) *Breeding for Robustness in Cattle*, Wageningen Academic Publishers

40   Panel on Animal Health and Animal Welfare (2009) 'Scientific opinion on the overall effects of farming systems on dairy cow welfare and disease', *The EFSA Journal*, vol 1143, pp1–38

41   Oltenacu, P. A. and Algers, B. (2005) 'Selection for increased production and the welfare of dairy cows: Are new breeding goals needed?', *Ambio*, vol 34, no 4–5, pp311–315

42   Hare, E., Norman, H. D. and Wright, J. R. (2006) 'Survival rates and productive herd life of dairy cattle in the United States', *Journal of Dairy Science*, vol 89, pp3713–3720; Holstein Association USA (2006) *Holstein Breed of the Future Committee's Report to 2006 National Convention*, Sioux Falls, South Dakota

43   Wragg, S. (2008) 'Holsteins need hybrid vigour to boost health', *Farmers Weekly*, 5 December 2008, pp45–47

44   Heins, B. J., Hansen, L. B. and Seykora, A. J. (2006) 'Fertility and survival during first lactation of crossbred dairy cows sired by bulls from Swedish, Norwegian, and French red breeds compared to pure Holstein cows', paper presented to the Eighth World Congress on Genetics Applied to Livestock Production, 13–18 August 2006, Belo Horizonte, Brazil, www.wcgalp8.org.br

45   Defra Science Directorate (2008) *Developing Technologies to Improve the Fertility of Dairy Cows*, Research Project Final Report, AC0205, UK; Trickett, S. (2009) 'Why some cows never turn a profit', *Farmers Weekly*, 25 September 2009; *Farmers Guardian* (2009) 'Dairy Event 2009: Cows make profit from 3rd lactation', *Farmers Guardian*, 17 September; for Swedish cows born in 1998, see: Hultgren, J. and Svensson, C. (2009) 'Heifer rearing conditions affect length of productive life in Swedish dairy cows', *Preventive Veterinary Medicine*, vol 89, no 3–4, pp255–264

46   Hansen, L. B. (2006) 'Monitoring the worldwide genetic supply for dairy cattle with emphasis on managing crossbreeding and inbreeding', paper presented to the Eighth World Congress on Genetics Applied to Livestock Production, 13–18 August 2006, Belo Horizonte, Brazil, www.wcgalp8.org.br

47   Trickett, S. (2009) 'UK inbreeding risk is low', *Farmers Weekly*, 28 August, p33; *Farmers Guardian* (2009) 'O-Man dominates dairy proofs', *Farmers Guardian*, 18 August

48   Garnsworthy, P. C. and Thomas, P. C. (2005) 'Yield trends in UK dairy and beef cattle', in R. Sylvester-Bradley and J. Wiseman (eds) *Yields of Farmed Species*, Nottingham University Press, Chapter 20

49   Pryce, J. E., Coffey, M. P. and Brotherstone, S. (2000) 'The genetic relationship between calving interval, body condition score and linear type and management traits in registered Holsteins', *Journal of Dairy Science*, vol 83, pp2664–2671

50   Tamminga, S. (2000) 'Issues arising from genetic change: Ruminants', in W. G. Hill et al (eds) *The Challenge of Genetic Change in Animal Production, Occasional Publication British Society of Animal Science (BSAS)*, no 27, BSAS, pp53–62

51  Wragg, S. (2007) 'Education at heart of plan to tackle mastitis in cattle', *Farmers Weekly*, 19 October, p43
52  Bradley, A. J. et al (2007) 'Survey of the incidence and aetiology of mastitis on dairy farms in England and Wales', *Veterinary Record*, vol 160, no 6, pp253–258
53  Capion, N., Thamsborg, S. M. and Enevoldesen, C. (2008) 'Conformation of hind legs and lameness in Danish Holstein heifers', *Journal of Dairy Science*, vol 91, no 5, pp2089–2097
54  Kujala, M., Pastell, M. and Soveri, T. (2008) 'Use of force sensors to detect and analyse lameness in dairy cows', *Veterinary Record*, vol 162, no 12, pp365–368
55  Swalve, H. H., Alkhoder, H. and Fiji, R. (2009) 'Relationships between disorders of the bovine hoof and fertility in dairy cattle herds in Northern Germany?, in M. Klopčič et al (eds) *Breeding for Robustness in Cattle*, Wageningen Academic Publishers, The Netherlands, pp161–168; König, S. et al (2009) 'Genetic analysis of claw disorders and relationships with production and type traits', in M. Klopāiā et al (eds) *Breeding for Robustness in Cattle*, Wageningen Academic Publishers, pp181–189
56  Alves, C. G. et al (2007) 'Sensitivity of adult females of the Holstein, Brown Swiss and Girolando breeds to the hoof affections in the Northern of the State of Pernambuco', *Medicina Veterinária* (Brasil), vol 1, no 1, pp14–18
57  Haskell, M. J. et al (2006) 'Housing system, milk production and zero-grazing effects on lameness and leg injury in dairy cows', *Journal of Dairy Science*, vol 89, pp4359–4266; Somers, J. G. C. J. et al (2003) 'Prevalence of claw disorders in Dutch dairy cows exposed to several floor systems', *Journal of Dairy Science*, vol 86, pp2082–2093; Weary, D. M., Flower, F. C. and von Keyserlingk, M. A. G. (2008) 'Lameness in dairy cattle – new research on gait and housing', in *Proceedings of the 41st Annual Conference of the American Association of Bovine Practitioners*, Charlotte, North Carolina, 25–27 September 2008, pp60–63
58  Flower, F. C. and Weary, D. M. (2006) 'Effect of hoof pathologies on subjective assessments of dairy cow gait', *Journal of Dairy Science*, vol 89, pp139–146; Thomsen, P. T. (2009) 'Rapid screening method for lameness in dairy cows', *Veterinary Record*, vol 164, pp689–690
59  Flower, F. C., Sanderson, D. J. and Weary, D. M. (2006) 'Effects of milking on dairy cow gait', *Journal of Dairy* Science, vol 89, pp2084–2089
60  Miglior, F. and Sewalem, A. (2009) 'A review on breeding for functional longevity of dairy cow', in M. Klopčič et al (eds) *Breeding for Robustness in Cattle*, Wageningen Academic Publishers
61  Whay, H. R. et al (2003) 'Assessment of dairy cattle welfare using animal-based measurements', *Veterinary Record*, vol 153, pp197–202; Webster, J. (2005) *Animal Welfare: Limping towards Eden*, Blackwell Publishing, pp89–90
62  Scientific Committee on Animal Health and Animal Welfare (2001) *The Welfare of Cattle Kept for Beef Production*, European Commission
63  Hunt, J. (2009) 'DNA details to improve bull buying', *Farmers Weekly*, 8 May 2009, p41
64  Phocas, F. (2009) 'Genetic analysis of breeding traits in a Charolais cattle population segregating an inactive myostatin allele', *Journal of Animal Science*, vol 87, pp1865–1871
65  Marchant, J. N. et al (2000) 'Timing and causes of piglet mortality in alternative and conventional farrowing systems', *Veterinary Record*, vol 147, pp209–214
66  Whitney, M. (2009) 'Managing highly prolific sows', *The PigSite*, May 2009, www.thepigsite.com
67  Hypor (2008) 'Controlling stillbirth losses', *The PigSite*, November 2008, www.thepigsite.com

68  Trickett, S. (2009) 'Simple changes can boost piglet survival', *Farmers Weekly*, 3 April, p37; Baxter, E. M. et al (2009) 'Indicators of piglet survival in an outdoor farrowing system', *Livestock Science*, vol 124, no 1/3, pp266–276

69  Canario, L. et al (2006) 'Between-breed variability of stillbirth and its relationship with sow and piglet characteristics', *Journal of Animal Science*, vol 84, no 12, pp3185–3196

70  Baxter, E. M. et al (2008) 'Investigating the behavioural and physiological indicators of neonatal survival in pigs', *Theriogenology*, vol 69, no 6, pp773–783; Roehe, R. et al (2009) 'Genetic analyses of piglet survival and individual birth weight on first generation data of a selection experiment for piglet survival under outdoor conditions', *Livestock Science*, vol 121, pp173–181

71  Wischner, D. et al (2009) 'Characterisation of sows' postures and posture changes with regard to crushing piglets', *Applied Animal Behaviour Science*, vol 19, pp49–55

72  Scientific Panel on Animal Health and Welfare (2007) *Scientific Report: Animal Health and Welfare Aspects of Different Housing and Husbandry Systems for Adult Breeding Boars, Pregnant, Farrowing Sows and Unweaned piglets*, European Commission; Scientific Panel on Animal Health and Welfare (2007) *Annex to the EFSA Journal*, vol 572, pp1–13

73  Binns, S. H. et al (2001) 'Risk factors for lamb mortality on UK sheep farms', *Preventive Veterinary Medicine*, vol 52, no 3/4, pp287–303; Defra, Scottish Executive and Welsh Assembly Government (2003) *Outline of an Animal Health and Welfare Strategy for Great Britain*, UK, Section 4.1; Meat and Livestock Commission (2002) *Sheep Yearbook 2002*, Meat and Livestock Commission

74  Welsh, C. S. et al (2006) 'Threshold model analysis of lamb survivability in Romney sheep', *New Zealand Journal of Agricultural Research*, vol 49, no 4, pp411–418

75  Safari, E. et al (2005) 'Analysis of lamb survival in Australian Merino', in *Application of New Genetic Technologies to Animal Breeding: Proceedings of the 16th Conference of the Association for the Advancement of Animal Breeding and Genetics*, Noosa Lakes, Queensland, Australia, 25–28 September 2005, pp28–31; Hatcher, S., Atkins, K. D. and Safari, E. (2009) 'Phenotypic aspects of lamb survival in Australian Merino sheep', *Journal of Animal Science*, vol 87, pp2781–2790

76  Morel, P. C. H., Morris, S. T. and Kenyon, P. R. (2008) 'Effect of birthweight on survival in triplet-born lambs', *Australian Journal of Experimental Agriculture*, vol 48, no 6/7, pp984–987

77  Stafford, K. J. et al (2007) 'The physical state and metabolic status of lambs of different birth rank soon after birth', *Livestock Science*, vol 111, no 1/2, pp10–15

78  Hindson, J. C. and Winter, A. C. (2002) *Manual of sheep diseases*, second edition, Blackwell Publishing

79  Sawalha, R. M. et al (2006) 'Estimates of genetic and non-genetic parameters for survival traits of Scottish Blackface lambs', paper no 04-18 presented to the Eighth World Congress on Genetics Applied to Livestock Production, 13–18 August 2006, Belo Horizonte, Brazil, www.wcgalp8.org.br

80  Hatcher, S., Atkins, K. D. and Safari, E. (2009) 'Phenotypic aspects of lamb survival in Australian Merino sheep', *Journal of Animal Science*, vol 87, pp2781–2790

81  Morel, P. C. H., Morris, S. T. and Kenyon, P. R. (2008) 'Effect of birthweight on survival in triplet-born lambs', *Australian Journal of Experimental Agriculture*, vol 48, no 6/7, pp984–987

82  Burns, J. (2000) 'Four teats good – for profit', *Farmers Weekly*, 1 September, p40

83  Trickett, S. (2009) 'Selection of ewes helps avoid anthelmintic resistance', *Farmers Weekly*, 6 March, p33

84  See also discussion in Conington, J. and Dwyer, C. (2009) 'Breeding for easier-managed sheep', in *Darwinian Selection, Selective Breeding and the Welfare of Animals*, UFAW International Symposium 2009, Bristol, 22–23 June; Macfarlane, J. M., Matheson, S. M. and Dwyer, C. M., (2009) 'Genetic parameters for lamb birth difficulty, vigour and sucking ability in Suffolk sheep', *Darwinian Selection, Selective Breeding and the Welfare of Animals*, UFAW International Symposium 2009, Bristol, 22–23 June

85  *Veterinary Record* (2008) 'News & reports', *Veterinary Record*, vol 163, no 6, 9 August, p173

86  Le Helloco, M. (2009) 'A new breed enters layer market', *Poultry World*, August, p20

87  Sherwin, C. M. et al (2009) 'The consequences of artificial selection of layer hens on their welfare in all current housing systems', *Darwinian Selection, Selective Breeding and the Welfare of Animals*, UFAW International Symposium 2009, Bristol, 22–23 June

88  Cooper, O. (2009) 'Wise management can avoid winter pitfalls', *Poultry World*, October, pp30–31

89  Durham, S. (2009) *Breeding Gentler Laying Hens that Still Produce Eggs to Industry Standard*, US Department of Agriculture press release, 10 June 2009; Muir, W. M. (1996) 'Group selection for adaptation to multiple-hen cages: selection program and direct responses', *Poultry Science*, vol 75, no 4, pp447–458; Muir, W. M. and Bijma, P. (2006) 'Incorporation of competitive effects in breeding programs for improved performance and animal well-being', paper presented to the Eighth World Congress on Genetics Applied to Livestock Production, 13–18 August 2006, Belo Horizonte, Brazil, www.wcgalp8.org.br

90  Sandøe, P. et al (1999) 'Staying good while playing God – the ethics of breeding farm animals', *Animal Welfare*, vol 8, pp313–328

91  Lawrence, A. et al (2009) 'Robustness in dairy cows: Experimental studies of reproduction, fertility, behaviour and welfare', in M. Klopčič et al (eds) *Breeding for Robustness in Cattle*, Wageningen Academic Publishers, pp55–65

92  See also discussion in Twine, R. (2007) 'Searching for the 'win–win'? Animals, genomics and welfare', *International Journal of Sociology of Food and Agriculture*, vol 15, no 3, pp8–25

93  McKay, J. C. et al (2000) 'The challenge of genetic change in the broiler chicken', in W. G. Hill et al (eds) *The Challenge of Genetic Change in Animal Production*, *Occ. Publi. Br. Soc. Anim. Sc. (BSAS)*, no 27, BSAS, pp1–7

94  Miglior, F., Muir, B. L. and Van Doormaal, B. J. (2005) 'Selection indices in Holstein cattle in various countries', *Journal of Dairy Science*, vol 88, pp1255–1263

95  Villanueva, B. (2004) 'Managing genetic resources in selected and conserved populations', in G. Simm et al (eds) *Farm Animal Genetic Resources*, BSAS Publication 30, Nottingham University Press, pp113–132

96  See calculations of input costs and output of high- and lower-yielding dairy breeds in Darwent, N. (2009) 'Understanding the economics of robust dairy breeds', paper presented to the Beyond Calf Exports Stakeholders Forum, Compassion in World Farming and RSPCA, www.calfforum.org.uk/

97  The end result of this approach might be to engineer pain-free animals for factory farms; see Shriver, A. (2009) 'Knocking out pain in livestock: Can technology succeed where morality has stalled?', *Neuroethics*, vol 2 no 3, pp115–124

98  See the aspiration to provide a 'good life' for 'each and every farm animal used for our benefit' in Farm Animal Welfare Council (2009) *Farm Animal Welfare in*

*Great Britain: Past, Present and Future*, FAWC
99 Cobb-Vantress, *CobbSasso250™ Sales Brochure*, www.cobb-vantress.com, accessed October 2009; Aviagen (2008) *Introducing the Ross Rowan*, www.aviagen.com, accessed September 2009
100 Steinfeld, H. et al (2006) *Livestock's Long Shadow: Environmental Issues and Options*, Food and Agriculture Organization of the United Nations, Rome; McMichael, A. J. et al (2007) 'Food, livestock production, energy, climate change, and health', *Lancet*, vol 370, pp1253–1263; World Cancer Research Fund and the American Institute for Cancer Research (2007) *Food, Nutrition, Physical Activity, and the Prevention of Cancer: A Global Perspective*, World Cancer Research Fund; Compassion in World Farming (2008) *Global Warning: Climate Change and Farm Animal Welfare*, www.ciwf.org.uk; Powles, J. (2009) 'Commentary: Why diets have to change to avert harm from global warming', *International Journal of Epidemiology*, vol 38, no 4, pp1141–1142

# 4

# Productivity and Welfare: Animal Behaviour

## 4.1 Background and context: The abolition of the family

### 4.1.1 Historical understanding of animals' social bonds

A famous painting by the English Victorian artist Sir Edwin Landseer, *Wild Cattle of Chillingham* (1867), depicts a family scene. A white bull, cow and calf are shown against a wild and mountainous landscape. The strong, stern bull as paterfamilias dominates the painting with a look of alert intelligence and courage as, with raised head and horns, he scans the horizon for signs of danger to his family. The cow and calf stand below in his shelter, the cow's expression gentle and attentive, her muzzle protectively placed on her young calf's back.[1] For all its limitations in realism, this painting is remarkable as a very rare example of the celebration of the social bonds of animals of a farmed species.

Early naturalists took it for granted that animals had feelings associated with their behaviour towards offspring and mates, if only for a limited period during the mating season or when their young were relatively helpless. The 18th-century English naturalist Gilbert White was impressed by what he termed the *storge* (στοργη) of animals, using the Greek word for the natural affection between parents and children.[2] While noting that the behaviour he observed originated in 'instinct', he describes the 'tender attachment' of a field mouse disturbed with her young, the 'tender assiduity' of parent house-martins, the 'great fury' of the male mistle-thrush defending his nest, and how every hen who hatched chicks becomes for a while 'the virago of the yard ... and will fly in the face of a dog or sow' in defence of her brood.[2]

A century later, Darwin in *The Descent of Man* (1871) argued for the evolutionary continuity of the mental and moral characteristics of humans and other animals. He quoted with approval a contemporary view that no one 'who reads the touching instances of maternal affection, related so often of the women of all nations, and of the females of all animals, can doubt that the principle of action is the same in the two cases'.[3] Sexual selection, in his theory, involved 'ardour in love, courage and the rivalry of the males, and on the powers of perception, taste and will of the female', even if without conscious deliberation on the animal's part.[3,4]

In animal husbandry from earliest times animal reproduction inevitably has been managed for human use rather than according to the preferences of the animals. Male calves have always been removed from their protesting mothers when they were needed for meat, a process analogous to natural predation. But the industrial farming age has brought a new level of regimentation into animals' lives. In spite of our ancient understanding of animals' social bonds, farming practice has come to pay less and less attention animals' natural behaviour when this is in any way inconsistent with human requirements for the speedy, streamlined and cost-effective delivery of animal products.

## 4.1.2 The modern division of labour

The animal family group is at best irrelevant to large-scale animal husbandry. The relationship between mother and offspring is maintained normally only while it is the most cost-efficient method of feeding the young. For production efficiency, animals are grouped into production units of the same age, function and often gender. In the most industrialized pig production systems, gestating sows are kept in one shed, sows suckling piglets in another, recently weaned piglets in another and pigs being grown to their slaughter weight, in segregated age groups, in others. Dairy cows and calves are separated shortly after the birth of the calf, piglets are removed from their mothers and weaned after a month or less. Chicks never see their parents or indeed any adult chicken. Their lives are spent with thousands of others who were hatched on the same day as themselves. Their biological parents never see any offspring. Hatcheries incubate eggs on an industrial scale, the large automated ones hatching up to 1.5 million chicks per week in four equal hatches, with 'biologically smart' systems to adjust the concentrations of oxygen and carbon dioxide for the different phases of the incubation and hatching process.[5]

Humans seem to be fascinated by the breeding behaviour of wild animals. The immensely popular television documentaries on science and natural history convey that there is something heroic about the Darwinian struggle, the unpredictability, of reproduction in the wild. The animals are depicted as having intentions, preferences and attachments. In contrast, relatively little is known or communicated to the public about the natural behaviour of farmed species (apart from the perennial fascination with lambing in spring). As animal behaviour (ethology) developed as a professional branch of science during the 20th century, and as farm animal husbandry became industrialized, interest in the natural behaviour of domesticated animals seems to have been lost.[6] One of the major 20th-century figures in the science of animal behaviour, Konrad Lorenz, gave detailed descriptions of the friendships, courtship, nesting, egg-laying, incubating and parenting behaviour of wild and semi-wild greylag geese in his book *Here I Am – Where Are You?*, based on scientific research although intended for the general public.[7] It is impossible to imagine a fraction of this research effort being devoted to domestic poultry. Nevertheless they too, when given the opportunity, select nest sites, make nests, lay and incubate eggs, communicate with, protect and teach their chicks for several weeks or months.

Today the social and maternal behaviour of farmed animals is most typically studied only when it can be shown to be relevant to increasing productivity or tackling a production problem. This is partly understandable because industrial farming has so greatly reduced the scope for the expression of animals' natural behaviour. However, it may also have made it appear scientifically legitimate to ignore the subjective experiences of the animals in modern animal reproduction systems.

## 4.2 Natural behaviour versus farming practice

### 4.2.1 What we know about farm animals' natural behaviour

The main farmed species are social animals, naturally living in groups, and they have evolved with the necessary abilities for group living. These include the ability to recognize different individuals, to communicate, to form bonds and understand relationships with and between others, and to look after their young in their species-specific ways. Research in brain imaging is showing evidence suggesting that the basic brain mechanisms involved in recognition, interpretation of emotional cues, social bonds, attraction and mate choice are to some extent conserved across mammalian species. Being with a familiar individual reduces stress in animals such as rodents, birds, sheep and monkeys, as in people. Like primates, sheep appear to have specialized cells in their temporal and frontal cortices that encode face identity. They can remember images of 50 sheep faces for up to two years and they respond emotionally to images of familiar sheep.[8,9] They become very vocal when separated from flockmates, and researchers conclude that their apparently conscious awareness of other individual sheep may indicate that they have 'a highly developed requirement for social interaction and therefore a sophisticated sense of social awareness'.[9,10]

In spite of thousands of years of domestic use and decades of intensive breeding, the basic behaviour patterns and motivations of livestock have not changed qualitatively from those of their wild ancestors.[6,11-13] It is not unusual to hear the comment 'but they know no different', given as a justification for restricting the behaviour of animals, but this seems to be incorrect. Farmed pigs and chickens can revert to breeding in wild or semi-wild conditions without difficulty.

#### 4.2.1.1 Cattle

The wild ancestor of the Western breeds of cattle (*Bos taurus*), the auroch, became extinct in the 17th century in Europe but the social behaviour of some of the few remaining feral cattle herds has been studied. Cattle typically live in small herds that may include both male and female animals, but males tend to form separate groups and older males are often solitary outside the breeding season. A cow would usually have two of her offspring with her, one calf and one yearling. Before calving, the cow separates herself from the herd and hides her calf in vegetation for a few days before the calf follows her back to the herd. The calf suckles often, at first about five to eight times a day, decreasing to three to five times a day as it gets older. After about three weeks the calf starts to spend more time with other calves and the herd often establishes a 'crèche' which it guards. Calves are generally weaned at about 8 to 11 months old and cows may not wean their yearling calves until the next calf is born, or even after.[11] The attachment between mother and daughter may still be apparent at the time the daughter's first calf is born.[14]

Cattle are thought to be able to recognize up to 50–70 individuals and there is a hierarchical relationship between each member of the herd and each of the others. Particular cows form long-lasting friendships, so we can assume that it matters to them which other cattle they are with and whether they have a familiar social environment. Heifers are less afraid of a new situation when they are with others than when they are alone, and they apparently notice when a companion is stressed.[15,16] When the cows' social group is disrupted as a result of regrouping by the farmer, they can show signs of disturbance for three days.[17]

### 4.2.1.2 Pigs

The natural behaviour of pigs has been studied in wild boar herds and in groups of feral and free-ranging domestic pig herds. The social behaviour of domestic pigs when they are released into a natural environment is very like that of wild boar. The basic social unit consists of a sow and her litter, often joining with others to form a group of two to four sows, who are often related, and it is thought that pigs can recognize up to 20–30 individuals.[12,15] Unknown sows rarely join the group and there is an established hierarchy within it. When males leave the sow group they either live solitary or form a male group, and rejoin sow groups during the breeding season. The young may stay with the sow until they are sexually mature, at around 1.5 years for wild boar and at seven months of age in domestic pigs, even after the sow has her next litter. Pigs often have special neighbours when foraging. Pigs who know each other greet by making nose-to-nose contact, while grunting, and groom each other if they know each other really well.[12,15] Farmed pigs kept in a group establish social stability by their understanding of each other's behaviour and by working out which pigs are more aggressive and dominant.[18]

When a sow living in natural conditions is about to give birth, she walks a considerable distance (up to several kilometres) to select a suitably isolated and protected nest site. She carries grass, other vegetation and twigs to build a nest, which can take up to ten hours to complete, and if she can she will completely cover herself in the nest material before giving birth. The sow and piglets stay in or near the nest for up to two weeks before returning to the herd; but from a few days old the piglets will start to follow the sow when she leaves the nest to go on foraging trips. The piglets are gradually integrated into the herd and they

© Compassion in World Farming

**Figure 4.1** *Free-range sows and young foraging in woodland*

are weaned by about four months of age, as the frequency of suckling decreases. The piglets start to eat substantial amounts of solid food from about five weeks old, while continuing to suckle.[12]

### 4.2.1.3 Chickens

Chickens in natural conditions live in small groups. Jungle fowl, the ancestor of domestic chickens, live in flocks of 4 to 30 adults, either in mixed-sex flocks, in small male flocks or in groups of one male with a few hens. Birds in one group tend to stay quite close together and synchronize foraging, resting and preening. Males have important functions in watching for danger and in keeping the group together by calling and pecking to indicate a food source, and sometimes they will lead a female to investigate a potential nest site (domestic cockerels may also show this behaviour). To find a nest site, a hen may walk a considerable distance and explore several potential sites before deciding on one. She then scrapes a hollow and builds a raised edge to the nest before laying. She lays several eggs in the same nest and then stops laying and starts to incubate the clutch. Domestic hens will lay in nest boxes (or other sites) where other hens have already laid and, when 'broody', will incubate eggs laid by other hens. However, free-range domestic hens kept with a cockerel can also seek out secluded nest sites in vegetation where they incubate and hatch a dozen chicks unnoticed by their owners. Chicks start to communicate with their mother by peeping calls before hatching. They imprint on the hen in their first day after hatching and follow her, learning how to select suitable foods. They are kept warm and dry under the hen's wings when necessary.[13]

A mother hen is very attentive to her young for several weeks, teaching and protecting them as they forage in a group and calling them when she finds a food item. Experiments have shown that a mother hen actively tries to discourage her chicks from eating what she considers to be the 'wrong' food.[19] Later, in free-range conditions, she encourages the chicks to fly up to branches to roost at night. The hen and chicks may stay together for some purposes, such as ranging and foraging, for several weeks.

### 4.2.1.4 Behavioural restrictions in commercial animal production

The natural sexual and parenting behaviour of farmed species does not meet the predictability and efficiency required in large-scale animal production. Industrial farming has controlled and restricted this behaviour to the minimum that is required for procreation to be carried out. Some of these restrictions and their consequences are listed in Table 4.1.

**Table 4.1** *Restriction of natural social and reproductive behaviour of livestock animals in commercial farming practice*

| Type of disruption of behaviour | Examples in conventional animal production (practices vary within and between countries and regions) |
|---|---|
| Early or abrupt separation of mother and offspring (immediate separation or earlier than in natural conditions) | • Calves born to dairy cows (immediate separation)<br>• Piglets (early separation)<br>• Beef suckler calves<br>• Some lambs |
| Complete maternal deprivation | • Calves born to dairy cows<br>• Chicks (hatcheries and same-age rearing) |
| Prevention of nest-building behaviour | • Sows/gilts in farrowing crates or housed without straw<br>• Laying hens |
| Mothers prevented from finding secluded nest or birth site | • Sows/gilts in farrowing crates<br>• Dairy cows<br>• Laying hens |
| Disruption of mother–offspring relationship in suckling period | Farrowing crates |
| Stress caused to young from handling and mutilations | • Tail-docking of piglets and lambs<br>• Clipping or grinding teeth of piglets<br>• Castration of piglets, lambs and calves |
| Early weaning from milk | Piglets, dairy calves, some beef suckler calves |
| Prevention of natural mating or mate choice | Artificial insemination and embryo transfer |
| Prevention of natural social groupings | • All species (with exception of beef suckler and sheep herds)<br>• Breeding pigs kept in gestation and farrowing crates<br>• Young calves kept solitary or in veal crates |
| Disruption of established social bonds | Forced 'mixing' (putting together unfamiliar animals) and forced separation of all mammalian species |
| Prevention of natural social behaviour of males | Solitary and sometimes close confinement of breeding boars and bulls |

## 4.2.2 Farrowing crates: The automation of motherhood

On an industrial pigmeat production unit, the only natural social grouping that survives is that of the individual sow and her suckling piglets. The commercially ideal sow is one who lies passively on her side for two to four weeks, presenting her teats to her piglets and enabling them to move rapidly towards their future marketable weights. A sow who does this is referred to as having 'good maternal behaviour' and scientific research is being directed to finding genes that will enable the selection of sows that show 'maternal behaviour' in farrowing crates, where substantial elements of natural maternal behaviour have been effectively eliminated.

The farrowing crate (see Table 4.2) is an industrialized version of the farrowing nest that a sow would choose and construct in natural conditions, and was estimated in 2009 to be used for 83 and 95 per cent of farrowing sows in the US and European Union (EU), respectively.[20]

The farrowing crate disrupts the normal relationship between sow and piglets. The piglets compete and fight for teats (the more so if there are more of them) and their sharp eye teeth often damage the sow's teats and each other's faces. To compensate for these husbandry-induced problems, most piglets have their teeth either clipped or ground down and their tails cut off in the first days of life, without anaesthetic. As the lactation proceeds, studies of cortisol levels

**Table 4.2** *Comparison of conditions in a farrowing crate and in natural farrowing*

|  | Farrowing crate | Natural conditions |
|---|---|---|
| Site | Adjacent to other sows | Secluded place away from herd |
| Size | Sow cannot turn around and has difficulty standing up, lying down or adjusting her position | No space restriction |
| Flooring | • Concrete or perforated/slatted<br>• No bedding | • Lined with vegetation<br>• In farm conditions, sows use straw if provided |
| Sow behaviour[20–22] | • Hormones initiate nest-building activity<br>• Goes through nest-building movements even if no bedding material (paws and noses at floor)<br>• Higher heart rate and levels of stress hormone than in wider pen | Hormones initiate nest-building activity |
| Sow and piglets[20,21,23–26] | • Sow cannot move away from piglets<br>• Piglets' teeth may damage sow's teats and each others' faces<br>• Teeth clipping/grinding of piglets<br>• Tail-docking of piglets<br>• Sow cannot conserve body condition by avoiding piglets<br>• Piglets cannot socialize with other litters<br>• Piglets removed abruptly from sow and weaned | • Sow and piglets start to leave nest from a few days after birth<br>• Gradual integration into herd and weaning |

show that the sows find the demands of the increasingly insistent piglets stress-ful,[23] and sows are more likely to savage a piglet to death when they are confined in a crate rather than being kept loose in a pen.[24]

Farrowing crates also prevent the socialization of the piglets with other pigs. Studies in Canada showed that when sows were allowed to get away from their piglets ('get-away' crates), the sows that were lightest and had the larger litters got away the most often, doubtless because they needed to conserve their body condition, but remained responsive to piglets' distress calls. Sows allowed to 'get away' and mix with a couple of other sows chose to spend 14 hours a day away from their piglets. Piglets allowed to mix with other litters chose to spend 40 per cent of their time in the pens of other litters by the end of the commercial lactation period. The result was that these piglets ate more and fought less after separation from their mother and weaning.[25,26]

The pig breeding industry continues overwhelmingly to use farrowing crates for indoor sows on the grounds that they reduce the number of piglets crushed by sows, as well as minimizing the space needed per farrowing and the labour needed for cleaning. At the same time, several types of less restrictive systems have been developed. These range from semi-crate systems that can be opened up a few days after farrowing, to larger individual pens with straw or individual hutches within a larger strawed communal area, and have been shown to deliver the same or similar numbers of weaned piglets per sow per year.[20,27,28]

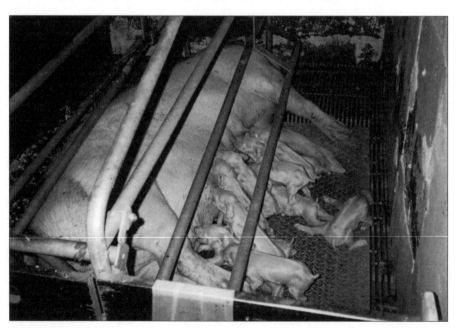

© Compassion in World Farming

**Figure 4.2** *The farrowing crate – and the piglets have already had their tails docked*

### 4.2.3 Mutilation of young animals

Some selective breeding practices, such as breeding for large pig litters or breeding sheep to have long woolly tails, have created husbandry problems that are typically dealt with by mutilation. A mutilation has been defined by the UK's Royal College of Veterinary Surgeons as a procedure that involves interference with the sensitive tissue or bone of an animal for non-therapeutic reasons.[29] The most common mutilations of tail-docking, teeth-clipping, castration (see section 4.2.6) and removal of horn buds are carried out within a few days or weeks of an animal being born, usually by a stockperson and without anaesthesia. Laws and practices vary internationally; but the mutilation of older animals often requires a veterinarian using local anaesthesia (although injection of anaesthetic may itself be painful).

The distinction between the pain relief needed at different ages used to be justified by the now scientifically discredited belief that very young animals feel less pain. Probably the distinction has much to do with the fact that very young animals are not capable of putting up much resistance. While many in the pig and sheep industry internationally maintain that tooth cutting or grinding, tail-docking and castration are essential and only minimally or only temporarily painful, there is much scientific evidence that they cause considerable pain, which can be lasting.[30] Film footage that would shock many people, showing castration, tail-docking, teeth-clipping and ear notching or tagging of piglets, and castration, de-horning and tail-docking of cattle, all without anaesthesia, can now be seen by the public on the internet.

---

**BOX 4.1 THE UK'S ADVERTISING STANDARDS AUTHORITY AND TEETH-CLIPPING**

In May 2009 the Advertising Standards Authority (ASA), whose role is to police the veracity of advertising claims in the UK, ruled in favour of a newspaper advertisement placed by the farm animal protection organization Compassion in World Farming (CIWF). CIWF's advertisement showed a piglet with the caption: 'What noise does a piglet make when its teeth are cut off with pliers – without anaesthetic? Same as you.' Members of the pig industry complained to the ASA that the advertisement was misleading because tooth-clipping does not cause distress if done properly. The ASA considered the evidence on the pain caused by tooth-clipping cited by the EU's Scientific Veterinary Committee in 1997 and the European Food Safety Authority in 2007 and ruled that CIWF's advertisement was not misleading.[31]

---

### 4.2.4 Separation and weaning

Early weaning, abrupt weaning and separation of offspring from the mother are practices that occur in much of the world's farming. Weaning involves a change of diet, loss of social bonds with the mother, mixing with unfamiliar animals for rearing or for transport for sale or slaughter, and a move to an unfamiliar environment. It thus confronts the young animal with a number of new and unfamiliar factors at once.[32]

Commercial pig production weans piglets very much earlier than would be natural, often at three to four weeks old and sometimes earlier (weaning piglets under three weeks old is illegal in the EU, although some are removed from their mother and put on automatic milk feeders at a few days old). They are removed and weaned abruptly at an age when they would still be suckling and are still socially dependent on the sow.[33] For the sow, this would be equivalent to the natural situation of having all her piglets die of disease or be predated at once, and may leave her with discomfort in her udder. The producer's objective after weaning is to get her back into gestation within as few days as possible. One method of speeding this process is to inject the sow with gonadotrophin a few hours before her piglets are removed.

Piglets show a number of signs of stress and distress when they are removed from their mothers and weaned.[32,33] They often stop eating, develop diarrhoea and producers have difficulty keeping them gaining weight as required. Researchers have analysed the calls of piglets and sow when they are separated. The piglets have a distress call which the sow responds to, and when they hear her grunt they redouble their own calls. Piglets rarely call when they are with the sow; but studies found that they called at a rate of eight calls a minute on the first day of weaning and separation, and those weaned younger call more often.[34] Those weaned at seven days old spent more time trying to jump out of the pen, presumably to get back to their mothers, and showed little interest in eating. Some piglet behaviour was described as 'loss of will to live'.[35] One of the signs that piglets are stressed by early weaning is that they develop various abnormal behaviours related to their motivation to suck. They often engage in 'belly nosing', which is a stereotyped behaviour probably related to the way in which piglets massage a sow's udder, and they chew each other's tails and ears, all of which can cause serious injuries.[36]

Cows and calves have been separated by their owners from time immemorial. This has been done in order to milk the cow, or in order to sell or kill the calf or the cow, or both. In addition, people have always known that the cow and calf very much dislike being separated, becoming agitated, calling and searching for each other. Because of the very high demand for dairy products, somewhat more than half of all calves that are born in Europe are intentionally reared without their mothers because they are born to dairy cows rather than being the offspring of beef suckler cows. The mortality of dairy-born calves reared without their mothers can be high: 5 per cent or more.[37] (For the destruction of male dairy-breed calves at a few days old because they are not economic for meat production, see section 8.4.2 in Chapter 8.)

Calves reared without their mothers are typically fed on milk replacer for five to seven weeks before being weaned. They are often kept in individual stalls or hutches for their first weeks of life to isolate them from the infections they are prone to, and later in groups of same-age calves. In the EU, individual housing is legal up to eight weeks of age; but the calf must be able to see and hear other calves, although it cannot touch them. Young calves are generally very playful, play-fighting, running, prancing and mounting, behaviour prevented by individual housing. Some male dairy calves are transported to veal production units at a couple of weeks old. Veal crates, in which the calf cannot turn around and is typically fed a liquid diet low in iron to keep the flesh white, are still legal in North America, although not in the EU. Veal calves reared in isolation from both mother or other calves are easily alarmed and have reduced weight gain compared to calves reared in groups.[38]

Researchers on dairy farming have debated how to reduce the distress of the inevitable separation of the dairy cow and her calf, as this poses dilemmas. The most common practice is to remove the calf immediately after it has drunk the essential colostrum (or even before, and colostrum fed by hand); this is thought to reduce distress because the cow and calf have not yet bonded strongly. An alternative is to leave the calf with the cow for a little longer, which is known to have social and physical benefits for calves. They have more weight gain, better social relationships with other cattle later in life, lower incidence of diarrhoea, lower incidence of redirected suckling behaviour, such as sucking at other calves, and better immune systems, and there are also benefits for the cow's health.[36,39] The disadvantage is that the cow and calf may be more strongly bonded and give more signs of distress when they are separated.[39,40]

Beef calves are typically separated from their mothers at around six months old, although sometimes as young as two to three months old in North America, if this is seen as economically advantageous. The separation causes evident distress to both and animal scientists have suggested various procedures to reduce distress, such as 'fence-line' separation or a two-stage process that includes fitting a plastic anti-sucking device into the calf's nostrils. Studies in Ireland have shown that the immune function and levels of stress hormones in beef calves abruptly weaned after seven months with their mothers are altered for as long as seven days, and the researchers captured an image of the moment when a barn full of cows all strained their heads in one direction towards where they had left their calves.[41] Adding to the stress of separation, calves are sometimes castrated and dehorned shortly before weaning and both calves and lambs are often transported long distance for sale or slaughter immediately after removal from their mothers.

### 4.2.5 Bulls, boars and rams

Adult male farm animals used for breeding are generally more important to the farm's overall profit, more dangerous and potentially troublesome, more expensive, larger and far fewer than breeding females or their offspring. However, males are under the same performance pressures as breeding females. If a breeding male fails to mount and to produce quality semen on demand he will be rejected and sent for slaughter. Male breeding animals are often overlooked in discussions of animal welfare because their numbers are so much fewer and, probably, because the activities of many of them are invisible in semen banks and stud farms. Animal scientists do carry out considerable research on these males, but it tends to be concerned with performance and semen quality, and how their housing and management might affect this, rather than on how the animal experiences his life.

Male animals are used in breeding in a number of ways. They can be kept on farm for natural mating or for producing semen for artificial insemination (AI). Semen collection on farm is routine in pig farming, where AI using fresh semen is widely practised. They are also used on farm to induce and synchronize oestrus in groups of female pigs and sheep and to detect oestrus in female pigs and in cows before they are artificially inseminated. These 'teaser' males are often vasectomized in order to avoid unplanned inseminations.

Even in industrialized animal breeding, the natural sexual behaviour of the animals unexpectedly retains a vital auxiliary role. In a system dominated by AI, the physiological impact of a female in oestrus or of a rival male is often necessary to facilitate semen collection from bulls and boars. A male of the species is also the most effective oestrus detection device yet invented. Boars are also used, behind fences, as potential rivals to stimulate the behaviour of other boars. Sows that are inseminated by AI may be given 'nose-to-nose' contact with a boar across a barrier to induce her 'standing' response while the semen catheter is inserted at her other end.

The aggression shown by a bull, boar or ram tends to be respected by farmers as a sign of his essential trait of 'high libido'. As a semen machine, a male is thoroughly tested before being set to work, his sperm-production ability is built up with a high-protein diet and attention is paid to reducing sources of stress that could affect his libido and sperm production. He is tested for transmissible diseases; his legs and feet are checked for the ability to mount; his teeth are checked for the ability to keep up his feed intake; his scrotal circumference is measured; his testes are squeezed to assess firmness; and a sample of his semen is taken to assess the quantity, fertility and motility of his sperm. A semen sample can be obtained by electroejaculation from a bull restrained in a crush. In this procedure an electrode is inserted in the bull's anus and the voltage increased until semen is obtained, and if it is not up to standard he will be culled. The effects of breed, age and heritability of the libido of breeding males is a subject of scientific study. A boar used for AI on farm can be expected to father 6000 piglets in a year; to select those suitable for the task, one breeding company offers libido-testing of young boars, grading them from 'Timid' to 'Excellent Worker'.[42]

An ideal mature ram will inseminate 100 ewes in a breeding season. A mature bull could be asked to mate with up to 40 cows during a two-month breeding season (although fewer if the cows' oestrous cycles have been synchronized hormonally because he would need to work faster). Because conception rates after AI are quite poor for Holstein dairy cows, in a large dairy herd a 'sweeper' bull may be required to serve up to 200 cows in a year. Large and aggressive males are a potential management problem and, when not working, many boars and bulls are kept solitary and often in barren surroundings. In 2007 some EU countries reported that boars were kept in crates.[28] Males used for frequent semen collection are kept in relatively confined quarters so that it is easier to handle them.

Hundreds of bulls and boars are kept in AI centres and stud farms where their semen is collected, treated with diluents, preservatives and antibiotics, and distributed for use. Cattle semen collection is more centralized because bull semen can easily be frozen. To produce the semen, the male is trained to mount a dummy female, sometimes encouraged by the use of pheromones or the physical presence of another male or a female in oestrus. The dummy is used in conjunction with a semen collection vessel or an artificial vagina, guided and aided by the human operator. A bull can go through this procedure every two or three days, amounting to over 100 semen collections per year, and a proven bull may last for several years performing this function. It is possible that electroejaculation may sometimes be used to get valuable semen from an old or lame bull no longer able to mount the dummy.

Bulls can still be seen on pasture with organic beef suckler cows, and some outdoor pig breeders leave males and females loose together; but this is increasingly seen as inefficient and hit-or-miss. Boars and bulls consume costly feed and their performance needs to be optimized. A bull is a 'poor reproductive manager' in business terms and he is increasingly being superseded by AI. AI offers a wider choice of up-to-date genetics and greater control by animal owners.

## 4.2.6 Castration: Removing gender

While male characteristics are celebrated in breeding animals, in meat animals they are seen as a nuisance or a source of economic loss. Ram- or boar-like characteristics in growing meat animals makes them harder to manage and their meat has sometimes been found to have a nauseating smell ('boar taint' or 'ram taint'), resembling urine, when cooked, if they have reached puberty. Slaughterhouses or consumers may refuse to buy them. Neutering also avoids unplanned mating, unwanted sexual behaviour and the waste of energy on developing sexual characteristics.

The neutering of meat animals to improve meat quality was an ancient practice, long before the development of pain-killing drugs. In past times in England, as well as the routine castration of male pigs intended for meat, female pigs intended for meat would be cut open, spayed, stitched up, and the wound dressed with tar.[43] Today, heifers being grown for beef in crowded feedlots are often spayed to avoid mounting behaviour that causes injuries; because spaying reduces growth rate, they may also be implanted with growth hormones in jurisdictions where this is allowed. Alternatively, the progesterone-type drug melengestrol acetate (MGA) may be added to beef heifers' feed to suppress oestrus. Cockerels were caponized as late as the 20th century by cutting into the abdomen and pulling out the testicles without pain relief. In the first half of the 20th century in England, the synthetic oestrogen compound stilboestrol was used for caponizing male chickens before these methods were banned and the specialized meat chicken strains were developed that led to the modern broiler.[44] Castration is thus a long-standing tradition in farming and until recently the rest of society asked few questions about it.

The methods used and the regulation of castration vary between countries depending on local jurisdiction and guidelines, or there may be no regulation. In Britain it was still legal in 2010 for a stockperson (or other non-veterinarian) to castrate young animals without anaesthetic (calves up to two months old, lambs up to three months old and piglets up to seven days old).[45] Calves, lambs and piglets are castrated by one of three methods:

1  A tight rubber ring is placed across the neck of the scrotum, cutting off the blood supply, causing the tissue below the ring to die and fall off. This method is often used for castrating lambs in their first week of life and is allowed in Britain without anaesthetic only up to seven days old, presumably because it is recognized to be painful.
2  A knife is used to cut into the scrotum to expose and then cut the spermatic cords and pull out the testes (in the EU the law specifies that the tissues must be cut rather than torn). This is the method routinely used for piglets and can also be used for lambs and calves.
3  A 'bloodless castrator' or crusher (a 'Burdizzo' clamp) is placed across the neck of the scrotum and instantaneously crushes the nerves and blood vessels leading to the testicles. This method is used for calves and lambs, sometimes in combination with the rubber ring method for lambs. Beef calves are often castrated by the Burdizzo at a few days old. This method is believed to be immediately extremely painful (the animals show 'an obvious pain response') but in the longer term the least painful method with the least complications such as infection.[46]

While the UK and Republic of Ireland voluntarily stopped castrating most piglets towards the end of the 20th century (because commercial fast-growing pigs were slaughtered at a younger age), in most pig production countries it has been routine and in the EU an estimated 100 million male pigs were surgically castrated annually by 2007.[47] Young piglets are very small and helpless and they can easily be picked up and either held, suspended or clamped upside down for castration in their first days of life by one stockperson using a knife.

Terminology used by those animal scientists and veterinarians who have studied the reactions of lambs, calves and piglets to castration include 'severe pain and distress'; pain deduced from 'abnormal postures (immobility)', 'alternate lifting of the hind legs', 'statue standing', repeated lying down and standing up, writhing and kicking on the ground, sliding on their hindquarters, tail-wagging; 'behaviour indicating pain for several weeks', 'a burst of intense pain', 'acute pain for up to two hours, followed by chronic inflammation, sepsis and pain until the affected parts fall off and healing occurs'. The screams of piglets at the first and second cut of the knife have been interpreted as 'indictors of pain and suffering' and their behaviour is altered for several days.[30,45,47]

In Europe there is now a momentum to end the surgical castration of piglets without anaesthesia. The EU set up PIGCAS, a research and policy programme whose 2007 stakeholder forum heard that castration without anaesthesia and post-operative analgesia is a 'painful' and 'stressful' event 'at any age', not acceptable from an animal welfare point of view.[47] In The Netherlands, a major pig-producing country, farmers and retailers implemented an agreement that pigs are not castrated without general anaesthesia, with a complete end to castration envisaged by 2015.[48] Other Northern European countries are moving towards requiring anaesthesia or ending all surgical castration of piglets, and Switzerland has a system combining a pre-surgical analgesic injection with anaesthesia.[49] Even with general anaesthesia, the procedure involves some distress, risk and pain. Immunocastration – for example, by vaccination against gonadotrophin-releasing hormone (GnRH) – has been successfully trialled in Sweden and Switzerland as a means of removing 'boar taint' from the meat of male pigs and is used to castrate around 25 per cent of piglets in Australia.[47,48,50]

Some scientists dispute whether boar taint is genuinely a problem in more than a few per cent of male pigs and suggest that those carcases could be identified without difficulty at the slaughterhouse (using an 'electronic nose') or that lines of breeding boars without boar taint could be selected. Research suggests that reducing stress and fighting among pigs and improving their cleanliness could also reduce the levels of the chemicals skatole and androstenone, (a hormone found in sweat), which cause boar taint.[47] Boar taint and ram taint and the management problems caused by male behaviour can be largely avoided by slaughtering meat animals below the age of sexual maturity.

## 4.3 The impact on animals

### 4.3.1 What animals want: Behaviour and subjective experience

An American primatologist has described a wild female baboon who knew the relationships within the herd of goats belonging to an African village so well that at night she would carry a bleating goat kid to its mother kept in another barn.[51] The baboon clearly knew what the kid and the mother goat wanted. In the pursuit of production efficiency, we have had to remove most of the behavioural choice and autonomy from farmed animals and have had to ignore much of the social behaviour that they might 'want'. The baboon story shows that this is not only a modern phenomenon.

Does it matter that we disrupt and prevent the natural behaviour of animals? Are their lives impoverished by being prevented from carrying out their natural sexual and parenting behaviour and experiencing the emotions associated with it? Are autonomy and choice important to them? There is plenty of evidence that their ancestors' evolved behaviours are still important to domesticated animals, whether or not they are kept in conditions that allow them to be expressed. A hen will 'work' to get to a nest site to lay her egg.[52] A sow shows measurable signs of stress when she cannot build a nest.[20,22] Cows and calves seek and call for each other when they are separated and the health and social development of the calf is affected.[39–41] Oxytocin, a neurochemical involved in attachment, is released in calves when they suck milk from their mothers, but not when they drink milk from a bucket.[32] Piglets show more abnormal behaviour if they are weaned too young, and fight less when their weaning is managed more in accordance with the natural behaviour of pigs.[26,33] In experiments to control which bull mated with a cow by fitting electronic shock-collars to the bulls, some cows pursued the 'wrong' bull, apparently out of personal preference.[53]

We know that the relationship between mother and young depends on the evolved behaviour of the species in relation to their environment – for example, whether they hide in undergrowth for their first days (as do calves) or whether they immediately follow their mother (as do lambs). Many evolved behaviours and motivations, such as nest-building by hens and sows, are hard-wired to the extent that the animal does not have to be taught them and tries to carry out the behaviour even when confined in a cage or a crate. But this does not mean that the motivations and the relationships are not experienced subjectively. Because these behaviours are essential to the survival of the species, it is far more likely that the animal is rewarded by emotional satisfaction in doing them and that the animal feels unpleasant frustration when they are prevented. If farming methods restrict animals' lives to the extent of preventing them from carrying out most natural behaviour, as is the case with industrially farmed poultry, pigs and dairy cows, it is hard to escape the conclusion that we are knowingly depriving them of enjoyment and subjecting them to frustration and anxiety.

An important factor in the scientific approach to farm animal welfare is the domination of animal behaviour science by the psychological school of behaviourism for much of the 20th century. In the behaviourist view, the subjective experience of animals should not enter into the science of animal behaviour because it could not be studied in a scientifically rigorous way. While behaviourism should have been seen as a method, not a dogma, it was naively (or conveniently) interpreted in a scientistic manner as implying that 'science says' that animals have no subjective experiences that we need to take account of.

When the modern science of the study of animal behaviour, or ethology, was created in the early 20th century, reproductive behaviour was one of the main areas of observation and theorizing. The emphasis was on establishing innate, or 'instinctive', patterns of behaviour and the stimuli that elicited them in their evolutionary context. This behaviour could be explained, it was believed, without reference to any conscious choice on the part of the animals involved; but the scientists assumed that the animals' behaviour had a subjective importance to them because otherwise they would not be sufficiently motivated to carry it out. Most of the early 20th-century ethologists believed at a personal level that animals' behaviour, including parenting and bonding with mates, is accompanied by subjective experiences but they maintained that it was too difficult, or impossible, to study them scientifically.[4] When writing for a general public readership, the Nobel Laureate Konrad Lorenz described geese as experiencing both love and grief.[7]

In recent years, the somewhat one-dimensional perspective of behaviourism is being broadened by a renewed scientific interest in animals' emotions. Neurobiological methods that can track brain activity are now showing that animals' attachment and social bonding are not figments of an 'anthropomorphic' view of animals. If the neurotransmitter oxytocin is blocked in rats and other species, they fail to look after their young or have normal social relationships with others rats.[54] The contemporary zoologist Bernd Heinrich, in his study of ravens, 'suspects' that ravens fall in love simply because to maintain their long-term pair bond would require an emotional reward.[55]

There is also increasing scientific interest in animals' cognition and decision-making abilities. Research is revealing that more and more species of animals turn out to perform feats of reasoning and conscious decision-making (such as selection between tools) that scientists were unaware of even a few decades ago. Considering farmed species alone, it has been shown that pigs are capable of consciously deceiving others about the location of food; young chicks can make decisions based on counting numbers of objects and can make mental images of objects that are out of sight; and young dairy heifers are emotionally rewarded when they succeed in working out how to open a gate to get to food. French scientists conclude that sheep evaluate emotion-triggering situations (such as an unexpected event) in a similar way to humans, and can experience fear, anger, rage, despair, boredom, disgust and happiness.[56–58]

### 4.3.2 The effects of maternal deprivation

Animal behaviour scientists have become increasingly interested in the effects on offspring of the lack of normal maternal care. Long-term effects due to maternal deprivation or early weaning have been demonstrated or suggested for a number of species, including rats, mice, elephants, deer, cats, monkeys, chimpanzees, cattle, pigs and poultry, and include a reduced ability to manage stress. Newborn mice stressed by being removed from their mothers secreted abnormally high levels of the stress hormone corticosterone when they were adults, were less able to cope with stressful situations and had memory impairments. Similarly, animals that were born in the wild and therefore had normal maternal care appear to cope better with the later stress of captivity than animals born in captivity and lacking a normal rearing experience.[59]

'Weaning distress' in farmed animals is now a growing topic of study (see also section 4.2.4).[60] Early separation of pigs and poultry from the mother affects the physiology of the neurotransmitters dopamine and serotonin,[59] which are involved in regulating mood. Piglets abruptly removed from their mothers and mixed with other piglets tend to fight. British experiments have found that treating the walls and feeders of pig pens with maternal pheromone significantly reduced both the amount of time that weaned piglets spent fighting and fight injuries.[61]

Chicks receive no maternal care in modern poultry breeding. This may be a factor in one of the most intractable problems in commercial egg production: the tendency of hens to injure each other by pecking (a behaviour that is not seen in wild hens). Experiments have been carried out to compare the behaviour of domestic chicks that were brooded and cared for by a maternal hen for their first eight weeks of life with those that were reared without adults, as in normal commercial practice. Later in life, those reared by a mother hen were more sociable, formed a stable hierarchy in the group and were less nervous of new objects in their environment, while those not reared by a hen were 3.5 times more likely to feather-peck others.[62] A mother hen secretes a substance which is chemically similar to the pheromones produced by many mammals, which have a comforting effect on their young. Tests in France showed that a synthetic analogue of this secretion reduced stress in broiler chicks reared in commercial conditions with 12,000 chicks per shed.[63]

This evidence suggests that the typical methods used to manage farm animal reproduction, nearly all of which disrupts or eliminates a normal rearing environment, have more negative effects on the welfare of offspring than has been fully recognized in the past. At worst, we may be creating stress and distress to millions of young domesticated animals yearly from maternal deprivation and early weaning.

## 4.4 The professionals, the industry and the public

This chapter has discussed a number of well-known problems related to breeding methods that have important animal welfare implications, as well as production or economic implications. By 2009 some of these were being debated in Europe and to some extent also in North America, Australia and New Zealand, with the aim of finding commercially practical solutions.

### 4.4.1 Debates on practice and alternatives

The debate on farrowing crates seems to be following the earlier debate on gestation crates, for which workable alternatives have now been found. Initially, the industry continued to support gestation crates on the grounds that they prevented fighting in large groups of loose-housed sows, and that 'welfare' in gestation crates was therefore better. Modern large-scale pig production keeps sows in larger and more crowded groups than would occur in natural conditions, creating an unnatural social environment that leads to conflict unless well designed and managed with the sows' behaviour patterns in mind. However, commercially viable alternative group housing and feeding systems exist that are designed so that they avoid the sows needing to compete for food, water and lying areas,[64] and are facilitating what seems to be the inevitable phase-out of gestation crates in developed countries at least.

The pig industry in developed countries has understood that the farrowing crate has become publicly unacceptable and that alternatives needed to be found, although many in the industry continue to support crates for the 'welfare' of piglets. A considerable amount is now known about what is needed for loose farrowing systems that minimize the deaths of piglets. These include adequate space for both sow and piglets, adequate heating for the piglets, design that incorporates supports for the sow when she lies down from a standing position, and design to encourage the piglets to lie away from the sow.[20,65,66] However, well-designed loose farrowing systems take up more space than farrowing crates and are therefore seen as less economic. In the highly competitive global market in pig production, it may be that global or regional voluntary agreements or regulation, perhaps by the EU or the World Organisation for Animal Health (OIE), will be needed to create a 'level playing field' for producers.

Within the farrowing-crate system and the rearing of meat pigs in barren environments, tooth-clipping and tail-docking make sense in that they fit the animal to survive in a system that distorts natural behaviour. These mutilations are defended by the industry and some veterinarians on grounds of 'welfare.' In the EU, neither routine tooth-clipping nor tail-docking of piglets is lawful except as a last resort in order to prevent worse welfare problems. In fact, both practices are still routine. In 2007 over 90 per cent of piglets were tail-docked and in 2009 57 per cent of piglets covered by the British pig industry's quality assurance scheme were reported to be teeth-clipped and 63 per cent were tail-docked.[67] Veterinarians who give written approval for these mutilations, without anaesthetic, must believe that they are acceptable or the least bad alternative. In effect, they are supporting their clients in taking advantage of the flexibility in the law rather than recommending changes to husbandry. This gives indirect support to farming methods that lead to the problems that mutilations are intended to solve, such as the use of farrowing crates, over-large litters and barren environments.

Castration and tail-docking are entrenched in traditional farming practice. In England, Wales and Scotland, official Codes of Recommendations for welfare make it clear to farmers and stockpeople that they should carefully consider whether mutilations are necessary before carrying them out. It is not yet clear how far these recommendations are changing farmers' practice. In 2008 the UK's Farm Animal Welfare Council (FAWC) recommended that tail-docking and castration of lambs should not be a routine procedure and that the whole food chain should work to end the practice, but the sheep industry was far from welcoming to this suggestion.[68,69] Tail-docking of lambs is defended as essential for 'welfare' in order to avoid the worse suffering that could be caused by flystrike. Teeth-clipping and tail-docking are also viewed as essential for the 'welfare' of piglets and sows and the pig industry refers to them as 'veterinary' procedures.[67] A further motivation may be that these mutilations have tradi-tionally been essential for an animal to be accepted for sale and farmers fear being left with uncastrated or undocked animals that no one is willing to buy.

Scientific evidence does not support an age limit for the ability to feel pain, and there seems no scientific reason why it should be illegal for a non-veterinarian to castrate a dog, cat or horse while this is allowed for farmed animals. In these cases it seems more likely that the law has been used to legitimize centuries of farming practice rather than being based on science or even on public acceptability.

## 4.4.2 The public, policy-makers and the future

Members of the animal production industry tend to criticize the public for making judgements (such as unfavourable judgements on the farrowing crate) based on emotion rather than on science. In this view the public is judging illogically, possibly because they have become 'detached from how their food is produced'. But animal welfare as an area of public policy and concern is not only about scientific evidence. The more important element has probably always been society's view of what is an acceptable way to treat an animal. To the general public not involved in large-scale animal production, there is something very disturbing about a gestation crate, a farrowing crate, a veal crate and a battery cage. These seem to violate some concept of decent treatment for a sentient creature, irrespective of the scientific arguments put forward by animal science professionals and the farming industry that these systems are actually in the welfare interests of the animals. Animal protection organizations are able to appeal to this instinctive revulsion to lobby for voluntary or legislative change.

In 2008 an opinion survey by the University of Michigan found that 69.2 per cent of respondents across the US said that they would vote for a ban on gestation crates in their state of residence if such a referendum were on the ballot paper. There was no difference between responses based on age, gender, income or education or on whether livestock and pig production were economically important in the state concerned.[70] In New Zealand in 2009 there was public outrage after a television programme showed sows in gestation crates, which are still legal and used during at least part of the pregnancy for almost half of the country's sows. The sows were filmed screaming and biting the bars of crates that were barely larger than their bodies.[71]

In many cases government advisory bodies such as the UK's FAWC and New Zealand's National Animal Welfare Advisory Committee are not in a position to insist on major changes to established farming practice. Governments are unwilling to bring in legislation unilaterally that will be perceived as putting their own farmers at a disadvantage in world markets. But it would be feasible for a large trading block, such as in the EU, to prohibit the sale of meat produced using either farrowing crates or mutilations without anaesthesia (the EU already bans the sale of cattle meat that has been produced with the use of growth-promoting hormones for food safety reasons). As recommended by the FAWC in 2008,[68] the large British food retailers could immediately reduce the perceived commercial necessity of mutilations by specifying that their suppliers should not use them.

Farrowing crates, mutilation of offspring and early weaning and separation from mothers could be eliminated from farming, but they would require a change in consumers' behaviour, a lower consumption of animal products, and a willingness to pay a higher price for them. Society would need to make it economically advantageous for farmers to manage animals in a way that takes their feelings into account, rather than being economically rewarded for ignoring them.

## Notes

1   For this and other depictions of farm animals, see Moncrieff, E. (2006) *Farm Animal Portraits*, Antique Collectors' Club
2   White, G. (1788–1789) *Natural History of Selborne*, Penguin Books, 1977
3   Darwin, C. (1871) *The Descent of Man, and Selection in Relation to Sex*, Introduction by J. Moore and A. Desmond, Penguin Books, 2004
4   Burkhardt, R. W. Jr. (2005) *Patterns of Behaviour: Korad Lorenz, Niko Tinbergen, and the Founding of Ethology*, University of Chicago Press
5   Hamminga, B. (2009) 'The hatchery of the future', *World Poultry* news online, 10 September, www.worldpoultry.net; *World Poultry* (2009) 'Cobb Vantress Brazil selects smart incubation', *World Poultry* news online, 1 May 2009, www.worldpoultry.net; Petersime NV (2009) *Synchro-Hatch™* sales leaflet, February, www.petersime.com, accessed May 2009
6   An exception is the BBC Natural History Collection film *Beasts of the Field*, narrated by Desmond Morris, BBC Enterprises Ltd, 1992
7   Lorenz, K. (1988, 1992) *Here I Am – Where Are You? The Behaviour of the Greylag Goose*, translated by R. D. Martin, Harper Collins,1992
8   Kendrick, K. M. (2006) 'Introduction: The neurobiology of social recognition, attraction and bonding', *Philosophical Transactions of the Royal Society, B*, vol 361, pp2057–2059; Kendrick, K. M. (1997) 'Animal awareness', in J. M. Forbes et al (eds) *Animal Choices*, Occasional Publication no 20, BSAS, pp1–7; da Costa, A. P. et al (2004) 'Face pictures reduce behavioural, autonomic, endocrine and neural indices of stress and fear in sheep', *Proceedings of the Royal Society: Biological Sciences*, vol 271, pp2077–2084; Kikusui, T., Winslow, J. T. and Mori, Y. (2006) 'Social buffering: Relief from stress and anxiety', *Philosophical Transactions of the Royal Society, B*, vol 361, pp2215–2228
9   Kendrick, K. M. et al (2001) 'Sheep don't forget a face', *Nature*, vol 414, pp165–166; Kendrick, K. M. (1997) 'Animal awareness', in J. M. Forbes et al (eds) *Animal Choices*, Occasional Publication no 20, BSAS, pp1–7
10  Rutter, S. M. (2002) 'Behaviour of sheep and goats', in P. Jensen (ed) *The Ethology of Domestic Animals: An Introductory Text*, CABI Publishing, pp145–158
11  Bouissou, M.-F. et al (2001) 'The social behaviour of cattle', in L. J. Keeling and H. W. Gonyou (eds) *Social Behaviour in Farm Animals*, CABI Publishing, pp113–145; Hall, S. J. G. (2002) 'Behaviour of cattle', in P. Jensen (ed) *The Ethology of Domestic Animals: An Introductory Text*, CABI Publishing, pp131–143; Fraser, A. F. and Broom, D. M. (2004) *Farm Animal Behaviour and Welfare*, CABI Publishing, third edition, Chapter 15; Veissier, I., Lamy, D. and le Neindre, P. (1990) 'Social behaviour in domestic beef cattle when yearling calves are left with the cows for the next calving', *Applied Animal Behaviour Science*, vol 27, pp193–2000
12  Jensen, P. (2002) 'Behaviour of pigs', in P. Jensen (ed) *The Ethology of Domestic Animals: An Introductory Text*, CABI Publishing, Wallingford, UK, Chapter 11; Jensen, P. (2001) 'Parental behaviour', in L. J. Keeling and H. W. Gonyou (eds)

*Social Behaviour in Farm Animals*, CABI Publishing, Wallingford, UK, Chapter 3; Gonyou, H. W. (2001) 'Social behaviour of pigs', in L. J. Keeling and H. W. Gonyou (eds) *Social Behaviour in Farm Animals*, CABI Publishing, Chapter 6

13  Keeling, L. (2002) 'Behaviour of fowl and other domesticated birds', in P. Jensen (ed) *The Ethology of Domestic Animals: An Introductory Text*, CABI Publishing, Chapter 7; Mench, J. and Keeling, L. J. (2001) 'The social behaviour of domestic birds', in L. J. Keeling and H. W. Gonyou (eds) *Social Behaviour in Farm Animals*, CABI Publishing, Chapter 7; Popescu, C. (2009) pers comm

14  Young. R. (2003) *The Secret Life of Cows*, Farming Books and Videos Ltd

15  Fraser, A. F. and Broom, D. M. (2004) *Farm Animal Behaviour and Welfare*, CABI Publishing, third edition, Chapter 15

16  Hall, S. J. G. (2002) 'Behaviour of cattle', in P. Jensen (ed) *The Ethology of Domestic Animals: An Introductory Text*, CABI Publishing, pp131–143; Bouissou, M.-F. et al (2001) 'The social behaviour of cattle', in L. J. Keeling and H. W. Gonyou (eds) *Social Behaviour in Farm Animals*, CABI Publishing, pp113–145

17  von Keyserlingk, M. A. G., Olenick, D. and Weary, D. M. (2008) 'Acute behavioral effects of regrouping dairy cows', *Journal of Dairy Science*, vol 91, no 3, pp1011–1016

18  Mendl, M. and Erhard, H. W. (1997) 'Social choices in farm animals: To fight or not to fight?', in J. M. Forbes et al (eds) *Animal Choices*, BSAS Occasional Publication no 20, pp45–53

19  Nicol, C. J. and Pope, S. J. (1996) 'The maternal feeding behaviour of hens is sensitive to perceived chick error', *Animal Behaviour*, vol 52, pp767–774

20  Johnson, A. K. and Marchant-Forde, J. N. (2009) 'Welfare of pigs in the farrowing environment', in J. N. Marchant-Forde (ed) *The Welfare of Pigs*, Springer, Chapter 5

21  Bergeron, R., Meunier-Salaün, M.-C. and Robert, S. (2009) 'The welfare of pregnant and lactating sows', in L. Fuacitano and A. L. Schaefer (eds) *Welfare of Pigs from Birth to Slaughter*, Wageningen Academic Publishers, Chapter 3

22  Jarvis, S. et al (2002) 'Pituitary-adrenal activation in preparturient pigs (*Sus scrofa*) is associated with behavioural restriction due to lack of space rather than nesting substrate', *Animal Welfare*, vol 11, pp371–384

23  Jarvis, S. et al (2006) 'The effect of confinement during lactation on the hypothala-mic–pituitary–adrenal axis and behaviour of primiparous sows', *Physiology and Behavior*, vol 87, no 2, pp345–352; Edwards, S. (2008) 'Balancing sow and piglet welfare with production efficiency', London Swine Conference, Ontario, *The PigSite*, July, www.thepigsite.com/

24  Scottish Agricultural College (undated) *Sow Welfare and Piglet Mortality*, Livestock Research Notes, SAC reference number 521112; 521129, SAC

25  Pitts, A. D. et al (2002) 'Alternative housing for sows and litters: Individual differ-ences in the maternal behaviour of sows', *Applied Animal Behaviour Science*, vol 76, no 4, pp291–306

26  Weary, D. M. et al (2002) 'Alternative housing for sows and litters: Part 4. Effects of sow-controlled housing combined with a communal piglet area on pre- and post-weaning behaviour and performance', *Applied Animal Behaviour Science*, vol 76, no 4, pp279–290

27  Arey, D. and Brooke, P. (2006) *Animal Welfare Aspects of Good Agricultural Practice: Pig Production*, Compassion in World Farming Trust

28  Panel on Animal Health and Welfare (2007) 'Scientific report on animal health and welfare aspects of different housing and husbandry systems for adult breeding boars, pregnant, farrowing sows and unweaned piglets', European Food Safety Authority, *The EFSA Journal*, vol 572, pp1–107

29　Royal College of Veterinary Surgeons (1987) *Report of Working Party Established by RCVS Council to Consider the Mutilation of Animals*

30　Advocates for Animals (2006) *Painful Reality: Why Painful Mutilations of Animals Must Be Reviewed*, Advocates for Animals; National Animal Welfare Advisory Committee (2005) *Animal Welfare (Painful Husbandry Procedures) Report* and *Code of Welfare No 7*, MAF, New Zealand Government; Farm Animal Welfare Council (2008) *FAWC Report on the Implications of Castration and Taildocking for the Welfare of Lambs*, FAWC; Marchant-Forde, J. N. et al (2009) 'Postnatal piglet husbandry practices and well-being: The effects of alternative techniques delivered separately', *Journal of Animal Science*, vol 87, pp1479–1492; Kluivers-Poodt, M., Hopster, H. and Spoolder, H. A. M. (2007) *Castration under Anaesthesia and/or Analgesia in Commercial Pig Production*, Wageningen University and Research Centre

31　Advertising Standards Authority (2009) *Adjudication 20 May 2009*, Compassion in World Farming

32　Weary, D. M., Jasper, J. and Hötzel, M. J. (2008) 'Understanding weaning distress', *Applied Animal Welfare Science*, vol 110, no 1/2, pp24–41

33　Held, S. and Mendl, M. (2001) 'Behaviour of the young weaner pig', in M. A. Varley and J. Wiseman (eds) *The Weaner Pig: Nutrition and Management*, CABI Publishing, pp273–297

34　Weary, D. M., Ross, S. and Fraser, D. (1996) 'Vocalizations by isolated piglets: A reliable indicator of piglet need directed towards the sow', *Animal Behaviour*, vol 52, no 6, pp1247–1253; Weary, D. M. and Fraser, D. (1997) 'Vocal response of piglets to weaning: Effect of piglet age', *Applied Animal Behaviour Science*, vol 54, pp153–160

35　Worobec, E. K., Duncan, I. J. H. and Widowski, T. M. (1999) 'The effects of weaning at 7, 14 and 28 days on piglet behaviour', *Applied Animal Behaviour Science*, vol 62, pp173–182

36　Newberry, R. and Swanson, J. (2001) 'Breaking social bonds', in L. J. Keeling and H. W. Gonyou (eds) *Social Behaviour in Farm Animals*, CABI Publishing, Chapter 11

37　Weeks, C. (2007) *UK Calf Transport and Veal Rearing*, Compassion in World Farming

38　Bouissou, M.-F. et al (2001) 'The social behaviour of cattle', in L. J. Keeling, H. W. Gonyou (eds) *Social Behaviour in Farm Animals*, CABI Publishing, pp113–145

39　Flower, F. C. and Weary, D. M. (2003) 'The effects of early separation on the dairy cow and calf', *Animal Welfare*, vol 12, pp339–348

40　Stehulová, I., Lidfors, L. and Spinka, M. (2008) 'Response of dairy cows and calves to early separation: Effect of calf age and visual and auditory contact after separation', *Applied Animal Behaviour Science*, vol 110, no 1/2, pp144–165

41　Hickey, M. C., Drennan, M. and Earley, B.(2003) 'The effect of abrupt weaning of suckler calves on the plasma concentrations of cortisol, catecholamines, leukocytes, acute-phase proteins and in vitro interferon-gamma production', *Journal of Animal Science*, vol 81, no 11, pp2847–2855

42　*Pig Progress* (2009) 'UK: New boar quality assurance scheme', *Pig Progress* online news, 22 June, www.pigprogress.net/

43　Trow-Smith, R. (1957) *A History of British Livestock Husbandry to 1700*, Routledge and Kegan Paul

44　Whittle, T. E. (2000) *A Triumph of Science*, Poultry World Publications

45　See examples cited in Advocates for Animals (2006) *Painful Reality: Why Painful Mutilations of Animals Must Be Reviewed*, www.advocatesforanimals.org (see Appendix for summary of UK practice and regulations as of 2006)

46  Farm Animal Welfare Council (2008) *FAWC Report on the Implications of Castration and Taildocking for the Welfare of Lambs*, FAWC; Stoffel, M. H. et al (2009) 'Histological assessment of testicular residues in lambs and calves after Burdizzo castration', *Veterinary Record*, vol 164, pp523–528

47  European Food Safety Authority (2004) *Opinion of the Scientific Panel on Animal Health and Welfare on a Request from the Commission Related to Welfare Aspects of the Castration of Piglets*, EFSA, July 2004; Panel on Animal Health and Welfare (2004) *Report on Welfare Aspects of the Castration of Piglets*, EFSA; PIGCAS (2007) *Report of Stakeholder Forum*, PIGCAS

48  ter Beek, V. (2008) 'Europe moves away from conventional castration', *Pig Progress*, vol 24, no 8, pp12–13; Harris, C. (2008) 'Balancing pig welfare, castration and boar taint', *The PigSite*, December, www.thepigsite.com; *The PigSite* (2009) 'Is this the end of castration?' *The PigSite*, News Desk, 8 May, www.thepigsite.com

49  *Pig Progress* (2009) 'Swiss castration method', *Pig Progress online*, 15 August, www.pigprogress.net

50  Zamaratskaia, G. et al (2008) 'Effect of a gonadotropin-releasing hormone vaccine (Improvac™) on steroid hormones, boar taint compounds and performance in entire male pigs', *Reproduction in Domestic Animals*, vol 43, no 3, pp351–359; Harris, C. (2009) 'Boar taint vaccine improves more than welfare', *The PigSite*, Newsletter, July, www.thepigsite.com; Merks, J. W. M. et al (2009) 'Genetic opportunities for pork production without castration', *Animal Welfare*, vol 18, pp539–544

51  University of Delaware (2009) 'Baboons benefit from strong social networks, expert says', *ScienceDaily*, May 9, www.sciencedaily.com

52  Dawkins, M. (1998) *Through Our Eyes Only? The Search for Animal Consciousness*, Oxford University Press, Chapter 5

53  Lee, C. et al (2008) 'Behavioral aspects of electronic bull separation and mate allocation in multiple-sire mating paddocks', *Journal of Animal Science*, vol 86, pp1690–1696

54  Kendrick K. M. (2006) 'Introduction: The neurobiology of social recognition, attraction and bonding', *Philosophical Transactions of the Royal Society, B*, vol 361, pp2057–2059, and work cited; Jin, D. et al (2007) 'CD38 is critical for social behaviour by regulating oxytocin secretion', *Nature*, vol 446, pp41–45; Szalavitz, M. (2008) 'Cuddle chemical could treat mental illness', *New Scientist*, 17 May, pp34–37

55  Balcombe, J. (2006) *Pleasurable Kingdom: Animals and the Nature of Feeling Good*, Macmillan, citing Heinrich, B. (1999) *Mind of the Raven: Investigations and Adventures with Wolf-Birds*, Harper Collins

56  Held, S. et al (2002) 'Foraging pigs alter their behaviour in response to exploitation', *Animal Behaviour*, vol 64, no 2, pp157–165; Held, S. et al (2000) 'Social tactics of pigs in a competitive foraging task: The "informed forager" paradigm', *Animal Behaviour*, vol 59, no 3, pp569–576

57  Rugani, R. et al (2009) 'Arithmetic in newborn chicks', *Proceedings of the Royal Society, B*, vol 276, pp2451–2460; Regolin, C. L., Vallortigara, G. and Zanforlin, M. (1995) 'Object and spatial experimentation in detour problems by chicks', *Animal Behaviour*, vol 49, no 1, pp195–199

58  Hagen, K. and Broom, D. M. (2004) 'Emotional reactions to learning in cattle', *Applied Animal Behaviour Science*, vol 85, pp203–213; Veissier, I. et al (2009) 'Animals' emotions: Studies in sheep using appraisal theories', *Animal Welfare*, vol 18, pp347–354

59  Latham, N. R. and Mason, G. J. (2008) 'Maternal deprivation and the development of stereotypic behaviour', *Applied Animal Behaviour Science*, vol

110, no 1/2, pp84–108; Novak, M. A. et al (2006) 'Deprived environments: Developmental insights from primatology', in G. Mason and J. Rushen (eds) *Stereotypic Animal Behaviour: Fundamentals and Applications to Welfare*, second edition, CABI, Wallingford, UK, pp153–189; Murgatroyd, C. et al (2009) 'Dynamic DNA methylation programs persistent adverse effects of early-life stress', *Nature Neuroscience*, vol 12, no 12, pp1559–1566; *Nature* (2009) 'Neuroscience: Early stress marks genes', *Nature*, 12 November, vol 462, p140

60  Dybkjær, L. (ed) (2008) *Early Weaning: Special Issue of Applied Animal Behaviour Science*, vol 110, no 1/2

61  Guy, J. H. et al (2009) 'Reduced post-mixing aggression and skin lesions in weaned pigs by application of a synthetic maternal pheromone', *Animal Welfare*, vol 18, no 3, pp249–255

62  Perré, Y., Wauters, A.-M. and Richard-Yris M.-A. (2002) 'Influence of mothering on emotional and social reactivity of domestic pullets', *Applied Animal Behaviour Science*, vol 75, no 2, pp133–146; see also Rodenburg T. B. et al (2009) 'The effect of selection on low mortality and brooding by a mother hen on open-field response, feather pecking and cannibalism in laying hens, *Animal Welfare*, vol 18, pp427–432

63  Madec, I. et al (2008) 'Broilers (*Gallus gallus*) are less stressed if they can smell a mother odorant', *South African Journal of Animal Science*, vol 38, no 3, pp201–206

64  An example is Ontario Pork (2009) 'Making the switch to group housing', *The Pigsite*, Newsletter, 24 August, www.thepigsite.com

65  Pedersen, L. J. (2009) 'Important pen features and management in farrowing pens for loose-housed sows', *The Pig Site*, May, www.thepigsite.com, citing Pedersen, L. J. (2008) *Farrowing and Lactating Sows in Non-Crate Systems,* Arnhaus University

66  Marchant, J. N. et al ( 2000) 'Timing and causes of piglet mortality in alternative and conventional farrowing systems', *Veterinary Record*, vol 147, pp209–214; Johnson, A. K. and Marchant-Forde, J. N. (2009) 'Welfare of pigs in the farrowing environment', in J. N. Marchant-Forde (ed) *The Welfare of Pigs*, Springer, Chapter 5

67  Fowler, F. (2008) *Structure of the UK Pig Industry*, British Pig Executive (BPEX); Commission Directive 2001/93/EC amending Directive 91/630/EEC Laying Down Minimum Standards for the Protection of Pigs; Panel on Animal Health and Welfare (2007) 'The risks associated with tail biting in pigs and possible means to reduce the need for tail docking considering the different housing and husbandry systems', *The EFSA Journal*, vol 611, pp1–13

68  Farm Animal Welfare Council (2008) *FAWC Report on the Implications of Castration and Tail Docking on the Welfare of Lambs*, FAWC

69  *Farmers Weekly* (2008) 'Advice on docking and castration is "unfortunate"', *Farmers Weekly*, 4 July 2008, p13

70  Tonsor, G. (2009) 'Understanding consumer support for a gestation crate ban', Michigan State University, *The Pig Site*, April, www.thepigsite.com

71  TVNZ (2009) *Sunday Programme: Comic Tackles Pig Welfare*, 17 May

# 5

# Companion Animal Breeding: Ideal Standards

## 5.1 Background and context: Breeding for work and whim

### 5.1.1 Then and now: The creation of dog breeds and standards

A late 19th-century *Punch* cartoon captioned 'Dog fashions of 1889' pictures a pug with corkscrew tail waddling through the park enveloped in folds of skin, a bulldog with fangs and tongue protruding from his outsized jaw, terriers and dachshunds crawling along the ground like huge elongated lizards, a small hairy dog resembling a hedgehog, an enormous hound the size of a pony and a micro-dog barely visible to the naked eye.[1] People have long ridiculed the breeding of animals to fit some human whim. A 1911 book by the dog breeder The Honourable Mrs Neville Lytton described 'certain types of modern dogs' as 'monstrosities'.[2] Both the caricatured excesses and the criticism are familiar today. The dog adjudged 'Best in Show' at the British 2007 Crufts dog show and watched by 6000 people at the event and by millions on television was Araki Fabulous Willy, a Tibetan Terrier who would not have looked out of place in the cartoon of 100 years earlier. His body and legs were invisible under a curtain of hair that reached to the ground all around him and his head needed to be held firmly upward by his lead to allow the audience to see his face underneath its coverings.

The explosion in the creation, differentiation and refinement of dog, cat and other domesticated animal breeds coincided with urbanization, the appearance of a prosperous middle class and the decline in the use of working dogs during the 19th and 20th centuries.[1,3] A 16th-century British author identified 17 varieties of dog by function, such as bloodhound, greyhound, turnspit, shepherd's dog and 'comforter'. By 1800 Sydenham Edwards's *Cynographia Britannica* identified only 15 'permanent' breeds and numerous cross breeds.[1] Over the course of the 19th century in France, the number of identified breeds increased from around 24 to around 200.[3]

The underpinnings of these changes were the systematization of the records of dogs, and later of their parentage, and competitive shows to exhibit and judge them. Dog shows were held from 1865 onwards in Paris, and from the 1880s the organization of shows was taken over by the Société Centrale for the 'improvement' of dog breeds. Guard dogs, sheep dogs and mountain dogs were now being kept in Paris.[3] In England, the first dog show with over 1000 entries was held in Chelsea in 1863 and by 1899 there were 380 shows in the year, some regional or small town events, but including Kennel Club shows and the Crufts dog show (at that time Crufts was a private commercial event, taken over by the Kennel Club in the 1940s). These shows aimed to show specimens of model dogs of each breed and to discourage the breeding of non-pedigree dogs. Non-pedigree dogs started to become unacceptable, referred to as 'curs', 'mongrels', 'useless' and 'rubbish'. It was agreed that a careless choice of pet could reflect badly on the owner since no one could 'now afford to be followed about by a mongrel dog'.[1]

As still happens today, certain breeds could become fashionable after endorsement by high-status owners. The pug breed was revived because it had aristocratic admirers and the perceived aristocratic Fox Terrier breed had its own 19th-century periodical, *Fox-Terrier Chronicle*, covering the activities of the Fox Terrier elite (both dogs and owners). This included regular features on 'Gossip', 'Visits' (matings) and 'Debutantes' (dogs making a first appearance at a dog show).[1]

Dog breeding for shows has always been seen as a competitive sport and pastime. A 'breed standard' became the blueprint and the brand label that allowed the dog fanciers to differentiate their chosen breed from others, and to create points of difference between dogs of the breed that were easy to identify and compete on. As a result, breeders tended to breed for these points. An example was the remodelling of the collie (a very popular breed, deemed aristocratic) for exaggerated heads with long pointed noses in the 1890s such that these were described as 'greyhound type', with an 'inane, expressionless look', according to a contemporary.[1] By the beginning of the 20th century the little spaniels with long ears, round eyes and pointed noses seen in numerous 17th- and 18th-century portraits had become the snub-nosed, dome-headed, bulbous-eyed King Charles Toy Spaniel of today, with drooping ears set nearly half way down the head. In the early 20th century some of these toy spaniels were bred with almost concave facial profiles ('nostrils almost sunk into the skull') and were criticized as a 'noseless atrocity'; they often died ('providentially') before adulthood as a result of cleft palate or other lethal abnormalities.[2] (The King Charles Spaniel is now differentiated from the very popular Cavalier King Charles Spaniel, which has a nose but has accumulated breeding-related health problems; see section 6.2 in Chapter 6.)

The bulldog was also remodelled in the 19th century after the traditional bull-fighting breed was in danger of dying out following the legal abolition of bull-baiting in 1835. The new model bulldog of 1899 looked more like the tank-like, massive-headed modern bulldog than the lithe, longer-legged bulldog pictured in 1805.[1] As late as the 1850s, the artist Jemima Blackburn painted her bulldog, Doll, as agile in the Scottish Highlands, without the bandy legs that were to come.[4] Some believed the new model bulldog's body should correctly be 'out at the shoulder', while others saw the bulldogs exhibited in shows as 'disgusting abortions' which were 'deformities from foot to muzzle' and incapable of attacking a bull. Dockleaf, a champion new bulldog of the 1890s, indeed collapsed after walking a couple of miles.[1]

The exaggeration of dog breed points for competitive showing and branding purposes was therefore well established by the end of the 19th century. Separate from the show dogs, the selection of working dogs for ability and functional conformation would have needed to be as rigorous as selection for the show ring. In Thomas Hardy's *Far from the Madding Crowd* (1874), a young dog learning the sheepdog's craft drives Farmer Oak's sheep over a cliff in an excess of zeal. He is 'considered too good a workman to live' and is shot, probably without passing on his genes.[5]

Breeding of dogs (or cats, rabbits, mice and rats) to meet human specifications has always involved selecting the more desirable and culling the unwanted, whether the selection was for work or for showing. Well before the 19th century, breeders advised that, when a bitch gave birth to puppies, 'choose them you intend to preserve, and throw away the rest' and recorded of a litter that three were so chosen and 'the rest hanged, because not liked'.[6] The same differentiation between 'off types' and the 'true-to-type', and the pursuit of the ideal type defined by the breeder, is still made today. As a popular modern manual on dog reproduction tells us: 'Every good breeder has in his mind's eye a picture, no matter how ill-defined the picture might be, of what he is aiming towards.'[7]

## 5.1.2 The cat, mouse and rabbit 'Fancy'

The 19th-century enthusiasm for remoulding animals into new breeds and varieties (termed the 'Fancy') also encompassed cats, mice and rabbits, among other species. Unlike the case of dogs, originally differentiated by working function, the fancy breeders concentrated largely on finding new combinations of coat colour, length and texture and eye colour rather than the huge differences in size and shape that had already been created over centuries in dog breeds. Cat shows and societies developed in the later 19th century in England. Foreign cat breeds, particularly the Persian and Siamese, were imported to England towards the end of the century and became popular, possibly because they offered the fanciers some definite points of difference to breed to.[1] The Cat Fanciers' Association in the US and the Governing Council of the Cat Fancy in the UK were founded in the first decade of the 20th century. They established registers and stud books and organized shows.[8]

In Britain, fancy rabbit breeding started in the early 19th century (for fur and flesh, as well as for showing) and by the 21st century there were 50 recognized breeds and over 500 varieties. Around 1000 shows per year exhibit and judge rabbits against their breed standards. The mouse fancy existed from the 18th century in Japan (in particular, the 'waltzing mouse' which suffered from a damaging genetic mutation) and arrived in Europe and the US in the later 19th and early 20th centuries. Forty recognized fancy mouse breeds and 200 varieties exist in the UK today. The rat fancy today includes some hairless and tailless varieties whose mutations are linked to health problems. For these reasons the National Fancy Rat Society (UK) bars them from their shows, although they are bred for show in the US.[9] By the later 20th century the foremost inventors of mouse and rat breeds were no longer the fancy, but the scientists who create rodent strains for experimental purposes (see Chapter 12).

## 5.1.3 Global dog standards

Pedigree dog organizations, dedicated to breeding, registering and judging in championship shows, exist all over the world operating under essentially the same rules and procedures. The Fédération Cynologique Internationale (FCI), based in Belgium, is the world canine authority and has affiliated or partner 'Kennel' or 'Canine' or 'Cynologic' organizations in 84 countries (excluding the US, Canada and the UK, but including the world's major emerging economies of India, China and Brazil). The affiliated national organizations reported the registration of over 2 million puppies in 2006, around half of which were from Europe. Excluding the non-affiliated US and UK, the largest regional breeders of pedigree registered puppies in 2006 were France, Russia, Italy and Spain in the European region; Japan, Taiwan and Korea in the Asian region; and Brazil, Argentina and Mexico in the Americas. In total, the FCI authorized over 6000 championship shows worldwide in 2006, nearly 10,000 judges and nearly 7000 breed clubs.[10]

In China, which has a long tradition of dog breeding, the China Kennel Union operates under FCI rules, issues pedigrees and official Kennel names, and in 2008 ran nine all breed championship shows in different regions of China, and a Labrador Retriever and Golden Retriever speciality show in Beijing. In Finland, over 10 per cent of the population participates in or attends competitive dog shows based on the dog's appearance. The UK developed the world's largest single dog show (Crufts), involving 23,000 dogs and 160,000 visitors in 2008.[11]

**Table 5.1** *World regional activity in pedigree dogs registered under the Fédération Cynologique Internationale in 2006 (rounded figures)*

|  | Number of puppies registered | Number of breed clubs | Number of championship shows | Number of accredited judges |
|---|---|---|---|---|
| Europe (excluding UK) | 1,050,000 | 4800 | 3700 | 6900 |
| Asia | 700,000 | 1200 | 480 | 190 |
| Americas (excluding US and Canada) | 230,000 | 330 | 2000 | 370 |
| Australia and New Zealand | 74,000 | 650 | 140 | 2000 |
| Africa (South Africa) | 22,000 | 0 | 40 | 260 |

*Source:* FCI[10]

## 5.2 Modern breeding to design

### 5.2.1 Dog breeds and pedigrees

There may be 500 million dogs in the world, the majority free-living in Africa, Asia and South America. 40 species of canids have been identified, either wolf-like or fox-like. The domestic dog is one of the species of wolf-like canids and genetic analysis has shown that all domestic dog breeds originate from the grey wolf (*Canis lupus*), although dogs can hybridize with certain wild canid species such as the coyote. Selective breeding by humans has now created the estimated 400 distinct breeds of dog in existence globally today. The UK Kennel Club recognizes approximately 210 breeds. The American Kennel Club recognizes just over 160 breeds and provides standards for a further 60 or so 'rare breeds' that are not yet recognized.[12]

All dog breeds are unnatural and sometimes bizarre biological entities, created and maintained for the benefit of people rather than of dogs. Charles Darwin, a dog enthusiast, noted in *The Variation of Animals and Plants under Domestication* (1868) the 'distinct and abnormal origin' of dog breeds compared to other known members of the Canid family. He thought it self-evident that 'Such extreme forms as thoroughbred greyhounds, bloodhounds, bulldogs, Blenheim spaniels, terriers, pugs, etc.' were too unnatural ever to exist 'in a wild state'.[13] Since then, the number of breeds have multiplied further with the creation of variations on existing breeds. Remarkably, any person or group of people is free to try to invent a new breed, start a breed registry or a breed society, certify pedigrees, produce a 'standard' that mimics the official Kennel Club standards, and hold dog shows where dogs are judged against the chosen standard.

A dog that appears to belong to a defined and recognized breed is usually referred to as a 'purebred' or 'pedigree', although the dog may not in fact be listed on a certified pedigree. The certified registered pedigree of a dog, recorded in a stud book of a breed society or Kennel Club, is the quality assurance mark for dogs sold or exhibited as members of the breed. In developed countries, the large majority of owned dogs are of specified breeds (estimated 75 per cent in the UK and 67 per cent in France[14]). The belief that a dog or cat that appears to be of a defined breed, and possibly has a 'pedigree', is of superior quality to one who is of no breed seems to be widespread in human society.

In reality, the pedigree of either a human or a dog means simply that the ancestry ('family tree') is known and recorded. In the case of dogs, the ancestry is required to be restricted to individuals whose ancestry is similarly recorded and of the same breed, which means that all dog breeds and varieties are closed breeding groups. In contrast to human pedigrees, dog and cat breeds additionally require that all the animals should have a similar appearance, temperament, motivations and abilities. Their height, weight, head shape and size, body shape, tail, coat colour and length, ears, legs, feet, nose colour, eye colour, and more are specified in often minute detail. All this is set out in a breed standard – according to the UK Kennel Club, this is the 'blueprint of the ideal specimen in each breed approved by a governing body'.[15] Some breed societies will not allow full registration of a puppy that fails to conform to some aspect of the breed standard, such as coat colour.

## 5.2.2 Breeds, lifestyle and consumer choice

Why do so many of us prefer a dog of a specified breed, and preferably one with a pedigree? Originally dog breeds were classified in functional groups, such as gundogs, guard dogs, herding dogs, spitz dogs (pulling sleds, etc.), terriers, spaniels, hounds and toy dogs.[16] The Kennel Clubs have continued to use a version of these traditional groupings: hound, gundog, terrier, utility, working, pastoral and toy groups, although their contemporary relevance for many of the breeds has almost disappeared (the 'utility' group still includes the bulldog, poodle and Shih Tzu).

Today the proliferation of dog breeds offers the consumer a wide range of dog attributes. We are offered a perfect match to our needs. Those who promote dog breeding can claim with justification that there is a breed out there to fit into every lifestyle and reflect the values and aspirations of any person. Breeds are branded according to their looks, behaviour and personality. A-to-Z lists of the breeds and their attributes are available for people engaged in the search for 'the right companion' or 'the perfect pet'. Acquiring a pedigree dog is therefore promoted as a lifestyle choice and also a wise purchasing decision because of the predictability and uniformity of the package on offer. Dog breed listings inform the consumer about size, exercise and grooming requirements, behaviour with children, need for attention and stimulation, and more. The Labrador Retriever, perhaps the world's most popular companion dog breed, we are told 'adores children' and has 'a strong will to please'.[17]

One reason why breeds seem to have such importance for the pet-owning public may be the moral and social values they are felt to reflect and that are often endorsed in the breed standards. The Pekinese is described as an 'aristocrat'. The Labrador Retriever is 'a real gentleman' and 'a bit of a country squire at heart'. Other dog breeds are 'noble', 'regal', 'dignified', 'proud', 'courageous', 'wise', 'gay', 'merry', 'benevolent', 'kindly', 'saucy', 'jaunty', 'elegant', 'forbidding', 'fearless' or 'indomitable'.[17] People may feel judged by their dog's breed. Pedigree dogs of a perceived 'aristocratic' breed have been targeted by popular revolutionaries throughout history.[3] Breeds are also marketed on their 'origin' story that validates their special status, whether royal, exotic or heroic, however little relevance it may have to the circumstances of the urban dog of today. Thus the Pekinese were palace guards in China, the Afghan hound a hunter in the mountains of Central Asia, the Basenji a palace dog of the Pharaohs, the Borzoi the wolf-hunter of the Tsars, and pugs an ancient breed of China, imported to Europe by merchants of the Dutch East India company in the 16th century and entering the English court with William and Mary in 1688.[17]

A breed may be an artificial biological entity; but maintaining it and its characteristics is a major lifetime preoccupation for many breeders. Some are described as doing a devoted, or even heroic, service to dogs by promoting, showing and 'improving' what they refer to as 'their breed'.[18] But breeds, shows and prizes are a sport and a preoccupation of people rather than of dogs. Dog shows may be very uncomfortable places for dogs (and they sometimes collapse from heat stress). When dogs interact, it is clear that they have no sense of each other as belonging to a 'breed'. A dog can have no concept of, or interest in, winning a title in a dog show (apart from the dog's normal enjoyment of human praise and companionship). Whether his or her size, colour, eyes, nose, ears, coat and leg length conform to the breed standard for 'his' breed is immaterial to the dog, provided that they are functional.

## 5.2.3 The most popular dog breeds

According to their annual registration statistics, in 2007 the Kennel Club (London) registered around 270,000 dogs, while the American Kennel Club registered over 800,000. 12 breeds each registered over 5000 dogs with the Kennel Club in London (KC) and 14 breeds each registered over 10,000 dogs with the American Kennel Club (AKC).[19] (The popularity of a breed as judged by Kennel Club registrations in a particular year does not necessarily correspond to the relative number of owned dogs of that breed, because fashions change over the lifetime of a dog and a significant proportion of dogs are bred outside the KC auspices.)

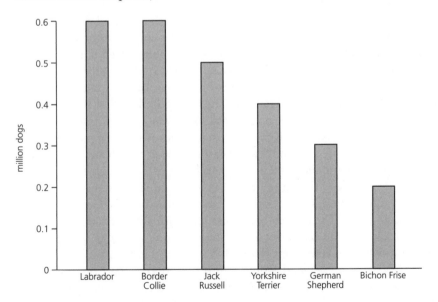

*Source:* Pet Food Manufacturers Association (2008, 2009)[14]

**Figure 5.1** *The six most-owned dog breeds in the UK in 2008 as assessed by the pet food industry*

**Table 5.2** *Estimates of popularity of dog breeds*

| Rank (descending order of popularity) | Number of dogs of breed in UK, 2008[14] | Kennel Club UK registrations, 2007[19] | American Kennel Club registrations, 2007[19] |
| --- | --- | --- | --- |
| 1 | Labrador retriever | Labrador retriever | Labrador retriever |
| 2 | Border Collie | Cocker Spaniel | Yorkshire Terrier |
| 3 | Jack Russell Terrier | English Springer Spaniel | German Shepherd |
| 4 | Yorkshire Terrier | Staffordshire Bull Terrier | Golden Retriever |
| 5 | German Shepherd | German Shepherd | Beagle |
| 6 | Bichon Frise | Cavalier King Charles Spaniel | boxer |
| 7 | Rottweiler/Dalmatian | Golden Retriever | dachshunds |
| 8 | Cocker Spaniel/Shih Tzu | Border Terrier | poodles |
| 9 | Labradoodle/Golden Retriever | West Highland White Terrier | Shih Tzu |
| 10 | greyhound or whippet/ Chihuahua | boxer | bulldog |

According to the UK pet food manufacturers (whose dog and cat food market was worth UK£1.9 billion in 2008), the top three dog breeds owned are the Labrador Retriever, the Border Collie and the Jack Russell Terrier.[14] It is notable that these three most popular dogs were originally bred for work, and probably many of the Border Collies are still working sheepdogs, not registered with the Kennel Club. But the majority of dogs of originally working breeds are now kept as domestic companions, including the popular Labrador Retriever and the Jack Russell Terrier, originally bred to hunt and kill.

The statistics on pedigree dog registrations in the UK and the US during 2007–2008 gives some insight into our breed-owning motivations. The Labrador Retriever is by any measure the most popular breed in both the UK and the US, with twice as many Kennel Club registrations as any other breed. This could be seen as logical since the Labrador is bred and marketed to be devoted to people and family friendly. The high popularity of the Yorkshire Terrier in the US can also be seen as logical for urban and apartment living. A marked difference between UK and US preferences is that the bulldog breed has become much more popular over the last decade in the US and in 2007 was on the top ten list nationally and in over half of the 50 largest cities.[19]

More surprisingly, the large breeds were the most registered in some of America's largest cities. 45 out of the 50 largest cities had the Labrador as the most popular breed. The top ten breeds in New York City were mainly smaller or toy breeds; but the Labrador is still number one choice. Chicago had a higher proportion of large dogs (Labrador and German Shepherd at the top), including the Rottweiler and Dobermann. Los Angeles had the bulldog as number two favourite after the ubiquitous Labrador, and otherwise a slight majority of small and toy dogs. The bulldog was also popular in Boston (ranked sixth), where four of the top five registrations are large breeds.[19]

The American Kennel Club analysis of past registrations shows that both fashion and practicality have dictated the consumer's choice of breeds since the early 20th century. Dog breed choices have mirrored our work habits and lifestyle. For example, dogs with a high requirement for grooming were most popular during the 1940s, but currently 48 per cent of the dogs registered are of the 'low grooming' type. Dogs that need a lot of exercise make up nearly half of those registered today, possibly due to the popularity of human fitness routines. The popularity of some toy breeds, including the Cavalier King Charles Spaniel, French bulldog and Brussels Griffon, has increased several-fold in the last decade; toy dogs are nearly 30 per cent of registrations today. The movie industry has started several breed fashions over the years.[19]

## 5.3 Breed standards

Breed standards define the physical characteristics of the breed ideal in minute detail and are used to judge dogs in competitive shows. As the examples below illustrate, many of the exaggerated features that have long been criticized in pedigree dog breeds as potentially damaging to health or well-being are actually required features of the breed standard. Standards that are so prescriptive have the almost inevitable effect of restricting the number of dogs used for breeding, risking inbreeding and genetic disease (see Chapter 6). In the UK this came to a wider public attention in 2008 through a television exposé of health problems in pedigree dogs;[20] as a result, in 2009 the Kennel Club revised its breed standards with the aim of discouraging the most exaggerated features that could lead to disease or disability.[21] The following examples from the UK Kennel Club (KC) and the American Kennel Club (AKC) breed standards current during 2008 give an insight into how these ideals moulded dog breeds into what they had become by the first decade of the century.

### 5.3.1 Standards for size and shape

Toy dogs, today exemplified by the popular Yorkshire Terrier and Chihuahua, have existed for millennia and today's breed standards are designed to ensure that they remain very small. The Chihuahua standard states that if two dogs are 'equally good in type the more diminutive [is] preferred'. For miniature dachshunds, the standard states that it is of the 'utmost importance' that dogs over 5kg (11lb) are not given prizes.[17,22]

The dachshund is the best-known example of a dog currently required to have exaggeratedly short front legs and a long back. Dachshunds are pictured with their ribcages almost touching the ground.[17] The AKC and KC standards for the dachshund requires the dog to be 'Low to ground, long in body and short of leg', while 'appearing neither crippled, awkward, nor cramped in his capacity for movement'. The short forearm must not 'bend forward or knuckle over' and, when moving forward, the feet must not 'swing out, cross over or interfere with each other'.[17,22,23]

The Basset Hound is also required to be short-legged and close to the ground, with the upper forearm 'inclined slightly inward', but not so much as to 'prevent free movement' or 'to result in legs touching each other'. The bulldog should be 'a delightfully ugly dog' with a 'low-swung body'. The head should be 'massive' but not so large as to 'make the dog appear deformed, or interfere with its powers of motion'. With bowed legs, the gait of the bulldog should be 'peculiarly heavy and constrained' and 'shuffling'. The shoulders of the short forelegs should give the 'appearance of being "tacked on" to the body'; but the shortness of the legs should not 'cripple him'.[17,23]

## 5.3.2 Loose skin, flat faces and long hair

Certain breeds are required to have loose skin and skin folds on the face or body. For the Basset Hound, pictured with folds of loose skin on neck, chest and forelegs, 'A certain amount of loose skin is desirable', and the head may 'wrinkle noticeably' when the head is lowered. According to the AKC: 'A dry head and tight skin are faults.' The ears should be 'extremely long' reaching 'well beyond' the end of the muzzle. The Shar Pei breed has 'superabundant' skin wrinkles on face, neck and body as a puppy, 'loose skin' and a 'frowning expression' (see Figure 6.2 in Chapter 6). The dog's eyes appear sunken within the facial skin folds, but the 'function of eyeball or lid' must be 'in no way disturbed by surrounding skin, folds or hair'.[17,22,23]

Certain breeds are required to have wide flattened faces and short noses, referred to in veterinary terminology as 'brachycephalic' breeds. These include the popular breeds of bulldog, pug, Pekinese and boxer. Because of the shortening of the skull, their faces also have abundant skin folds. The bulldog's face should be short and wrinkled, the nose 'as short as possible' and 'set back deeply between the eyes', with the lower jaw 'projecting considerably' in front of the upper jaw and turning up. The boxer similarly must have a muzzle only two-thirds the width of the skull, with a protruding upper jaw and a wrinkled face. The AKC standard depicts the ears cropped and the tail docked. The pug's flat head and its neck are covered in rolls of loose skin; wrinkles should be 'clearly defined' or even 'large and deep', with a roll of skin across the bridge of the nose. While the bulldog's eyes are sunken in skin folds, the pug's eyes are 'very large', 'globular', and 'prominent' (see Figure 6.1 in Chapter 6).[17,23]

Several breeds have long hair reaching to the ground and covering the face, and the Yorkshire Terrier, Shih Tzu and Maltese Lap Dog need their head hair tied up in a bow. The Briard, Lhasa Apso, Hungarian Puli, Old English Sheepdog and the Komondor are pictured in the breed standards with their eyes partly or wholly obscured by long hair. The Dandie Dinmont Terrier should have a 'top knot' of hair falling over the eyes. The Skye Terrier's hair should 'veil' the forehead and eyes. In contrast, the Chinese Crested Dog is hairless ('a breed for the connoisseur') except for a long crest and mane of head hair, tail hair and long hair on the lower leg and feet.[17]

## 5.3.3 Upholding the standards

The KC licenses over 2000 breed shows (as well as over 1000 agility, obedience and field events) annually in the UK. The judges are the people who uphold the

**Figure 5.2** *Lhasa Apso with long head hair tied back off the eyes and nose*

© Colin Seddon

breed standards and their judgements on the 'exhibits' or 'specimens' presented to them are published. Judges are therefore of great importance in interpreting the breed standards and influencing the direction of breeding.

Judges' reports show a readiness to enforce the minutiae of the breed standards and to encourage physical uniformity within the breed. One judge reported in 2008: 'I was very disappointed at the lack of correct heads... All breeds must comply to type at the very least in head and expression. Skull proportions, muzzle, shape and set of eye and leathers have to fit the standard or it [the dog] is not representative of that breed.' Another found that 'One or two could do with more divergence between the planes of the skull and the muzzle' and 'there is still quite a variation in the ratio of length to height'. Other faults found were 'far too many light and round eyes'; not enough of 'a frowning expression created by heavy brows'; 'quite a few heavy untypical heads'; bitches 'looking at the top side of the height standard'; and too many 'long pointed faces' that 'have no place in this breed'. Judges also assessed the dogs on 'soundness' and were ready to lecture and penalize those that had exhibited dogs with hampered walking ability.[24]

## 5.3.4 Docking and cropping

The breed standard for certain breeds in some countries includes the obligatory or optional tail-docking, ear-cropping and removal of dew-claws. Cosmetic ear-cropping has long been illegal in the UK, but the AKC standard describes the boxer's ears as 'customarily cropped, cut rather long and tapering'.[23] Tail-docking for cosmetic reasons was upheld in the KC breed standards ('customarily docked') until the practice became illegal in 2007 for dogs in England and Wales and, separately, Scotland. In England and Wales there is an exception for certified 'working dogs', a loophole that may be being exploited.[25] Dew-claw removal is still legal in the UK and veterinarians may be asked to carry this out to conform to breed standards.[26]

## 5.3.5 Cat breeds and breed standards

Most cats born are not deliberately 'bred' to a standard but there are indications that cats of defined or novelty breeds for showing and sale are becoming more fashionable. In the UK, the aim of cat breeding has been defined by the Governing Council of the Cat Fancy (GCCF) as being:[27]

- *to perpetuate the breed concerned as a distinct and recognizable 'breed';*
- *to improve the quality of the breed as measured against the standard; and*
- *to gain success on the show bench.*

Unlike dogs, cats do not generally cooperate with human tasks and have been subjected to far less selective breeding than dogs. Historically in Europe cats were free-ranging, of low status compared to dogs, and their mating hard to control. Early 'fancy' cat breeding in Europe and North America concentrated on visual features such as the long coat of the imported Persian or the exotic look of the imported Siamese, without attempting to make the kind of changes in size and shape that have differentiated the Chihuahua from the Great Dane dog breeds. Only a small proportion of owned cats are 'pedigrees' (estimated at 8 per cent for the UK in 2008[14]) and the extreme products of the cat breeders' art are rarely seen on the streets.

The US Cat Fanciers' Association (CFA) recognizes and produces breed standards for 40 breeds.[28] Some of these are not recognized by equivalent associations in other countries; for example, the British GCCF does not recognize breeds that involve a 'structural anomaly', such as the Japanese Bobtail or the Pixie-Bob (additional digits and a very short tail) or the American Curl (a deformation of the ear), or hairless or miniaturized breeds.[27] In the second half of the 20th century cat breeders began to change the size and shape of cats to conform to specific points in redesigned breed standards and to invent new cat breeds. The Persian and Siamese breeds, imported by Western cat fanciers and very popular around the turn of the 20th century, were changed almost beyond recognition by the end of the 20th century.

The 19th-century Persian cat resembled a typical domestic cat except for having an unusually long and thick coat. Since then, the Persian's face has become flattened or even concave, the nose barely visible in profile. The 2009 Breed Standard of the CFA requires that 'the head is round and massive' and 'When viewed in profile, the prominence of the eyes is apparent and the forehead, nose and chin appear to be in vertical alignment.' A cat is disqualified, however, for 'Deformity of the skull resulting in an asymmetrical face and/or head'.[28] What is now called the 'traditional' or 'doll-faced' Persian with a normal facial structure has been eliminated from the cat show world by the modern breed standard.

The Siamese cats imported to England around the 1890s were of strong and stocky build, similar in shape to the typical domestic cat, with round heads (their squints and kinked tails were subsequently bred out). Their main value was in the trademark dark-brown and white coat pattern and their bright blue eyes. From the 1960s, breeders remodelled the Siamese body to become long and thin, the head elongated into 'a long tapering wedge', the ears hugely enlarged ('strikingly large') and set obliquely at 45 degrees on the sides of the head. In profile, the head is specified as 'a long straight line … from the top of the head to the tip of the nose'[28] (the result has been described by a British veterinarian as resembling the fictional monster in the 1984 movie *Gremlins* rather than a domestic cat[29]). The Siamese typical of the 1950s are now called 'traditional' or 'apple head' Siamese and have been eliminated from shows by the modern breed standard.

Recessive genes for colouration have been discovered and used to create new coat varieties of the Siamese and Persian breeds. Cat breeders have not always been tolerant of unexpected diversity and the Persian breed was originally required to have a coat of a single solid colour. In 1904 the *Cat Review* recommended that breeders should 'chloroform' any Persian kitten born with more than one colour in the coat, lest they should 'ruin their strain both in value and reputation'.[30]

Over the last 50 years, cat breeders have created new breeds based on rare natural mutations that have been noticed by chance and subsequently bred for. Examples are the Scottish or American Fold, carrying a developmental mutation where some kittens develop a folded-down ear, or the absence of tail of the Manx cat. Where the mutated gene is dominant, some kittens do not inherit the mutation and are ineligible for showing.

Other recognized new breeds include the Ragdoll, very large and passive, the Devon and Cornish Rex breeds, with curly coats, elongated bodies and oversized ears intended to convey a 'pixie' or 'other planet' look, and the hairless Sphynx breed (a 'suede-finish mutant'[31]), which needs regular cleaning of the skin and ears.[28] Other unrecognized but commercially successful breeds include the Munchkin, a breed with very short legs due to a dwarfism mutation.

## 5.3.6 Novelties and designer crosses

Consumer demand for novelty pets is met by the continuous invention of new breeds or variations on existing ones. Outside the realm of recognized breeds, commercial dog and cat breeders have created miniature dogs, designer crosses (such as Labradoodles and puggles) between two different dog breeds, and new breeds derived from hybridization with wild canids and felids. Celebrity-endorsed 'teacup' versions of some of the toy breeds, particularly Chihuahuas, Yorkshire Terriers, poodles or Pomeranians, have been reported to sell for a few thousand pounds sterling as puppies and can be replaced when they grow too big to be carried in a pocket.[32] Other novelties are dogs and cats that either are, or appear to be, crosses with wild species, such as the 'wolf-dog' Tamaskan[33] and the Bengal and Savannah cats. Both the CFA and the GCCF have a policy of not recognizing new breeds derived from wild species.

## 5.3.7 Breeds and magazine readers

Popular magazines for dog owners offer a wide range of features and information about dogs and their behaviour and welfare but their content is dominated by features on, and pictures of, dogs of defined breeds. The magazines operate as a consumer marketplace for breeds and the exaggerated features required by the breed standard may be pictured without comment: a Basset Hound with ears almost touching the ground, a bulldog with outsized jaw and tiny eyes, bandy-legged and resembling a furry toad, or a St Bernard ('these gentle giants really become part of the family') lying apparently exhausted, with tiny triangular eyes, bloodshot and half covered by the third eyelid.[34] One popular dog magazine in the UK, *Dogs Today*, has consistently run campaigns about the health impact of exaggerated breed features and genetic disease and regularly includes features intended to educate its readers and breeders about breeding and health, while continuing to market breeds. Cat magazines, in contrast, while they carry features and sales advertisements on pedigree and novelty breeds, depict mainly non-breed cats.

Dog magazine readers, on occasion, can be as devoted as any Victorian fancier to the concept of breed purity. The puggle, the designer cross of the pug and the Beagle breeds, has been described as 'unnatural' and 'disgusting' (and perhaps threatens the pedigree breeders' market for puppies). Other crosses of pedigree breeds, marketed as the 'Westiepoo', 'Labradoodle', 'Cavapoo', 'Pekepoo', 'Yorktese', 'Pomchi' and others, were 'ridiculous mongrel dogs', their creation leading to 'indiscriminate mating and diluting of popular breeds' – indeed, 'absolutely no reputable breeder would crossbreed two breeds deliberately'.[35]

## 5.4 Breeding practices

### 5.4.1 Selection and inbreeding

The essence of any dog or cat breed or strain is that all the animals resemble each other closely. Creating or refining a breed towards the standard's ideal involves restricting the gene pool to those animals with the most desired traits. In order to achieve this, the mating of first cousins and of half siblings has been considered normal, if not essential, to attain the desired 'type', and mating of full siblings or parents and offspring is not unknown. This is not new; Old Foiler, a famous Fox Terrier born in 1870 when the breed was becoming very fashionable, had full siblings for both his parents and his grandparents, making each of his four pairs of great-grandparents identical.[7] In the genetic lottery of dog breeding, inbreeding is often considered worth the risk, and a popular UK guide to dog breeding tells us that 'Inbreeding is a sharp and powerful tool' in experienced hands that 'offers the best means to perpetuate the desirable qualities of particular dogs'.[7] New breeds created by utilizing a rare mutation or imported animals are often based on a very few founders.

Studies of pedigree dogs registered with the Kennel Club (UK) up to the end of 2006 found that typically only around 10 per cent of all male dogs and around 20–30 per cent of all females were used for breeding. The 'popular' males (those who produced 100 or more offspring each) were just a few per cent of that 10 per cent of males. Some of these stud dogs had produced up to 2000 offspring.[36] In Finland, the proportion of registered males that were used for breeding the three popular breeds of German Shepherd, Labrador Retriever and Golden Retriever had fallen to 6 per cent or fewer by the end of the 20th century (see section 6.2.1 in Chapter 6).[37]

### 5.4.2 Breeding methods: Choosing partners

The breeding of pedigree dogs, including the choice of mates, the mating process and the documentation involved, is a serious and complex transaction, recalling the control of human marriages typical in earlier human societies. For professional breeders, as opposed to puppy farmers, breeding is a legally attested, commercialized and somewhat ritualized undertaking. The perceived quality of any offspring will reflect on the reputation and career of the stud dog and his breeder or owner within the breeding community, and so the entire process of choice of partners and breeding is tightly controlled.

The dogs (or at least the stud dog) would be expected to have proved themselves in the show ring before being chosen for breeding, and comparatively few breeding males are considered of the top quality that attracts other breeders to use him. The stud dog has an undeniable prestige, and only 'approved' bitches are allowed access to his services. But males set to work as stud dogs may become less suitable for living as a household pet, and it is recommended that he be housed outside in a kennel.[7] Little is known about the mate preferences and mate choice of male and female dogs in natural

conditions, but modern breeding for pedigree purposes has certainly eliminated it.

The pedigree breeding procedure involves the owner of the bitch in
researching the pedigrees and show successes of available studs, applying to the
one of her choice, having her bitch approved (or rejected) on grounds of
suitability, health-checking the bitch for sexually transmitted disease and
antibiotic treatment if required (the stud has already had all his disease tests),
and then taking or shipping the bitch to the stud-owner's kennels, which may
mean shipping the bitch alone by air. The mating process itself can be highly
controlled, with the owners each holding their own animal to ensure that the
process goes smoothly without injury and that insemination has occurred.
Disputes can arise as to the stud dog's fertility if a pregnancy does not result or,
later, about the identity of the father if the puppies do not turn out to the
owner's satisfaction. DNA confirmation of parentage may be required. A
contract is usually required in which the conditions for payment of the stud fee
are set out (payment may be in money or by transfer of one of the resulting
puppies, or both).[7] Registration of the puppies with the breed society or Kennel
Club requires a declaration by both owners that the mating took place.

## 5.4.3 Breeding methods: Homing the puppies

The sport of dog-showing requires the production of numerous puppies in
order for selection to continue but this entails finding homes for those which
the breeder does not wish to retain. The typical age at which puppies are sold is
eight weeks, and from the point of view of natural behaviour this constitutes
an early separation from the social group of mother and littermates. It is
known that the puppy benefits socially from staying with his or her litter for a
month longer than this in learning how to interact well with other dogs, but an
older puppy integrates less easily into the new home. Puppies bred in puppy
farms (puppy mills) and sold from pet shops may have had an even shorter
time with their mothers and little contact with people, and they are more likely
to show extreme fear of new environments and have impaired social skills.[38]

Relocated puppies experience 'a series of traumatic events',[38] including the
abrupt separation from the mother and the unfamiliar surroundings and
people they encounter. Research shows that puppies are often distressed by
being left alone in their new homes. Pet shop puppies studied in France had a
tendency to wake their new owners at night by activities such as whining,
howling, scratching at the door, wandering around the home and destroying
objects, in some cases continuing for at least two weeks after being bought.
Puppies given a collar treated with dog-appeasing pheromone, a hormone
secreted by bitches in the first weeks after giving birth, settled down very much
faster than the control group. Some puppies only became calm at night when
allowed free access to their owners' bedroom or allowed to sleep with another
dog. The puppies studied had spent between three days and two months in the
pet shop before being sold to their new owners.[38,39]

## 5.4.4 Induced abortions and unwanted puppies

Bitches who have mated with the wrong dog or at the wrong time ('mismating') may be treated with synthetic anti-progestins or oestrogens to prevent the pregnancy from proceeding or to cause abortion. The ethical justification for this is presumably to avoid the birth of a litter of unmarketable puppies or to spare the bitch's health, but the treatments are known to increase the likelihood of pyometra (a life-threatening infection of the uterus) and of bone marrow aplasia (causing life-threatening anaemia).[40,41] A survey of veterinary records between 1995 and 2007 in the UK has shown that the use of oestrogens for mismating increases the risk of pyometra by over sixfold, concluding that 'more than 85 per cent of pyometras occurring within four months of [oestrogen] treatment are iatrogenic'.[40]

Some puppies or kittens are inevitably born that lack an essential aspect of the breed standard, or have an obvious inherited disorder. Thus, it was a practice in the past to kill puppies that were white-coated boxers, Rhodesian Ridgebacks lacking the distinctive back ridge, or Dalmatians deaf in both ears (a recognized genetic disorder of the breed).[42] The KC Code of Ethics of September 2008 requires that no healthy puppy is killed, and that those not conforming to breed standards should be found homes.

## 5.4.5 Artificial insemination and optimizing investment

Competitive and commercial pressure to achieve the most desirable and most efficient mating make it more likely that breeders will turn to 'assisted' reproduction methods. Artificial insemination (AI) is seen as offering predictability, choice and the opportunity of breeding in situations where the stud dog is incompetent, old, unwell or dead, or alternatively if either he or the bitch is unwilling, risking the injury of valuable animals. The UK's KC, however, normally restricts AI to imported semen or stored semen from stud dogs that are dead,[43] and it has been suggested that some breeders ship bitches out of the UK for the procedure to be performed.

AI involves depositing semen either into the vagina using a catheter (most commonly when the semen is fresh or chilled) or into the uterus (most commonly when the semen is frozen/thawed, when its lifetime is shorter). AI into the uterus can be 'trans-cervical' (non-surgical, using a catheter and endoscope) or surgical, under general anaesthesia. The KC (UK) strongly discourages surgical insemination, citing the Royal College of Veterinary Surgeons' advice that it can be justified only for exceptional reasons and that it 'carries many disadvantages for the bitch and is unlikely to be carried out in the best interests of any particular dog'.[43] Ironically, AI may come to be seen as increasingly necessary in future in order to rescue the gene pool of many inbred breeds (see Chapter 6).

AI is more commonly used in the US, as is surgical insemination. The AKC allows AI routinely on application, provided that a veterinarian is used for extraction, insemination and certification when extended or frozen/thawed semen is used.[43] Breeders can also use fresh semen when both dogs are present. DIY AI kits and 'how to' videos are available to dog owners who want to use fresh semen and vaginal insemination, possibly using a 'teaser' female to aid semen collection. As with livestock animals, AI requires accurate oestrus detection, which may require taking several blood samples. Commercial dog breeding companies offer a professional package of sperm-testing and home blood-testing kits to determine the bitch's progesterone levels, claiming a possible conception rate of over 90 per cent. They point out that these technologies save money, increase efficiency and 'maximize the reproductive capacity of our brood females', as well as allowing semen to be extended and used for more than one insemination.[44]

### 5.4.6 Commercial breeding: Puppy farms (puppy mills)

The public appetite for pedigree dogs and 'must-have' designer cross-breeds, novelties and 'hypo-allogenic' pets makes an attractive market opportunity.[45] Kennel Club rules put limits on the use of breeding females; for example, in the UK, the KC requires that a bitch is not mated at under one year old, has a maximum of six litters in her breeding lifetime and is only used for breeding up to eight years of age.[46] Licensed dog breeders are similarly limited under the Breeding and Sale of Dogs (Welfare) Act 1999 to a maximum of six litters per bitch, a minimum mating age of one year and a minimum time of 12 months between litters. Commercial puppy production is carried out to supply pet shops and internet sales, often by unlicensed breeders, but also by licensed breeders and occasionally by pedigree breeders registered with Kennel Clubs. Many of the reports of farmed puppies originate from new owners who find that the puppy has serious and costly health problems that sometimes lead to death within a few days or weeks, or serious behaviour problems. In a French study, 21 of 100 puppies received by a pet shop during the study period were returned for 'medical reasons', their eventual fate unknown.[39]

A 2009 review of the regulation of dog breeding in Wales (human population 3 million) found that there were 249 unlicensed dog-breeding establishments.[47] Puppy farms that avoid regulation in Ireland export puppies to Scotland and England. Investigations by the Humane Society of the United States (HSUS) have shown that commercial puppy farming is carried on in thousands of operations in the US, some selling puppies through apparently upmarket pet shops and internet sites, including those that have celebrity customers. Large commercial breeding operations can hold several hundred dogs in tiers of wire cages. In 2008, nearly 700 dogs were confiscated from a large puppy farm in Tennessee, and in 2009 an investigation of puppy farming in Pennsylvania found one couple in charge of 200 breeding dogs and puppies. Kept on wire mesh floors, the breeding bitches were unable to walk when released onto solid ground surfaces. Commentators were shocked that the dogs were being treated 'like livestock'.[45,48] Internet sites, showing dozens of attractive puppies of numerous breeds, and upmarket pet shops can offer an image far removed from the often squalid breeding conditions that have been exposed in the UK and the US.

The advice reiterated by dog protection organizations is that puppies should only be bought when the puppy can be visited with its mother, and the breeder has all the documentation on pedigree, health tests and vaccinations to hand (although these can on occasion be forgeries). In the UK nearly half of dogs are reported to be purchased from breeders, private advertisements, pet shops and the internet rather than rescued or acquired from friends and family.[49]

## 5.5 Benefits and costs, sustainability and the future

### 5.5.1 Benefits and costs to people and animals

Pedigree dog breeding (either of show dogs or working dogs) is a sport that undoubtedly gives pleasure and leisure activity to people within the professional dog breeding community. The commercial breeding sector can provide puppy farmers with a good income that they might not otherwise have. It is also true that a larger section of the public is fascinated by pedigree dogs, visits dog shows, and watches shows such as Crufts on television. From these points of view, pedigree dog breeding could be said to have advantages if only for a relatively small section of human society.

It is more difficult to argue that dog breeding produces any benefit to dogs or to human society as a whole. Breeding dogs, or other companion animals, to conform to a standard specification is done for the benefit of people, not the benefit of dogs, and has a number of unwelcome results for the animals (as discussed in Chapter 6 and 8):

- *Damaging effect on health, physical functioning and well-being of the animal.* The damage can be due to the inbreeding that is used to achieve and maintain the breed type or to unnatural features related to shape, hair, skin or eyes that are considered to be features of the breed. Animals are being bred that are unsustainable in the sense of their health and physical functioning, and these aspects of breeding are increasingly coming to be seen as ethically unacceptable by society. Unfit companion animals also cost their owners both in financial terms and in emotional distress (see Chapter 6).
- *Mismatch between the animal's behaviour and its role in human society.* Animals produced and kept as household companions almost inevitably have their natural behaviour restricted in order to fit in with human needs and lifestyles. Pedigree breeding increases this problem when the behaviour selected for the breed – for example, hunting (or fighting) – makes the dog less suitable as a companion animal and a possible danger to people, especially children. It can also happen that unwanted characteristics, such as 'bad temper', are unintentionally bred into dogs by breeders who are selecting for points of the dog's appearance. This mismatch also subjects

the animal to frustration, boredom and possibly to fear or punishment due to its inability to fit in with domestic life. Pedigree cats are often kept indoors for their entire lives.

- *Dog breeding, whether for 'breed improvement', for showing or for profit increases the population of unwanted dogs.* Pedigree breeding promotes the view that dogs are consumer goods, to be acquired and disposed of on demand. Unwanted dogs of fashionable or once-fashionable breeds often end up in dog rescue centres. Their accidental cross-bred offspring have a low market value and are even more likely to become surplus to requirements. Surplus dogs and cats create nuisance and expense for people, and the animals suffer when they become homeless or are kept caged in rescue centres (see section 8.5 in Chapter 8).

## 5.5.2 Is pedigree breeding necessary?

Chapter 6 discusses the reforms to breed standards and to breeding goals and practices that Kennel Clubs, breeders and veterinarians have been debating increasingly urgently over the last years. A further legitimate question is whether it is in the interest of dogs and of society as a whole to continue producing dogs of defined breeds even under reformed practices (the question applies equally to cats and other companion animals). It is even harder to make a case for creating additional or novel breeds. In overall terms, neither animals nor human society benefit from our irrational obsession with 'breed'.

In what circumstances are dogs of a defined breed needed? There may continue to be a small demand for working dogs with specific breed-related characteristics, such as those used by the military, the police or as sheepdogs or other helper dogs such as guide dogs. But working dogs are a minority of the dog population in developed countries (with the possible exception of New Zealand, where the majority of owned dogs are sheepdogs[12]). Outside these functions, it is hard to make the case that society as a whole benefits from the existence of defined breeds of dogs or cats. The most important social function of the large majority of dogs and cats is in providing companionship. This has little relationship to the breed definition of dogs and no relevance to the breed definition of cats.

The marketing of brand-name dogs or cats, with supposed special characteristics, encourages more people to decide to acquire an animal than would otherwise make that decision. Many of these decisions turn out not to be sustainable for the household or person concerned, to the disadvantage of both the person and the animal. Without a change in public perception of the value of breeds and pedigrees, the marketing of breeds on the basis of their appearance, celebrity endorsement or perceived rarity is likely to become more intensive in consumer societies. This market trend will probably continue whether or not reforms to the regulated sector of dog breeding are made, until public perceptions change.

## Notes

1 Ritvo, H. (1987) *The Animal Estate: The English and Other Creatures in the Victorian Age*, Harvard University Press, Chapter 2

2 Lytton, J. N. (The Honourable Mrs Neville Lytton) (1911) *Toy Dogs and their Ancestors: Including the History and Management of Toy Spaniels, Pekingese, Japanese and Pomeranians*, Duckworth & Co, London

3 Kete, K. (1994) *The Beast in the Boudoir: Petkeeping in Nineteenth-Century Paris*, University of California Press

4 Fairley, R. (ed) (1988) *Jemina: The Paintings and Memoirs of a Victorian Lady*, Canongate

5 Hardy, T. (1874) *Far from the Madding Crowd*, Penguin Books,1994, Chapter V

6 Thomas, K. (1983) *Man and the Natural World: Changing Attitudes in England 1500–1800*, Penguin Books

7 Jackson, R. (2000) *Dog Breeding: The Theory and the Practice*, Crowood Press

8 See histories given on the websites of the Cat Fanciers' Association, www.cfa.org, and the Governing Council of the Cat Fancy, www.gccfcats.org

9 Organizational histories and information given on the websites of the British Rabbit Council (www.thebrc.org); the National Mouse Club (www.nationalmouseclub.co.uk); and the National Fancy Rat Society (www.nfrs.org).

10 FCI (Fédération Cynologique Internationale) *FCI Statistics*, www.fci.be/stats.aspx, accessed July 2008

11 China Kennel Union website, www.cku.org.cn/english/index.html, accessed July 2008; Liinamo, A.-E. and van Arendonk, J. A. M. (2006) 'Genetic parameters of show quality and its relationship with working traits and hip dysplasia in Finnish hounds', paper 10-10 presesnted ot the Eighth World Congress on Genetics Applied to Livestock Production, 13–18 August, Belo Horizonte, Brazil, www.wcgalp8.org.br; Crufts website at www.crufts.org.uk, accessed July 2008

12 Stafford, K. (2006) *The Welfare of Dogs*, Springer, The Netherlands; Lindblad-Toh, K. et al (2005) 'Genome sequences, comparative analysis and haplotype structure of the domestic dog', *Nature*, vol 438, pp803–819; websites of the Kennel Club (London) and the American Kennel Club

13 Darwin, C. R. (1868) *The Variation of Animals and Plants under Domestication*, first edition, second issue, vol 1, John Murray, p34

14 Pet Food Manufacturers Association (2008, 2009) 'Statistics of pet ownership and pet food market data', www.pfma.org.uk; Colliard, L. et al (2006) 'Risk factors for obesity in dogs in France', *Journal of Nutrition*, vol 136, pp1951S–1954S

15 Kennel Club (London) (undated) 'Glossary of terms', www.thekennelclub.org.uk

16 Bradshaw, J. W. S. et al (1996) 'A survey of the behavioural characteristics of pure-bred dogs in the United Kingdom', *Veterinary Record*, vol 138, pp465–468

17 Kennel Club (2003) *Illustrated Breed Standards: The Official Guide to Registered Breeds*, revised edition, Ebury Press

18 As examples, see articles in *Dog World*, 27 June 2008, pp6–7.

19 Kennel Club (London) (2008) *Registration Statistics for all Recognised Dog Breeds – 2006 and 2007*, 27 March, Kennel Club, London; American Kennel Club (2008) *2007 Dog Registration Statistics* and *2007 Litter Registration Statistics*, March; American Kennel Club (2007) *AKC Registration Statistics: Fact Sheet*, AKC

20 Passionate Productions (2008) *Pedigree Dogs Exposed*, BBC Television, 19 August 2008

21 Kennel Club (2009) 'Kennel Club announces healthy new year regulations for pedigree dogs', press release, 12 January 2009

22 Kennel Club (London) Breed Standards online, www.thekennelclub.org.uk, accessed June 2008
23 American Kennel Club, Breed Standards online, www.akc.org/breeds/index.cfm, accessed June 2008
24 *Dog World* (2008) 'Show reports', *Dog World*, 27 June 2008
25 Horton-Bussey, C. (2009) 'Mocking the docking laws', *Dogs Today*, February, pp18–21
26 Goodman Milne, E. (2008) 'Removal of the dewclaws of dogs', *Veterinary Record*, vol 162, no 26, p868
27 Governing Council of the Cat Fancy (2009) *GCCF Breeding Policy: Guidelines for Healthy Breeding*, version 4, 14 May 2009
28 Cat Fanciers' Association, Inc 'Breeds and breed standards', www.cfa.org/breeds.html , accessed July 2008 and June 2009
29 Milne, E. (2007) *The Truth about Cats and Dogs*, Book Guild Publishing
30 Cat Fanciers' Association (undated) *Cinderella Story: History of Bicolor and Calico Persians*, www.cfa.org
31 *The Veterinary Record* (2008) 'For better or worse? BVA AWF forum considers breeding, and electric shock collars: News and reports', *The Veterinary Record*, vol 162, no 23, pp736–737
32 Beck, C. (2006) 'Designer dogs bred to die', *Daily Express*, 3 February, pp34–35
33 *Dogs Today* (2009) July, pp24–25
34 *Dogs Today* (2007) June, p21; *Your Dog* (2008) July, p40; *Your Dog* (2008) July, p33
35 *Dogs Today* (2007) June, p34
36 Calboli, F. C. F. et al (2008) 'Population structure and inbreeding from pedigree analysis of purebred dogs', *Genetics*, vol 179, pp593–610
37 Mäki, K. et al (2001) 'Population structure, inbreeding trend and their association with hip and elbow dysplasia in dogs', *Animal Science*, vol 73, pp217–228
38 Gaultier, E. et al (2009) 'Efficacy of dog-appeasing pheromone in reducing behaviours associated with fear of unfamiliar people and new surroundings in newly adopted puppies', *Veterinary Record*, vol 164, pp708–714
39 Gaultier, E. et al (2008) 'Efficacy of dog-appeasing pheromone in reducing stress associated with social isolation in newly adopted puppies', *Veterinary Record*, vol 163, pp73–80
40 Whitehead, M. L. (2008) 'Risk of pyometra in bitches treated for mismating with low doses of oestradiol benzoate,' *Veterinary Record*, vol 162, pp746–749
41 Acke, E., Mooney C. T. and Jones, B. R. (2003) 'Oestrogen toxicity in a dog', *Irish Veterinary Journal*, vol 56, no 9, pp465–468; Conrado, F. de O. et al (2009) 'Use of lithium carbonate in the treatment of a suspected case of oestrogen-induced bone marrow aplasia in a bitch', *Veterinary Record*, vol 164, pp274–275
42 Wood, J. L. N. (1997) 'Deafness – the disease and the research', in *Hereditary Diseases in Dogs: What Are They and What Can Be Done*, Proceedings of a Symposium of the Animal Health Trust, the British Veterinary Association Animal Welfare Foundation and the RSPCA, April 1997, pp12–15
43 Kennel Club (London) (2007, updated 2009) *Information Guide: How to Breed Dogs Using Artificial Insemination*, Kennel Club, London; Royal College of Veterinary Surgeons (2005) *Advice Note 8: Canine Surgical Artificial Insemination*, November, UK; American Kennel Club (2009) 'Registration information: Artificial insemination', www.akc.org , accessed June 2009
44 Camelot Farms, www.camelotfarms.com, accessed July 2008
45 Smalley, S. (2009) 'A (designer) dog's life', *Newsweek*, 13 April
46 Kennel Club (2007) *Information Guide: Breeding from Your Bitch*, London, 8 June

47  *Veterinary Record* (2009) 'Review of dog breeding rules in Wales', *Veterinary Record*, vol 165, no 21, p610

48  Humane Society of the United States (2008) 'Nearly 700 puppies rescued from Tennessee puppy mill', News release, 26 June 2008; Alfonsi, S. and Gerstein, T. (2009) *Puppies 'Viewed as Livestock' in Amish Community, Says Rescue Advocate; Exclusive Access: Cutting-Edge Facilities or Puppy Factories?*, ABC News Nightline, 27 March 2009; Redpath, K. (2008) 'Puppy trafficking', *Dogs Today*, December, pp26–28

49  Pet Food Manufacturers Association (2008, 2009) 'Statistics of pet ownership, UK', www.pfma.org.uk

# 6

# Companion Animal Breeding: Welfare, Professionals and Owners

## 6.1 Background and context: Clouds over pedigree dog breeding

In 1994 *Time* magazine in the US published a cover story entitled 'A terrible beauty'.[1] The article described how a couple bought an apparently healthy Golden Retriever puppy from a reputable breeder, complete with pedigree and American Kennel Club registration. Within a year the puppy had developed pain from osteochondritis, a hereditary bone condition requiring surgery, then severe hip dysplasia in both hips, also inherited, also requiring surgery, plus severe allergies, dry skin and a poor coat. The article went on to claim that one in four of America's 'purebred' dogs had a genetic disorder, listing hip dysplasia in the majority of German Shepherd Dogs, eye disorders in the majority of collies, deafness in Dalmatians, heart disease in Great Danes and Newfoundlands, and inability to give birth naturally in bulldogs, amounting to 300 known inherited conditions in all. By 1999 in America, the number of genetic diseases in pedigree dogs was listed as 500.[2]

In 1999, a veterinarian commented in the scientific journal *Animal Welfare* that the hundreds of known genetic diseases among dogs worldwide 'are man-made diseases, and, as such, largely preventable'.[3] Another pointed out that 'traits that are best regarded as defects have actually been included in breed standards' and gave examples where the standard directly contributed to a disease condition, such as birth difficulties caused by the very large head required for a bulldog.[4] Over the next years both veterinarians and animal welfare organizations published criticisms of the damaging effects of breed standards and inbreeding.[5–8] In 2006 the Canadian Veterinary Medical Association stated its concern about the 'continuation of breeds whose structure or characteristics inherently cause health problems'.[5] In 2007, at the start of the annual Crufts dog show, an article entitled 'Should Crufts be banned?' was published by one of the leading London daily newspapers.[9]

In mid 2008, a veterinarian told the British Veterinary Association's Animal Welfare Foundation annual discussion forum that 'The veterinary profession is indirectly condoning welfare problems caused by genetic malformations in pedigree animals when it accepts them as typical breed-related conditions' and that current breeding practices had caused the 'devolution' (as opposed to adaptive 'evolution') of the modern dog.[10] At the end of 2008, following a widely discussed British television exposé of health problems and inbreeding in pedigree dogs,[11] the BBC decided not to televise the next Crufts dog show because of the health status of some breeds that would be shown there. This was after many years when the BBC had devoted several hours of entirely celebratory live coverage annually to the four-day event.

By 2009 all the leading UK organizations involved with dog health and welfare, including the British Veterinary Association, the British Small Animal Veterinary Association, the UK Kennel Club (KC), the Royal Society for the Prevention of Cruelty to Animals (RSPCA), the Dogs Trust, the Companion Animal Welfare Council, the Universities Federation for Animal Welfare, and the Associate Parliamentary Group for Animal Welfare had set up or completed reviews on pedigree dog breeding.[12] Reviews of pedigree cat breeding were initiated by the Feline Advisory Bureau and the RSPCA .

For many years before this time professionals were aware of the health problems of pedigree dog breeds (and some cat breeds). Veterinary textbooks routinely contained long lists of breed predispositions and inherited conditions. Although in some countries, such as in Scandinavia, the Kennel Clubs had tighter requirements for the health testing of parent dogs than in Britain or North America, the pedigree dog problem was essentially global. During this time the dog-owning public continued to choose dogs of breeds that were known to have health problems and breeders continued to breed them.

## 6.2 Pedigree dog breeds and their health

### 6.2.1 Inbreeding

Inbreeding has always been a favoured method of animal breeders seeking to create or modify a breed or strain to obtain particular desired traits. Inbreeding increases the likelihood that an animal will inherit a copy of the same allele (alternative form of a gene) from each parent because the parents are related and have each inherited it from a common ancestor. It therefore increases the likelihood that animals that are homozygous for deleterious recessive mutations will be born and suffer the effects of the mutation. In the case of dogs and cats, breeders continued to show and breed from animals that carried genetic disease because they had desirable breed and show traits.

Analysis of dog genomes has confirmed that the creation of dog breeds resulted in tight breed-specific population 'bottlenecks'[13] and that even within breeds, because of the different lines selected by different breeders, there is genetic differentiation between populations.[14] An analysis of pedigrees between 1970 and 2006 was carried out by the Kennel Club (London) and Imperial College London to ascertain the extent of inbreeding. In nearly all breeds there were extremely inbred dogs (see Table 6.1) – for comparison, the theoretical inbreeding coefficient of an animal whose parents are half-siblings is 12.5 per cent. The study calculated effective population sizes that ranged

**Table 6.1** *Inbreeding in selected popular dog breeds, calculated over six and seven generations*

| Breed | Proportion of dogs with inbreeding coefficient greater than 10% | Mean inbreeding coefficient | Maximum inbreeding coefficient found |
|---|---|---|---|
| boxer | 16% | 4.8% | 50% |
| bulldog | 18% | 5.7% | 41% |
| Golden Retriever | 8.2% | 3.5% | 39% |
| German Shepherd | 12% | 3.3% | 47% |
| Labrador retriever | 5.2% | 2.4% | 39% |
| English Springer Spaniel | 6.0% | 3.3% | 38% |

*Source:* Calboli et al (2008)[15]

from 33 to 76 individuals for various breeds, although there might be tens of thousands of dogs registered. The effective population size was 114 for the very popular Labrador Retriever breed, for which there were twice as many dogs as for any other breed.[15]

The fact that so many breeds now exist makes it more likely that some breeds are numerically quite small and register relatively few litters each year. This makes inbreeding almost inevitable unless either the dogs themselves or their semen are transported internationally.[4,15]

## 6.2.2 Genetic and breed-related problems in dogs

The best-documented breed-related health problems of dogs are a direct result of breeding for a particular physical conformation or are the unintentional result of inbreeding. They cover many aspects of the dogs' anatomy and physiology: the skeleton, eyes, heart, breathing, skin, cancer risk, neurological problems and deafness. A 2009 scientific review for the Dogs Trust found that each of the 50 most popular dog breeds in the UK had 'at least one aspect of their physical conformation which predisposes them to a heritable defect'.[16] The popular German Shepherd breed, noted in the show ring for an exaggeratedly sloping back and crouching rear legs, has one of the highest numbers of inherited defects, and in 2004 a veterinary textbook listed around 110 conditions for which the breed had a known or a possible predisposition.[17]

### 6.2.2.1 Hip and elbow dysplasia

'Dysplasia' denotes an abnormality in growth. Hip dysplasia is a malformation of the hip joint so that the head of the femur does not fit properly into the hip socket and results in joint looseness, bone loss, inflammation and arthritis. It can cause considerable pain and lameness requiring surgery. Being disorders of bone growth, hip and elbow dysplasia are most prevalent in larger and fast-growing dogs, and historically the breeds most affected were the German Shepherd, the Golden and Labrador Retrievers, the Rottweiler and other large breeds such the Dobermann, Irish Setter, Flat-Coated Retriever, boxer and St Bernard (see Table 6.2).

**Table 6.2** *High prevalence of hip dysplasia in some popular or once popular dog breeds across countries (direct comparisons between different countries are difficult because of different testing regimes and ages of testing)*

|  | Belgium 2002–2006 | Finland 1988–1999 | Sweden 1972–1988 | US 2005* | UK 1997 |
|---|---|---|---|---|---|
| German Shepherd | 23% | 33–46% | 22–35% | <25% | <50% |
| Golden Retriever | 25% | 32–41% | 20–28% | 25% | ~50% |
| Labrador retriever | 22% | 25–32% | 18–25% | <25% | 25–40% |
| Rottweiler | 10% | 32–45% | 15–35% | 25% | 20–25% |
| boxer | 16% | 28–40% | – | <25% | 40% |
| Old English Sheepdog | 5% | – | – | 25% | 50% |
| Shar Pei | 21% | – | – | 25% | <50% |

*Note:* * There is evidence that prevalence figures in the US may be affected by selective submission of X-rays.[18]
*Source:* Coopman et al (2008)[18]

Schemes to X-ray and score hips and elbows are now common internationally, intended to allow breeders not to breed from dogs that have these inherited problems. Testing is compulsory for Kennel Club registration in Finland and Sweden, and in the UK a voluntary scheme was set up by the British Veterinary Association and the Kennel Club (London) in the 1980s (from 1978 for German Shepherd Dogs). The X-ray procedure requires the dog to be anaesthetized, so the need for these tests in itself has created a welfare cost.

The British hip dysplasia testing scheme assigns a cumulative 'breed mean score' to each breed on the basis of the submitted X-rays. Assuming both hips score the same, a total score of 20 would indicate a mild degree of hip dysplasia and a total score of 64 would indicate a gross degree of hip dysplasia,[19] and a score of zero indicates normal hips. Typically only dogs being considered for breeding have X-rays submitted for scoring, and so the scores at best only cover a small proportion of all the dogs in the breed, and there is evidence that the 'worst' X-rays are not submitted because the diagnosis is obvious.[6,18] As of November 2007, 22 breeds, or 18 per cent of the breeds scored, had a breed mean score of 20 or over. Breeds with scores over 30 were the bulldog and Otterhound (both score 43), Russian Black Terrier (39), Clumber Spaniel (38) and Sussex Spaniel (37), and there is often a wide range of scores within a breed. Only 18 bulldogs had been hip-scored since the start of the scheme, although the breed mean score from those few dogs was one of the highest.[20] Evidence from Finland, Sweden and the US shows that if breeders give priority to test scores rather than to the dogs' appearance, there can be rapid improvement,[21–23] and mandatory testing is likely to come in the UK.

### 6.2.2.2 Eye disorders

A standard textbook published in 2000 on veterinary ophthalmology lists 100 dog breeds associated with one or more of seventeen eye and eyelid conditions or groups of conditions.[24] These eye conditions include cataracts, the very

**Table 6.3** *Number of breeds listed in 2000 as affected by common inherited eye disorders*

| Breed-related disorder | Number of breeds |
| --- | --- |
| Eyelid defects (various) | 58 |
| Hereditary glaucoma | 20 |
| Cataract | 75 |
| Retinal dysplasia (malformation or detachment) | 25 |
| Degeneration of retina | 44 |

*Source:* Gelatt (2000)[24]

painful condition glaucoma and defects of the retina, including retinal detachment and progressive retinal degeneration, all of which can lead to blindness. In addition, many breeds suffer from eyelid and eyelash conditions that cause inflammation and pain, and may require surgery.

A largely voluntary eye testing scheme in the UK is run by the British Veterinary Association (BVA), the Kennel Club and the International Sheep Dog Society (ISDS) with the intention that dogs used for breeding should show 'no evidence of hereditary eye disease'.[25] Many of the most popular dog breeds such as the Springer Spaniel, Cavalier King Charles Spaniel, Staffordshire Bull Terrier, Labrador and Golden Retrievers, German Shepherd, collies, Jack Russell Terrier and the poodles are included under the scheme. Many breeds are under investigation for other eye conditions not yet certified for the breed under the scheme, and increasing numbers of DNA tests for carriers are available.[25,26]

There are several unpleasant eye conditions whose main cause is some required features of the breed, such as head shape and facial skin folds. Depending on breed requirements, the dog's eyes may either bulge from the head or be sunken within skin folds. The bulging eyes of some Pekinese and pug dogs are partly due to their very shallow eye sockets as a result of the required flat face of these breeds. Breeders and veterinarians report that their eyes are easily damaged by accidental contact with any sharp object. Pugs' eyes have even been reported to fall out under stress or excitement.[4,6,27]

Eyes that are bulbous or surrounded by skin folds can have eyelids rolling inwards (entropion), causing the eyelashes to scratch and often ulcerate the eyes and sometimes requiring surgery. The Pekinese suffers from nasal fold trichiasis, where facial hair irritates the surface of the eye. 'Diamond eye' (macropalpebral fissure) affects breeds with drooping folds of skin on the eyelid, such as the Clumber Spaniel, bulldog, Shar Pei and Neapolitan Mastiff and may require surgery. These distressing and painful conditions have been caused by intentional breeding for skin folds and an abnormal eye shape.[6,17]

### 6.2.2.3 Skin diseases
Breeding for shortened faces and legs has the effect of increasing the amount of loose and folded skin on the dog's body. Dogs bred to have loose skin and skin

© Colin Seddon

**Figure 6.1** *Pug, showing short nose, skin folds on face and body, bulbous eyes and tightly curled tail*

folds are most likely to suffer from skin-fold dermatitis (intertrigo), as documented in veterinary textbooks. Skin-fold dermatitis is caused by friction between skin surfaces and can lead to ulceration, exudation of pus and fluid, surface infection by bacteria and a foul smell. The Boston Terrier, bulldog, Pekinese, pug and Persian cats are affected in the skin folds on their faces. The Cocker Spaniel, Springer Spaniel and St Bernard are affected in their lip folds. The Shar Pei breed, which has perhaps the most exaggeratedly loose skin of all breeds, is affected in body skin folds.[28] In the case of the bulldog, veterinarians know that intertrigo 'may occur due to intentional breeding for excessive skin folding'.[17]

A number of breeds are predisposed to several other skin diseases. The West Highland White Terrier is known to veterinarians for the prevalence of skin problems that include the *Malassezia* yeast infection, skin infection by the *Demodex* mite, and inherited seborrhoea (overproduction of oil by the skin, leading to scaling, flaking and infections).[28] Boxers have a 5.8 times increased risk of allergic skin disease compared to the normal dog population. The Old English Sheepdog, bred to have copious fur on its feet, has a 28.9 times increased risk of pododemodicosis (infection of the feet by the *Demodex* mite).[17]

**Figure 6.2** *Shar pei, showing facial skin folds and sunken eyes*

© Colin Seddon

Excessive skin folds and loose skin sometimes require surgery, or 'skin tacking', in breeds such as the Shar Pei. In the UK, the Kennel Club (KC) and the Royal College of Veterinary Surgeons have agreed that skin tacking operations can be reported by veterinarians to the KC and the dogs cannot be submitted for shows without special permission. The KC has stated that it wishes to see an end to the need for the practice;[29] but this may require a radical reform of breed standards that require skin folds.

### 6.2.2.4 Heart disease

Certain breeds have a very much increased risk of heart disease compared to the general dog population (see Table 6.4). The risk of the heart condition dilated cardiomyopathy is four times increased for purebred dogs compared to mixed-breed dogs. A reported 59 per cent of Cavalier King Charles Spaniels over four years of age in the UK and 40.6 per cent in France have heart murmurs indicative of heart valve disease, although most of the dogs do not develop heart failure as a result.[17,30] Heart failure can cause the sudden death of young Great Danes.[6]

**Table 6.4** *Increased relative risk of selected cardiovascular diseases in some popular dog breeds*

| | AS | ASD | EC | DC | PDA | PE | PS | SSS | VSD | TofF |
|---|---|---|---|---|---|---|---|---|---|---|
| boxer | 9.3 | 25.0 | | | | 1.5 | | 2.6 | | |
| bulldog | >5 | | | | | | 12.9 | | 5.0 | |
| Cavalier King Charles Spaniel | | | 20.1* | | | | | | | |
| Chihuahua | | | 5.5 | | 2.8 | | 3.7 | | | |
| Dobermann | | | | 33.7 | | | | | | |
| Fox Terrier | | | | | | | 10.5 | | | 22.0 |
| Golden Retriever | 6.8 | | | | | 7.4 | | | | |
| Great Dane | | | | 6.0†, 24.0†† | | | | | | |
| Pekinese | | | 4.1 | | | | | | | |
| poodle (toy) | | | 3.1 | | 6.7 | | | | | |
| poodle (miniature) | | | 2.8 | | 5.9 | | | | | |
| Rottweiler | 5.4 | | | | | | | | | |
| Shih Tzu | | | 3.3 | | | | | | 3.3 | |
| Springer Spaniel | | | | | 4.0 | | | | 5.0 | |
| West Highland White Terrier | | | | | | | 4.2 | | 13.4 | 14.1 |

*Notes:* A value greater than 1 indicates an increased risk for the breed compared to the general dog population. Hence, a value of 5 would indicate a fivefold increased risk for the breed compared to the general dog population.
* Mitral valve disease. † Compared to purebred dogs as a whole. †† Compared to non-breed dogs. AS = aortic stenosis; ASD = atrial septal defect; EC = endocardiosis; DC = dilated cardiomyopathy; PDA = patent ductus arteriosus; PE = pericardial effusion; PS = pulmonic stenosis; SSS = sick sinus syndrome; VSD = ventricular septal defect; TofF = tetralogy of Fallot.
*Source:* Gough and Thomas (2004)[17]

### 6.2.2.5 Brachycephalic breeds and large heads

Flat-faced breeds are known as 'brachycephalic' (short-headed) and frequently suffer from 'brachycephalic upper airway syndrome'. When the length of the skull and jaw bones are shortened by selective breeding for a short head, the skin and soft tissue of the face and mouth are not necessarily reduced in the same proportion, potentially obstructing the dog's airway. Brachycephalic syndrome is described by veterinarians as 'A group of anatomical deformities which lead to respiratory compromise in brachycephalic breeds' that is 'likely to be a consequence of selective breeding to certain facial characteristics'.[17] Commonly affected short-faced breeds include the Pekinese, pug, Boston Terrier, boxer and bulldog. The deformities include stenotic (very narrow) nostrils, a soft palate that is too long and therefore obstructs breathing, deformities of the larynx that obstruct the trachea (windpipe) and an incompletely developed (hypoplastic) trachea that is too narrow to supply enough air during exercise.

Dogs with the syndrome often snore and breathe noisily and with difficulty, sometimes lose consciousness and have more difficulty if they exercise or get overheated. As a result, surgery may be needed to cut off some of the soft palate (soft palate resection) and to cut off some nasal cartilage to open the nostrils. One winner of Crufts 'Best in Show' prize reportedly had previous surgery for a breathing problem and was placed on an ice pack during the show.[11] This raises the question of whether 'best' should denote the healthiest and best-functioning dog or the dog that best conforms to an artificial breed standard.

The brachycephalic breeds are also more predisposed to heart disease, possibly because they find it difficult to breathe through their obstructed airways. A four-year-old champion bulldog died during the 2007 Crufts show, possibly as a result of the high temperature in the National Exhibition Centre.[31] An additional consequence of the standard's requirement for the bulldog to have a very large head is that caesarean section is now considered a normal method of birth for bulldogs, meaning that the breed in its present form is no longer viable without veterinary intervention.

### 6.2.2.6 Chondrodysplastic, toy, miniature and giant breeds

Dogs are predisposed to problems with their backs and legs if they have very short legs, disproportionately long backs, or if they are very small, with very fine legs. The effects range from a limited ability for exercise to severe pain and disability. The dogs may have to be prevented from climbing stairs or jumping to protect them from potential damage. Patella luxation (kneecap dislocation) is inherited in a number of mostly small breeds, including the miniature and toy poodles, Yorkshire Terrier, Pomeranian, Pekinese, Chihuahua, Boston Terrier, Basset Hound, Shih Tzu, Silky Terrier and Lhasa Apso.[32]

Chondrodystrophoid or achondroplastic breeds are those with disproportionately short and bowed limbs. These features are the result of dwarfism, a genetic abnormality in the development of cartilage and bone. Chondrodystrophoid breeds include the dachshund, Basset Hound, Beagle, French bulldog, Lhasa Apso, Pekinese, Pomeranian, Shih Tzu and Welsh Corgi, among others.

Chondrodystrophoid breeds are at risk of intervertebral disc disease. In the early 1990s, disc-related problems were thought to affect one quarter of dachshunds in America.[33] Because of the abnormal development of cartilage, the inner layer of the disc protrudes (herniates) and presses on the spinal cord. This happens at a relatively young age and often at several sites along the back, causing mild to intense pain and often requiring surgery. In severe cases it causes paralysis and permanent nerve damage.[32,33] The twisted tail of the pug breed ('double curl highly desirable', according to the 2003 standard[34]) results in some dogs being born with malformed vertebrae (hemivertebrae) or spina bifida.[17,32]

Small dog breeds, and especially the Cavalier King Charles Spaniel, are prone to what is termed the Chiari-like malformation. This occurs essentially because the dogs have been bred to have a skull that is too small for the brain. The result is that the lower part of the brain protrudes into the spinal column and the increased pressure leads to cavities of cerebrospinal fluid forming in the spinal cord (syringomyelia). Syringomyelia can cause extreme pain. Estimates are that between half and 90 per cent of the Cavalier King Charles Spaniel breed have the malformation and at least half of these develop syringomyelia. A study of clinically normal Cavalier King Charles breeding dogs in France using ultrasound imaging and computer tomography found that all the dogs had the Chiari-like malformation and 43.7 per cent had syringomyelia.[35]

There has been a second wave of miniaturization of the recognized toy breeds for celebrity 'pocket' use, sometimes bred from the runts of a litter. These 'teacup dogs' have a number of health problems. These include breaks to their delicate legs, stomachs that are too small to take in sufficient food, jaws too small for their teeth, dislocating kneecaps, heart problems, and caesarean sections for giving birth because of the small pelvis.[36] At the other end of the size scale, large and giant breeds of dog, such as the Irish Wolfhound, Great Dane, Rottweiler and St Bernard, are particularly prone to painful bone tumours, affecting 4.4 per cent of Great Danes and 5.3 per cent of Rottweilers. Bone tumours are associated with rapid bone growth when young dogs of the large breeds are growing very fast, and with bone stresses due to weight bearing.[37]

### 6.2.2.7 Hereditary deafness

Hereditary deafness is associated with breeding for white, piebald and 'merle' (speckled) coat colours in particular breeds. Dogs deaf in only one ear can function normally; however, breeding from deaf dogs is obviously risky. Dalmatians and Border Collies are particularly affected but deafness also affects the black-and-white speckled English setter, the bull terrier, dappled dachshunds and merle Chihuahuas (and the 'merle' mutation is also associated with eye problems). Hearing ability can now be tested in puppies of a few weeks old by the brainstem auditory-evoked response (BAER) method. The British Dalmatian Club discourages owners from breeding from deaf bitches and advises that owners ask the veterinarian who performs the BAER test to kill any puppies found to be deaf in both ears.[38]

Rates of deafness in Dalmatians have been very high in the past. In 2004, surveys in the US and Switzerland suggested that between 9.4 and 18 per cent of Dalmatians were deaf in one ear and between 7 and 8 per cent were deaf in both ears.[39] For Border Collies in England tested up to 2002, 2.3 per cent were deaf in one ear and 0.5 per cent deaf in both ears. Collie puppies born to a deaf mother were 14 times more likely to be deaf.[40] A 2008 study of merle dogs of several breeds in the US found that 9 per cent were deaf either in one or both ears and 15 per cent of those homozygous for the merle gene were deaf in both ears.[41]

*6.2.2.8 Breed-related diseases under investigation*
Genetic and breed-related diseases in dogs continue to emerge, and a large number are under investigation. By mid 2009, the American Kennel Club's Canine Health Foundation was funding research on diseases affecting 127 breeds and the Animal Health Trust in England was researching new genetic tests for diseases affecting 40 breeds. Distressing conditions such as canine degenerative myelopathy (a fatal disease of the spine that affects German Shepherds, Rhodesian Ridgebacks, corgis and boxers) and 'exercise-induced collapse' that affects retrievers are known to be related to mutations that are now widespread in the breeds.[42]

## 6.3 The breed-related behaviour of dogs

### *6.3.1 Bred for action and reaction*
The large majority of owned dogs need to be capable of fitting into modern domestic life and being contented with a fairly inactive lifestyle. But this is far from the behaviour that many dogs have been bred for. Breed standards and the show world still categorize dog breeds around their traditional working groups, and modern dogs who will be household companions show breed-related behaviour characteristics of their working ancestors. Dogs that have been bred to guard, hunt, search, herd or, worse, fight may cause problems either to their owners or to strangers, children and other animal owners. Canids are predators, but selection has deliberately sharpened this existing motivation in some breeds. Small, popular and harmless-looking dogs of terrier breeds were originally selectively bred to kill. Traits related to the working role, such as predation, territorial defence, aggression, wariness of strangers, attack in response to a perceived threat, pursuit of a scent, chasing and herding have been deliberately bred in over generations. Owners then have to prevent behaviour that is a genetic component of the dog.[43] Frustration, boredom, fear, anxiety and sometimes punishment result from the conflict between the dogs' evolved and breed-specific behaviour and their owners' needs and expectations.

To compound the problem, 'bad temper' may have been unintentionally bred into some dogs, while their breeders were focused on breed standards of appearance. This has led to 'a genetic predisposition to higher levels of aggression' in Cocker Spaniels, according to the Companion Animals Welfare Council in 2006.[8] A professional dog behaviourist writing in *Your Dog* magazine noted that there are 'frightening numbers of dogs from breeds traditionally renowned for their good temperaments – such as boxers, Labradors (particularly black ones) and Golden Retrievers – displaying seriously aggressive patterns of behaviour ... [as a result of] less than scrupulous breeding'. Terriers originally bred for fighting may show 'a particularly relentless and severe form of aggression' towards animals and, sometimes, people.[43] Complaints in magazines for dog owners suggest that uncontrolled dogs in public are a constant danger: a toy poodle killed by a greyhound; Jack Russell

Terriers who pick fights with any dog in sight; two show dogs attacked and one killed by suspected fighting dogs while walking in the park.

Researchers at the Anthrozoology Institute at the University of Southampton assessed a range of popular breeds for traits categorized as 'aggressivity', 'reactivity' (excitability, excessive barking and demand for attention) and 'immaturity' (playfulness, destructiveness). Each of these three traits could cause problems for dogs in a domestic setting (and the behaviour trait of snapping at children appeared in more than one category). Many of the small and toy breeds, including the Yorkshire Terrier, Chihuahua and Shih Tzu, were rated as high in reactivity and average in aggressivity. These three are among the numerically largest owned breeds in the UK (with Yorkshire Terrier at number four by some estimates). Other popular breeds such as the Jack Russell Terrier, Border Collie, Cocker Spaniel, Corgi and West Highland Terrier were rated high in both aggressivity and immaturity. A highly significant genetic association has been found for obsessive compulsive disorder (flank and blanket-sucking) in Dobermanns.[44]

Kennel Clubs and breeders do point out to potential buyers that some breeds are hard to control by inexperienced owners and that others need a working activity or a rural environment in order to be happy. But professional breeders may have a genuine conflict of interest. In order to produce a sufficient number of puppies to enable them to select the 'best' for show and breeding dogs, the general public needs to be induced to keep buying the puppies that are not to be retained.

### 6.3.2 Dog bites

Estimates from Europe are that between 9 and 18 people per 1000 are bitten by a dog annually. Surveys in the US in 2001–2003 indicated that a similar proportion, 15 per 1000, or 4.5 million people, were bitten annually. Children are at least twice as likely to be bitten as adults. Estimates from the US are that 1 in 20 dogs will bite people and between 10 and 15 people die annually from dog bites. In the UK, 5000 postal workers need medical attention for dog bites per year.[45,46]

Pit Bull Terriers and large dogs such as Rottweilers and German Shepherds are most often identified as likely to bite, but in fact the statistics on which breeds are dangerous biters are very unclear.[46] It appears that people are bitten by dogs of a wide range of breeds, including popular ones such as the collie, the Springer Spaniel, Golden Retriever, dachshund and Jack Russell Terrier. In a study between 2002 and 2004 in County Cork, Ireland, none of the dogs most frequently reported as biting were of breeds most often associated with aggression, such as the Staffordshire Bull Terrier, Rottweiler or Dobermann. The dogs with the highest 'bite rate' (the number of bites divided by number of dogs of that breed) included the Papillon and Pekinese. The dogs with the lowest bite rate included the Staffordshire Bull Terrier, closely related in appearance and origin to the Pit Bull Terrier. The breed most often reported as biting was the collie, the most popular breed in the study area.[45] But although large dogs may not be the most frequent biters, their bites can do more damage and in recent years in England children have been killed by fighting-breed dogs owned by the family.

### 6.3.3 Fighting breeds

The Dangerous Dogs Act of 1991 in Great Britain prohibited 'types' of dog, including dogs of the type of the Pit Bull Terrier, the Japanese Tosa, Dogo Argentinos and the Fila Brazilieros. This allows a judgement to be made on whether a particular dog's characteristics meet the prohibited type and can include cross-bred dogs. Under the 1991 Act, all such dogs were to be destroyed, while an amendment in 1997 allowed the courts to have discretion on this and for some dogs to be exempted from destruction if they were assessed not to be a danger to the public. The UK Department for Environment, Food and Rural Affairs provides guidance, based on an American Breed Standard of 1977, for judging whether a dog has enough characteristics (such as 'shoulders wider than the rib cage at the eighth rib') to be considered a Pit Bull type.[47] Pit Bull Terriers quite closely resemble American Staffordshire Terriers or (in England) Staffordshire Bull Terriers, both recognized breeds with fighting tendencies that are acknowledged by the Kennel Clubs in their descriptions of the breeds. Behavioural characteristics of fighting dogs, selected over centuries, include their 'grab and hold' style of attack, their rapid arousal to attack, without giving warning and ignoring signs of submission, and their 'gameness' – the willingness to fight to the death. They have been bred to need human attention and they fight for the reward of praise.[48]

Because of the lack of clarity about whether dogs are dangerous as a breed (or type), rather than as individuals, the RSPCA, the British Veterinary Association and the Kennel Club (London) oppose breed-specific legislation, as does the Humane Society of the United States (HSUS). The legislation is very unpopular with many dog owners. Dog magazines print a constant stream of letters and opinion pieces excoriating the legislation, 'irresponsible' dog owners, local authorities, the RSPCA and the general public and in support of the Staffordshire Bull Terriers who may get unjustly identified as fighting dogs. There are several cases of dogs who have or perhaps have not attacked, have been sentenced to destruction and then reprieved after court cases involving expert testimony by animal behaviourists and conducted by specialist lawyers.

Increasing numbers of the Pit Bull type of dog have been bred in the UK for fighting or for 'status' purposes and dog rescue shelters in Britain started to fill up with abandoned Staffordshire Bull Terrier types and crosses. Dogs have been trained, often by unpleasant means, to be openly aggressive on the streets, as well as for fighting.[49] After the killing of a child in 2007, 300 dogs of the 'illegal' type were handed in to local police in Merseyside for assessment and around one third were found to be 'Pit Bull types' and surrendered by their owners.[50]

Historically, dogs have always been bred and trained to defend their owners and the owners' property aggressively against trespass or theft and to project their owners' power and status. The 'status' and fighting dogs of the 21st century are an unwelcome new manifestation of this on the crowded inner-city streets. The dog-owning community and animal protection organizations argue, probably rightly, that the breed of a dangerous dog should be irrelevant; but they may have prepared the ground for this type of categorization themselves. It would be hard to be more focused on the significance of 'breed' than the dog-owning community is itself. If breeds are clearly defined, with clearly defined physical and behavioural characteristics deliberately created by breeders, it is easier for legislators to target them. To criticize the breed ideology with respect to 'dangerous breeds' only, while endorsing the importance of breed-specific behaviours in other recognized breeds, seems inconsistent.

---

### Box 6.1 Dog fighting

The breeding of fighting dogs, mainly Pit Bull Terriers, and their illegal use for dog fighting is an underground activity in Europe and the US. Dog fighting is illegal in the UK and in 50 US states, and in nearly all those states it is a felony rather than a misdemeanour.[51] In 2007 the BBC exposed a dog-fighting network operating across the UK, Ireland and Finland. After fights described as 'bloodbaths', the dogs who lost or were too badly injured to move were drowned or electrocuted. Some of the surviving dogs were heavily scarred. A dog supplier in Finland described a good dog as one who is 'wild' and 'crazy' and will fight from the beginning to the end until he dies.[52]

The US dog-fighting ring operated by the American football star Michael Vick, who was sentenced to 23 months in prison in 2007, received national publicity both for the celebrity element and because of the cruelty that was exposed. Vick kept around 50 Pit Bull Terriers at Bad Newz Kennels. Dogs that failed to fight adequately were beaten or disposed of by being shot, hanged, electrocuted or drowned. Unusually, the judge ordered each dog to be evaluated individually instead of requiring all to be destroyed. After evaluation by animal behaviourists, only one was found to be too aggressive to be re-homed and was humanely destroyed. The remainder were either placed in foster homes or animal sanctuaries, depending on how aggressive they were towards other dogs, and one became a certified hospital therapy dog. After serving his sentence, and paying for the dogs' rehabilitation, Michael Vick became a campaign adviser on dog fighting for the HSUS.[53]

---

## 6.4 Pedigree cat breeds and their health

Although cats have been subject to much less intensive selection into breeds than have dogs, analogous health problems have emerged in the breeds that exist. These are related to the extreme conformation required by the breed standard, or related to the inbreeding and the spread of damaging genes within the breed. Some breeds of cat are now almost unviable except in a protected indoor environment and some breeds are less able to give birth unaided. Cats with excessively long coats, or hairless, would probably no longer be able to survive the feral outdoor lifestyle that most cats are able to revert to in case of need. Because of the relatively smaller numbers of animals involved, research results and evidence for breed-related health problems in cats are inevitably sparser than for the dog breeds, but the trend is evident. In 2009 a feline veterinary journal described the extent to which we have deformed the faces and skulls of severely brachycephalic Persian cats as 'appalling' and 'truly grotesque.'[54]

Cat breeders operate a relatively high level of inbreeding. In 2009, the UK Governing Council of the Cat Fancy (GCCF) recommended that the inbreeding coefficient should be limited to 20 per cent calculated over six generations and that 25 per cent calculated over eight generations or more was 'perfectly acceptable'. Males up to 40 per cent inbred were considered acceptable. The GCCF does not normally allow the 'active' registration (i.e. for breeding) of kittens resulting from either parent–offspring or full sibling matings, except for particular approved purposes.[55]

## 6.4.1 Flat faces and bulging eyes

The Persian, still one of the most popular pedigree cat breeds, has been bred to have an excessively short face. In extreme cases, the cat has a concave face so that the tip of the cat's nose may be higher than the lower part of the eyes and the upper canine teeth are rotated to an almost horizontal position.[54,56] The breed is now subject to some of the same types of problem as the brachycephalic Pekinese or pug dog breeds, including narrowing of the nostrils and upper respiratory tract that can lead to difficulties in breathing. The bulbous eyes are more prone to injury and disease, including disorders of the eyelid and cornea and the inability of the tear duct to drain away the normal tear production (epiphora).[6,17,54,57] The Cat Fanciers' Association (CFA) considers a wet face 'normal' for the breed, and recommends daily face washing.[58]

In the second half of the 20th century the Burmese breed was also selectively bred for a shorter ('contemporary') face, although less extreme than the Persian. During the 1980s this resulted in one breeding line of Burmese cats in which 25 per cent of kittens born had a lethal malformation of the face and died shortly after birth.[59]

## 6.4.2 Difficulty giving birth

Cats bred to have abnormally shaped heads or bodies are more likely to have difficulty giving birth (dystocia), sometimes requiring surgery. A 1995 study at the University of Bristol of nearly 3000 litters found that brachycephalic breeds (such as the Persian) and the dolichocephalic breeds (such as the Siamese) had relatively high levels of dystocia. Dystocia affected 18.2 per cent of Devon Rex litters, compared to 0.4 per cent in a colony of mixed-breed cats. Overall, dystocia was 22.6 times more likely in pedigree litters compared to mixed-breed cats.[60]

### 6.4.3 Abnormal hair, ears and tails

Excessively long hair or hairlessness makes it likely that a cat will be unfit to live a normal life by spending time outdoors. The CFA recommends that the 'long, flowing coat' of the Persian breed requires a protected indoor environment.[58] The hairless Sphynx breed has insufficient protection against cold and sun to lead a normal outdoor life and needs washing to remove the secreted oil that would normally be absorbed in fur.[56,61] The Devon Rex (very short curly coat) is 80 per cent more likely than ordinary domestic short-haired cats to carry the *Malassezia* yeast that causes skin disease.[62] The mutation that causes the 'folded' ear of the Scottish or American Fold breeds also causes abnormal cartilage and bone development (osteochondrodysplasia), which can result in painful lameness and misshapen limbs.[17,56,63]

### 6.4.4 Spread of genetic diseases

Increasing numbers of genetic diseases, caused mainly by recessive mutations, are spreading through the pedigree cat breeds, some affecting a number of related breeds. Degeneration of the retina (progressive retinal atrophy, resulting in blindness) is now a recognized disease of several breeds, including the Abyssinian, Somali and Persian.[64,65] One of the main causal genes in Abyssinian and Somali cats has been identified and is carried by 13 per cent of the Abyssinian cat population in Sweden and 7 per cent in the US.[65] Siamese cats suffer from inherited glaucoma, a painful condition thought to be related to eye shape.[8]

Burmese cats are 3.7 times more likely to develop diabetes than the general cat population.[66] Persians and a derived breed, the Exotic Shorthair, have a high incidence of inherited polycystic kidney disease, causing kidney failure. This is now thought to affect around 40 per cent of Persians and has spread to several other breeds, transmitted as a dominant gene. A recessive gene identified in Abyssinian and Somali cats causes pyruvate kinase deficiency, leading to anaemia. Genetic tests are available for some of these diseases, which should enable breeders to avoid breeding from cats that are carriers.[67] The large-sized Maine Coon breed, reported to have originated in rugged farm cats in North America, but now a show breed, suffers from inherited haemophilia, hip dysplasia (affecting perhaps half of the breed) and hypertrophic cardiomyopathy. Male Maine Coons have died post-operatively from bleeding after castration.[17,68,69]

Behavioural problems that suggest severe anxiety or stress, such as obsessive chewing of wool (pica) or other objects, are more common among pedigree cats and especially the Siamese and breeds that derive from them.[70] Stress and anxiety may also reflect the fact that many valuable pedigree cats are kept permanently in restrictive conditions indoors. There is evidence that Siamese and Persian cats are selected and managed to interact more with their owners than are non-pedigree cats;[70] as well as being more likely to be kept indoors, they may receive more attention from their owners as 'special' or valuable animals. Greater emotional dependence on people may well not be to the cat's advantage.

## 6.5 Professionals and owners

### 6.5.1 Apportioning responsibility

The fact that some pedigree dogs and cats have been subjected to pain and distress in the pursuit of breed-specific characteristics has appeared all the more scandalous and embarrassing because these problems arise from a community that claims to be breeding out of a love of the animals concerned, or the love of a breed. There seems no doubt that the public has been given to believe that a pedigree dog or cat is of superior quality to a non-breed animal and that Kennel Club registration should guarantee this quality. At the point where we are now, insurers' estimates (see Table 6.5) strongly suggest that the non-breed dog, living longer and requiring less treatment, is a healthier animal.

The health problems of pedigree dogs have been known to professionals, including veterinarians, breed societies, breeders and animal protection organizations, for decades. Some continue to maintain that the serious problems are small scale, localized and the responsibility of a minority of 'irresponsible' breeders. In this view the problems can be solved with more careful testing for disease, the avoidance of inbreeding and the reform of some breed standards to remove the most exaggerated features.

An important consideration for any plan of reform is what sanctions are held by the professionals. In Britain and the US, society has no specific rules limiting how people may modify animals by selective breeding. In the absence of legislation, neither veterinarians nor Kennel Clubs can entirely prevent breeders from selecting for any traits that they wish, or from using any degree of inbreeding that they wish. Kennel Clubs can influence strongly the direction

**Table 6.5** *Lifetime and non-routine veterinary costs per year for selected breeds and non-breed (mongrel) in UK, 2006*

|  | *Average lifetime (years)* | *Non-routine annual veterinary and other treatment costs (UK£)\** |
|---|---|---|
| bulldog | 8 | 890 |
| Great Dane | 10 | 1396 |
| Rottweiler | 12 | 467 |
| boxer | 12 | 431 |
| English Springer Spaniel | 12 | 414 |
| Jack Russell Terrier | 12 | 306 |
| Labrador retriever | 13 | 204 |
| poodle-cross | 16 | 204 |
| non-breed (mongrel) | 16 | 102 |

*Note:* \* Essential veterinary costs are taken to be the same for all breeds at UK£301 annually.
*Source:* K9 Magazine (2006) February, citing Churchill insurance company *Annual Cost of a Dog* report

of breeding by refusing to register or admit to shows any dogs whose parents have not tested clear of certain inherited conditions or who have closely related parents. They can set breed standards that avoid the most damaging traits and they can exclude breeds that have damaging exaggerated traits or persistent health problems from winning prizes. They have been much criticized for failing to do these things in the past. But there is the possibility that breeders who disagree with any Kennel Club rules will continue to operate outside the Kennel Club registry and show circuit.

## 6.5.2 Veterinarians and scientists

Veterinarians have long been aware of the health problems of pedigree dogs but are in a difficult position because their human clients can leave them if they dislike their advice, reducing the veterinarians' influence even further. As two British veterinary associations put it in 2008: 'There is also little doubt the profession as a whole has been aware of these issues but has largely chosen to deal with specific problems in individual animals rather than tackle the root cause.'[71] In addition, pedigree dogs and their breeders provide a substantial proportion of a veterinary practice's clients and the further development of 'corrective' surgery, such as opening the narrow nostrils of puppies of brachycephalic breeds,[42] may provide a good customer base for some veterinarians in some countries.

Since the 1970s, veterinarians have been involved with breed societies and Kennel Clubs in Europe and the US[72] in dog health-testing schemes. But the impact of a testing regime in improving the health of dogs depends upon the cooperation of breeders, unless breed societies make them compulsory, and veterinarians cannot compel cooperation. On the brachycephalic syndrome, veterinarians have commented: 'Selective breeding programmes to remove these anatomical deformities would be the ideal long-term approach to this problem';[73] but unless they enter the public debate, they are not in a position to make this happen.

The geneticists who study dog breeds may have a different perspective in that their primary interest is generally in fundamental genetics or in elucidating the genetics behind diseases that affect people, rather than the suffering that the diseases may cause to dogs or cats. The small and well-differentiated genetic pools created by the world's 400 dog breeds and the inherited defects associated with them are a goldmine for genetic research. For this reason, scientists tend to take the existence of genetic disease in dogs and cats as a given, rather than a man-made problem to be solved. Thus the journal *Nature* reported in 2005 that Maine Coon cats could become 'the first useful large animal model' for the familial hypertrophic cardiomyopathy in humans because this disease is common in the breed.[68] It should be added that the genetic investigation of disease in dogs and cats, whether this is done to reduce disease in animals or in people, is likely to involve experimental breeding and the experimental use of cats and dogs.

## 6.5.3 Kennel Clubs and breeders

Kennel Clubs are often identified by the public as organizations that should promote dog health and welfare and responsible dog ownership – perhaps unfairly, as their original function was to promote the sport of dog breeding and showing. Possibly in response to modern criticism, the UK's KC explicitly states its mission as the promotion of the interests of all dogs and 'dedicated to the health and welfare of dogs'. Similarly, the American Kennel Club ('the nation's premier advocate for dogs and the people who love them') in April 2009 introduced registration for mixed-breed dogs to be entered for events such as agility trials.

Kennel Clubs have been criticized for registering dogs whose parents are known to have hereditary defects, for upholding extreme physical (or behavioural) features in breed standards, and for failing to make health checks a condition of registration. In response to their own and others' concerns, the KC instituted a higher level of registration (the Accredited Breeder Scheme), with mandatory health checks on parent dogs as a condition of registering puppies. These initiatives led to more criticism from both sides of the debate. Those who wanted reform exposed inconsistencies and failures to enforce the rules. Some breeders argued that a requirement to test all parent dogs was unnecessary and would unacceptably limit the number of animals that could be used for breeding. Some breed societies continue to defend characteristics in dog and cat breeds that many in society no longer find acceptable. Making an analogy with human marriage norms, the general public finds the close inbreeding of dogs and cats shocking. While the KC, under criticism, forbade the mating of full siblings or of parents and offspring, many breeders mate quite close relatives routinely (referred to as 'line breeding').

There have been questions over the determination of some breeders to reduce inherited disease and increase transparency. Maintaining a line can be very important to breeders and the Companion Animal Welfare Council found that, even with the evidence that at least half the Cavalier King Charles Spaniel breed is affected by syringomyelia, breeders could strongly oppose moving away from what is perceived as breed purity or ceasing to breed from an affected line or breed of dogs.[74] In 2004 the KC asked a large number of breeders to participate in a health survey, which included causes of illness and mortality in their dogs. The response was patchy, considering the seriousness of the issues to professional breeders: 24 per cent overall and with a range between breeds of from 4.5 to nearly 65 per cent. For one breed, *Dogs Today* reported that 890 questionnaires were distributed and only three completed ones submitted for analysis.[75]

In the absence of legislation, breed societies and Kennel Clubs may have had insufficient sanctions to change the behaviour of breeders. By 2009, the KC proposed to government that the rules of the Accredited Breeder Scheme should be made a legal requirement for all dog breeders.[76] The future will tell the success and acceptability of the new breed standards issued by the KC in

2009, which include such innovations as the requirement for the Pekinese breed to have a defined muzzle. Breeders are currently still at liberty to sell puppies of a defined breed, and even issue 'pedigrees', without registering them with any breed society. In the case of the very popular but disease-afflicted Cavalier King Charles breed, it is estimated that as many puppies are produced outside the breed registration system as within it.[74]

There is a wide range of behaviour within the dog-breeding community, which includes a hobby or breed-enthusiast section, an entirely commercial section and gradations in between. When breeders acknowledge that excessive breeding to type has caused problems, it is notable that they tend to assign blame to others. A distinction is often made between 'responsible' breeders who include themselves and other 'irresponsible' breeders who have caused any problems that exist.

### 6.5.4 Dog owners

Pedigree dogs, including those with exaggerated features and health defects, continue to be produced because the public continues to want them. Even obvious health problems do not seem to prevent this. An article in *The Field* in 2007 told readers 'pugs are now Society's top dog', listing the breed's celebrity endorsements, and added the comment: 'they apparently find it very difficult to breathe – in fact they constantly snuffle and snort'.[77] Dog owners continue to buy dogs of breeds that are prone to early and sudden death from heart disease or other afflictions,[6,78] while deploring the problem, showing that their attitude is a complex one. There seems to be no relationship between the popularity of a breed, as judged by the number of puppies registered annually, and the number of inherited defects in the breed.[16] The public continues to buy pedigree puppies (and to a lesser extent kittens) rather than adopting a dog from a rescue centre.

A section of the dog-owning community in the UK at least has been active in demanding reform in pedigree dog breeding. *Dogs Today*, a British magazine for dog owners, has campaigned tirelessly against the KC and the Crufts show and in favour of reform of pedigree dog breeding, and publicized scandals such as the suffering caused by the spread of syringomyelia through the Cavalier King Charles breed.[78,79]

## 6.6 The future of pedigree breeds

### 6.6.1 Proposed solutions

The dog-breeding community's core belief – that over 400 dog breeds can continue to exist and to be genetically differentiated, with minimal regulation of their genetics and without negative effects on dog welfare – appears increasingly unsustainable. By 2009 in the UK there was a strong move by the companion animal professionals and policy-makers to oversee and regulate companion animal breeding and to consider whether certain existing breeds should be discontinued in their present form.

The 1987 European Convention for the protection of pet animals (Council of Europe Treaty Series 125) has provided a set of objectives for reform, either voluntary or through regulation. Around 20 European countries have either ratified or signed the Convention (the UK has not and in 2004 the Kennel Club expressed opposition to the UK becoming a signatory, preferring self-regulation by the breeding community[80]). Article 5 of the Convention makes the general statement that 'Any person who selects a pet animal for breeding shall be responsible for having regard to the anatomical, physiological and behavioural characteristics which are likely to put at risk the health and welfare of either the offspring or the female parent',[81] which all breeders could be expected to agree with.

In 1995 a Multilateral Consultation by the Convention's signatories agreed a detailed resolution that aimed to ensure the implementation of Article 5. This called for a reform of dog and cat breed standards to remove abnormal or exaggerated features, suggesting that legislation might be necessary to prohibit certain breeds if the reform of breed standards was not sufficient to solve the problem.[82] While some critics of the current situation urge the implementation of the 1995 resolution, many breeders are opposed to this as it would probably involve the end of some breeds in their present form.

The type of breed characteristics that the resolution wanted to see ended included:

- extremes of size or weight;
- extreme shortness of nose or skull;
- extremely long back compared to leg length;
- bowed or abnormally positioned legs;
- abnormally deep-set or protruding eyes;
- abnormal positioning of teeth;
- excessively long ears;
- excessive skin folds;
- physical abnormalities and defects, such as hairless or tailless animals;
- coat colours such as white or 'merle' associated with deafness and eye disorders.

In the UK in 2008, the Companion Animal Welfare Council (CAWC) suggested three possible strategies for a voluntary approach to solving 'ancestral problems':[83]

1 selective breeding within a breed to attempt to eliminate the problem (trying to breed out a defect, while avoiding inbreeding);
2 crossing with another breed or breeds (outbreeding);
3 ceasing to breed at all from potential carriers, even if this meant that particular lines in the breed or the whole breed might be discontinued.

One of the major problems that any voluntary approach would encounter is the 'ideology of breed purity' which many breeders subscribe to. Veterinarians have long proposed that some breeds need to be 'out-crossed' with other suitable breeds in order to increase genetic diversity or to change conformational or behavioural traits, or reduce inherited disease. Some breeds also have healthy and less exaggerated breeding lines of working dogs that do not currently win prizes but could become the reformed 'breed standard'. It is likely that most breeders would prefer the current strategy of continuing to select within their existing breeds and lines, reducing inherited health problems by testing potential parents. This is essentially the strategy that would follow from the 2009 reform of KC breed standards requiring, for example, that only a Pekinese dog with a muzzle would meet the breed standard and so win prizes. Whether this strategy would actually work, within the narrow genetic base of some existing breeds, is not yet known.

The CAWC pointed out that the three voluntary strategies depend on the relative importance of breed purity and animal welfare in the mind of breeders:[83]

- If breed purity is the main priority, strategy 1 above wins.
- If breed purity is less important, strategy 2 can be tried.
- If animal welfare is the main priority, strategy 3 wins.

The first two strategies also have the disadvantage that unwanted and probably unhealthy puppies would almost certainly be produced during the period of experimental breeding and crossing, unsuitable for either showing or breeding and with low market value.

## 6.6.2 A need for regulation

Dog and cat breeding may not change enough, and fast enough, without a radical change in the thinking of breeders and the animal-buying public, and may need legislation. Dog and cat breeds are now lifestyle commodities; as with other commodities, the most reliable way that society can control their quality (and protect their welfare) is by law, unless voluntary reform is successful.

Effective regulation of breeding, either by voluntary agreement or by law, could include provisions such as the following:

- mandatory licensing and breeding records for pedigree dogs and cats used for breeding – a high breeding licence fee would be a useful disincentive to breeding;
- a prohibition of the sale of puppies and kittens through pet shops or other than at their mother's home;
- mandatory health checks on parent dogs, including all genetic defects known to exist in the breed, and recording of the test results;

- prohibition of the use of dogs for breeding that are affected by damaging genetic mutations;
- legally enforced limitations on dog and cat conformation as proposed in the European Convention's resolution on Breeding of 1995;
- financial incentives (for example by a reduction in the breeding licence fee) to limit inbreeding to 3 per cent over ten generations;[84]
- prohibition of matings that produced an inbreeding coefficient of 20 per cent or more over five generations.[84]

These regulations would need to be extended, as far as possible, to all dogs used in licensed breeding operations, whether or not they were registered with a breed society or Kennel Club.

### 6.6.3 Ending the ideology of breed

Underlying the welfare problems associated with pedigree pet breeding is our obsession with breed itself, fostered by the pet industry. Breeds exist for the benefit of people, not of animals. The existence of distinct breeds encourages the search for unique and exaggerated characteristics and drives the inbreeding that produces these characteristics. It encourages the view of animals as commodities rather than as sentient individuals. It encourages commercial mass production of puppies in puppy farms. It encourages over-breeding and contributes to the problem of unwanted and homeless dogs and cats (see section 8.5 in Chapter 8).

There are few good reasons in modern society for differentiating companion dogs and cats into breeds with defined characteristics. Pedigree dogs and cats, in general, have no innate superiority and are typically less healthy than non-breed animals. The maintenance and creation of breeds may come to be seen as a piece of self-indulgence that society could well dispense with, without losing much of economic or cultural importance. The professionals have so far seemed reluctant to argue this point explicitly with the public and it may be reasonable for the dog (and cat) professionals to attempt first to achieve change by education and persuasion. If they cannot achieve this, it may be time for animal protection organizations to start public campaigning on the slogan 'Breed is bad'.

### Notes

1   Lemonick, M. D. (1994) 'A terrible beauty', *Time Magazine*, 12 December
2   Arman, K. (2007) 'Animal welfare: A new direction for Kennel Club regulations and breed standards', *Canadian Veterinary Journal*, vol 48, pp953–965
3   Bedford, P. G. C. (1999) 'Genetics and animal welfare in the world of the pedigree dog', *Animal Welfare*, vol 8, p311
4   McGreevy, P. D. and Nicholas, F. W. (1999) 'Some practical solutions to welfare problems in dog breeding', *Animal Welfare*, vol 8, pp329–341
5   Canadian Veterinary Medical Association (2006) *Position Statement: Purebred Dog Breeding*, adopted March 2006

6    Milne, E. (2007) *The Truth about Cats and Dogs*, Book Guild Publishing
7    Advocates for Animals (2006) *The Price of a Pedigree: Dog Breed Standards and Breed-Related Illness*, Advocates for Animals
8    Companion Animal Welfare Council (2006) *Breeding and Welfare in Companion Animals: CAWC's Report on Welfare Aspects of Modifications, through Selective Breeding or Biotechnological Methods, of the Form, Function or Behaviour of Companion Animals*, CAWC
9    Cuddy, B. (2007) 'Should Crufts be banned?', *Daily Telegraph*, 7 March (note that there appears to be a typographical error in the number of breed-related diseases stated in this article)
10   *Veterinary Record* (2008) 'For better or worse? BVA AWF forum considers breeding, and shock collars: News and reports', *Veterinary Record*, 7 June, pp736–737
11   Passionate Productions (2008) *Pedigree Dogs Exposed*, BBC Television, 19 August 2008; 'Pedigree dogs plagued by disease', BBC News online, 19 August, http://news.bbc.co.uk/
12   Reports published in 2009 include Rooney, N. and Sargan, D. (2009) *Pedigree Dog Breeding in the UK: A Major Welfare Concern? An Independent Scientific Report Commissioned by the RSPCA*, RSCPA; Associate Parliamentary Group for Animal Welfare (2009) *A Healthier Future for Pedigree Dogs: The Report of the APGAW Inquiry into the Health and Welfare Issues Surrounding the Breeding of Pedigree Dogs*, APGAW; Bateson, P. (2010) *Independent Inquiry into Dog Breeding*, Patrick Bateson, University of Cambridge
13   Lindblad-Toh, K. et al (2005) 'Genome sequences, comparative analysis and haplotype structure of the domestic dog', *Nature*, vol 438, pp803–819
14   Björnerfeldt, S. et al (2008) 'Assortative mating and fragmentation within dog breeds', *BMC Evolutionary Biology*, vol 8, no 28, www.biomedcentral.com/1471-2148/8/28
15   Calboli, F. C. F. et al (2008) 'Population structure and inbreeding from pedigree analysis of purebred dogs', *Genetics*, vol 179, pp593–601
16   Collins, L. M. et al (2009) 'Conforming to standards: A review of inherited defects as a consequence of physical conformation in pedigree dogs', in *Darwinian Selection, Selective Breeding and the Welfare of Animals*, UFAW International Symposium 2009, Bristol, 22–23 June 2009; Asher, L. et al (2009) 'Conformational disorders in dogs – analysing the association with breed standards,' *Veterinary Journal*, vol 182, pp402–411
17   Gough, A. and Thomas, A. (2004) *Breed Predispositions to Disease in Dogs and Cats*, Blackwell Publishing
18   Coopman, F. et al (2008) 'Prevalence of hip dysplasia, elbow dysplasia and humeral head osteochondrosis in dog breeds in Belgium', *Veterinary Record*, vol 163, pp654–658; Paster, E. R. et al (2005) 'Estimates of prevalence of hip dysplasia in Golden Retrievers and Rottweilers and the influence of bias on published prevalence figures', *Journal of the American Veterinary Medical Association*, vol 226, no 3, pp387–392
19   Foster, J. (1996) *Hip Dysplasia in Dogs: A Guide for Dog Owners*, reprinted by the BVA Animal Welfare Foundation from *You & Your Vet* (1996)
20   British Veterinary Association/Kennel Club (2007) *Hip Dysplasia Scheme – Breed Mean Scores at 01/11/2007*; British Veterinary Association/Kennel Club (2005, 2006) *Hip Dysplasia Scheme – Breed Mean Scores at 01/01/2006 and at 10/10/2005*
21   Mäki, K. et al (2002) 'Genetic variances, trends and mode of inheritance for hip and elbow dysplasia in Finnish dog populations', *Animal Science*, vol 75, pp197–207; Mäki, K. et al (2005) 'The effect of breeding schemes on the genetic response of canine hip dysplasia, elbow dysplasia, behaviour traits and

appearance', *Animal Welfare*, vol 14, pp117–124; Leppanen, M. and Saloniemi, H. (1999) 'Controlling canine hip-dysplasia in Finland', *Preventive Veterinary Medicine*, vol 42, pp121–131

22  Leighton, E. A. (1997) 'Genetics of canine hip dysplasia', *Journal of the American Veterinary Medical Association*, vol 210, pp1471–1479

23  Swenson, L., Audell, L. and Hedhammar, Å (1997) 'Prevalence and inheritance of and selection for hip dysplasia in seven breeds of dogs in Sweden and benefit–cost analysis of a screening and control programme', *Journal of the American Veterinary Medical Association*, vol 210, pp207–214

24  Gelatt, K. N. (2000) *Essentials of Veterinary Ophthalmology*, Lippincott Williams & Wilkins

25  Crispin, S. et al (2008) 'Hereditary eye disease in dogs', *In Practice*, vol 30, January, pp2–14, updated by BVA and Kennel Club, February 2009, www.bva.co.uk/public/documents/Hereditary_Eye_Disease_In_Dogs.pdf, accessed June 2009

26  American Kennel Club Canine Health Foundation (2009) *Linkage and Direct DNA Canine Genetic Tests Offered 4/22/09*, www.akcchf.org/research/genetic_tests.pdf, last accessed June 2009

27  *Dogs Today* (2008) July, p74

28  Hill, P. B. (2002) *Small Animal Dermatology: A Practical Guide to the Diagnosis and Management of Skin Diseases in Dogs and Cats*, Butterworth Heinemann

29  *Veterinary Record* (2008) 'Notification of "skin tacking" in dogs: News and reports', *Veterinary Record*, vol 162, no 16, 19 April, p496

30  Serfass, P. et al (2006) 'Retrospective study of 942 small-sized dogs: Prevalence of left apical systolic heart murmur and left-sided heart failure, critical effects of breed and sex', *Journal of Veterinary Cardiology*, vol 8, no 1, pp11–18

31  Hancock, D. (2007) 'The great pedigree dog swindle', *Dogs Today*, May, pp23–25

32  Atlantic Veterinary College and the Canadian Veterinary Medical Association (1998, revised 2004) *Canine Inherited Disorders Database*, Atlantic Veterinary College, University of Prince Edward Island and the Canadian Veterinary Medical Association

33  Luttgen, J. P. (1993) *Canine Invertebral Disk Disease*, Dachshund Club of America, www.dachshund-dca.org/discbook.html, last accessed June 2009

34  Kennel Club (2003) *Illustrated Breed Standards: The Official Guide to Registered Breeds*, revised edition, Ebury Press; see also revised standards in Kennel Club (2009) 'Review of breed standards', News release, 12 January

35  *Dogs Today* (2009) *How Can We Save the Pedigree Dog?*, Supplement, January 2009; Couturier, J., Rault, D. and Cauzinille, L. (2008) 'Chiari-like malformation and syringomyelia in normal Cavalier King Charles Spaniels: A multiple diagnostic imaging approach', *Journal of Small Animal Practice*, vol 49, no 9, pp438–443; Lewis, T. W., Woolliams, J. A. and Blott, S. C. (2009) 'Optimisation of breeding strategies to reduce the prevalence of inherited disease in pedigree dogs', *Darwinian Selection, Selective Breeding and the Welfare of Animals*, UFAW International Symposium 2009, Bristol, 22–23 June 2009

36  Beck, C. (2006) 'Designer dogs bred to die', *Daily Express*, 3 February, pp34–35

37  Morris, J. and Dobson, J. (2001) *Small Animal Oncology*, Blackwell Science; Rosenberger, J., Pablo, N. V. and Crawford, P. C. (2007) 'Prevalence of and intrinsic risk factors for appendicular osteosarcoma in dogs: 179 cases (1996–2005)', *Journal of the American Veterinary Medical Association*, vol 231, no 7, pp1076–1080

38  British Dalmatian Club (undated) 'Hearing', www.britishdalmatianclub.org.uk/, accessed June 2009

39   Cargill, E. J. et al (2004) 'Heritability and segregation analysis of deafness in US Dalmatians', *Genetics*, vol 166, no 3, pp1385–1393; Muhle, A. C. et al (2002) 'Further contributions to the genetic aspect of congenital sensorineural deafness in Dalmatians', *Veterinary Journal*, vol 163, no 3, pp311–318

40   Platt, S. et al (2006) 'Prevalence of unilateral and bilateral deafness in Border Collies and association with phenotype', *Journal of Veterinary Internal Medicine*, vol 20, no 6, pp1355–1362

41   Strain, G. M. (2009) 'Prevalence of deafness in dogs heterozygous or homozygous for the merle allele', *Journal of Veterinary Internal Medicine*, vol 23, no 2, pp282–286

42   American Kennel Club Canine Health Foundation (undated) *Funded Research News*, www.akcchf.org/research/?nav_area=research, accessed June 2009

43   Price, C. (2008) 'Nature or nurture?', *Your Dog*, July, pp7–8

44   Bradshaw, J. W. S. et al (1996) 'A survey of the behavioural characteristics of pure-bred dogs in the United Kingdom', *Veterinary Record*, vol 138, pp465–468 (for estimates of the most owned breeds, see Pet Food Manufacturers Association (2008, 2009) 'Statistics of pet ownership, UK', www.pfma.org.uk/); Dodman, N. H. et al (2010) 'A canine chromosome 7 locus confers compulsive disorder susceptibility', *Molecular Psychiatry*, vol 15, pp8–10

45   O'Sullivan, E. N. et al (2008) 'Characteristics of 234 dog bite incidents in Ireland during 2004 and 2005', *Veterinary Record*, vol 163, no 2, pp37–42

46   Sacks, J. J., Kresnow, M.-J. and Houston, B. (1996) 'Dog bites: How big a problem?', *Injury Prevention*, vol 2, pp52–54; Gilchrist, J. et al (2008) 'Dog bites: Still a problem?', *Injury Prevention*, vol 14, no 5, pp296–301; American Veterinary Medical Association (2001) 'A community approach to dog bite prevention', *JAVMA*, vol 218, no 11, pp1732–1748

47   Department for Environment, Food and Rural Affairs (Defra) (2009) *Dangerous Dogs Law: Guidance for Enforcers*, Defra; Defra (2003) *Types of Dog Prohibited in the UK*, Defra

48   McMillan, F. D. and Reid, P. J. (2009) 'Selective breeding of fighting dogs: What have we created?', *Darwinian Selection, Selective Breeding and the Welfare of Animals*, UFAW International Symposium 2009, Bristol, 22–23 June 2009

49   BBC3 Television (2009) *My Weapon Is a Dog*, 21 May 2009

50   *Dogs Today* (2007) May, pp10–13

51   Humane Society of the United States (undated) *Dog Fighting: Factsheet*, www.humanesociety.org, accessed June 2009

52   BBC Television (2007) *Dog Fighting Undercover*, Panorama, 30 August

53   Schulte, B. (2008) 'Saving Michael Vick's dogs', *Washington Post*, 7 July; Gorant, J. (2008) 'What happened to Michael Vick's dogs', *Sports Illustrated*, 23 December; Rhoden, W. C. (2009) 'Humane Society sees Vick as an ally, not a pariah', *New York Times*, 21 May

54   le Bars, C. F. (2008) 'Abnormalities in pedigree cats', *Veterinary Times*, vol 38, no 22, p14; Copping, J. (2009) 'Inbred pedigree cats suffering from life-threatening diseases and deformities', *Sunday Telegraph*, 15 March; Veterinary Record (2009) 'FAB takes a stand against breeding for extreme phenotypes in cats', *Veterinary Record*, vol 165, no 25, p733; Schlueter, C. et al (2009) 'Brachycephalic feline noses: CT and anatomical study of the relationship between head conformation and nasolacrimal drainage system', *Journal of Feline Medicine and Surgery*, vol 11, pp891–900 (see photographs of degrees of brachycephalia in Persians)

55   Governing Council of the Cat Fancy (2008) *GCCF Breeding Policy: Guidelines for Healthy Breeding*, version 4, 14 May

56   Steinger, A. (2007) 'Breeding and welfare', in I. Rochlitz (ed) *The Welfare of Cats*, Springer, Dordrecht, Chapter 10

57  Glaze, M. B. (2005) 'Congenital and hereditary ocular abnormalities in cats', *Clinical Techniques in Small Animal Practice*, vol 20, no 2, pp74–82; Bouhanna, L. and Zaram J. (2001) 'Feline corneal sequestration: Study of etiology on 39 cases', *Pratique Médicale & Chirurgicale de l'Animal de Compagnie*, vol 36, no 5, pp473–479

58  Cat Fanciers' Association 'Persian breed profile', www.cfa.org/breeds/profiles/persian.html, accessed June 2009

59  Noden, D. N. and Evans, H. E. (1986) 'Inherited homeotic midfacial malformations in Burmese cats', *Journal of Craniofacial Genetics and Developmental Biology*, Supplement 2, pp249–266

60  Gunn-Moore, D. A. and Thrusfield, M. V. (1995) 'Feline dystocia: Prevalence, and association with cranial conformation and breed', *Veterinary Record*, vol 136, no 14, pp350–353

61  Cat Fanciers' Association 'Breed profile for Sphynx', www.cfa.org/breeds/profiles/Sphynx.html, accessed June 2009

62  Bond, R. et al (2008) 'Carriage of *Malassezia* spp yeasts in Cornish Rex, Devon Rex and domestic short-haired cats: A cross-sectional survey', *Veterinary Dermatology*, vol 19, no 5, pp299–304

63  Chang, J. H. et al (2007) 'Osteochondrodysplasia in three Scottish Fold cats', *Journal of Veterinary Science*, vol 8, no 3, pp307–309

64  Rah, H. C., Maggs, D. J. and Lyons, L. A. (2006) 'Lack of genetic association among coat colors, progressive retinal atrophy and polycystic kidney disease in Persian cats', *Journal of Feline Medicine and Surgery*, vol 8, no 5, pp357–360; Djajadiningrat-Laanen, S. C. et al (2002) 'Progressive retinal atrophy in Abyssinian and Somali cats in the Netherlands (1981–2001)', *Tijdschrift voor Diergeneeskunde*, vol 127, no 17, pp508–514

65  Menotti-Raymond, M. et al (2007) 'Mutation in CEP290 discovered for cat model of human retinal degeneration', *Journal of Heredity*, vol 98, no 3, pp211–220

66  McCann, T. M. (2007) 'Feline diabetes mellitus in the UK: The prevalence within an insured cat population and a questionnaire-based putative risk factor analysis', *Journal of Feline Medicine and Surgery*, vol 9, no 4, pp289–299

67  Bonazzi, M. et al (2007) 'Prevalence of the polycystic kidney disease and renal and urinary bladder ultrasonographic abnormalities in Persian and Exotic Shorthair cats in Italy', *Journal of Feline Medicine and Surgery*, vol 9, no 5, pp387–391; University of California, Davis *Genetic Test Services for Cats*, www.vgl.ucdavis.edu/services/cat, accessed June 2009; Barrs, V. R. et al (2001) 'Prevalence of autosomal dominant polycystic kidney disease in Persian cats and related-breeds in Sydney and Brisbane', *Australian Veterinary Journal*, vol 79, no 4, pp257–259

68  *Nature* (2005) 'A purrfect model?: Research highlights', *Nature*, vol 438, 8 December, pp714–715

69  Brown, R. (2008) 'Haemophilia in Maine Coon cats', *Veterinary Record*, vol 163, no 22, p667

70  Halls, V. (2009) 'Playing detective', *The Cat*, spring, pp30–31; Turner, D. C. (2000) 'Human–cat interactions: Relationship with, and breed differences between, non-pedigree, Persian and Siamese cats', in A. L. Podberscek, E. S. Paul and J. A. Serpell (eds) *Companion Animals and Us: Exploring the Relationships between People and Pets*, Cambridge University Press, pp257–271

71  Paull, N. J. and Hall, E. J. (2008) 'Breeding of pedigree dogs', *Veterinary Record*, vol 163, no 16, p491

72  Bell, J. S. (2006) 'American breed clubs and health initiatives', in E. A. Ostrander, U. Giger and K. Lindblad-Toh (eds) *The Dog and Its Genome*, Cold Spring Harbor Laboratory Press, pp31–45

73  Martin, M. W. S. and Corcoran, B. M. (1997) *Cardiorespiratory Diseases of the Dog and Cat*, Blackwell Science, Library of Veterinary Practice

74  Companion Animal Welfare Council (2008) *Fixing Ancestral Problems: Genetics and Welfare in Companion Animals Focusing on Syringomyelia in Cavalier King Charles Spaniels as an Example*, Report of the Companion Animal Welfare Council Workshop, Tuesday, 29 April 2008, House of Lords

75  Kennel Club (2006) 'KC/BSAVA purebred dog health survey', News release, Kennel Club, 15 August; Kennel Club (2006) *Individual Breed Results for Purebred Dog Health Survey*, Kennel Club, 18 August; *Dogs Today* (2008) August, p72

76  *Veterinary Record* (2008) 'Kennel Club launches review of UK pedigree dog breeds', *Veterinary Record*, vol 163, no 16, 18 October, p464

77  Muir, M. (2007) 'Lots of pugs and kisses, darling', *The Field*, July, pp62–64

78  *Little Black Dog Book*, supplement to *Dogs Today* (2007), July; see also owners' accounts of the health problems of their dogs

79  *Dogs Today* (2007) June, p36; Redpath, K. (2008) 'Is this the end of the Cavalier?', *Dogs Today*, November, pp14–16

80  Kennel Club (2004) *Memorandum of Evidence Submitted to the Sub-Committee on the Draft Animal Welfare Bill of the Environment, Food and Rural Affairs Committee of the House of Commons*, 7 September, para 13.1

81  Council of Europe, Treaty Office (1987) Documents relating to the Convention for the Protection of Pet Animals, ETS 125, 1987

82  Council of Europe (1995) *Report of the Meeting of the Multilateral Consultation on the European Convention for the Protection of Pet Animals (ETS 125)*, Strasbourg, 7–10 March 1995

83  Companion Animal Welfare Council (2008) *Approaches to Tackling Genetic Welfare Problems in Companion Animals*, Report of the Companion Animal Welfare Council Workshop, 9 October 2008, Westminster, CAWC

84  Horton-Bussey, C. (2008) 'Sum-thing has to be done!', *Dogs Today*, December, pp14–16

# 7
# Sports Animals: Breeding Gladiators

## 7.1 Background and context: Breeding, racing and betting

### 7.1.1 Gladiators and money: The value of the industry

Animals used in spectator sports, such as racehorses and greyhounds, are often described as 'athletes'. Greyhounds are 'superlative canine athletes', according to the Society of Greyhound Veterinarians.[1] But in the way that society utilizes and views them, racing greyhounds and racehorses are more like gladiators. Like gladiators, their participation is only partly voluntary and they are disposable when their success or utility ends. Like gladiators, they sometimes die in the cause of the sport. Animal gladiators occupy an ambiguous region in human society where admiration, enthusiasm, instrumentalism and sometimes cruelty are combined. They are not expected to interact with humans in the home and are not bred for suitability as companion animals. Yet they (or at least those that perform successfully) are much admired as individuals and their success is identified with ours. Some are made into legends. At the least, the successful ones are respected as valuable commodities.

Breeding the animal gladiators is a game of skill and chance. The primary breeding goal is to produce an animal that wins races but it is the human owner who actually wins, not the horse or dog. It is fair to assume that horses and dogs have not evolved to understand the concept of winning a race, much less a monetary prize, and it seems unlikely that they spend the night before the Gold Cup worrying about whether they are going to win. Humans have capitalized on the animals' evolved and selected motivation to run fast: they run to escape a predator, to keep up with a running herd, to catch and kill prey, or merely for the enjoyment of exercise or of obtaining praise from owners and handlers.

By the end of the 20th century, racing horses and dogs existed in large part to be a medium for public betting, involving large sums of money. According to the British Horseracing Authority, flat and jump racing together contribute nearly UK£3 billion to the economy, including tax revenues of nearly UK£300 million, and results in UK£10 billion in off-course betting and UK£104 million in prize money.[2] Greyhound racing, a much smaller and less wealthy sport in

Britain, in 2008 generated betting of UK£2.9 million and UK£11 million in prize money.[3] The deregulation of gambling has considerably reduced the number of people who attend greyhound races because other gambling media became available. In spite of this, in 2006 in England, over 3 million people annually attended dog races and around 6 million people attended horse races.[4]

More importantly for owners, the animals earn money from winnings, sales and stud fees. Breeding and training racehorses and racing dogs can be described as a partly large-scale and industrialized, partly enthusiast activity. In the US, professional thoroughbred breeding expanded from being a home-based business of a few very wealthy owners in the southern states at the start of the 19th century to 'agricultural corporations that involve vast sums of money and sizable staffs of people' by the mid 20th century.[5] However, many smaller breeders do not expect to make significant amounts of money and in the UK there are fewer than 10,000 'active' racehorse owners.[2]

## 7.1.2 Historical breeding of greyhounds and racehorses

In the thousands of years during which horses have been bred by people for various functions, racing was far from being the most essential. Much of the work of horses was high status in that it involved carrying the great, the warlike and the victorious through their careers. Horse breeding up to the 20th century was an essential activity, rather than the recreation it has become today. It provided horses for cavalry, riding and carriage work and until the advent of the motor vehicle a good horse had the importance, value and relative price of a high-performance car today, Oliver Cromwell in 1643 offered to pay the owner of a premium horse 'all that you ask for that black you won last fight'.[6] Horses were national assets. In 1915, when Britain needed cavalry horses during World War I, an official show of Thoroughbred stallions was organized to find suitable sires for cross-breeding, with a prize donated by the king.[7] In 1916 the National Stud was founded essentially as a state-owned Thoroughbred breeding operation.

People have also been betting on the running abilities of specialized animal athletes for centuries, if not millennia. By the 16th century in England, the precursor to organized horseracing took the form of 'matches' where two members of the gentry or aristocracy made a wager as to which of their horses would win over a prescribed course. Horses were being bred for racing and betting as well as their other main purposes; Thomas Blunderville's *The Art of Ryding and Breaking Greate Horses* (1566) lists breeds of 'Great Horses' suitable for war, smaller 'ambling horses' for general travelling purposes, another breed used only for draught or burden, owned by 'plain country men', and then 'a race of swift runners to run for wagers or to gallop the buck'.[6] Aristocracy and royalty operated breeding studs and there is early evidence of selection and record-keeping and the use of imported Arab, Turk or Spanish stallions to modify the local horse breeds long before the Thoroughbred racehorse breed was established.[8] The racecourses of Newmarket, Ascot and Epsom started business in the 17th to 18th centuries when racing became the 'Sport of Kings' and racehorse breeding became a powerful enthusiasm with the aristocracy and sporting gentry from then until the 21st century.

The Thoroughbred breed originated as a local English variant of the fast and light North African and Middle Eastern horse typically known as Arabs, Barbs (from the Barbary or North African coast) or Turks.[8] The breed was created specifically for racing, and was developed by importing stallions and using them to breed from native, cross-bred or sometimes Barb mares. The genetic pool of the breed became closed in 1791 when the General Stud Book was created, and a pedigree recorded in the General Stud Book came to define a horse's membership of the Thoroughbred breed. There is now an effectively closed population of Thoroughbreds globally of around 300,000 individuals.[9]

Hunting dogs with an appearance similar to greyhounds have been bred for thousands of years and were depicted in ancient Egypt. Medieval depictions of hunting and domestic scenes show that greyhounds were popular with the aristocracy in Europe, were kept in kennels, wore collars and even received veterinary attention to their mouths and legs (sometimes apparently under protest). Hunting with hounds was identified as an aristocratic pursuit, and in England before the Norman Conquest the poor were forbidden to own greyhounds.[10] Both horses and greyhounds have long been considered superior animals and human helpers, distinguished by characteristics of loyalty and nobility, who will 'win for you'.

Modern greyhound racing on tracks originated in hare-coursing, a 'blood sport' of competitive chasing and killing of hares; latterly hares were brought to the event in boxes and released for the purpose. The most prestigious event in English hare-coursing was the Waterloo Cup, the last event taking place in 2005 amid scenes of minor civil disturbance, a few days before the legislation to prohibit hare-coursing came into force. From the 1920s, greyhound racing on circular tracks in pursuit of a mechanical hare was introduced in Britain and the US and became an exceptionally popular spectator sport and betting medium, attracting 15 million spectators in Britain per year in its heyday around 1960.[4]

According to the early chronicler of racing greyhounds James Matheson, until the 1920s greyhound breeding was 'in the hands of men and women to whom money was no object' and greyhound rearing in the north of England was 'a great industry'. These people contracted 'puppy rearers' who in turn placed pregnant bitches and their puppies in 'walks', the term for small farmers or cottagers in remote rural districts. The 'puppy rearer' would be paid '£1 per sapling delivered fit and well at Carlisle station', ready for serious training. In the south of England, a system of greyhound rearing by small farmers and dairymen in large paddocks was used. Breeding bitches were mated in the late autumn so that they would give birth in January and their puppies could race successfully in the autumn of the following year.[11] These dogs were not companion animals, and in the absence of modern veterinary treatments both natural selection and human selection probably ensured that only the most healthy and promising puppies survived to breed.

### 7.1.3 The hereditary principle and the Thoroughbred

Starting centuries before modern genetics, the breeding of racing horses has always relied on a belief in the transmissible traits of outstanding individuals and families, the horses' prestige mirroring that of their generally wealthy owners. Racehorses of note in the 17th and 18th centuries had to have Arabian, Turkish or Barb ancestry. Inheritance of traits was generally thought to be through males. The racehorse breeder Federico Tesio famously commented in his 1958 book *Breeding the Racehorse*: 'The Arabs say that the mare is like a sack which gives back what has been put into it. This is not strictly true, but neither is it strictly false.'[12] Tesio was following a long line of thinking about the inheritance of traits, in which the male 'influence' was thought to carry the important characteristics of the offspring while the female provided the physical material; according to Aristotle, the ideal offspring would be almost a replica of his father.[8]

The origin of the Thoroughbred breed has long been a subject of debate, legend, record and, latterly, genetic analysis, and discussion in the early 20th century included speculation on the breed's descent from horses imported by Solomon in the 10th century BCE and from the African zebra.[13] According to the General Stud Book, today's global Thoroughbred breed is descended from a small number of North African or Middle Eastern stallions imported to England in the early 18th century, particularly the three males known as the Darley Arabian (acquired by Thomas Darley in the North African port of Aleppo), the Byerley Turk (possibly captured from a Turkish officer by Captain Byerley in the late 17th century), and the Godolphin Arabian (possibly born in the Arabian Peninsula and acquired by Lord Godolphin in the early 18th century). These three stallions are celebrated as the 'foundation sires' of the breed. Racehorse breeding probably reached America with the importation to Virginia in 1730 of the stallion Bulle Rock, who had both the Darley Arabian and the Byerley Turk as ancestors.[13]

The ancestry of the modern population of Thoroughbreds in England and Ireland has been studied by statistical analysis of their pedigrees combined with DNA microsatellite analysis of their relationships.[9] This showed that the genetics of the modern population derives from very few horses. The results identified 158 founder horses born before 1750, about equal numbers of males and females who were responsible for 81 per cent of the genetics in the 1990 sample of Thoroughbreds. On this analysis, the most significant founders to the 1990 generation were the Godolphin Arabian (born 1725), the Darley Arabian (born 1700), the Ruby Mare (born 1742), the Curwen Bay Barb Mare (born 1693) and the Byerley Turk (born 1675). By the mid 19th century, only the sire lines of the Godolphin Arabian, the Darley Arabian and the Byerley Turk remained, and today the Darley Arabian sire line alone is responsible for

95 per cent of the paternal lines in the modern population through his famous great-great grandson Eclipse (born 1764). The top 20 founder females were responsible for 89 per cent of the modern female lines.[9] Subsequent analysis of mitochondrial DNA markers and pedigrees showed that there is considerable uncertainty over the recording of maternal ancestry and that unsung native mares, including Irish and Scottish breeds, had an important maternal influence on the creation of the Thoroughbred.[14]

## 7.1.4 Approaches to breeding winners

In the absence of genetic tests, breeders concentrated on breeding from winners or the families of winners and this is still the strategy today. The famous horse Flying Childers, born in 1715, was a son of the Darley Arabian. His brother, Bartlett's Childers, was considered useless for racing but fathered the second 'great' racehorse Eclipse, born in 1764 and never beaten. Eclipse (who came close to being gelded because of his bad temper) was the father of three Derby winners and in total his offspring won 344 races. The never-beaten St Simon, born in 1881, was mated with 775 mares, 554 of whom gave birth to foals who subsequently won a total of 571 races.[15] The skeletons of St Simon and his son Persimmon were duly presented to the Natural History Museum by their owners the Duke of Cumberland and King Edward VII, respectively.[16] Federico Tesio in 1958 listed several examples from the 18th to the 20th centuries of winning horses who were also the parents of winners, but noted that two offspring of the same parents could also have completely different racing abilities. (Tesio also read an account of Mendelian genetic theory by chance during a train journey in 1906 and concluded that it provided a 'revelation' of why breeding produced uncertain results.)[12]

Other racehorse breeding theories that pre-date modern genetics include Bruce Lowe's *Breeding Race Horses by the Figure System* (1898), which identified the properties of different 'families' of the original foundation mares of the breed and scored them according to the number of winners that they had in the Derby, Oaks and St Leger. The biological statistician Francis Galton (1822–1911) constructed a 'stamina index' for racehorses on the basis of their ancestors' running form. The French ex-military officer Vuillier proposed a system in the 1920s that allowed the breeder to calculate the required 'dosages' of particular pedigrees that would produce the desired racehorse and make decisions about which stallion and mare to breed from (the Aga Khan is said to have used the 'dosage' method in planning matings in his stud farm).[15]

Some famous male racehorses failed to live up to expectations as transmitters of success to the next generation, a fact that 19th- and 20th-century breeders accepted but had no explanation for. The top American racehorse of the 1880s, Salvator, was 'undefeated' at four years old and 'the idol of the entire turf world', but when he was retired to stud 'he failed utterly to reproduce himself' in spite of being sent the very best mares to inseminate. Lexington (1850–1875), one of the most famous American Thoroughbred sires, fathered 600 offspring, of which one third were winners[17] – a relatively low return on investment. A study of the racing performance ratings of over 30,000 Thoroughbreds during the mid 20th century found that the average rating of stallions was 42 per cent higher than that of the colts they fathered.[18]

An inevitable consequence of breeding animals with the sole aim of winning is that there must be more individuals that are average or below average than those that prove outstanding for the required task. Because the task is competitive, it is logically impossible to breed only winners. This would be true even if genetic science were eventually able, by DNA analysis or even cloning, to ensure that only the 'winning genes' were transmitted. The ethical problem then arises that the individual horses are being bred and trained to take part in a never-ending human-devised competition or lottery, in which many will inevitably fail to satisfy the requirements.

## 7.2 Industry practices: The use of racehorses and greyhounds

### 7.2.1 The uses of Thoroughbreds

The Thoroughbred was developed for maximum sprinting speed over a relatively short distance of 1 to 2 miles in flat racing and also for running 3 to 4.5 miles in jump racing. Today's Thoroughbred is tall, with fine long legs, and can be over 17 hands (1.7m) in height, compared to up to 16 hands for the equivalent American Standardbred, a breed developed to create a fast but sturdier horse currently used for harness and trotting racing.

Thoroughbred racing horses are produced and managed in yearly batches and are all considered to be of the same age, dated 1 January of the year they are born (1 August in the Southern Hemisphere). At one year old they are offered in the yearling sales. Flat racers begin being raced in their two-year-old season but jump racers are required to be physically more mature and may begin being raced at four years old. The flat race horses are assessed on the results of their two-year-old and three-year-old race season results. Jump races include hurdle races and steeplechases such as the Grand National.

### 7.2.2 The breeding business

The success of top-performing sports animals is often a prelude to a longer and much more lucrative (for the owner) use as a breeding animal. Male horses and racing dogs are therefore not castrated, or at least not until their racing and breeding potential have been ascertained, except for those used for jump racing. Successful flat-race Thoroughbreds are often withdrawn from racing young, after the three-year-old race season, and spend the rest of their working lives in a stud farm. Very successful racehorses such as Nijinsky and Affirmed, who both won the Triple Crown, can be used for breeding for 20 years after being retired from racing. Sea the Stars won six major races in a row in 2009, promising an estimated UK£100 million in stud earnings.[19]

Some contemporary 'top sires' who have had at least three 'crops' of three-year-old racehorses in successful operation, recorded by the American Jockey Club in 2007, can have offspring who in total earn their owners winnings of as much as US$20 million to $30 million. The stud fees charged for stallions range from a moderate US$2500 up to US$30,000–$40,000 dollars and, exceptionally, as much as US$225,000. Stallions that are mated successfully with a large number of mares in their breeding lives for large stud fees are thus highly profitable for their owners, who may be individuals or syndicates. A stallion who fathers 500 foals could earn his owners millions of dollars, and up to US$1 million in a single season. While the majority of North American Thoroughbred stallions were mated with between a handful and 50 mares, a small minority were mated with well over 100 mares in a year.[20]

With so much at stake, the reproduction of racing animals is intensive and highly controlled, although the rules for Thoroughbred breeding forbid artificial insemination and embryo transfer. A stallion may be transported around the world for use in breeding and a few are used year round during the breeding seasons of the Northern and Southern Hemispheres. Hormone treatment is used to advance or induce oestrus, induce parturition or abort a pregnancy. If twins are conceived, one of them is generally destroyed in the uterus by manipulation and compression. Thoroughbred mares during the breeding season are assessed daily by veterinarians for follicle development and oestrus and subsequently reassessed to confirm pregnancy. Racing greyhounds are produced by artificial insemination, and the trainers of female horses and greyhounds used in performance administer hormones to suppress oestrus when this interferes with their behaviour during racing. In non-Thoroughbred sports horses, such as the Standardbred and the Quarter Horse breeds, artificial insemination is common and more rarely embryo transfer is used with valuable mares. In 2005, over 14,000 horse embryos were reported to have been transferred globally, the majority in the US and Brazil.[21]

## 7.2.3 Breeding for speed

A statistical analysis of Thoroughbred racing performance between 1952 and 1977 found that the genetic potential for speed was increasing by 1 per cent a year for the population as a whole, although this was not showing up in faster winning times in the major races (the 'Cunningham Paradox').[18,22] For practical purposes this should be of no importance to the industry, since in most cases a winning horse only has to be faster than the average of the age group he or she is running with, not faster than the previous generation of horses.

Winning may depend very much on a horse's management and training, an expensive commodity that may currently cost well over UK£10,000 per year, and the offspring of highly rated stallions are likely to have more money spent on them. A 2007 study of racehorses' lifetime prize money and stud fees has concluded that while racing ability (as judged by lifetime earnings from winnings) is heritable, the environmental effects such as good and expensive training account for over 90 per cent of the observed variation in results. There is almost no consistent relationship between the amount of the stud fee and the amount of lifetime earnings of the stallion's offspring.[23] Hence there may be no reliable advantage in paying US$20,000 rather than $2000 for a stallion's fee.

Much research continues to try to identify the genetic or environmental basis of racing success by examining race records and pedigrees. Some of the findings are unsurprising: times are slower on muddy surfaces and faster when the prize money is large; winning horses have large hearts that are able to process larger quantities of oxygen. The genetic basis of speed and endurance remains to be fully elucidated although at least one 'speed gene' has been identified in Thoroughbreds. A possible genetic clue has been found in certain mitochondrial genes in racehorses that code for proteins involved in metabolism in humans, and that could influence fitness and stamina in horses.[24] Since mitochondrial DNA is inherited only from the female line (via the mother's egg cell), this would put the mare rather than the stallion in the forefront of the inheritance of some winning traits. It is even possible to speculate that today's intensive training regimes are counterproductive, given the very high rates of exercise-induced injuries in young horses. Some of the potentially fastest horses may be damaged before they can achieve their potential.

Biotechnology is currently not an option in Thoroughbred breeding, since foals can only be registered if they are the result of natural mating. Although attitudes in the Thoroughbred industry towards reproductive technology could change, racing profits depend on breeding and betting on winners rather than on betting on speeds, and the long-established and costly traditional breeding system may act as a barrier against change. At the other end of the biotechnological spectrum, performance horses have been cloned experimentally by nuclear transfer, starting in Italy in 2003 and the US in 2005, using horse oocytes from slaughterhouses. The first cloned foal born in the US was the result of 400 attempts and the only survivor, after a longer than normal gestation, from six pregnancies. However, cloning by the current method of nuclear transfer does not produce a true genetic copy because the mitochondrial genes of the clone are contributed mostly or entirely by the oocyte that is used to produce the reconstructed embryo. If mitochondrial genes turned out to be an important factor in racing success, cloning by transfer of nuclear DNA would not transfer them to the cloned offspring. Researchers might be motivated to use the newer technology of mtDNA replacement, leading to further invasive experimentation on horses.[25]

### 7.2.4 The greyhound industry

The major greyhound-racing countries are the US, Australia, Ireland and the UK. As with racehorses, the dog racing business involves breeders, trainers, track owners and bookmakers. Possibly even more than in horseracing, the industry is founded on betting; as the Society of Greyhound Veterinarians has put it: 'greyhound racing is staged largely as a gambling medium'.[26] In the UK, there can be over 1400 separate races per week of which around one third are organized by the British Bookmakers Afternoon Service (BAGS), held on weekday afternoons with few spectators, solely as a vehicle for off-track betting. Online gambling has divorced dog racetracks from the betting business and reduced attendance, and both economics and public concerns about the welfare of the dogs are currently putting UK dog racing under pressure.

Compared with the sport of horseracing, greyhounds are relatively inexpensive to buy, train and maintain. Young racing greyhounds sell from a few hundred pounds sterling in Britain (although a top racing dog may cost UK£20,000) and the cost of rearing a puppy to the time that it can be sent to a race track is currently around UK£1250.[3,27] The majority of racing dogs are now owned by their trainers, not by members of the general public.[4] Up to 80 per cent of the dogs raced in England are bred in Ireland, according to the Associate Parliamentary Group on Animal Welfare report *The Welfare of Greyhounds* (2007).[26]

By 2006, around 11,000 new greyhounds were registered annually to race on regulated tracks in the UK (not counting dogs already racing) and around the same number leave racing every year. Up to 4000 additional dogs are raced on tracks outside the regulated system.[26] In the US, over 26,000 greyhound puppies were registered to race with the National Greyhound Association (US) in 2003, although this number may be only 76 per cent of the number of greyhound puppies born in the previous year.[28] (In each of the major racing countries, several thousand greyhound puppies born annually are never used for racing; see sections 7.3.2.3 and 8.2 in Chapter 8.) Racing greyhounds typically stop racing at three or four years old, if not earlier, and can live for 14 years.[26]

## 7.2.5 Greyhound selection and breeding

Greyhounds, like racehorses, are selected for breeding on the basis of their own or their relative's winning performance, and produced both by commercial suppliers and in what may be quite small-scale operations by owners and trainers. In the UK, the Greyhound Breeders Forum provides detailed records on the performance of potential sires and dams and calculations of the inbreeding involved in any potential mating. It advises that the 'object is to produce high-class greyhounds that will make the grade, thus eliminating the chances of having to re-home inferior animals at such an early age'.[27]

Highly regarded stud dogs are very widely used and celebrated for their contribution to the sport. Top Honcho was one of the best-regarded greyhound sires of the 1990s, born in Australia in 1993 and used for breeding in Ireland until his death in 2007. His father, Head Honcho, won 13 of his 15 races and was rated as the top Australian greyhound stud over several years. According to industry-compiled records, Top Honcho produced 9936 offspring, of which 21 per cent were run in major races[29] and included several of the most successful racing dogs in England and Ireland of his time. Top Honcho's pedigree

**Table 7.1** *Examples of breeding by some top-rated greyhound bitches of 2008*

| Races run (dates) | Races won | Number of litters (dates) | Number of offspring | Number of highly rated offspring (ran in major events) |
|---|---|---|---|---|
| 36 (2001–2002) | 24 | 5 (2003–2006) | 38 | 31 |
| 7 (2001) | 1 | 7 (2000–2005) | 42 | 28 |
| 8 (2003–2004)[†] | 2 | 3 (2005–2006) | 23 | 11 |
| 0[‡] | – | 4 (2003–2007) | 28 | 16 |

*Notes:* † Daughter of Top Honcho.
‡ Grand-daughter of Top Honcho.
*Source: Greyhound Data*[29]

includes the famous Australian dog Temlee, born in 1972, who was raced for 15 months and 37 races before breaking a bone on track. Temlee appears seven times in Top Honcho's pedigree.[29] Female racing dogs are also capable of working very hard for their owners, both on the track and in breeding (see Table 7.1). The mother of one of 2008's top-rated bitches, born in 1994, had produced 61 offspring in nine litters by January 2004.[29]

Since the early 1990s, the use of artificial insemination (AI) has become much more common, and by 2003 accounted for 86 per cent of the National Greyhound Association-registered puppies born in the US, and 70 per cent of the puppies being produced by frozen/thawed semen.[28] As we have seen in the case of food production animals, achieving a high conception rate with AI requires precise knowledge of the time of ovulation, which involves blood testing the bitch to ascertain levels of progesterone. Surgical insemination is more likely to be used when the semen is frozen/thawed (although surgical insemination is not considered permissible for routine use by veterinarians in the UK (see section 5.4.5 in Chapter 5). The disadvantages of AI for greyhound bitches are the invasive procedures (drawing blood for testing, possible surgery involving general anaesthesia), but there may be advantages in avoiding other stresses, such as transport to a stud, that are involved in 'natural' mating.

## 7.3 The impact on animals: Survival of the fittest

The main welfare concerns about the methods and strategies of breeding racing horses and dogs can be summarized as:

- over-breeding of animals compared to the number that will be successfully used in the sport;
- short working lifetimes and early deaths due to unsuitability or early injury;
- levels of injury and deaths in training and racing;
- the continuous production by the industries of surplus or rejected animals that need to be re-homed by the public or destroyed (see section 8.2 in Chapter 8);

- breeding for physical characteristics, such as speed, that are likely to increase injuries;
- breeding and management for behavioural characteristics that make the animals less suitable for 'second careers' or re-homing;
- a historical acceptance in the industry that injuries and deaths are a normal part of the sport.

## 7.3.1 Racehorses

### 7.3.1.1 Over-breeding and wastage

A competitive breeding industry inevitably produces more animals than turn out to be useful for the purpose: in this case, winning races. The annual production cycle that fuels the yearling sales and the established schedules of two-year-old and three-year-old flat racing require a constant supply of new recruits. The number of recorded Thoroughbred foals born in Britain and Ireland increased from 2004 to 2008 and was over 18,000 per year by 2008, produced from around 750 stallions and nearly 31,000 mares. In the US, up to 35,000 Thoroughbred foals are registered with the Jockey Club annually (33,500 in 2008), bred from nearly 3000 stallions and 52,000 mares.[30]

A British study from Cambridge University Veterinary Department of 1022 Thoroughbred foals up to three years old appears to be the only public systematic study of the UK horseracing industry's usage and wastage. This showed that only 47 per cent of the non-exported horses were still being entered for races at age three (see Table 7.2).[31]

A study of 1804 horses from Queensland, Australia, also showed 'high wastage'. Only 46 per cent were still being raced two years after their first race and nearly 30 per cent were raced for only one year or less.[32] In the US, Jockey Club records at 2006 showed that only 70 per cent of registered foals raced at least once, with an average of 16 or 17 races in the horse's racing lifetime. These statistics indicated average racing lifetimes of under three years (although the averages may be lowered by the fact that some fillies with a 'high-fashion pedigree' are likely to be withdrawn from racing early for breeding purposes).[33]

**Table 7.2** *Production and usage of 1022 Thoroughbred foals born in 1999 up to age three*

| Started training at age 2 or 3 in Britain or Ireland | Percentage of 2-year-olds in training never raced | Total horses in training in Britain and Ireland aged 3 years | Percentage of 3 year olds in training never raced | Exported | Died, destroyed or untraceable |
|---|---|---|---|---|---|
| 55% of cohort (562 horses) | 39% | 45% of cohort | 24% | 28% of cohort | 9% of cohort or 13% of horses not exported |

*Source:* Wilsher et al (2006)[31]

### 7.3.1.2 Speed, injuries and deaths

For the very reason that racehorses have been designed for running, they are in danger of being overworked or even 'raced to death'. The public collapse on track of Best Mate at Exeter racecourse in 2005 (from a heart attack), after winning the Gold Cup three times, of the 2006 Kentucky Derby winner Barboro in the Preakness Stakes the same year (from a broken leg), and of Eight Belles as she just failed to win the Kentucky Derby in 2008 (from two broken legs) caused a general, if temporary, public revulsion and questioning of the ethics of horseracing. These special cases caught public attention, but in fact injuries and deaths are not uncommon. 2 out of 29 horses died in a single jump race at Aintree in April 2008 (the Topham Chase); the nine-year-old Time To Sell fell after jumping a 5 foot obstacle in the 43rd race of his life and the seven-year-old In The Long Grass hit the top of the eighth fence and turned a somersault, in the 25th race of his life and his third race in a month.[34]

At the high-profile annual jump races such as the Grand National and the Cheltenham Festival in England, deaths occur in most years (see Table 7.3). Steeplechases have a sevenfold greater risk of death compared to flat races and horses are nearly five times more likely to fall on the first occasion that they run a hurdle race.[35,36]

Dozens of scientific and veterinary studies have shown that horses that run faster, farther and more often, in training or on racetracks, are more likely to be injured and killed, mainly from muscle and bone injury.[36,37] A 2006 study from the University of Liverpool Veterinary Clinical Science Department examined the circumstances, using race videos, of 109 cases of fatal fractures of the lower legs of horses on UK racecourses over two years up to January 2001.[38] More than 75 per cent of fractures were spontaneous and not caused by a fall or a collision. Sixty-six per cent of foreleg fractures were in the leg that the horse was leading with at the time. Horses were more likely to sustain a fatal fracture if: they were doing well in the race; their jockeys were encouraging them to go even faster in the ten seconds before the fracture; they had been reluctant to start the race.[38]

According to the British Horseracing Authority (BHA) in 2009, the rate of fatal injury at races is 2 per 1000 runners: 0.6 per 1000 in flat racing, and 4 per 1000 in jump racing.[39] The BHA does not take account of horses subsequently

**Table 7.3** *Deaths or fatal injuries in high-profile jump races, the UK*

|  | 2009 | 2008 | 2007 | 2006 |
|---|---|---|---|---|
| Grand National (single race) | One died on course (heart failure); one collapsed, revived with oxygen | One | One | One |
| Cheltenham Festival races (four days) | One | One | Two | Nine + two injured and subsequently destroyed |

*Source:* Kennedy (2008);[35] BBC News reporting of Grand National, 2009; Animal Aid[40]

Reproduced by permission of Animal Aid

**Figure 7.1** *A fall on the racetrack*

destroyed after the race meeting due to injuries sustained at the track, so the total death rate is undoubtedly higher. Independent measures from 1990 to 1999 indicated fatalities of from 1 per 1000 runners in flat racing, 5 per 1000 runners in hurdle racing, and 7 per 1000 runners in steeplechases. This means that for a jump race meeting that involves 500 horses, such as the Cheltenham Festival, it is statistically likely that a horse will die.[35] A Canadian survey of data from two racetracks in Ontario concluded that a cumulative death rate of one or two horses per week 'should be considered typical'.[41] Four horses died during the 2010 Cheltenham Festival.[40]

Training at a correct level increases bone strength; but excessive training at speed makes fractures more likely. A study from the Animal Health Trust at Newmarket recorded 148 cases of exercise-induced leg fracture during the training runs of 1178 Thoroughbreds over two years and found that those horses that were exercised the most within a month at a canter or gallop were more at risk of injury. 56 of the fractures occurred in 335 horses in the study that were entered into training as yearlings, when they had immature skeletons.[42] 'Shin soreness' (inflammation of the metacarpus) in young Thoroughbreds is common, and is considered a 'major animal welfare concern, and a cause of industry wastage'.[43,44] Studies from the University of Melbourne and the University of California have likewise shown that the accumulation of high-speed exercise, by training or racing, increases the risk of death from catastrophic leg injury.[45]

Steeplechasing makes great demands on the horse's bones, muscles and tendons. Arkle, born in 1957, was considered 'the greatest [steeple]chaser ever', and won 22 out of the 26 races he was entered for over a four-year racing lifetime. In 1966 the pedal bone in his hoof cracked during the King George VI chase and he could 'scarcely hobble' from the course. He was destroyed four years later at the age of 13 due to increasing joint pain.[19]

The animal protection organization Animal Aid monitored English racecourses over 12 months from March 2007 in order to record fatal injuries, and posted these deaths on the internet as they occurred. In total, 161 deaths were recorded, an average of three per week, which may be an underestimate since not all racecourses could be fully monitored. Animal Aid estimates that deaths that occur at the racecourse account for well under half of all deaths attributable to training or racing injuries or for commercial reasons. During the 12 months monitored, ten racecourses had two or more deaths in a single day, two named jockeys each rode seven horses that were fatally injured during a race, and two named trainers were the trainers of seven and six of the horses that died, respectively.[40] The relationship between speed and injury means that some will regard speed as a breeding goal as ethically very questionable. Others argue that the genotype merely sets the limit as to how fast a horse can run, and that it is the training methods and other environmental factors that determine whether the horse can reach that speed and whether it can be done safely.

### 7.3.1.3 Breeding and robustness

The Thoroughbred Breeders Association has a mission statement that includes 'the improvement of British bred horses as judged by success achieved on the racecourse', raising concern that current breeding goals may be too narrow. There are increasing questions from within as well as outside the industry as to whether Thoroughbred breeding goals are now sufficiently focused on the durability of the horses.

The American Jockey Club research foundation said in 2008 that 'the consensus of a broad representation of industry leaders was that Thoroughbreds today tend to be less sound, rugged and durable than in the past'. One indicator was the fact that the average number of races run by a Thoroughbred in 2006 was only 6.4 compared to 11 in 1960[33] (although this may also be related to large increases in the number of horses bred and available to race). The Jockey Club's Welfare and Safety Summit of 2008 had concerns that the very large number of mares that some stallions are mated to may have affected the genetic diversity, health and quality of the breed.[46]

A contribution to the 2008 workshop of the British Association for Animal Science on the welfare of animals in sport detailed the areas of concern among experts about the deterioration of the quality of Thoroughbreds over the last several decades, including:[47]

- increased fragility;
- decreasing soundness;
- less good bone;
- less good respiratory system ('wind'): 80 per cent of two year olds in training develop airway inflammatory disease;
- reduced disease resistance;
- increased nervousness and harder to train;
- corrective surgery allows 'basically unsound' horses to be sold and entered for training.

Between 10 and 20 per cent of racehorses develop the condition known as dorsal displacement of the soft palate (DDSP), possibly due to exercise-induced inflammation, in which the soft palate obstructs the airway when the horse is running. In order to maintain the horse's respiratory and running performance, the owner may decide to have the soft palate reduced by surgery or a tongue-tie may be used during training and racing. A tongue-tie is a length of cloth looped around the horse's tongue and then tied firmly under the jaw so that the tongue is held down on the floor of the mouth, serving to increase significantly the horse's air intake and earnings from winnings. Thoroughbreds are also predisposed to cervical vertebral stenotic myelopathy (compression of the spine, a cause of 'wobbler syndrome'), found to affect 1.3 per cent of Thoroughbreds born in stud farms surveyed in 2000–2006 and usually leading to euthanasia.[48]

The breeding and management of Thoroughbreds for extreme athleticism, and their possible injuries, can make them psychologically or physically unsuitable for any other purpose. Some ex-racing Thoroughbreds are unable to adapt to another way of life and humane destruction can be the 'only sensible course'. About 90 per cent of the horses taken in by the Thoroughbred Rehabilitation Trust in the UK come from multiple post-racing homes,[47] suggesting that they have been unable to fit into any of them satisfactorily.

### 7.3.1.4 Intensive breeding versus natural behaviour
The intensive nature of racehorse breeding is inconsistent in many ways with the natural reproductive behaviour of horses. Horses are social animals living in herds, typically in a home range covering a large area. Within the herd the breeding groups consist of a mature stallion and several mares (the 'harem band').[49,50] Unlike some other domesticated animals, in natural conditions a stallion stays with his group of mares all year round, protecting and herding

them. The foals suckle for up to a year and stay with their natal band for up to three years, before dispersing to other stallion bands or to form bachelor bands. Foals are born in spring, after an 11 month gestation, and their mothers come back into season typically nine days after foaling (the 'foal heat') and generally become pregnant again at this time. In natural conditions the stallion will know his mares well and will only mate with the familiar mares of his band. When the mares are coming into oestrus the stallion monitors their reproductive condition by their behaviour (such as approaching him, standing with tail raised) and by smell and taste, and he is able to assess when they are willing to mate.[49,50]

Horses under modern management of stud farms are asked to adapt to practices that are very different from these natural behaviour patterns. Fillies and colts are often segregated at weaning, and horses are often kept individually stabled. Stallions are usually kept isolated for life. During their rearing, stallions have no learning experience of social interaction with fillies and mares and a stallion is expected to mate with unknown mares and even with mares who may not be in oestrus and are therefore unwilling or hostile.[50] Typically, the mare will be transported to the stud farm before her foal is due and kept there until she is confirmed to be pregnant again, when she is returned to her owner with the foal. Multiple veterinary checks for oestrus and ovulation and sessions of 'teasing' or 'trying' the mare are often needed. 'Teasing' refers to introducing the mare to an (unfamiliar) stallion to assess her response to him across a partition, in controlled conditions requiring two handlers, and a mare not in oestrus can react aggressively to a stallion's approach. Often the teaser stallion used is of lower value than the stud stallion because of the risk of being injured by the mare.

Intensive stud farms may operate three mating sessions a day. If judged to be in oestrus, the mare is taken to the stallion under strictly controlled conditions, requiring up to four handlers, and the proceedings may be videoed for proof of covering. In order to protect both the mare and the valuable stallion, elaborate precautions are taken and the mare may be equipped with a selection of the following: a neck guard with biting roll (to protect her if the stallion bites her); an ear or nose 'twitch' to control her; a withers pad; 'covering boots' (to prevent her injuring the stallion if she kicks him); a 'breeding roll' placed under her tail to increase the stallion's distance and avoid internal injury; a tail bandage (to keep it out of the way); and possibly she has one foreleg tied up, or is tied with hind-leg hobbles to prevent her from lunging forwards away from the stallion; occasionally, tranquillizing drugs may be used. A 'twitch' is a form of clamp put on the sensitive nose area and twisted painfully if the animal moves. Many mares have young foals at the time of mating and the foals may have to be temporarily removed for 'teasing' or mating.[50] All these interventions are likely to increase stress and could decrease the chance of a successful mating.

Foals are normally weaned at six months old, isolated and kept separately from their mothers or from other adult horses. Both the mare and the foal can be very disturbed by abrupt weaning. Less drastic methods such as batch weaning ('paddock weaning') are believed to be less damaging, where a group of foals and their mothers are brought up together in a paddock and the mares are removed one by one each day.[50] Surveys of foals weaned by a number of methods have found that as many as 30 per cent can develop stereotypic oral behaviours indicative of stress, such as wood-chewing and crib-biting, as well as mouthing and nosing other horses and foals, stereotypic pacing and weaving.[51]

Natural mating systems, where the stallion is left on range or pasture with familiar mares, would probably achieve higher conception rates than 'in-hand' mating. But in a natural system the stallion mates several times with each mare during her oestrus, a wasteful procedure that limits the number of mares he can impregnate during a season. As a result, 'breeders feel the need to control events to protect the investment made, maximize the number of mares covered per season and minimize the risk of injury to stock'.[50]

To suit foaling dates to the racing calendar, it is common to advance the Thoroughbred mare's natural breeding season by using artificial lighting, sometimes supplemented by hormone treatment. Foals born earlier in the year will be (often but not always) more effective when they are first raced at two years old and more attractive in the yearling sales. Breeding mares are treated with progesterone-type drugs such as Regumate for a number of reasons related to reproduction control: for suppressing oestrus, for encouraging normal oestrous cycling, for timing ovulation (for the efficient use of stallions), and for maintaining pregnancy. 'Twin reduction' involves the mare in several days of intramuscular injections with antibiotics, an intravenous analgesic on the day the unwanted foetus is killed, followed by months of oral progesterone treatment.

Thoroughbred breeding may be an area where artificial insemination might have a positive impact on the well-being of horses by removing some of the stresses associated with transport and in-hand mating at stud farms. Currently the Thoroughbred racing industry does not permit it. Whatever vested interests may be involved in this policy, it is also true that some breeders retain, or claim to retain, the ancient belief that the process of natural mating in some way transmits energy and winning abilities to the offspring.[12,52]

## 7.3.2 Greyhounds

### 7.3.2.1 Breeding goals, stress and injuries

The speed of greyhounds, as measured by racing times, is moderately heritable and a study of over 40,000 Irish greyhounds from 2000 to 2003 concluded that greyhounds were becoming faster.[53] Intensive breeding for speed has designed greyhounds as sprinting machines, and this has created physiological and physical peculiarities in greyhounds compared to other breeds. The blood of young healthy greyhounds of nine to ten months, before their training begins, has higher concentrations of haemoglobin, more red blood cells and fewer white cells than other breeds; the differences are due to breed (genotype), not to training. Young greyhounds have lower levels of the thyroid hormone thyroxine, related to metabolic rate and heat control, than other dogs. Normal racing dogs have a larger heart than other dog breeds or non-racing lines of the breed and the heart becomes larger with training. Greyhounds with apparently enlarged hearts and heart murmurs are sometimes thought to have heart disease, but these are normal features of healthy young dogs of the breed.[54] Their legs have also been designed for their task. Compared to the Pit Bull Terrier (bred for fighting), the greyhound has relatively stiff, brittle limb bones, whereas the Pit Bull Terrier's limb bones have a higher resistance to failure.[55]

Racing subjects the greyhound to extreme physiological stresses. There are 'major physiological changes' in greyhounds, including temperature, blood and heart output, immediately before and during a race.[56] Their level of physiological and psychological stress during the race means that it is a 'not uncommon' problem for young and excitable greyhounds to be unable to pass urine for some time after each race and needing to be catheterized in order to empty the bladder.[57]

As with racehorses, the design of the greyhound for speed inevitably brings injury. Greyhounds can accelerate to a speed of 65km/hour (40 miles/hour) in a few seconds,[56] and have been known to reach 45 miles/hour. The weight of greyhounds increased by 10 per cent between 1970 and 2008 and the speed at which races are run has increased by about 2 per cent, mainly because of changes to the tracks.[58] The dogs exert large stresses on their limbs as they corner, leaning left into the bend to counter the centrifugal force on their bodies. Cornering potentially damages bone, muscle, tendons and ligaments, and makes limb fractures in greyhounds 'very common ... due to stresses of cornering to the left'.[58,59] The greyhound is even considered a 'naturally occurring animal model' of fatigue fracture of the foot bones, due to the compressive loading that occurs on bends.[60] Higher weights and speeds increase the force on the dogs and the impact if they collide with each other as they bunch on bends, or with any other object. In the view of the Associate Parliamentary Group on Animal Welfare (APGAW) in London, older racetracks were not designed for the increased weight and speed of modern greyhounds.[26]

This British parliamentary review also concluded that some greyhounds are now being bred 'for speed rather than longevity and endurance'.[26] Trainers consider that injuries are a normal part of the greyhound's work; they are 'unfortunately ... part of greyhound racing'[57] and 'the physical stresses of racing mean that every greyhound will, at some point, sustain some form of injury'.[61] Indeed, the primary role of veterinarians at race meetings has been to provide first aid and euthanasia for dogs injured on the track.[26] As with racehorses, some will conclude that the relationship between speed and injury makes speed a highly questionable breeding goal, while others will see speed and safety as separate issues, with safety determined largely by management of dogs and design of tracks.

Studies of re-homed and older greyhounds have found that they have a disposition to a bleeding disorder, due to an abnormally low level of platelets (particles that form blood clots) in their blood, and up to 15 per cent bleed profusely after minor injury or surgery. A study of retired racing greyhounds in the US reported in 2007 that the most common diseases among these dogs were skeletal (affecting over 30 per cent of the dogs) and that 6.2 per cent of retired racing greyhounds develop bone cancer (osteosarcoma), which is related to bone stress.[62] Racing greyhounds are more likely to develop bone cancer than any other breed, including the Rottweiler and Great Dane breeds which are known to be predisposed to the disease.[63] In breeding racing whippets, the quest for speed has produced increasing numbers of 'double-muscled' ('bully') whippets, homozygous for the mutated myostatin gene that controls muscle growth. While whippets heterozygous for the mutation are among the fastest, homozygous dogs are grossly over-muscled and subject to muscle cramping, and may be destroyed at a young age.[64]

### 7.3.2.2 Selection for behaviour
Greyhounds or their ancestors have been selected for millennia as hunting dogs and according to the Kennel Club (London) the breed is 'obviously possessed of an insatiable instinct to chase and kill'.[65] In addition, this motivation is deliberately increased in race training and any greyhound that lacks enough of it will be rejected by trainers. Rejected or 'retired' greyhounds are considered by many to be good household companions, calm, friendly and somewhat indolent, but the chase-and-kill motivation remains strong and means that they are a continuing danger to small animals such as domestic cats when re-homed.

### 7.3.2.3 Over-breeding and wastage
Historically, the greyhound industry produced and disposed of large numbers of surplus dogs annually, but precise numbers have been difficult to obtain because there was no obligation to record the disposal of dogs and puppies. The APGAW in London stated in 2007 that the industry regulatory body 'has consistently failed to provide reliable data about the numbers of dogs involved in the industry, about what happens to dogs at the end of their racing career and about incidence and frequency of injury'.[26]

Calculations based on National Greyhound Association (NGA) records indicate that nearly 12,000 racing dogs and nearly 6000 puppies were unaccounted for in the US in 2001, and presumed destroyed.[56] While this is a high number, it represents a large reduction in wastage during the 1990s, probably as a result of the falling popularity of the sport and increasing public criticism (see Table 7.4). The US industry denies that there is now a high wastage of greyhounds and stated in 2008 that 90 per cent of puppies born were subsequently registered to race, and 90 per cent of retired greyhounds were re-homed (adopted) or used for breeding after racing.[66]

The APGAW estimated that in Britain an average of 2478 young dogs per year registered to race are never raced and probably 'a significant number' of these are destroyed (puppies born in Ireland could increase this figure;

**Table 7.4** *Numbers of NGA greyhound puppies produced in the US and probable outcomes, 1991 and 2001*

|  | Puppies born | New dogs registered to race | Dogs homed (adopted) | Dogs used for breeding | Racing dogs presumed destroyed | Puppies presumed destroyed |
|---|---|---|---|---|---|---|
| 1991 | 52,479 | 38,430 | 1000 | 3000 | 33,930 | 14,049 |
| 2001 | 32,698 | 26,797 | 13,000 | 1800 | 11,997 | 5901 |

*Source:* Stafford (2006)[56]

6000–12,000 puppies bred to supply the British market may be unaccounted for annually). Adding the 11,000 racing greyhounds who leave the regulated industry yearly, England and Wales produce a 'surplus' of 13,478 greyhounds per year that need to be re-homed, used for breeding or otherwise disposed of. These figures may be an underestimate because of the existence of racetracks outside the regulated sector and because of the greyhound trade that operates between England and Ireland.[26]

## 7.4 The professionals, the public and the future: Unnecessary breeding?

A competitive sport such as dog and horse racing has two features that almost inevitably involve wastage of animals:

1  Breeding for speed and competitive racing at maximum speed inevitably will result in an increased level of accident and injury.
2  Competitive breeding and competitive racing inevitably involve over-breeding in order to select the most useful and, consequently, wastage of the less useful or injured animals.

These lead to the question: is it necessary for society to continue to produce single-purpose high-speed animals for betting and spectator sport?

### 7.4.1 Public criticism and industry response

There is unlikely to be agreement in the near future between those who accept the traditional values of animal racing and those who view the industry as an unjustifiable exploitation of the animals' potential for speed, to the detriment of animal welfare. The racing industry argues that it is doing what needs to be done, financially and organizationally, to extend the working lifetime of racing animals, reduce injuries and premature deaths, and re-home the large majority of animals not wanted for racing or breeding (see section 8.2 in Chapter 8).

Racing Thoroughbreds and greyhounds are produced as raw material for the racing, betting and breeding industries with a single purpose in view: the ability to win or be placed. We knowingly organize race meetings, such as the Cheltenham Festival, where there is a statistical probability that one of the horses running will be killed. This level of instrumentality is not unusual in animal production, and is normal in the food animal and laboratory animal breeding industries. Both horse and dog racing were developed in an era when respect for the well-being of animals was of little public concern. But some industry practices are now coming into conflict with contemporary attitudes to the proper treatment of dogs and horses. This is only a slow-growing conflict of attitudes in society. In the UK, for example, the BBC has continued to give the major horseracing events such as the Grand National and the Epsom Derby the same uncritical celebratory coverage that it used to accord to the Crufts dog show.

Historically it has always been the case that many of the Thoroughbreds born have not been considered useful for racing and horses have throughout history been injured or killed in accidents or worked to death during their use in war, sports, performance or in courier or draught work. But dog and horse racing today are merely sports, albeit with considerable business and tax implications for both individuals and governments, and arguably not necessary activities for society to pursue if the welfare costs appear too high. The result is that the regulatory authorities for both sports are under pressure to reduce over-breeding, injuries, deaths and wastage. The APGAW stated its belief that 'the greyhound industry should accept that the breeding of large numbers of dogs to supply their industry should be of major concern to that industry'.[26]

Some in the racing industries believe that the criticism is unfair and misplaced. The chairman of the British Greyhound Racing Board has deplored the 'extreme [animal] welfarists' and their 'ignorant abuse' of the industry.[67] But a well-known British greyhound trainer considered in 2007 that 'in greyhound racing, often the last consideration is the greyhounds'.[57] Some in the industry are working to reduce the number of dogs retired at two or three years old though injury because otherwise 'you never get rid of the backlog of greyhounds needing homes'.[57]

Similarly, public pressure has encouraged the British Horseracing Authority to publish overall figures of deaths on racetracks (although not of subsequent deaths), to introduce additional safety features such as a 'bypass track' beside the fences at the Grand National, and to investigate cases of unusual numbers of deaths at a racetrack. The British greyhound industry body in 2008 claimed to spend one third of its annual budget on welfare, including supporting veterinary attendance at events and the Retired Greyhounds Trust, and improving tracks.[68] The North American industry similarly claims to spend millions of dollars supporting greyhound adoption.[66] Some industry professionals deplore the appeal to 'emotion' rather than 'science' by the public and animal protection organizations that are critical of the industry's treatment of animals;[69] but in reality the same public and animal protection organizations provide an important 'sink' that absorbs the surplus animals produced and discarded every year by the racing industries.

## 7.4.2 The veterinary profession and the industry

Veterinarians are highly involved in the horseracing and greyhound industries and may share the racing interests of their clients or employers, while attempting to maintain professional independence. Veterinarians have to negotiate a route between an assessment of the interests of the animal and the interest of the animal users, if these do not coincide. A veterinarian on duty at a race meeting is permitted to destroy a seriously injured horse or dog without waiting for permission from the owner or insurer, who may not be present at the scene. Veterinarians may also be asked by owners to destroy healthy but unwanted horses or greyhounds (see also section 8.2 in Chapter 8).

In the past, veterinarians attending greyhound races have been employed by the racetrack whose welfare standards they are overseeing and, according to Lord Donoughue's review of the British greyhound industry in 2007, many felt that their independence was compromised – for example, withdrawing a dog who they believed was not fit to race could interfere with the race schedule and hence the racetrack profitability.[4] New government guidelines proposed in 2009 would require all dog race meetings to be attended by a veterinarian who would examine all dogs for their fitness to race.[70] The wastage and unrecorded disposal of racing horses and dogs has become of concern to the veterinary profession and was the subject of the annual discussion forum of the British Veterinary Association's Animal Welfare Foundation in 2007.[71]

## 7.4.3 Alternatives for the racing industry

The breeding and use of sentient animals primarily for racing and as a betting medium has inherent ethical problems. Greyhounds can live to more than 12 years of age and horses live into their 20s; but many are discarded by the racing industry at less than five years old. What happens to the dogs or racehorses that turn out not to be suited to the job that they have been produced for, or have come to the end of their often short working lives? Unlike food production animals, there is a very limited market in most developed countries for horse or dog meat. The issue of how we dispose of, and how we could limit, the number of surplus or reject animals that we breed is discussed in Chapter 8.

New solutions need to be found to maintain the racing industries for those who want to use them, while minimizing injury and ensuring a long and healthy life for the animals. Some will believe that these aims are contradictory, and that only the phasing out of live racing will end the exploitation of the animals. Others will see solutions in better breeding programmes and better regulation of training and racing. If the industry and breeders prove unable to ensure high welfare for life, an alternative solution would be to replace live sport by virtual racing. Modern computer game technology is capable of reproducing every element of racing and betting, including stud books and form books, and providing a lifelike reproduction of the experience of watching a live race. Virtual racing could continue to be watched at race tracks for those who so wished and thus continue to provide a good day, or night, at the races.

## Notes

1   Watts, M. (2005) 'In the running?', *Veterinary Record*, vol 156, p474
2   British Horseracing Authority (2008) *Fact Sheets*, www.britishhorseracing.com/inside_horseracing/media/2.5.7.1.asp?item=001579, accessed August 2009
3   Greyhound Racing Board of Great Britain (undated), Information on website, www.thedogs.co.uk/default.aspx, accessed October 2008
4   Lord Donoughue of Ashton (2007) *Independent Review of the Greyhound Industry in Great Britain*, British Greyhound Racing Board and the National Greyhound Racing Club
5   Mitchell, F. J. (2006) *Great Breeders and Their Methods: The Hancocks*, Russell Meerdink Company
6   Gilbey, Sir W. (1889, 2000) *Concise History of the Shire Horse*, J. Barnes (ed) Beech Publishing House
7   *Nature* (1915) vol 94, January, p597
8   Russell, N. (1986) *Like Engend'ring Like: Heredity and Animal Breeding in Early Modern England*, Cambridge University Press
9   Cunningham, E. P. et al (2001) 'Microsatellite diversity, pedigree relatedness and the contributions of founder lineages to thoroughbred horses', *Animal Genetics*, vol 32, pp360–364
10  Menache, S. (2000) 'Hunting and attachment to dogs in the Pre-Modern period', in A. L. Podberscek, E. S. Paul and J. A. Serpell (eds) *Companion Animals and Us: Exploring the Relationships between People and Pets*, Cambridge University Press, pp42–60; Thomas, K. (1983) *Man and the Natural World: Changing Attitudes in England 1500–1800*, Penguin Books
11  Matheson, J. (1929) *The Greyhound: Breeding, Coursing, Racing, Etc.*, reprinted by Vintage Dog Books
12  Tesio, F. (1958, 2005) *Breeding the Racehorse*, edited and translated by Edward Spinola, foreword by John Hislop, J. A. Allen & Company
13  *Nature* (1904) 'The evolution of the horse', *Nature*, vol 70, 21 April, p520; *Nature* (1902) 'The origin of the Thoroughbred horse', *Nature*, vol 67, 25 December, p187; *Nature* (1905) vol 72, 24 August, p395
14  Hill, E. W. et al (2002) 'History and integrity of thoroughbred dam lines revealed in equine mtDNA variation', *Animal Genetics*, vol 33, pp287–294
15  Willett, P. (1966) *An Introduction to the Thoroughbred*, Stanley Paul
16  *Nature* (1914), vol 93, 25 June, p436
17  Hildreth, S. C. and Crowell, J. R. (1926) *The Spell of the Turf: The Story of American Racing*, J. B. Lippincott Company; Harrison, L. H. and Klotter, J. C. (1997) *A New History of Kentucky*, University Press of Kentucky
18  Gaffney, B. and Cunningham, E. P. (1988) 'Estimation of genetic trend in racing performance of thoroughbred horses', *Nature*, vol 332, pp722–724
19  Magee, S. (2001) *Complete A–Z of Horse Racing*, Channel Four Books; BBC (2009) 'Sea the Stars in historic Arc win', BBC Sport online, 1 October, http://news.bbc.co.uk/sport
20  American Jockey Club (2008) *Statistical Tables for 2007: 70 Per Cent Starters Sires by Starters, at 3rd July 2007; Average Starts per Starter at 3rd July 2007; Breeding Statistics: 2007 Breeding Year/2008 Foaling Year*
21  Thibier, M. (2006) *Data Retrieval Committee Annual Report*, December, International Embryo Transfer Society, www.iets.org/pdf/data_retrieval/december2006.pdf
22  Simm, G. et al (2005) 'Limits to yield of farm species: Genetic improvement of livestock', in R. Sylvester-Bradley and J. Wiseman (eds) *Yields of Farmed Species*, Nottingham University Press, pp123–141

23 Wilson, A. J. and Rambaut, A. (2008) 'Breeding racehorses: What price good genes?', *Biology Letters*, vol 4, pp173–175

24 Hill, E. W. et al (2010) 'A sequence polymorphism in MSTN predicts sprinting ability and racing stamina in Thoroughbred horses', *PLoS ONE* 5(1), e8645, doi:10.1371/journal.pone.0008645; Harris, S. P. and Turrion-Gomez, J. L. (2006) 'Mitochondrial DNA: An important female contribution to thoroughbred racehorse performance', *Mitochondrion*, vol 6, pp53–66

25 Galli, C. et al (2003) 'A cloned horse born to its twin dam', *Nature*, vol 424, p635; 'US–French team clone horse', *CBS News*, 28 April 2005; Evans, M. J. et al (1999) 'Mitochondrial DNA genotypes in nuclear transfer-derived cloned sheep', *Nature Genetics*, vol 23, no 1, pp90–93; Tachibana, M. et al (2009) 'Mitochondrial gene replacement in primate offspring and embryonic stem cells', *Nature*, vol 461, no 7262, pp367–372

26 Associate Parliamentary Group for Animal Welfare (2007) *The Welfare of Greyhounds: Report of the APGAW Inquiry into Welfare Issues Surrounding the Racing of Greyhounds in England*, APGAW

27 British Greyhound Racing Board Welfare Committee 'The greyhound breeder', www.greyhoundbreedersforum.org/welfare.htm, last accessed June 2009

28 Greyhound Racing Association of America (2008) *Media Kit* online, www.gra-america.org, accessed September 2008; Camelot Farms (2009) *Breeding and Insemination Statistics*, www.camelotfarms.com/national_greyhound_stats2.php, last accessed October 2009

29 *Greyhound Data*, www.greyhound-data.com/index.htm?z=GXyOf4, last accessed September 2008

30 British Horseracing Authority (2008) *British Racing Statistics 2008*; Jockey Club (America) (2009) *2009 Online Factbook*

31 Wilsher, S., Allen, W. R. and Wood, J. L. N. (2006) 'Factors associated with failure of Thoroughbred horses to train and race', *Equine Veterinary Journal*, vol 38, no 2, pp113–118

32 More, S. J. (1999) 'A longitudinal study of racing thoroughbreds: Performance during the first years of racing', *Australian Veterinary Journal*, vol 77, no 2, pp105–112

33 Grayson-Jockey Club Research Foundation (2008) *Statistics on Durability/Soundness Indicators*, Welfare and Safety of the Racehorse Summit, Lexington, 17–18 March 2008

34 Animal Aid (2008) 'Grand National meeting kills two more horses', News release, 4 April 2008

35 Kennedy, M. (2008) 'Horse racing: The need for consideration of the ethics of exposure to risk', presentation at Animal Athletes: Welfare of Animals in Sport, Scottish Centre for Animal Welfare Sciences Workshop, Moredun Research Institute, 24 September 2008, www.bsas.org.uk/downloads/WAS_009_WAS_MarkKennedy.pdf

36 Pinchbeck, G. L. et al (2003) 'Case-control study to investigate risk factors for horse falls in hurdle racing in England and Wales', *Veterinary Record*, vol 152, pp583–587

37 Parkin, T. (2008) 'Problems, investigations, results, impact', presentation at Animal Athletes: Welfare of Animals in Sport, Scottish Centre for Animal Welfare Sciences Workshop, Moredun Research Institute, 24 September 2008; Wood, J. L. N. et al (2005) 'Sports injuries: Epidemiological studies in racehorses', in E. J. L. Soulsby and J. F. Wade (eds) *Proceedings of a Workshop on Sporting Injuries in Horses and Man: A Comparative Approach*, Lexington, 23–25 September 2004, Havemeyer Foundation Monograph Series no 15, 2005

38  Parkin, T. D. et al (2006) 'Analysis of horse race videos to identify intra-race risk factors for fatal distal limb fracture', *Preventive Veterinary Medicine*, vol 74, no 1, pp44–55; Parkin, T. D. et al (2004) 'Horse-level risk factors for fatal distal limb fracture in racing Thoroughbreds in the UK', *Equine Veterinary Journal*, vol 36, no 6, pp513–519

39  British Horseracing Authority (2009) *Injuries and Fatalities*, www.britishhorseracing.com/inside_horseracing/about/whatwedo/veterinary/injuries_fatalities.asp, accessed June 2009

40  Animal Aid *Race Horse Death Watch*, www.horsedeathwatch.com; Stansall, D. (2008) *Race Horse Deathwatch: The First Year*, Animal Aid

41  Cruz, A. M. et al (2007) 'Epidemiologic characteristics of catastrophic musculoskeletal injuries in Thoroughbred racehorses', *American Journal of Veterinary Research*, vol 68, no 12, pp1370–1375

42  Verheyen, K. et al (2006) 'Exercise distance and speed affect the risk of fracture in racehorses', *Bone*, vol 39, no 6, pp1322–1330

43  Evans, D. L. (2007) 'Welfare of the racehorse during exercise training and racing', in Waran, N. (ed) *The Welfare of Horses*, Kluwer Academic Publishers, Dordrecht, pp181–201

44  Verheyen, K. L. et al (2005) 'Training-related factors associated with dorsometacarpal disease in young Thoroughbred racehorses in the UK', *Equine Veterinary Journal*, vol 37, no 5, pp442–448

45  Boden, L. A. et al (2007) 'Risk factors for Thoroughbred racehorse fatality in flat starts in Victoria, Australia (1989–2004)', *Equine Veterinary Journal*, vol 39, no 5, pp430–437; Anthenill, L. A. et al (2007) 'Risk factors for proximal sesamoid bone fractures associated with exercise history and horseshoe characteristics in Thoroughbred racehorses', *American Journal of Veterinary Research*, vol 68, no 7, pp760–771

46  Grayson-Jockey Club Research Foundation and Jockey Club (2006) *Proposed Strategic Plan: Recommendations of the Welfare and Safety of the Racehorse Summit*, Lexington, 16–17 October 2006

47  Humble, C. (2008) 'The Thoroughbred Rehabilitation Centre', presentation at Animal Athletes: Welfare of Animals in Sport, Scottish Centre for Animal Welfare Sciences Workshop, Moredun Research Institute, 24 September 2008, www.bsas.org.uk/downloads/WAS_001_WAS_CarrieHumble.pdf

48  Barakzai, S. Z. et al (2009) 'Use of tongue ties in thoroughbred racehorses in the United Kingdom, and its association with surgery for dorsal displacement of the soft palate', *Veterinary Record*, vol 165, pp278–281; Barakzai, S. Z., Finnegan C. and Boden, L. A. (2009) 'Effect of tongue tie use on racing performance of Thoroughbreds in the United Kingdom', *Equine Veterinary Journal*, vol 41, no 8, pp812–816; Oswald, J., Love, S., Parkin, T. D. H. and Hughes, K. J. (2010) 'Prevalence of cervical vertebral stenotic myelopathy in a population of thorough-bred horses', *Veterinary Record*, vol 166, pp82–83

49  Waran, N. K. (2001) 'The social behaviour of horses', in L. J. Keeling and H. W. Gonyou (eds) *Social Behaviour in Farm Animals*, CABI, Wallingford, UK, pp247–274; McDonnell, S. M. (2002) 'Behaviour of horses', in P. Jensen (ed) *The Ethology of Domestic Animals*, CABI, pp119–129

50  Davies-Morel, M. C. G. (2008) *Equine Reproductive Physiology, Breeding and Stud Management*, third edition, CABI

51  Cooper, J. and McGreevy, P. (2007) 'Stereotypic behaviour in the stabled horse', in N. Waran (ed) *The Welfare of Horses*, Kluwer Academic Publishers, pp99–124

52  Cassidy, R. (2002) *The Sport of Kings: Kinship, Class and Thoroughbred Breeding in Newmarket*, Cambridge University Press

53  Täubert, H., Agena, D. and Simianer, H. (2007) 'Genetic analysis of racing performance in Irish greyhounds', *Journal of Animal Breeding and Genetics*, vol 124, no 3, pp117–123

54  Shiel, R. E. et al (2007) 'Hematologic values in young pretraining healthy Greyhounds', *Veterinary Clinical Pathology*, vol 36, no 3, pp274–277; Marin, L. M. et al (2007) 'Vertebral heart size in retired racing greyhounds', *Veterinary Radiology and Ultrasound*, vol 48, no 4, pp332–334; Bavegems, V. et al (2005) 'Vertebral heart size ranges specific for whippets', V*eterinary Radiology and Ultrasound*, vol 46, no 5, pp400–403; Fabrizio, F. et al (2006) 'Left basilar systolic murmur in retired racing Greyhounds', *Journal of Veterinary Internal Medicine*, vol 20, no 1, pp78–82

55  Colborne, G. R. et al (2005) 'Distribution of power across the hind limb joints in Labrador Retrievers and Greyhounds', *American Journal of Veterinary Research*, vol 66, no 9, pp1563–1571; Kemp, T. J. et al (2005) 'Functional trade-offs in the limb bones of dogs selected for running versus fighting', *Journal of Experimental Biology*, vol 208, no 18, pp3475–3482

56  Stafford, K. J. (2006) *The Welfare of Dogs*, Animal Welfare Series vol 4, Springer

57  Jones, L. (2007) *Talking Greyhounds*, Corpus Publishing

58  Beary, D. (2008) '"Round the bend": Biomechanical challenges to the canine athlete', presentation at Animal Athletes: Welfare of Animals in Sport, Scottish Centre for Animal Welfare Sciences Workshop, Moredun Research Institute, 24 September 2008, www.bsas.org.uk/downloads/WAS_002_WAS_DenisBeary.pdf

59  Gough, A. and Thomas, A. (2004) *Breed Predisposition to Disease in Dogs and Cats*, Blackwell Publishing

60  Johnson, K. A. et al (2000) 'Asymmetric adaptive modeling of central tarsal bones in racing greyhounds', *Bone*, vol 27, no 2, pp257–263

61  Morris, D. (2009) *Training and Racing the Greyhound*, Publicity material, The Crowood Press

62  Vilar, P. et al (2008) 'Thromboelastographic tracings in retired racing greyhounds and in non-greyhound dogs', *Journal of Veterinary Internal Medicine*, vol 22, no 2, pp374–379; Couto, C. G. (2006) 'Evaluation of platelet aggregation using a point-of-care instrument in retired racing Greyhounds', *Journal of Veterinary Internal Medicine*, vol 20, no 2, pp365–370; Lord, L. K. et al (2007) 'Results of a web-based health survey of retired racing Greyhounds', *Journal of Veterinary Internal Medicine*, vol 21, no 6, pp1243–1250

63  Morris, J. and Dobson, J. (2001) *Small Animal Oncology*, Blackwell Science; Rosenberger, J., Pablo, N. V. and Crawford, P. C. (2007) 'Prevalence of and intrinsic risk factors for appendicular osteosarcoma in dogs: 179 cases (1996–2005)', *Journal of the American Veterinary Medical Association*, vol 231, no 7, pp1076–1080

64  Mosher, D. S. et al (2007) 'A mutation in the myostatin gene increases muscle mass and enhances racing performance in heterozygote dogs', *PLoS Genet*, vol 3, no 5, pe79; Shadan, S. (2007) 'Run, whippet, run', *Nature*, vol 447, p275; Harmon, A. (2007) 'As breeders test DNA, dogs become guinea pigs', *New York Times*, 12 June

65  Kennel Club (2003) *Illustrated Breed Standards*, Ebury Press

66  Greyhound Racing Association of America (2009) *Media Kit*, www.gra-america.org/media_kit/press/mediakit.html; *Adoption*, www.gra-america.org/the_sport/welfare/retirement.html, accessed November 2009

67  Hobbs, J. (ed) (2007) *Greyhound Annual 2008*, Raceform and the British Greyhound Racing Board, see Foreword by Lord Lipsey

68  Greyhound Racing Board of Great Britain (2009) *Welfare*, www.thedogs.co.uk/Welfare.aspx, accessed June 2009

69  *Animal Athletes: Welfare of Animals in Sport (Racehorses and Greyhounds)*,
    Report on the Scottish Centre for Animal Welfare Sciences Workshop chaired by
    Sir Colin Spedding and sponsored by BEVAT, Dogs Trust, UFAW, Fort Dodge,
    ISAE and BSAS, 24 September 2008, Moredun Research Institute, Edinburgh
70  Department for Food, Environment and Rural Affairs (2009) *Consultation on the
    Welfare of Greyhounds Regulations 2010*, Defra, April 2009
71  *Veterinary Record* (2007) 'News & reports: Welfare of racing greyhounds and
    horses', *Veterinary Record*, vol 160, no 20, May, pp674–675

# 8

# Surpluses and Rejects

## 8.1 Background: The scope of the problem

Society often feels uneasy about the disposal of unwanted animals that we have deliberately bred for our use. A famous *Punch* cartoon of 1909, entitled 'The Outcast', shows a gaunt, elderly horse, probably once a valued hunter or racer, arriving at the customs post on the dockside at Antwerp in Belgium. His label reads 'Hull to Antwerp' and he has been shipped from England to be sold to a Belgian slaughterhouse for horsemeat. The customs officer looks into the horse's eyes and asks: 'Have you anything to declare?' The horse looks back and answers, 'Nothing, except that I'm ashamed of my country.'[1]

Animal reproduction in the wild must compensate for high death rates through natural selection, and lives are often short. Far more young wild animals are born than can reach adulthood. Weak or unlucky offspring die from predation, disease, birth defects, death of a parent, starvation or exposure to harsh weather. When animals are bred by humans for food, companionship, work and sports we understand that some offspring and adults will fail to survive from unavoidable causes even with the best care possible. But beyond this, the breeding of animals by people often involves high levels of wastage that may be deliberate commercial policy or may be an inevitable result of over-breeding.

This chapter gives an overview of the impact on animals and society of some of the ways we produce and dispose of these surpluses and rejects, which include the following:

- discarded or surplus sports animals (greyhounds and Thoroughbred racehorses);
- by-product animals (male chicks and bull calves rejected as a result of extreme selection for egg or milk production);
- discarded breeding animals in food production (cull sows, cows, ewes, 'spent' hens, bulls and boars);
- over-breeding of companion animals (dogs and cats);
- surplus animals bred in zoos (see Box 11.2 in Chapter 11);
- surplus animals bred in laboratories (see Chapter 12).

Animals that are judged unsuitable for human uses or are past their best performance level have a low economic value. Their market value may be lower than the cost of disposing of them humanely. The well-being of surplus and reject animals is therefore a matter for concern.

## 8.2 Surpluses and rejects in the racing industries

### 8.2.1 Methods of disposal

In Ireland, 20,000 greyhounds were being bred annually by 2007 and Ireland supplied the majority of the dogs raced in England.[2] When a British Parliamentary group investigated the greyhound racing industry in 2007, it was estimated that 'at a minimum, a "surplus" of 13,478 dogs in England and Wales each year' were produced from the sector under the regulation of the British Greyhound Racing Board and an additional number were produced by the unregulated sector of the industry (see section 7.3.2.3 in Chapter 7). From the records that exist, it appears that nearly 5000 greyhound dogs and puppies are destroyed annually and this is likely to be 'a significant underestimation' of the total number.[3] Lord Donoughue's independent report, also in 2007, concluded that 'a significant number' of the annual 'massive exodus of greyhounds' from the industry, often with ten years of their life remaining, are destroyed and 'not always humanely'.[2]

In the US, a HBO *Real Sports* documentary in 2004 showed a farm where 3000 shot greyhounds were dug up two years earlier. Some informants alleged that the killing of unwanted greyhounds was sometimes carried out by clubbing or electrocution. The programme alleged that it was common practice for 'kill trucks' full of dogs for disposal to be taken out of the back of racetracks to be killed. The programme makers filmed a veterinary clinic ten miles (16km) from a racetrack, where trailers of healthy-looking greyhounds arrived and were unloaded, and their dead bodies subsequently dumped in a waste container.[4]

In England in 2006, an undercover investigation by the *Sunday Times* recorded unwanted greyhounds being delivered by trainers to a private house in Seaham, County Durham. There they were killed using a legally owned captive bolt gun (an instrument used to stun cattle in slaughterhouses) and buried in a field for a fee of UK£10 each. It was alleged that around 40 greyhound trainers used this dog disposal service and that more than 10,000

Table 8.1 *Greyhounds surplus and unaccounted for annually in the UK*

| Surplus or discarded from racing industry annually | Re-homed by Retired Greyhound Trust* | Re-homed by other charities | Kept by breeders, trainers or owners | Registered as to be returned to Ireland | Unaccounted for and presumed destroyed |
|---|---|---|---|---|---|
| 13,478 | 3500 | 1500 | 3000 | 750 | 4728 |

Note: * Funded by the Greyhound Racing Board of Great Britain.
Source: Associate Parliamentary Group on Animal Welfare (2007)[3]

dogs had been disposed of in this way, although the subsequent legal prosecution (on the grounds of unauthorized dumping of waste) concluded that the number had been lower.[5] As a result of the publicity generated by this disclosure, two enquiries were set up to investigate the greyhound industry and propose reforms that would reduce the number of surplus dogs destroyed.[2,3]

Veterinarians are often asked to destroy quite young and otherwise healthy racing greyhounds that have suffered injuries which are treatable and are not life threatening. Such injuries include the common injury of fracture of the central tarsal bone, which would require a rest of six months to one year before returning to racing, as well as veterinary costs. Although many veterinarians may find this ethically problematic, they suspect that if they refuse to cooperate the animal will be disposed of by less humane methods. Veterinarians may carry out euthanasia of greyhounds 'on demand' for this reason.[6]

There is little reliable information about what happens to individual racehorses discarded from the racing industry due to unsuitability, injury or increasing age. Some are passed from owner to owner and may be lucky enough to end up in a rescue shelter or rehabilitation centre, where some surplus horses are humanely destroyed. In the US, some are sold directly for horsemeat with no attempt to find an alternative home, avoiding the cost of humane destruction at the racing stables. A HBO *Real Sports* programme investigation in May 2008 showed evidence that young and healthy Thoroughbreds that fail to run well enough are transported directly from trainers' stables at racetracks to auctions, where they are sold to 'killer buyers' and then transported long distances to slaughterhouses in Canada and Mexico (a legal ban on horse slaughter within the US came into force in 2007). These can include previously well-known and successful racehorses.[7] At least 78,000 horses have been transported from the US to Canada and Mexico per year, according to investigations in 2008. Investigation by an animal protection organization of conditions of transport and slaughter within the US in recent years found horses dead in transport and others with severe injuries, including open leg fractures, missing hooves, gouged and bleeding faces, and eyes dangling out. Slaughter methods filmed in a slaughterhouse outside the US included stabbing a horse in the spine to paralyse it.[7,8] In economic downturns when private owners can no longer afford to keep the horses they bought or bred in better times, some prefer to sell to killer buyers rather than pay the costs of humane destruction and disposal.

## 8.2.2 Adoption and alternative uses after racing

The North American greyhound racing industry spends US$2 million annually on supporting the adoption of ex-racing dogs and believes that 90 per cent of greyhounds are adopted (re-homed) or retained by breeders, trainers or owners when they are withdrawn from racing, through the American Greyhound Council. The industry's stated aim is to re-home all 'eligible' greyhounds in future, leaving a minority, unsuited for adoption, to be humanely destroyed by licensed veterinarians.[9]

The greyhound industry in the UK was subject to political pressure as a result of the Seaham scandal and in 2007 the Minister for Sport stated that the industry had 'little time for complacency' before self-regulation was improved.[10] Under strengthened industry rules, the industry regulating body must be informed:[11]

- when a dog is retired;
- why a dog is destroyed, to include:
  - severe injury or illness;
  - an injury that was not considered economic to treat;
  - the dog was judged unsuitable as a pet;
  - no home or alternative placement could be found.

The Associate Parliamentary Group on Animal Welfare (APGAW) proposed that the racing registration fee could be increased and then refunded on proof that the dog had been treated humanely on retirement.[3] This would not, however, control the disposal of unpromising or unwanted puppies before the time when young greyhounds are first registered to race, which in the past may have amounted to 18–25 per cent of all puppies born in major greyhound racing countries.[12]

Horses are expensive animals to keep and few owners would be willing to keep an ex-racehorse in retirement without the horse being useful for some function. Although there are potentially a number of options for the use of Thoroughbreds when they are no longer considered suitable for racing, such as eventing, show-jumping and general leisure riding, horses typically live into their 20s and can live into their 30s. As in the case of racing greyhounds, it is unrealistic to expect that the large number of retired, injured or non-winning racehorses produced every year could be absorbed long term into the general horse-keeping population in good welfare conditions.

As discussed in Chapter 7, racing animals have been selectively bred and managed for high levels of exciting activity and for temperaments that may be unsuitable for non-racing functions. Greyhound trainers and veterinarians may see no alternative to destroying healthy young greyhounds that have relatively minor racing injuries if these dogs are not top grade racers and also are 'not very socialized and not housetrained'.[13] There may also be a mismatch of expectations between horse producers and the horse-buying public; breeders are more concerned with parentage and performance, whereas buyers may be looking for suitable temperament and trainability.[14]

### 8.2.3 Unsustainable levels of breeding

Changing the conditions of racing to reduce speed and injuries could in principle enable both dogs and horses to be used for racing for a longer proportion of their natural lifetimes, and thus reduce the number of animals entering and leaving the industry annually. The APGAW considered it feasible to extend greyhounds' working lives up to six or seven years of age by having more races for older, slower dogs and by making racetracks less likely to lead to injuries (better surfaces, avoiding tight curves). As the Society of Greyhound Veterinarians pointed out in their evidence to the enquiry, the main function of greyhound racing is to provide a medium for gambling, and the actual speed of the race is not necessarily important.[3] But it may be questioned whether being 'used to destruction' over a longer period of years would be a necessarily better outcome for the dogs or horses concerned.

The essential problem for the racing industry and society to solve is that racing involves an inherently unsustainable use of animals, inherited from an age when the unaudited disposal of unwanted dogs or horses was not a matter of public concern or public policy. If racing continues in its present form the public will need to continue taking care of its rejects either directly or indirectly, by adopting or funding the maintenance of an apparently endless supply of discarded racing animals. The Greyhound Racing Association of America has expressed the opinion that 'If animal rights groups really want to do something in the area of animal welfare, they should work constructively with the industry to maximize adoptions and secure a good home for every greyhound.'[15] This goal is surely the primary responsibility of the industry alone.

## 8.3 Decommissioned breeding animals in the food industry

### 8.3.1 Planned obsolescence

Animal farming has always had to take a 'use-and-dispose' approach to breeding animals, inevitable if the farmer is to make a living, but industrial farming has greatly increased the rate of disposal. Animals used for breeding in the food production industry are discarded for two main reasons: either because their reproductive performance or health is failing, or because their genes have become out of date. While, as discussed in Chapter 3, there is a high turnover of breeding animals for health reasons, the goal of the food industry for year-on-year genetic progress in performance means that animals are also subject to planned obsolescence.

Many producers may not be in a position to replace their breeding animals on schedule if they are still performing adequately. But the advice of experts to farmers is that if they want to achieve maximum genetic change in desired traits, they should change their animals regularly; boars should not be kept for more than one year or sows for more than three litters (about 1.5 reproductive years) for best results. Commercial pig-breeding companies change the boars used for semen production monthly in order to minimize genetic lag and ensure prompt incorporation of genetic improvements, and cattle-breeding companies replace 25–35 per cent of their semen-producing bulls annually.[16] Expert advice to farmers delivers a consistent message: any breeding animals that become less fertile and productive or have any health problems that will interfere with production must be culled in order to maintain the profitability of the business.

**Table 8.2** *Typical lifetime and potential natural lifespan of breeding livestock*

|  | Typical age of culling in commercial farming | Potential lifespan |
|---|---|---|
| Sows | 2.5–3 years | 15 years |
| Ewes | 6 years or earlier | 10–15 years |
| Dairy cows | 5–6 years or earlier | 20 or more years |
| Broiler breeders and laying hens | 14–18 months (single laying period)* | 6–10 years |

Note: * If laying hens are force moulted and used for a second or third laying period, they may be culled at over two years old.

We have seen in Chapter 3 that the reproductive lifetime of livestock is short, often due to exhaustion, ill health or failing fertility. Table 8.2 compares typical working lifetimes with the potential natural lifetime of the species, kept in good conditions.

## 8.3.2 Physical condition and low market value

The best quality chicken, cattle and pig meat comes from younger animals that are slaughtered before they have reached full physical maturity. Bred for the maximum productive output, discarded breeding animals are not in the best physical condition and have a relatively low value for meat. Often the animals have been selected for culling because they have persistent health problems, such as lameness. Breeding ewes, for example, will be culled if they have had a prolapse of the uterus, mastitis, chronic foot-rot or loose teeth. The UK Farm Animal Welfare Council (FAWC) assessment of farm quality assurance schemes of 2005 pointed out a 'major omission' in these schemes related to cull animals. The FAWC recommended that welfare of low-value cull animals should be ensured to the same standard as that of every other individual of the species and that their treatment should not deteriorate as their market value falls.[17] In practice, their physical condition and their low value may mean that cull animals suffer more than fitter animals would do during handling and transport for slaughter.

At the end of their laying period, 'spent hens' may be worth little more than the cost of disposing of them. They have been selectively bred for high output of eggs, not for muscle production, and they are often emaciated by the end of their intensive laying period (see section 3.2.6 in Chapter 3).[18] After they have been sold to the processor, farmers 'do not seem to care what happens to spent hens after that', in the view of a US poultry scientist,[19] and many 'are subjected to welfare insults' such as stress, fear and broken bones.[20]

Because of their very high output of eggshells, the bodies of modern laying hens can become depleted of calcium, making their bones brittle. This occurs in any housing system (see also section 3.2.6); but battery-cage hens also get no exercise, meaning that their bone strength is significantly lower than that of non-caged hens.[21] Cull battery hens are pulled out of their cages by their legs,

**Figure 8.1** *This 'spent' battery hen was bought from an English egg farmer by an animal welfare organization for re-homing in 2009. She had lost most of the feathers on her underside and on her back*

© J. Turner

the catchers often grabbing more than one hen per hand, and packed into crates for transport to the slaughterhouse. Recent British studies found that 24 per cent of battery hens had freshly broken bones caused by catching alone (compared to 10 per cent of free-range hens).[22] The process of transport, unloading at the slaughterhouse and hanging the hens by their feet for electrical stunning further increases the number of bone breaks. Most of the hens who die on the way to the slaughterhouse die from bone breaks during catching, crating and transport.[19,20,22] Some hens have few feathers left by the end of their laying period, increasing their risk of chilling during transport to slaughter.

An alternative method of slaughter is to stun and kill hens by gas while still in their crates, using a relatively high concentration of carbon dioxide (currently 30 per cent under UK regulations) or other gas mixtures, known as controlled atmosphere stunning (CAS). In some circumstances, the hens can be gas-killed in their sheds. Gas stunning has the advantage that hens do not have to be picked up or shackled, a procedure that probably causes pain to the many hens that have at least one broken bone. A US poultry scientist and industry adviser has pointed out that the shackling and electrical water-bath stunning method is especially problematic for laying hens because of their broken and fragile bones and because they are reactive on the shackles, struggling, flapping their wings and flexing their necks. This means that they are more likely to get 'pre-stun shocks' if their wings or necks hit the electrified water before their heads, and some hens miss the stunner altogether.[19] A disadvantage of the gas method is that carbon dioxide above 25–30 per cent concentration is very unpleasant for poultry to breathe because of its acidic effect on body tissues,[23] so it is important that only non-aversive gas mixtures are used.

Dairy cows of the highest-yielding and often bony breeds, such as Holsteins, also have a relatively low value for meat at the end of their lives. Dairy cows are also often lame and may have mastitis (see section 3.2.3 in Chapter 3). In 2008 the US public were made aware that sick or injured dairy cows unable to stand ('downer' cows) were being dragged, shoved and carried off trucks to slaughter, at a probable rate of nearly half a million per year, raising the possibility that some of these cows might be suffering from BSE (bovine spongiform encephalopathy) or other transmissible diseases. Undercover filming by the Humane Society of the United States (HSUS) showed slaughterhouse workers trying to make downer cows stand by using an electric cattle prod, a forklift truck and a water hose.[24]

### 8.3.3 Breeding for survival and longevity

The breeding of cows, ewes and sows who can survive and withstand the demands of modern farming for longer is an increasingly popular subject for scientific research.[25] In principle, if genes associated with longevity could be identified reliably and breeding companies and farmers produced longer-lived breeding animals, this would reduce the number discarded and sent to slaughter annually. Longer breeding lifetimes need to be the consequence of better health, not of greater workload – continuing to breed from a chronically lame cow, sow or ewe would be inhumane. It would be in the commercial interests of farmers to use animals who lived longer, but had a somewhat reduced annual output although, in some cases, farmers or breeding companies might find a conflict between longer-lived breeding animals and the desire for genetic change.

Unfortunately, any experimental or commercial breeding programmes are likely to result in by-product animals that are of the less desirable sex or the less desirable type, or both, which will need to be disposed of. For example, commercial breeding companies that produce lines of hybrid sows for breeding inevitably produce unwanted males of the same strain (see section 8.4.2 for unwanted dairy-breed male calves).

A 21st-century paradox is that breeding animals are decommissioned earlier in their lives in spite of the immensely increased potential of modern veterinary medicine to maintain health. The current short survival times, and the high rate of rejection, are primarily due to the production pressures put on the animals by cost competition in commercial farming. From the position of animal well-being alone, the simplest and most effective approach would be to take the pressure off the breeding animals by reducing the output required of them. In the case of dairy cows, some dairy producers are already moving in this direction by changing from the Holstein to dual-purpose breeds, such as the British Friesian or Montbeliarde, which have a lower milk output annually but are likely to remain healthier for longer and therefore reduce the annual outflow of discarded dairy cows.[26]

## 8.4 By-product offspring in the food animal industry

Modern animal breeding has developed highly specialized chickens and cattle for efficient production of either eggs/milk or meat, but not both. The large majority of male offspring in specialized egg- or milk-producing breeds are not used for breeding and have very limited value for meat, often making them an unwanted by-product of the industry.

### 8.4.1 Male chicks of egg-laying breeds

In developed countries, male chicks of egg-laying strains have no value for meat and are killed. Since the sex ratio of chicks is expected to be 50:50, this means that as many males are killed as females chicks are reared for egg laying – around 30 million per year in the UK and 330 million day-old chicks killed in the European Union (EU) annually[27,28].

After hatching, chicks of laying strains are placed on a conveyor belt to be sexed by skilled hatchery workers (the sexes may be 'coded' by differences in their feathering) and the males put into the destruction track. In countries where the killing of commercial male chicks in hatcheries is regulated, there are two main methods: instantaneous mechanical destruction (maceration) or gassing. Suffocation or crushing by throwing the chicks on top of each other into sacks or bins is not humane or legal in countries that have adequate animal welfare regulations.

According to the Humane Slaughter Association, the fastest and most humane method of killing day-old chicks is instantaneous mechanical destruction, although it is 'aesthetically unpleasant'.[29] In this method chicks on a conveyor belt are fed into rotating rollers which are fitted with either hard protuberances or blades and immediately crush or dismember the chicks as they reach the rollers. The effectiveness and humaneness of this method depends on the correct speed and rate of arrival of the chicks at the rollers, to avoid the rollers getting jammed or the chicks piling up in front or on top of the rollers. The alternative legal method in the EU is to gas the chicks with a high concentration of carbon dioxide. This stuns the chicks within several seconds, but not before they have shown signs of distress in breathing, because carbon dioxide is acidic and 'highly aversive' to birds at high concentrations.[29]

Killing chicks in hatcheries is not always ideally managed or regulated. Undercover investigations in a large US hatchery found that some chicks fell off the conveyor belt during the sex-sorting procedure and died on the floor, and others got trapped in the conveyor belt and were scalded during the automatic wash cycle of the trays at the end of the line. In 2009 the South African Poultry Association suspended the membership of a farm producing laying hens for investigation because of accusations that the farmer had for years disposed of 70,000 male chicks per week by dumping them alive outside and leaving them to die of exposure.[30]

## 8.4.2 Dairy bull calves

Dairy cows are required to give birth every 12–15 months in order to start a new lactation, and some of the calves born are inevitably surplus to market requirements. Modern dairy cows have been selected for large udders and little muscling, with the result that dairy calves are not suited to growing muscle and producing prime beef. The destruction of dairy bull calves because of their limited value for meat production has come to be seen as one of the most unacceptable aspects of modern animal breeding. Dairy bull calves take longer to grow to market weight, have inferior carcase conformation and worse survival rates in their first month than calves of specialized beef breeds.

Typically more than half of the dairy cows in a herd are inseminated with dairy bull semen (rather than by beef bulls; see section 2.2.5 in Chapter 2) because female dairy calves are required annually to replace worn-out cows in the milking herd. The annual replacement rate is very high (up to 30 per cent or more). But in the absence of sexed semen (see section 8.4.3.1), as many dairy bull calves are born as dairy heifers. In 2008 the Scottish Agricultural College estimated that in practice at least 35 per cent of pregnancies in dairy herds in the UK result in dairy bull calves: this could mean 175 potentially low-value male calves to be disposed of per year from a herd of 500 cows.[31]

In many countries male dairy calves are used to produce veal or are fattened in feedlots for up to a year to produce beef. In the UK veal is not popular, mainly because it is associated in the public mind with the inhumane use of veal crates. Some male calves are reared for beef, but the remaining unwanted calves are either transported at two or three weeks old for veal production in continental Europe or are destroyed by shooting at birth. While numbers vary widely depending on beef market conditions and the potential for exports, 100,000 or more male calves may be shot at birth annually in the UK.[32] In the US, illegal dumping of dead dairy calves was reported to be increasing in 2009, with one incident in California involving 30 dead calves stacked on a roadside, and around 100,000 'bobby calves' per year are transported to slaughter at a few days old. An undercover investigation of a slaughterhouse by the HSUS found some calves with remains of their umbilical cords still hanging from their navels, some apparently too weak to stand or injured during transport. Calves were kicked, slapped and repeatedly shocked with an electric prod in attempts to make them stand and walk. There was also evidence of inadequate stunning before slaughter and that calves were skinned while still alive.[33]

Depending on market demand in the milk industry, female as well as male dairy calves may become surplus. In Australia the Royal Society for the Prevention of Cruelty to Animals reported in 2009 that 900,000 unwanted dairy calves, both male and female, were being trucked long distance to slaughter annually, at around five days old. They are used to produce young veal, hides and other by-products.[33] In countries where there is little demand for goat meat, such as the UK, the male kids of milking goat breeds are also routinely destroyed at birth.

### 8.4.3 Ways of reducing the number of unwanted dairy bull calves

The long-distance transport and shooting of dairy bull calves has become of so much public concern in Britain that initiatives were developed by non-governmental organizations (NGOs) and the industry to try to reduce the numbers. There are two main ways in which a change in breeding practices could achieve this:

1    Using sexed semen whenever dairy cows are inseminated with dairy bull semen, to avoid the birth of male calves.
2    Using dairy cows that are less extreme in their conformation and closer to a dual-purpose breed. This would have two results:
     •    Male purebred dairy calves would be more suitable for beef.
     •    Cows would be somewhat longer-lived and healthier, which would reduce the number of dairy heifers needed annually as replacements. If fewer dairy replacements were needed, a higher proportion of the herd could be inseminated by beef bulls, producing calves very suitable for meat.

#### 8.4.3.1 Sexed semen

The X and Y chromosomes can be distinguished because the X chromosome is larger and laboratory sorting methods exist to produce cattle semen that contains only sperm bearing the X-chromosome, so that only female offspring are conceived. The current method of sorting cattle sperm (flow cytometry) is slow and therefore expensive; as a result the insemination dose used is ten times lower than that of normal sperm. Sexed semen produces a lower conception rate than unsorted semen and therefore it is recommended mainly for use on heifers who have not calved before, because they have higher conception rates than milking cows. This currently limits its application in the dairy industry. Similarly, bulls with desirable genetics but lower fertility are not suitable for semen-sorting.[31]

The uptake of sexed semen on a large scale in the dairy industry would therefore need the semen companies to produce more and cheaper sexed semen and from a greater range of bulls, but the technology already has the potential to reduce the number of unwanted male calves considerably. The Scottish Agricultural College estimated in 2008 that the number of dairy bull calves born in a herd annually could be reduced from 35 to 14 per cent of all calves by using sexed semen to inseminate all heifers.[31]

### 8.4.3.2 Breeding for dual purpose

Whatever the potential of sexed semen, it is essentially a technical fix and would entrench the existing overspecialization of dairy breeds that is at the root of the problem. The alternative solution would be to reform dairy cattle breeding so that both male and female calves have an economic function and an acceptable market value. This could mean using either fully dual-purpose cattle breeds or less extreme dairy breeds for milk production. The use of dual-purpose cattle for both milk and meat production would be the most effective solution and would eliminate the problem of low-value male calves, but the industry is unlikely to accept such a sudden change of emphasis in their breeding goals in the short term.

The UK food industry has made efforts to improve the meat value of dairy bull calves. In 2008, the Beyond Calf Exports Stakeholders Forum (involving a large number of organizations in the dairy industry, beef industry, retailers and animal protection NGOs) initiated supply chain schemes to reduce the killing or live export of bull calves. In some cases, dairy farmers were offered semen from particular dairy bulls that were capable of producing calves more suitable for beef production, together with a guaranteed sale of the male calves for rearing, and one large retailer offered to subsidize the cost of sexed semen. By 2009, this had succeeded in increasing the number of bull calves kept for rearing in the UK but the number shot at birth did not decrease (partly due to a disrupted export trade).[34]

## 8.5 Surplus companion animals: Dogs and cats

In many countries, including the UK and the US, more dogs and cats are bred than there are good long-term homes for them to live in. The reasons for this are various and include:

- accidental or careless over-breeding;
- deliberate breeding for sale or to produce pedigree animals for breeding and showing;
- decommissioning of pedigree breeding animals;
- a complex range of attitudes towards acquiring companion animals and responsibility for them.

The result of creating a surplus population of dogs and cats is suffering for animals that are either unwanted from birth, are abandoned or spend long periods of time in a shelter cage. Apart from the impact on the animals, considerable human and economic resources are spent controlling, collecting, caring for, assessing, re-homing and often destroying surplus dogs and cats, a cost often not borne by those who have contributed to the over-breeding. No one would suggest that over-breeding is the only reason why dogs and cats end up in rescue centres – others include an inability to manage the animal, perceived inconvenience caused by the animal, changes in the household or family, and more. But an essential ingredient is that cats and dogs do not have a scarcity value in society and this is related to the fact that there is a surplus population.

### 8.5.1 Dogs and cats collected, re-homed and destroyed

The US is estimated to have between 4000 and 6000 animal shelters that take in around 6 million to 8 million cats and dogs per year. Around 30 per cent of the dogs (but a very low percentage of cats) are subsequently reclaimed by their owners. Only around half of all the animals that enter shelters are subsequently re-homed and the rest are destroyed after attempts have been made to find their owners and assess their suitability for re-homing. A national survey of shelters in the mid 1990s found that 71 per cent of the cats taken in were destroyed.[35] US shelters and dog pounds may also sell dogs to veterinary schools and research institutes to be used in experiments or teaching, sometimes through dealers whose facilities are very poor (see Box 12.4 in Chapter 12).

In the UK, over 107,000 dogs were collected by local authorities in the year 2008/2009 and over 9000 were destroyed, according to surveys conducted for the Dogs Trust.[36] Every summer, cat protection charities take in boxes of unwanted kittens delivered to their doors or found abandoned. Most cat and dog breed societies also run rescue and re-homing operations for animals of their particular pedigree breed. The resources that society spends on the problem of companion animal overpopulation are illustrated by the effort put in by the large and long-established charity Cats Protection in 2008 (see Table 8.4).

In countries with less scope for companion animal regulation, methods of disposal are often less than humane and involve mass round-ups and destruction of cats and dogs, whether owned or not. Dogs and cats are also killed for meat and fur in East Asia, particularly in China. It has been estimated by the animal protection NGO Animals Asia that 13 million to 16 million dogs and 4 million cats per year are eaten in China (although a proposed animal welfare law would ban the practice). NGOs have photographed crates packed with cats and dogs in transport and at markets, some animals apparently heat-stressed, crushed and suffocating, and inhumane methods of slaughter.[37]

**Table 8.3** *Estimates of number of owned cats and dogs in the US and the UK*

| 'Owned' animals | UK population (2009, 2006)[38] | US population (2004)[39] | US not neutered[39] (2004) |
|---|---|---|---|
| Dogs | 8–10 million | 75 million | 20 million (27%) |
| Cats | 8–10 million | 96 million | 13 million (14%) |

**Table 8.4** *Human and financial resources expended by a British cat protection charity during 2008 (Cats Protection)*

| | |
|---|---|
| Total income | UK£36.4 million |
| Cats and kittens in care at any time | 6500 |
| Cats re-homed (adopted) | 55,000 |
| Cats neutered (with other organizations) | 151,000 |
| Expenditure on re-homing (adoption) | 73% of total |
| Expenditure on neutering | 18% of total |
| Staff and volunteers | 7200 |
| Volunteer-run branches in UK | 252 |
| Charity shops | 65 |
| Adoption centres | 29 |

*Note:* Figures over 1000 are rounded.
*Source:* Cats Protection Annual Review 2008 and website[40]

## 8.5.2 Unwanted pedigree dogs

Dogs are more likely to be used intentionally for breeding than cats. They are also more likely to be sold or bought and more likely to be of a defined pedigree breed. Estimates based on a US survey of owners in 1996 indicate that 82 per cent of the kittens born in that year were 'unplanned', compared to 43 per cent of the puppies. Only 18 per cent of the dogs that people acquired were rescued (stray, abandoned or from shelters) compared to 33.6 per cent of the cats, and 1 million more dogs than cats were acquired from breeders.[41] In 2008, 47 per cent of all owned dogs in the UK were reported as bought, either from breeders, pet shops, advertisements or the internet.[38]

Once-fashionable and newly fashionable dog breeds make up a sizeable proportion of those abandoned to public rescue centres, and others are taken in by breed society rescue centres. According to the HSUS, an estimated 25 per cent of stray and unwanted dogs in US animal shelters are 'purebreds'.[35] In the UK, the Dogs Trust reported in 2007 an influx of Staffordshire Bull Terriers and feared that the novelty cross-breeds such as Labradoodles and Cockapoos would follow.[36] In early October 2008, more than 200 stray or unwanted Chihuahua dogs were in need of re-homing from Los Angeles County's animal shelters.[42] Un-neutered 'purebred' dogs probably also contribute to the population of unwanted dogs because breed standards require that every male dog used for showing has 'two apparently normal descended testicles'. This must increase the risk of unplanned matings by pedigree dogs whose owners contemplate using them at some point for showing, accidentally producing low-value and unwanted cross-bred puppies.

Dogs are also handed over to rescue centres because their behaviour makes them unsuitable for domestic life or their owners cannot manage them. A survey of US animal shelters found that in 16 per cent of cases when owners requested a shelter to destroy their dog, they wanted the dog destroyed for behavioural reasons such as aggression towards people or other animals. More than half of the dogs for whom breed information was available were German Shepherds, Cocker Spaniels, Staffordshire Terriers, Labrador Retrievers, Chihuahuas, Chow Chows and Rottweilers.[43]

### 8.5.3 Cat and dog sterilization and contraception

The popularity of dogs and cats in modern society brings an inevitable need to control their reproduction closely, at the least in order to prevent the suffering that is caused by creating a surplus population. But there are potential losses to the animals, in terms of behavioural freedom, stress and pain involved in veterinary visits and invasive procedures, possible side effects and potentially further restriction of the gene pool. Where the balance of gain and loss lies from the point of view of the animals is a matter for debate, but in breeding companion animals in such large numbers we have put ourselves in the unenviable position of taking decisions over their life or death and their reproduction.

The majority of owned dogs and cats in developed countries are surgically neutered (although this is not the case everywhere – for example in Scandinavia[44]). Most veterinarians and companion animal welfare organizations recommend the routine neutering of companion dogs and cats, citing also the high risk of un-neutered female dogs developing pyometra as a consequence of repeated seasons without pregnancy, and the advantages in avoiding unwanted behaviour. In the UK and in Australia, 92 per cent of cats are neutered (although in the UK only 66 per cent are neutered by the age of 6–12 months, when they are sexually mature and could reproduce).[45] In some US states neutering/spaying programmes targeted at low-income owners and at homeless pets and feral cats have significantly reduced the number of animals that shelters destroy.[39] Some owners are strongly opposed to surgical neutering for a number of reasons, which could include wanting to show the animal or breed from the animal, dislike of interfering with the nature of the animal, viewing neutering as a mutilation, wishing to allow the animal behavioural freedom, and wishing to use a male dog for 'status'.

Non-surgical sterilization methods, similar to contraceptive drugs for humans, may have promise for reducing unwanted cat and dog populations because they could be offered at lower cost and would require less time and effort from owners. Possibilities that are being researched for dogs and cats include gonadotrophin-releasing hormone (GnRH) agonists or GnRH vaccines, both of which block the production of sex hormones that initiate the oestrous cycle, and zona pellucida vaccines, which prevent fertilization but do not prevent the oestrous cycle.[46,47] In developing countries where there are limited resources for surgical neutering clinics, programmes of chemical sterilization for male dogs have been carried out (for example in Mexico, Guatamala and Brazil). One chemical used is zinc gluconate, which is injected once into each testicle and causes atrophy of the testicle and permanent sterility.[48] All drug treatments raise issues of competent administration, injection-site reactions and any other damaging side effects.

Up to now it has typically been seen as the right of people who own dogs or cats to breed any number of animals that we wish. This right may be increasingly challenged in future by laws such as that of Los Angeles City Council, in force from April 2009, requiring all cats and dogs older than four months to be neutered. Exemptions to this law included police and guide dogs and also, more controversially, licensed breeders.[49] Breeders' organizations such as the American Kennel Club (AKC) and the Cat Fanciers' Association encourage their members to lobby against proposed legislation that would restrict cat and dog breeding. During the first half of 2009 the AKC issued 'legislative alerts' on proposals to restrict or further regulate breeding or to make neutering ('spay/neuter') compulsory in more than 20 legislatures, including Alabama, Arkansas, California, Chicago, Connecticut, Florida, Illinois, Indiana, Maryland, Minnesota, Montana, Nebraska, Nevada, New Hampshire, New York State, North Carolina, Ohio, Oklahoma, Oregon, Texas, Virginia, Washington State and West Virginia. The AKC described a West Virginia bill in March 2009 as: 'Similar to many bills introduced in legislatures across the country in 2009, HB 2843 is part of a radical national legislative agenda aimed at limiting the freedoms and liberties of Americans by attempting to restrict the number of animals they can own.'[50]

## 8.6 The professionals, the public and the future

### 8.6.1 The racing industries

Competition sports by their nature will always produce surpluses and rejects. One solution would be for the racing industries to take responsibility for the birth-to-death care of the animals that they produce and to set up and fund retirement homes that are capable of providing a high quality of life for all their discarded animals. Another solution would be to restrict the number of animals that can be bred so that this matches the ability of the public to absorb the annual outflow into good homes. The annual outflow could also be reduced in principle by the use of selective breeding and, potentially, genomics to increase the durability of the animals and reduce the number born that are unsuitable for racing.

The Associate Parliamentary Group on Animal Welfare (APGAW) concluded that it was 'highly unlikely' that all the dogs currently used in the greyhound racing industry could be re-homed and that 'the number of dogs required by the industry should therefore be substantially decreased' to make it possible to re-home the surplus. The APGAW believed that EU law would prevent the British government from putting legal restrictions on the number of greyhound puppies bred, but it suggested a number of measures (such as reducing injuries) that would keep greyhounds racing for a greater proportion of their lives.[3] Against this, it would not be acceptable to race injured or frail animals and thus dispose of them by 'natural selection' on the race track. Given that greyhounds can live for over 12 years and horses for well over 20 years, extending racing lifetimes might not be a sufficient solution to enable the public to absorb all the surplus animals into good homes. It is even questionable whether the public should be asked to carry out this service for the racing industries indefinitely.

In the short term, over-breeding could be discouraged by regulatory measures, such as licences for breeding and the requirement that the birth and death and changes of ownership of every animal bred or used in the industry should be documented (as is already required for ownership of motor vehicles). In the longer term, if the racing industries prove unable to provide good lifetime care for racing animals, society may need to intervene to phase out live racing.

### 8.6.2 Food animals

The main sources of surpluses and rejects in the food animal industries are the overspecialization of breeds for a single purpose and the excessive production pressures put on animals by economic competition. Overspecialization has made some animals less healthy and robust (such as high-yielding dairy cows) and others economically valueless (male chicks of laying breeds, dairy bull calves, 'spent' laying hens).

Many scientists and some farmers accept that the overspecialization of breeds has a negative impact on animals and on the public image of farming, and there is increasing interest in using more robust breeds of livestock. There is particular interest in using dairy cattle that can be used for both meat and milk production because of the evident health effects of overspecialization in the dairy industry and the unacceptable disposal of unwanted male calves. Less specialized and longer-living animals could also include chickens that are useful for both meat and egg production and sows that produce smaller litters over a longer breeding lifetime. A change to genuinely dual-purpose cattle and chickens could immensely improve animal welfare in the dairy and the chicken industries and remove some of the most obvious ethical objections to the industry. Both locally and internationally, there are numerous alternative breeds to choose from (see Chapter 9).

So far, progress towards reducing the high rejection rate of animals has been quite slow. Like any industry, the food industry and the breeding companies can only be expected to respond to market forces or to external regulation. Consumers are in the strongest position to create change by buying meat, milk and eggs from dual-purpose, healthy and long-lived animals (or alternatively by ceasing to buy these products until industry policies change). Since dual-purpose and slower-maturing animals may be more costly to produce, this probably means that consumers will need to pay more and consume somewhat less of the products. Farmers and breeders would also need to abandon their aim for year-on-year increases in genetic potential for higher productivity.

A linked question is how the animals are kept. It is not necessarily an advantage to a breeding animal to live for twice as many years in a battery cage, in a gestation crate or even in a barren and crowded indoor pen on a slatted floor. In the worst conditions of intensive farming and intensive breeding, a short life may be preferable. Part of the reform of farm animal breeding needs to be a reform of husbandry practices so that the animals are kept at stocking densities and in environments that avoid social stress and are consistent with the natural behavioural needs of the species.

### 8.6.3 Companion animals

Rejection and homelessness may cause as much suffering to dogs and cats as the genetic diseases of pedigree animals that are currently receiving increasing scientific attention. Some causes of homelessness, such as illness and death of the owner, are unavoidable but many animals are discarded voluntarily. The population of unwanted dogs and cats is a societal rather than a technical problem in developed countries since the resources to control breeding exist and are affordable for society as a whole. For developing countries, the problem is both societal and technical and there may be a need for scientists, pharmaceutical companies and drug regulators to develop and facilitate one-shot chemical sterilizing agents or contraceptive vaccines that are safe and painless in use. Unfortunately, the development of additional contraceptive methods in itself will involve potentially painful and distressing animal experiments and the wastage of some animals.

Society could choose to mandate and enforce a ban on the breeding of cats and dogs except under strict licence conditions, which could include an increased emphasis on breeding dogs with suitable behaviour traits for domestic living. Dogs and cats would acquire a scarcity value, and lead to a situation where rescue centres only needed to take in animals in exceptional circumstances, with a waiting list of new owners wanting to adopt them. There are no perfect solutions to managing the companion animal population but the importance of reducing the number of unwanted animals born is something that most people can agree on.

Part of the reason that society does not take the obvious steps to restrict the breeding of dogs and cats appears to be linked to our 'breed' culture, as discussed in Chapters 5 and 6. Breeders believe that they have a right to breed from cats and dogs as they wish and even to create and propagate a new breed or cross-breed. The public continues to buy pedigree or designer-cross puppies as companion animals rather than adopt dogs already in rescue centres and in need of new homes. Professional breeders have a vested interest in unrestricted breeding by those they refer to as 'responsible breeders' and in the continuance of pedigree breeds for showing and sale to the public (and very few breeders are likely to refer to themselves as 'irresponsible breeders'). Except in a few cases, such as some service dogs, the existence of dog and cat breeds is unnecessary for society and has become a negative factor in the relationship between people and companion animals.

## Notes

1    Reproduced in Gold, M. (1998) *Animal Century*, Jon Carpenter Publishing
2    Lord Donoughue of Ashton (2007) *Independent Review of the Greyhound Industry in Great Britain*, British Greyhound Racing Board and National Greyhound Racing Club
3    Associate Parliamentary Group for Animal Welfare (2007) *The Welfare of Greyhounds: Report of the APGAW Inquiry into Welfare Issues Surrounding the Racing of Greyhounds in England*, APGAW
4    HBO *Real Sports* with Bryant Gumbel, 23 November 2004
5    Foggo, D. (2006) 'Revealed: The man who killed 10,000 dogs', *Sunday Times*, 16 July; 'Man fined over greyhound deaths', BBC News online, 16 March 2007, http://news.bbc.co.uk
6    Watts, M. (2007) 'Everyday ethics: An injured greyhound', *In Practice*, January, p55; Guillard, M. J. (2000) 'Fractures of the central tarsal bone in eight racing greyhounds', *Veterinary Record*, vol 147, pp512–515; *Veterinary Record* (2007) 'Greyhound euthanasia', *Veterinary Record*, vol 161, p43
7    'Hidden horses', HBO *Real Sports* with Bryant Gumbel, 12 May 2008
8    Jenkins, N. (2008) 'More horses sent abroad for slaughter after US ban', *Associated Press*, 26 November 2008; Woodward, B. (2008) 'Thousands of US horses slaughtered in Mexico for food', *KHOU Houston*, 20 December 2008
9    American Greyhound Council, www.agcouncil.com/node/5, accessed July 2009; National Greyhound Association, *Media Kit*, www.gra-america.org/media_kit/press/mediakit.html, accessed September 2008
10   Suffcliffe, G. (2007) 'Government's view', *Greyhound Annual 2008*, J. Hobbs (ed), Raceform and the British Greyhound Racing Board
11   Greyhound Board of Great Britain (2009) *Rules of Racing*, as of 1 March 2009
12   Stafford, K. J. (2006) *The Welfare of Dogs*, Animal Welfare Series vol 4, Springer
13   Watts, M. (2007) 'Everyday ethics: An injured greyhound', *In Practice*, January 2007, p55
14   Hennessy, K. D., Quinn, K. M. and Murphy, J. (2008) 'Producer or purchaser: Different expectations may lead to equine wastage and welfare concerns', *Journal of Applied Animal Welfare Science*, vol 11, no 3, pp232–235
15   Greyhound Racing Association of America (2008) *Media Kit*, www.gra-america.org/media_kit/press/mediakit.html, accessed September 2008
16   See for example National Swine Improvement Federation (2001) *Application of Selection Concepts for Genetic Improvement*, Swine Genetics, Fact Sheet no 9, Purdue University Extension Service; Genus plc (2008) *Annual Report 2008*, Genus plc
17   Farm Animal Welfare Council (2005) *Report on the Welfare Implications of Farm Assurance Schemes*, FAWC
18   Sherwin, C. M. et al (2009) 'The consequences of artificial selection of layer hens on their welfare in all current housing systems', paper presented to Darwinian Selection, Selective Breeding and the Welfare of Animals, UFAW International Symposium 2009, Bristol, 22–23 June 2009

19  *World Poultry* (2007) 'Gas stunning reduces rejects in spent hen processing', *World Poultry*, vol 23, no 9, pp30–31

20  Tinker, D. B. et al (2004) 'Handling and catching of hens during depopulation', in G. C. Perry (ed) *Welfare of the Laying Hen*, CABI, Chapter 29; Knowles, T. G. (1994) 'Handling and transport of spent hens', *World's Poultry Science Journal*, vol 50, pp60–61

21  Whitehead, C. C. (2004) 'Skeletal disorders in laying hens: The problem of osteoporosis and bone fractures', in G. C. Perry (ed) *Welfare of the Laying Hen*, CABI, Chapter 23; Knowles, T. G. and Broom, D. M. (1990) 'Limb bone strength and movement in laying hens from different housing systems', *Veterinary Record*, vol 126, pp354–356; Abrahamsson, P. and Tauson, R. (1995) 'Aviary systems and conventional cages for laying hens', *Acta Agriculturae Scandinavica, Sect. A*, vol 45, pp191–203; Fleming, R. H. et al (1994) 'Bone structure and breaking strength in laying hens housed in different husbandry systems', *British Poultry Science*, vol 35, no 5, pp651–662

22  Cooper, O. (2009) 'Trials offer guide to safer handling of spent hens', *World Poultry*, June, pp36–37

23  Statutory Instrument 1995 No 731, The Welfare of Animals (Slaughter or Killing) Regulations 1995; Humane Slaughter Association (2005) *Gas Killing of Chickens and Turkeys: Technical Note 12*; European Food Safety Authority, Scientific Panel on Animal Health and Welfare (2004) 'Welfare aspects of the main systems of stunning and killing the main commercial species of animals', *The EFSA Journal*, vol 45, pp1–29

24  *Farmed Animal Watch* (2008) 'Hallmark update', *Farmed Animal Watch*, vol 8, no 8, 7 March, www.farmedanimal.net; Becker, G. S. (2008) *USDA Meat Inspection and the Humane Methods of Slaughter Act*, CRS report for Congress, 26 February, US; Kesmodel, D. and Zhang, J. (2008) 'Meatpacker in cow-abuse scandal may shut as Congress turns up heat', *Wall Street Journal*, 25 February, pA1

25  See, for example, Klopčič, M. et al (eds) (2009) *Breeding for Robustness in Cattle*, Wageningen Academic Publishers; Tarrés, J. et al (2006) 'Analysis of longevity and exterior traits on Large White sows in Switzerland', *Journal of Animal Science*, vol 84, pp2914–2924; Serenius, T. and Stalder, K. J. (2004) 'Genetics of length of productive life and lifetime prolificacy in the Finnish Landrace and Large White pig populations', *Journal of Animal Science*, vol 82, pp3111–3117; Lawrence, A. B., Conington, J. and Simm, G. (2004) 'Breeding and animal welfare: Practical and theoretical advantages of multi-trait selection', *Animal Welfare*, vol 13, ppS191–S196

26  Darwent, N. (2009) *Understanding the Economics of Robust Dairy Breeds*, Beyond Calf Exports Stakeholders Forum, Compassion in World Farming and RSPCA

27  *Poultry World* (2009) 'United Kingdom's egg industry', *Poultry World*, September, p22; Department for Environment, Food and Rural Affairs (2009) *Agriculture in the UK 2008*, Commodities, Defra

28  European Commission (2008) *Proposal for a Council Regulation on the Protection of Animals at the Time of Killing: Preamble*, COM(2008) 553 final, Brussels, 18 September 2008

29  Humane Slaughter Association (2005) *Instantaneous Mechanical Destruction*, Technical Note no 9; Humane Slaughter Association (2006) *Gas Killing of Chicks in Hatcheries*, Technical Note no 14; Council Directive 93/119/EC of 22 December 1993 on the protection of animals at the time of slaughter or killing, European Commission, Brussels; Statutory Instrument 1995 no 731, The Welfare of Animals (Slaughter or Killing) Regulations 1995, Schedule 11, Regulation 19, Killing of Surplus Chicks and Embryos in Hatchery Waste

30  Mercy for Animals (2009) *Hatchery Horrors*, www.mercyforanimals.org/
    hatchery, accessed September 2009; *World Poultry* (2009) 'SA Poultry Association
    suspends Boskop Layer farm', *World Poultry* news online, 9 September 2009,
    www.worldpoultry.net

31  Roberts, D. et al (2008) *Beyond Calf Exports: The Efficacy, Economics and
    Practicalities of Sexed Semen as a Welfare-Friendly Herd Replacement Tool in the
    Dairy Industry*, Report produced for Compassion in World Farming and the
    RSPCA, CIWF and RSPCA, www.calfforum.org.uk

32  Busuttil, L. (2008) '3000 bull calves a week shot because of Dutch importers'
    boycott', *Farmers Weekly*, 5 November, p10; Beyond Calf Exports Stakeholders
    Forum (2009) *Progress Report: Attitudes to Male Dairy Calves Are Becoming
    More Black & White*, www.calfforum.org.uk/; Weeks, C. (2007) *UK Calf
    Transport and Veal Rearing*, Compassion in World Farming

33  *The Record* (2009) 'Reward offered in calf case', *The Record*, Reed Fujii, 10
    February; HSUS (2009) *More Video of Abused Calves at Vermont Slaughter Plant*,
    2 November; RSPCA Australia (2009) *What Happens to Bobby Calves?*, Article
    ID 87, 19 October

34  Beyond Calf Exports Stakeholders Forum (2008) *Report on Conclusions and
    Recommendations*; Beyond Calf Exports Stakeholders Forum (2009) *Attitudes to
    Male Dairy Calves Are Becoming More Black & White*, Progress report,
    November. Both reports available at www.calfforum.org.uk

35  Humane Society of the United States (2010) *HSUS Pet Overpopulation Estimates*,
    HSUS; National Council on Pet Population Study and Policy (undated) *The Shelter
    Statistics Survey, 1994–1997*, www.petpopulation.org/statsurvey.html

36  Dogs Trust (2007) *Irresponsible Dog Owners Held Accountable for UK's Stray
    Dog Statistics*, News release; Dogs Trust (2009) *Shocking Stray Dog Figures Force
    Legislation Rethink*, News release

37  Animals Asia (2009) *Dog and Cat Eating*, www.animalsasia.org; World Chelonia
    Trust (2008) *Animal Markets in China*, www.chelonia.org; Gallagher E. (2009)
    'Barbaric Chinese cat market closed', *Mail on Sunday*,
    www.dailymail.co.uk/news/article-35012/Barbaric-Chinese-cat-market-
    closed.html, all accessed November 2009

38  Pet Food Manufacturers Association (2009) Statistics for 2009,
    www.pfma.org.uk/overall/pet-population-figures-.htm, accessed July 2009;
    Murray, J. K. et al (2010) 'Number and ownership profiles of cats and dogs in the
    UK', *Veterinary Record*, vol 166, pp163–169

39  Briggs, J. (2006) 'Estimate of spay/neuter surgeries in the United States and oppor-
    tunities for more affordable nonsurgical sterilization', in *Proceedings of the Third
    International Symposium on Non-Surgical Contraceptive Methods for Pet
    Population Control, 2006*, Session IV

40  Cats Protection (2008) *Annual Review 2008*, also information on website,
    www.cats.org.uk, accessed November 2009

41  New, J. C. Jr. et al (2004) 'Birth and death rate estimates of cats and dogs in US
    households and related factors', *Journal of Applied Animal Welfare Science*, vol 7,
    no 4, pp229–241

42  'Adoption event: More than 200 Chihuahuas need homes', *KNBC TV* news
    online, 3 October 2008, www.knbc.com

43  Kass, P. H. et al (2001) 'Understanding animal companion surplus in the United
    States: Relinquishment of nonadoptables to animal shelters for euthanasia',
    *Journal of Applied Animal Welfare Science*, vol 4, no 4, pp237–248

44  Murray, J. K. et al (2008) *The Neutered Status of UK Cats: Risk Factors and
    Prevalence*, www.svepm.org.uk/posters/2008/The%20Neutered%20Status%
    20of%20UK%20Cats.pdf; McGreevy, P. D. (2009) 'Challenges and paradoxes in

the companion-animal niche', in *Darwinian Selection, Selective Breeding and the Welfare of Animals*, UFAW International Symposium 2009, Bristol, 22–23 June 2009

45  Olson, P. (2006) 'Keynote address: Cats, canines and cures: the changing face of animal health', in *Proceedings of the 3rd Symposium on Non-Surgical Contraceptive Methods for Pet Population Control*, 9–12 November 2006, Alexandria, Virginia

46  Rhodes, L. and Moldave, K. (2002) *Contraception and Fertility Control in Animals*, AlcheraBio, for the Alliance for Contraception in Cats and Dogs (ACC&D)

47  Alliance for Contraception in Cats and Dogs (2006) *Proceedings of the 3rd Symposium on Non-Surgical Contraceptive Methods for Pet Population Control*, 9–12 November 2006, Alexandria, Virginia

48  Alliance for Contraception in Cats and Dogs (2009) *EsterilSol™/Neutersol® Frequently Asked Questions* and *Preliminary Statement on Infertile®*

49  Nolen, R. S. (2009) 'Los Angeles enacts mandatory pet sterilization law', *Journal of the American Veterinary Medical Association (JAVMA)*, online news, 1 April 2009, www.avma.org/onlnews/javma/apr08/080401j.asp

50  American Kennel Club (2009) *Legislative Alerts*, AKC website, www.akc.org; American Kennel Club (2009) 'West Virginia bill a radical attempt at limiting dog ownership', AKC website, www.akc.org, 17 March 2009

# 9

# Traditional, Rare and Fancy Breeds

## 9.1 Background and context: Breeding, survival and culture

### 9.1.1 Out of the mainstream: Traditional, rare and local

An account of the farrowing of a Large Black sow, written in England during the 1940s, makes the process sound easier than today when much research is devoted to improving the survival of piglets born in commercial farming. Each piglet born 'would lie on its side for a few seconds only – between 15 and 30 seconds by my watch – then rise to its feet and trot round and begin at once to suck from its mother. In an hour or so they had assumed that impudent, impish inquisitiveness that characterizes all little pigs, and were independent and adventurous.'[1] Large black pigs, hardy and suited to a free-range existence, are now a rare breed outside mainstream pig production.

On the Prince of Wales's organic farm in southern England, the breeds of pig are the Tamworth, a hairy russet-coloured breed with the upright ears and long snout reminiscent of its wild boar ancestor, and the Large Black. They are classified as rare native breeds in the UK National Database for Animal Genetic Resources and the Rare Breeds Survival Trust gives their conservation status as 'vulnerable'.[2,3] Today these two traditional breeds have speciality status. Between them there are just under 600 breeding females, compared to the 455,000 breeding females of commercial pigs used in the UK in 2007.[2,4]

In the wider world, the United Nations Food and Agriculture Organization (FAO) estimates that nearly 1 billion poor people in rural areas, accounting for over one third of the world's poor and 70 per cent of the rural poor, rely on mainly local breeds of livestock for their survival.[5] The international breeds of dairy and beef cattle, pigs, laying hens, meat chickens and sheep that make up the majority of the commercial animal production sector account for only 7 per cent of the 7616 breeds recorded in 2007 in the FAO's Global Databank of Animal Genetic Resources, while local breeds make up 86 per cent of the total.[6]

Animals of these traditional and local breeds typically survive on low inputs of feed, shelter and veterinary care and are less commercially productive, in terms of output per animal per year, than the breeds selected for the high-input, high-output systems of industrial farming. Increased demand for meat and milk in developing countries (predicted to double by mid century[7]) creates pressure for farmers to switch to higher-yielding imported breeds and more intensive methods in order to take advantage of the market (see Chapter 1). In addition, the need to reduce greenhouse gases from animal production globally is creating pressure from some policy-makers to use higher-yielding, more efficient animals. It is possible that today's traditional breeds which sustain millions of people in poor countries will disappear in their present form. This chapter explores the various rationales, that can be based on science, economics or culture, for supporting and promoting numerically small and distinctive breeds of domestic animal, and the implications for the quality of life of farmed animals as a whole.

The areas of livestock breeding and breed conservation that fall outside the mainstream commercial sector come under three overlapping categories:

1   traditional, local and minority breeds in developed countries;
2   breeding and collecting for the 'fancy' – that is, for appearance or showing as well as for utility;
3   traditional and local breeds in developing countries.

The preservation of minority or native livestock in developed countries is the mirror image of the mainstream livestock breeding industry. Relatively very small numbers of animals are involved. The emphasis is on preserving the past rather than on innovating for the market of the future. Cost-cutting is less important than heritage, aesthetics and conservation. The animals of the breed are considered rare and therefore special and in some senses to be preferred to the more common members of the species, and may have unusual characteristics.

In developing countries, traditional breeds of livestock are often relatively non-commercial; but they are essential to poor people's survival. In rich countries the traditional breeds of livestock are more likely to be alternative, niche or luxury brands. Industrial farming requires uniformity: animals that produce cuts of meat of almost identical size and shape and that are designed to fit into a standard-sized supermarket packaging tray. The alternative sector is more able to accept diversity. Their animals grow more slowly, challenging the speed-breeding culture of modern farming. Their products are supported by consumers disillusioned with the globalization and industrialization of farming who would rather pay more for meat from a rare or 'traditional' breed originating in the local agricultural landscape and history.

From the point of view of geneticists and conservationists, each gene pool of a breed is a subset of the genes of the species, and any of those genes that could be useful to people in the future need to be identified and stored. While the use of minority breeds is often, in developed countries, a reaction against modernity and a highly technological agriculture, their preservation paradoxically requires scientific and technological inputs such as genetic analysis, artificial insemination and the preservation of frozen sperm, eggs, embryos and DNA. The motivation behind the breeding and preservation of traditional, rare and fancy breeds is thus a complex mix that includes some nostalgia, the study and conservation of genetics, support for traditional ways of life, localism, sustainability and, in many cases, the desire to rear food animals more humanely.

## 9.1.2 The creation and decline of traditional breeds

Sales material for rare livestock products sometimes tells the consumer that the origin of the breed is 'lost in the mists of time', But in some cases the breed is a result of highly selective breeding in the more recent past. Many of the breeds that are now considered traditional in Western countries were in fact created in a frenzy of innovation and experimental cross-breeding during the 19th and early 20th centuries, either for food production or for the 'fancy'. In addition, many of what are now considered 'native' or 'traditional' breeds are at least partly 'exotic' in that they have at least part of their origins in animals imported by cross-breeders or collectors from a wide range of countries around the world. According to the historian of poultry breeds Joseph Batty, 'most breeds are "Foreign" when viewed historically'.[8] The only British livestock breeds that were not subjected to the attentions of breeders in the past 200 years were the Soay sheep of St Kilda and the Chillingham cattle.[9]

The 'standard' poultry breeds, for example, were created by a dedicated poultry-breeding and showing community in Britain from the mid 19th century (the 'Fowl Fever').[8] In this sense one essential difference between the supporters of rare breeds and the mainstream commercial community is at what point they choose to stop changing the breed to meet market demands. Many rare breed enthusiasts choose to stop around the early 20th century, before modern industrial breeding methods made today's rare breeds appear obsolete. At this point, they believed, many of the features of the breeds that made them hardy and long-lived were abandoned by those who bred animals suited to the emerging factory farms.

Joseph Batty's *Old and Rare Breeds of Poultry* describes how perfectly well-adapted and 'very useful' breeds were abandoned onto the 'scrap heap called Progress' because 'big business' took over farming. What had been household names in poultry, such as Anconas, Leghorns, Rhode Island Reds, Orpingtons, Plymouth Rocks and Wyandottes, became 'rare breeds' despite the fact that they were 'tried and tested, carried antibodies for fighting disease on free range, often developed for a specific purpose – laying, table or dual purpose'. From the mid 20th century, official farming policy favoured the new hybrid laying strains and the standard breeds were discarded as 'the march towards the creation of a nameless race [of commercial hybrids] continued'.[8]

Whether breeds are useful or obsolete varies with time. In the 18th century, older 'unimproved' native breeds such as the lop-eared Old English pig were themselves considered useless, obsolete and in need of improvement.[10] The 20th century considered obsolete many of the breeds created in the 18th and 19th centuries. The modern history of livestock breeding has been a continuous process of innovation to create more cost-effective animals that are faster maturing, more feed-efficient or visually attractive.

## 9.1.3 Innovation and standardization: Poultry breeds

Today's rare breed often started as yesterday's innovation, the most modern breed of the time. Robert Bakewell and the 18th-century breed improvers had little interest in the 'heritage' aspect of livestock except in the use of their genetics for innovation and commercialization. The Victorians who followed them were famously modernizers rather than conservers, nor wedded to native livestock. Breeders in Europe and North America imported chicken breeds created in Asia and further redesigned them for local use. Queen Victoria, a poultry fancier, acquired and exhibited some of the first Cochin chickens to arrive in England in 1845.[11] There was a 'flood of imports' of poultry in the mid 19th century from China, Japan, India, Java, Italy, Russia, South America, France, Germany, Holland, Belgium and Spain, among others. Breeders in Britain exchanged stock with breeders in North America, each making modifications to the breeds.[8,11]

In 1906, Sir Edward Brown's *Races of Domestic Poultry* described the specifically British 'races' as the Dorking, Sussex, so-called Indian (or Cornish) Game, Hamburgh, Redcap, Scots Grey and Orpington. By this date some specialization into chickens most useful for either egg laying or eating had already been made – for example by breeding out the motivation to sit and incubate a clutch of eggs and breeding in the ability to lay in winter. Brown listed around 70 breeds in all, including 30 laying (or 'non-sitting') breeds, which were medium sized, fast-growing and active, including the Ancona, Leghorn and Redcap, and most of which were non-native. The Hamburgh and the Redcap breeds were by this time capable of laying 220 eggs in a year, not so far from the 300 possible for a modern hybrid laying strain. Twenty breeds of meat ('table') chickens were listed, described as good mothers, larger in size, fairly rapid in growth, softer in flesh and less active, and included the Dorking, Sussex and Cornish Game. A characteristic of the traditional breeds was said to be their hardiness in all weathers and often their foraging ability, so that they could 'make their own living' and cost little in feed. The Redcap allegedly could be seen foraging in snow while being in full lay at the time.[11]

As described by Brown, 21 'general purpose' (dual-purpose) chicken breeds still existed in England at the start of the 20th century, good for producing both eggs and meat without 'excessive development' for either function. They were large in body, heavier in bone and therefore slower in growth than either the layers or the table breeds (and thus inconsistent with industrial requirements), and included the Orpington (created from both native and imported breeds around the 1880s), Langshan (imported from China in 1872), Plymouth Rock and Rhode Island Red (both created in the US during the 19th century from a mix of breeds, including orientals), Wyandotte, Cochin and the large Brahma (imported from India via US breeders in 1846).[11]

Breeds went in and out of fashion and some were bred for fancy points rather than utility. The Old English Game fighting breed, considered by the end of the 19th century the best 'table bird' because of its high proportion of breast meat, quick growth rate and small appetite, was also extremely hardy, roosted 'with impunity' in trees all winter, and was fearless in defence of chicks.[11] The legal abolition of cock-fighting led to the breed being drastically altered for the show ring as the Modern Game breed, the elongated neck and shortened body resembling a cartoon dinosaur.[8,12] In doing this, the breed lost the fighting bird's powerful breast muscles and became useless for meat production.[11] In the opposite direction, selection for breast meat had clearly begun by the start of the 20th century in the Cornish Game breed, whose exaggeratedly wide breast and short, thick, wide-set legs became the basis of the modern fast-growing international broiler chicken.

## 9.1.4 Standardization of pig breeds

Today's 'traditional' English pig breeds were also created in the 19th and early 20th centuries from many international sources. Pigs were 'daily altering their characteristics under the influence of some fresh cross', according to William Youatt's book *The Pig* (1847), and it was said that 'no two pigs are the same'.[13] Over only eight years, Prince Albert's pig herd was referred to variously as Bedfords, Yorkshires, Suffolks and Windsors.[10] The more prolific breeds of Chinese or Siamese pigs were imported and crossed with existing breeds. Some breeds disappeared.

The standardization of pig breeds was led by the National Pig Breeders' Association from 1884 and resulted in a much smaller number of closed pedigree breeds. By the 1920s the main breeds remaining were the Large and Middle Whites, Berkshire, Tamworth, Large Black, Essex, Wessex, Gloucester Old Spots, Cumberland and Long White Lop.[10]

In 1955 there was an official move to reduce the number of commercial breeds to a few or even to one, in the cause of production efficiency. The Howitt report to government saw the 'diversity of types' of pig as the industry's 'main handicap'. It recommended that the Large White, Landrace and Welsh should be the only breeds used and that an urgent programme of progeny testing of boars from these breeds should take place to develop sire lines to be used across the whole industry. The Large White became the basis for the modern commercial strains, and by 1973, when the Rare Breeds Survival Trust was established, what are now referred to as the traditional or rare breeds had become curiosities to be displayed at local agricultural shows. They had been 'left behind by the march of "progress" and the drive to produce a generic pig for least cost mass production'.[14]

## 9.1.5 Traditional breeds versus globalized agriculture

The preservation of the large number of traditional and minority breeds internationally has become part of the debate on, and resistance to, the spread of industrialized and globalized animal production. The main economic and social concern is the loss of locally adapted, low-input, low-output local breeds in developing countries that are displaced by the import of high-input, high-output specialized breeds originating in industrial countries.

According to the FAO's assessment of the *State of the World's Animal Genetic Resources* of 2007, 'the most significant [threat to livestock genetic diversity] is the marginalization of traditional production systems and the associated local breeds, driven mainly by the rapid spread of intensive livestock production, often large-scale and utilizing a narrow range of breeds'. The FAO sees the spread of the international high-input breeds designed for industrial production as both responding to the rising demand for animal products and facilitated by technologies for the global transfer of genetic material, and threatening a diversity of breeds resulting from thousands of years of human effort in breeding.[6,15]

By 1995, 600 known breeds of mammalian livestock had already ceased to exist.[16] According to the FAO in 2007, 20 per cent of all breeds were 'at risk' and one breed was being lost per month in the first years of the 21st century. The genetic basis of the world's livestock was becoming smaller, both because distinct local or minority breeds were disappearing and because the global commercial breeds themselves were losing genetic diversity as a result of inbreeding.[6] Diversity was thus being lost both between and within breeds.

## 9.1.6 What counts as a 'breed'?

'Breed' is one of the most relied-on concepts in the livestock industry, but it has proved difficult to define in the global context. Any particular population of animals within which genetic selection is made is likely to be referred to as a 'breed'. As a result, there is no definition of 'breed' that fits all circumstances.

For this reason the scientists and organizations advocating the preservation of breeds tend to leave the definition open to local interpretation. A 'breed' for purposes of conservation is defined by the FAO as: 'Either a subspecific group of domestic livestock with definable and identifiable external characteristics that enable it to be separated by visual appraisal from other similarly defined groups within the same species or a group for which geographical and/or cultural separation from phenotypically similar groups has led to acceptance of its separate identity'.[15] The FAO accepts that a 'breed' may not even be genetically distinct since 'They are constantly required to change in response to changes in market demand, and will at times be supplemented with bloodlines from other breeds.'[15] Broadly, the definition of a breed has one or more features of the following: a group of animals that are used for the same purpose, are distinguished in appearance by their breeder, have a more or less closed gene pool, or are used in a defined region or environment.

Essentially it has been accepted that a breed is what breeders, animal owners or governments say it is.[15] In developed countries the recognition of a breed may be related to pedigree, but in many cases internationally this would be irrelevant to local conditions. At one extreme, the UK's Rare Breeds Survival Trust requires 'evidence of continuous documented existence' and 25 years of recorded pedigree data for small breeds to be listed on its Watchlist.[3] In Ethiopia, on the other hand, the types of sheep vary depending on the environment they are kept in, the ethnic groups who keep them, and the methods of husbandry. They have been categorized into four main groups, the sub-alpine short fat-tailed, highland long fat-tailed, lowland fat-rumped and lowland thin-tailed, all visually distinct. These categories include 14 different sheep populations that are either traditionally recognized, phenotypically distinct or kept in distinct environments.[17]

## 9.2 Conservation practices: Recording and preserving animal genetic resources

### 9.2.1 Existing livestock breeds and their status

In 2007 the FAO produced a comprehensive assessment and rationale for the recording and control of livestock breeds, now relabelled as 'genetic resources for food and agriculture', listing 4068 local breeds of mammals and 1644 local breeds of poultry. The majority of these local breeds are in developing countries, but Europe and the Caucasus contain a greater number than any other one region. For around one third of all breeds there are no data on population, so it is not known how well or badly they are surviving. Where data exist, the FAO categorized 880 breeds of mammals and 607 breeds of domesticated birds as at risk.[6,15] For comparison, the inventory of farm animal genetic resources conducted for the UK in 2002 listed around 220 breeds of mammals (including equines) and around 240 breeds of poultry. Of these, 78 per cent of the mammal breeds were classified as 'rare' and 59 per cent of the poultry breeds were classified as 'rare' or at risk ('vulnerable', 'endangered' or 'critical').[2]

### 9.2.2 Global initiatives on breed conservation

Since the 1990s, the conservation of farmed animals has been an important part of international agreements on biological diversity. The 168 countries that

Table 9.1 *World number of local, regional and international breeds reported to the FAO*

|  | Local breeds[†] | Regionally used breeds[†] | Internationally used breeds[†] | Number of breeds known to be at risk or extinct[‡] |
|---|---|---|---|---|
| Cattle | 897 | 93 | 112 | 419 |
| Pigs | 541 | 25 | 33 | 273 |
| Sheep | 995 | 134 | 100 | 359 |
| Goats | 512 | 47 | 40 | 103 |
| Chickens | 1077 | 55 | 101 | 459 |

*Notes:* † Excluding extinct breeds.
‡ Extinct indicates that no breeding animals exist, although genetic material may have been preserved.
*Source:* FAO (2007)[15]

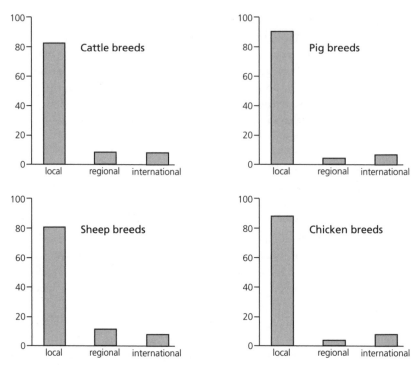

**Figure 9.1** *Percentage of existing breeds that are locally, regionally or internationally used*

*Source:* FAO (2007)[15]

have signed the 1992 Convention on Biological Diversity agreed to develop national strategies for the 'conservation and sustainable use' of all genetic resources that could be of actual or potential benefit to humans and, even more widely, to preserve local communities and 'traditional lifestyles' that are relevant to maintaining biological diversity. The Ninth Conference of Parties in 2008 further emphasized agricultural biodiversity.[18] The FAO has been coordinating global conservation efforts since 1990 and in 2007 initiated the Global Plan of Action for Animal Genetic Resources. In this context the management of genetic resources includes both local and commercial breeds and the genetic diversity within every breed.

By 2005 the majority of the countries that reported back to the FAO had programmes to conserve livestock genetic diversity and over one third had gene banks for cryopreservation of livestock genetic material. More than half of the participating countries in Europe and the Caucasus, East Asia, South Asia and the Americas reported that they had the capacity and infrastructure to preserve their breeds and a somewhat lower proportion were judged to be implementing plans. Not surprisingly, implementation was highest in developed countries, such as in North America and Europe, and also in major livestock-producing countries, including China, India and Brazil. Gene banks were well established

**Table 9.2** *Number of conservation breeding initiatives globally: Typically, over 90 per cent of these are for the conservation of local breeds*

| Method | cattle | sheep | goats | pigs | chickens | equines |
|---|---|---|---|---|---|---|
| In vivo | 324 | 261 | 109 | 120 | 194 | 149 |
| In vitro | 225 | 111 | 44 | 140 | 87 | 33 |

*Source:* FAO (2007, Table 78)[15]

in the Nordic countries, Central and Eastern European countries (Poland, Hungary and the Czech Republic), France and The Netherlands, among others. The world thus has hundreds of conservation efforts ongoing for local, regional breeds or international breeds, both though live breeding and through *in vitro* conservation (frozen sperm, embryos or other tissue) (see Table 9.2).[15]

Conservation programmes can involve a number of aspects, including finding, counting and categorizing the animals, live breeding programmes, the cryopreservation of genetic material such as sperm, embryos and DNA in tissue samples and, where possible, genotyping to establish both between-breed and within-breed diversity. By 2008, over 1000 breeds had been characterized genetically by DNA microsatellite markers.[19] In small populations of traditional or rare breeds, reproduction has to be managed to avoid mating close relatives (using either DNA markers or parentage records) and to breed out any diseases caused by damaging recessive genes that have already appeared.[20]

In the UK, the Rare Breeds Survival Trust (RBST) maintains a database of 'native' breeds (not all of native origin) and their conservation status. By 2009 the RBST had determined the effective population size, inbreeding coefficients and the genetic contribution of different founders in the pedigree for several numerically small sheep breeds, such as the Boreray, Soay, North Ronaldsay and Norfolk Horn, and used this information to select unrelated rams for semen collection in managed breeding programmes.[21] In Spain, dwindling numbers of the Alberes cattle breed of Catalonia live a semi-feral existence in the forests of the eastern Pyrenees and their preservation involves controlled breeding programmes to minimize inbreeding and the cryopreservation of semen and embryos.[22] In developing countries where exotic (Western) breeds are being imported, there have been attempts to prevent crossing with local breeds. Morocco, for example, designated zones for specified native breeds of sheep and restricted cross-breeding with imported sheep to separate zones.[23] It remains to be seen whether the active breed conservation programmes carried out in many developing countries will be enough to stem the tide of industrialized higher-yielding breeds as economies grow and small farmers can afford the extra inputs that Western breeds require.

There are many more minority, local or rare breeds than there are resources to monitor and preserve them. Scientists have suggested methods of prioritizing breeds for conservation that include the scientific, economic and what are called 'cultural' measures of value. These include genetic distinctiveness, distinctiveness of function, economic value of the breed traits, environmental or landscape value (for example in grazing use), disease resistance, cultural and historical value, and degree of endangerment.[15,16,24]

For some of the minority breeds in industrial countries, such as the Cornish, Plymouth Rock, Rhode Island Red and the Leghorn chickens, there may be no immediate need to have their genetics preserved. Their genes were co-opted long ago by the international breeding companies as the building blocks of the commercial hybrids for meat and laying chickens, now breeding annually in thousands of millions.[25,26]

## 9.2.3 Rationale for conserving livestock breeds

What are the arguments behind the drive to conserve minority livestock breeds? Although in many cases there is limited knowledge of how important either their genetics or their unique functional value to people or to ecosystems actually may be, two main groups of arguments are made. The first focuses on the role of traditional breeds in supporting an autonomous traditional way of life for people, which the introduction of modern commercial breeds and methods would disrupt. The second is about sustainable food production for the future in a changing environment. It is argued that traditional breeds:

• are better adapted to low-input agriculture, with resistance to heat, drought and parasites, and able to live on lower-quality diets;
• provide better economic support and food security for local communities;
• enable existing communities and husbandry methods to continue;
• are part of traditional cultures;
• are part of the property rights, knowledge and heritage of rural communities;
• carry genetics that may be essential for human use in the future (for example to cope with disease, climate change, economics or unforeseen changes to the environment).

High-yielding farm animals were typically developed to be productive in temperate climates and in relatively high-input systems. Native breeds in developing countries are adapted to be productive in local conditions of heat, drought, parasites and lower-quality feed. These conditions can cause suffering to high-yielding breeds that are not well adapted to survive them, and losses to their owners. The International Livestock Research Institute has pointed out that imported modern dairy cows that have replaced local breeds are at high risk of dying during droughts because they are not robust enough to walk long distances to water. Studies in South Africa have shown that cattle from imported Western breeds lose 15 per cent of their weight when they have no water for 24 hours, whereas the weight of local cattle is hardly affected.[15,27]

The international breeding companies hold stocks of the purebred animals that are the basis of the commercial breeds and are intended to provide a sufficiently wide gene pool from which to create new products in the future. These future needs could include adaptation to climate change or to the growing demand of consumers for free-range products; both of these demands are likely to need more robust animals able to adapt to varied environmental conditions. But there is evidence from a 2008 study of the allelic diversity in stocks of chickens held by the major breeding companies that they have captured only a small proportion of the genetics of the species. Each line of chickens studied had lost on average 60 per cent in the diversity of alleles compared to a hypothetical ancestral population, mainly because of the small number of the 'standard breeds' that were originally incorporated in the creation of the commercial hybrids of laying hens and meat chickens, and also due to inbreeding. The scientists concluded that non-commercial poultry breeds, including those in developing countries, probably still carry the now missing genes that the commercial sector may one day need.[25]

Examples do exist where neglected breeds are found to have important production traits, but generally this has been part of existing farming knowledge rather than derived from genetic analysis. In Britain the once-rare Lleyn sheep returned to greater favour because of its prolificacy and easy-care characteristics, desirable at a time when farmers need to reduce the cost of production.[28] The Wiltshire Horn sheep that sheds its fleece may provide an alternative to shearing, now desirable because of the very low value of wool.[28] Similarly, it is known that larger and heavier-bodied laying hens are better able to survive and produce well in outdoor conditions, compared to the commercial strains selected for smaller bodies that minimize their maintenance feed requirement.[29]

## 9.3 The impact on animals

### 9.3.1 Traditional breeds and quality of life

The level of well-being experienced by animals depends both on their genetics and on the husbandry conditions in which they are kept. In developed countries, animals of what are now rare and traditional breeds score highly on both those points. Supporters of traditional and rare breeds are often motivated by the desire to get back to a perceived more natural and more decent age of animal farming, where the animals' natural behaviour was in control and the animal was physically adapted to the outdoor environment. They are likely to be known as individuals, be given personal names, and may even have a status somewhere between a food-producing animal and a 'pet'. People who consume them expect them to have been given a high quality of life. They are not intended to be too commercial; if selective breeding for increased profitability becomes too effective in a traditional breed, it could make the breed less well adapted to its original environment and undermine the argument for its conservation and its special value.[20] For these reasons, the animals born in traditional and rare breeds today, given competent and responsible owners, have a considerably higher quality of life than animals born in the breeds used in the world's factory farms (see Box 9.1 for a summary).

It would be a mistake to take an over-romantic view of the quality of life, or death, of traditional livestock in developing countries or in pre-industrial societies anywhere. In late 19th-century England, Thomas Hardy's novel *Jude the Obscure* (1895) described the gruesome killing of a fattened household pig by country people at the start of winter. The pig would have been kept confined in a small outdoor pen. Jude, a self-educated man, is an appalled participant in the slaughter, while his wife Arabella urges that the pig must 'die slow' and that Jude is a 'tender-hearted fool' because 'poor folk must live'.[30] Suffering from starvation, dehydration, exposure to weather and untreated diseases and injuries affects food animals in developing countries today. Traditional methods of handling, transport and slaughter can be inhumane. But against this they may have more opportunities for natural behaviour, greater freedom from human interference and are less likely to experience the frustration, boredom, fear and social stress that characterize the factory farm.

## 9.3.2 Welfare dilemmas in rare and traditional breeds

Pre-industrial fancy livestock breeders, like the breeders of dogs and cats, wanted to produce interesting or exotic-looking animals and they experimented and designed accordingly. Breeding for the extremes of fancy features, as well as production features, has been a familiar theme through time, and these features were created for the benefit of the owner and fancier rather than that of the animal. Some of the Victorian breeding experiments produced huge combs on chickens that caused brain damage from their pressure on the head. Grossly fat pigs were bred and overfed for exhibition (a practice criticized by contemporaries).[10,12] Several of the fancy poultry breeds that survived to today, such as the Houdan, Sultan and Silkie, have excessive head feathering. The Poland hen (a breed described in the 17th century[11]) still has a cascading top-knot that almost completely obscures her vision and can compromise her behaviour, and the rare Large Black pig has drooping ears that entirely cover the eyes.

The control and management of the reproduction of rare and traditional breeds may on occasion be as invasive as the methods used in commercial animal production. Rare breed pigs grow to their slaughter weight more slowly and therefore the males intended for meat are castrated, often without anaesthetic (although pig castration is not permitted in the highest organic production standards, such as those of the Soil Association[31]). Traditional animal-keepers often use aprons on males to prevent mating, but less benign procedures can include castration without anaesthesia or using a cord to tie up the penis of a ram to the base of the scrotum.[32] Managed breeding programmes for endangered or small breeds have to control the choice of parents in order to avoid mating close relatives and often involve artificial insemination and sometimes the collection of embryos for frozen storage. Therefore conservation effort may impose a welfare cost on the animals of each generation in order to preserve the breed for human use in the future.

---

### BOX 9.1 THE QUALITY OF LIFE OF RARE BREEDS
### IN DEVELOPED COUNTRIES

Some advantages include:

- Breeds have high status because of their origin story and rarity.
- Animals are typically kept free range and at low stocking density.
- Animals are typically slower-growing and have a slower rate of reproduction.
- Rare breeds are not subject to intensive genetic selection for production; they avoid lameness, heart disease and other diseases of high-yielding breeds.
- Owners are likely to be committed to promoting natural behaviour.
- Consumers are likely to insist on extensive conditions and natural behaviour.
- Animals may be kept with minimal human interference (semi-feral populations).

Some disadvantages include:

- Traditional mutilations, such as castration, often continue.
- Fancy features of the breed may in some cases interfere with function or behaviour.
- Conservation breeding may be managed by invasive methods, such as artificial insemination and embryo collection.
- Semi-feral populations may suffer from starvation, illness and untreated injury.

---

## 9.4 Public policy, non-commercial breeds and the future

In developing countries the drive to conserve traditional breeds is associated with supporting the poor but in developed countries it tends to be associated with the wealthier sections of society. It is often a choice made possible by affluence to support sustainable farming methods and a better quality of life for the animals, as well as to avoid the perceived uniformity of the supermarkets. Rare breeds seem to offer a route back to a time characterized by an organic relationship between people and their livestock and, indeed, between different classes of society. The preservation of rare breeds may often be more about culture than about necessity. Probably the lives of the large majority of the British population and the large majority of its livestock population would be unaffected if some of the 44 breeds of equines and 84 breeds of sheep, mostly categorized as rare, distinctive or locally adapted, ceased to exist.

So, should people who have the choice support rare breeds of livestock in developed countries and the conservation of traditional and minority breeds in developing countries? From the point of view of the well-being of the animals, there are good arguments for doing that. Anyone who is concerned by the low level of animal welfare in the world's factory farms must welcome the preservation of rare breeds outside mainstream intensive animal production.

When imported modern breeds displace local and traditional breeds, they are generally kept in intensive conditions, even if on a small scale, subjecting them to overcrowding and restricting their behaviour. Genetic selection for maximum productivity has, in several cases, damaged the health of commercial breeds (see Chapter 3). In some developing countries the resources may well not exist to provide high-yielding animals of commercial breeds with the inputs that will keep them healthy. It is also possible, though not proven, that genes carried by these traditional animals could be used to avoid suffering among the commercially kept billions by conferring resistance to existing or future disease. The existing diversity of breeds locally and internationally means that farmers in developed countries have an alternative to the overspecialized single-purpose commercial breeds of dairy cows, laying hens and meat chickens whose health has been damaged by excessive selection for yield. If farmers and their customers chose, they could move to using hardy and dual-purpose traditional breeds.

Policy-makers are becoming more aware of the value of traditional livestock to poorer communities. They are less convinced than in the past that the right route to development in every case is to be found in industrial animal production.[33] But they still tend to believe that the escalating demand for animal products as countries develop and incomes increase is unstoppable and will require a correspondingly huge increase in output from the livestock sector globally during this century. In this future context, the most important issue for animal welfare is the genetic selection and husbandry of the animals within the commercial sector.

Support for the use of rare and traditional breeds can be a lever to improve the quality of life of the billions of nameless livestock that fill the world's supermarket shelves. Like the best organic farming, the use of rare and traditional breeds can challenge the 'use-and-dispose' culture of commercial animal breeding. Globally, to complement the international agreements and programmes on the conservation of farm animal 'genetic resources', we need international agreements and programmes for animal welfare that focus on the level of well-being experienced by the animals. These could include the phasing out of the most highly selected strains of food animals and investment in education and veterinary services for animal owners who continue to keep traditional breeds outside the mainstream commercial sector.

## Notes

1   Rogerson, S. and Tunnicliffe, C. (1949) *Both Sides of the Road: A Book about Farming*, Collins
2   Department for Environment, Food and Rural Affairs (2002) *UK Country Report on Farm Animal Genetic Resources 2002*, Defra
3   Rare Breeds Survival Trust (2008, 2009) *Watchlist*, www.rbst.org.uk, accessed July 2009
4   Department for Environment, Food and Rural Affairs (2008) *Agriculture in the UK 2007*, Defra
5   FAO (2007) *Global Plan of Action for Animal Genetic Resources* and *Interlaken Declaration on Animal Genetic Resources*, International Technical Conference on Animal Genetic Resources for Food and Agriculture, Interlaken, Switzerland, 3–7 September 2007; Steinfeld, H. et al (2006) *Livestock's Long Shadow: Environmental Issues and Options*, FAO

6   FAO (2007) *The State of the World's Animal Genetic Resources for Food and Agriculture – in brief*, D. Pilling and B. Rischkowsky (eds), FAO
7   Steinfeld H et al (2006) *Livestock's Long Shadow: Environmental Issues and Options*, FAO; World Bank (2007) *World Development Report 2008: Agriculture for Development*, World Bank, Overview and Chapter 2
8   Batty, J. (2006) *Old and Rare Breeds of Poultry*, fourth edition, Beech Publishing House
9   Hall, S. J. G. and Clutton-Brock, J. (1989) *Two Hundred Years of British Farm Livestock*, British Museum (Natural History)
10  Wiseman, J. (2000) *The Pig: A British History*, second edition, Duckworth
11  Brown, Sir E. (2004) *Races of Domestic Poultry: History and Development*, revised and edited by J. Batty, Beech Publishing House
12  Moncrieff, E. (1996) *Farm Animal Portraits*, Antique Collectors' Club; see Plate 96 for over-fattened pigs
13  Watson, L. (2004) *The Whole Hog: Exploring the Extraordinary Potential of Pigs*, Profile Books
14  British Pig Association (2002) *Traditional British Breeds: British Pig Breeds*, www.britishpigs.org.uk/trad.htm, accessed July 2008
15  FAO (2007) *The State of the World's Animal Genetic Resources for Food and Agriculture*, B. Rischkowsky and D. Pilling (eds), FAO, Rome
16  Ruane, J. (1999) 'A critical review of the value of genetic distance studies in conservation of animal genetic resources', *Journal of Animal Breeding and Genetics*, vol 116, no 5, pp317–323
17  Gizaw S. et al (2008) 'Indigenous sheep resources of Ethiopia: Types, production systems and farmers preferences', *Animal Genetic Resources Information (AGRI)*, vol 43, pp25–39
18  Convention on Biological Diversity (1992): see *List of Parties; Text of the Convention*; Ninth Conference of Parties, Bonn, May 2008, Decision IX/1, *In-Depth Review of the Programme of Work on Agricultural Biodiversity*
19  FAO (2008) 'Editorial: Measuring diversity', *Animal Genetic Resources Information (AGRI)*, vol 43, pI
20  Woolliams, J. A. (2004) 'Managing populations at risk', in G. Simm et al (eds) *Farm Animal Genetic Resources*, Nottingham University Press, pp85–106
21  Rare Breeds Survival Trust (2009) *Reports and Publications: Geneped Analysis*, www.rbst.org.uk
22  Fina, M. et al (2008) 'Characterisation and conservation programme of the Alberes cattle breed in Catalonia (Spain)', *Animal Genetic Resources Information (AGRI)*, vol 43, pp1–14; Jordana, J. et al (1999) 'Conservation genetics of an endangered Catalonian cattle breed (Alberes)', *Genetics and Molecular Biology*, vol 22, no 3, pp387–394
23  FAO (undated) *Protecting Animal Genetic Diversity for Food and Agriculture: Time for Action*, FAO
24  Hall, S. (2004) 'Conserving animal genetic resources: Making priority lists for British and Irish livestock breeds', in G. Simm et al (eds) *Farm Animal Genetic Resources*, Nottingham University Press, pp311–320; Defra (2006) *UK National Action Plan on Farm Animal Genetic Resources*, Defra
25  Muir, W. M. et al (2008) 'Genome-wide assessment of worldwide chicken SNP genetic diversity indicates significant absence of rare alleles in commercial breeds', *Proceedings of the National Academy of Sciences*, vol 105, no 45, pp17312–17317
26  Whittle, T. E. (2000) *A Triumph of Science: A 70 Year History of the UK Poultry Industry*, Poultry World Publications

27 'Livestock breeds face 'meltdown', BBC News online, 2 September 2007, news.bbc.co.uk; Hoffman, I. (2008) 'Livestock genetic diversity and climate change adaptation', presentation at the Conference on Livestock and Global Climate Change, Hammamet, Tunisia, 17–20 May 2008, www.bsas.org.uk/downloads/LGCC_procdings.pdf
28 Defra (2006) *UK National Action Plan on Farm Animal Genetic Resources*, Defra; Conington, J. and Dwyer, C. (2009) 'Breeding for easier-managed sheep', in *Darwinian Selection, Selective Breeding and Welfare*, UFAW International Symposium 2009, Bristol, 22–23 June
29 *Poultry World* (2009) 'Bodyweight puts profit back in free range', *Poultry World* , July, pp24–25
30 Hardy, T. (1895) *Jude the Obscure*, Macmillan, 1968, Chapter 10
31 Soil Association (2005) *Soil Association Organic Standards*, Revision 15, Chapter 13
32 Haile, A. et al (2008) 'Designing community-based breeding strategies for indigenous sheep breeds of smallholders in Ethiopia', in M. Tibbo (ed) *Animal Breeding in Developing Countries Context*, NCCR Trade Regulation IP-9 Workshop on Animal Breeding, Innovation, Trade and Proprietary Rights, Berne, 27–28 November 2008
33 For example, World Bank (2009) *Minding the Stock: Bringing Public Policy to Bear on Livestock Sector Development*, World Bank

# 10
# Pedigrees and Purity

## 10.1 Background and context: The value of pedigrees and purity

### 10.1.1 Aristocratic animals

In Anna Sewell's 1877 novel, the horse Black Beauty is saved by having been 'well-bred and well-born'. His father had a 'great name' and his grandfather had twice won the Cup at the Newmarket races. After years of exploitation and mistreatment by his various owners Black Beauty is in danger of being sent to slaughter for dog-meat, but instead ends up in a second-hand horse sale, full of other old, broken-down and lame animals and their often poverty-stricken sellers and buyers. In this sad scene the gentleman farmer Mr Thoroughgood recognizes Black Beauty as another gentleman, probably a Thoroughbred, and takes him home to start a better life. 'There's a deal of breeding about that horse', says Mr Thoroughgood.[1]

One of the most intriguing aspects of human interaction with animals is our concern with the definition of breeds and with breed (or species) purity and how this is related to the status of the animals and how we value them. Nearly all breeds created by humans and the breeding methods that have been discussed in previous chapters make use of the concepts 'purebred' and 'pedigree'. These terms are often used interchangeably and to imply some form of hereditary superiority compared to animals of the same species or type that are not thus endowed.

This is in striking contrast to current thinking about human society. The idea that a hereditary human aristocracy possesses some kind of genetic superiority as a result of a 'pedigree' would now be ridiculed – more often the opposite would be assumed to be true – and genetic diversity within human society is generally celebrated and encouraged. The stereotyping of different human populations according to inherited differences of appearance or behaviour that was entirely normal in the 19th and early 20th centuries has come to be considered obsolete and unacceptable. Parallel with the democratization of human society, animal breeders continue to be preoccupied with the stratification, definition and genetic purity of animals and breeds. An age-old preoccupation with genetic boundaries and genetic purity may also continue to influence scientific thinking about animal species.

The large majority of the billions of food production animals are anonymous hybrids, crosses to capture the desired characteristics of their often pedigree parents. The highest-value animals and those that win prizes at shows have pedigrees. Animals that have pedigrees are often those we admire most and acknowledge a personal relationship to (they often are given personal names). The British Pig Association stresses that only 'pedigree stock' are part of the conservation efforts for traditional pig breeds and has adopted the slogan: 'Without a pedigree it's just another pig.'[2] Like the 'prince of palfreys',[3] the Dauphin's horse in Shakespeare's *Henry V*, animals seen as high quality are often described as aristocrats of their species, reflecting the social status of their owners or breeders. As the historian of early livestock breeding Nicholas Russell has put it: 'The parallels between, on the one hand, the human obsession with title, hereditary position and social caste and, on the other, animal pedigrees, are too obvious to need emphasis.'[4]

Animal breeds, pedigrees and species have a scientific basis in genetics, but this genetic understanding is relatively recent. The pre-scientific understanding of breeds and their valuation seems to continue. While the Dauphin's fantasy ('his neigh is like the bidding of a monarch'[3]) is presented as ridiculous, it is still familiar. This chapter will give some examples of the scientific and the non-scientific uses of the concepts of pedigree and genetic purity in relation to breeds and species. It looks at how traditional but enduring concepts of blood and breed purity can affect our interaction with animals, and the outcomes for the animals.

## 10.1.2 Categorization, species and pedigrees in science

The human motivation to categorize and distinguish between types of animal is all around us. Experts and enthusiasts can identify a species of bird, or a breed of dog, sheep or cattle, at a glance. A major part of modern biology has centred on the identification of differences between species and with the recognition, collection and cataloguing of species of animal. Every week new scientific results are published on the discovery or identification of a previously unknown species or the reclassification of a species or subspecies.

The scientific understanding of species, subspecies and the boundaries between them is still very incomplete. Scientists are aware that the definition of a species is unclear and some even say that the understanding of evolution has made the concept itself outdated. On one analysis, around half of what are considered to be distinct species of animal are not reproductively independent lineages.[5] Although the species distinction between dogs and cats, for example, seems

> **BOX 10.1 THE DOMESTIC DOG IN ZOOLOGICAL NOMENCLATURE**
>
> Kingdom: Animalia
> Phylum: Chordata
> Class: Mammalia
> Order: Carnivora
> Family: Canidae
> Genus: *Canis*
> Species: *Canis familiaris*

entirely obvious, in many cases it is unclear whether animal populations should be classed as the same species or scientifically distinguished as sub-species. Where they come in contact, populations classified as subspecies or species sometimes hybridize. The potential of animals of different species or subspecies to hybridize varies considerably.

It is known that hybrids between animals that have too distantly related genetics have reduced fitness in an evolutionary sense, so that there is natural selection against hybrids. 'Outbreeding depression' typically, but not always, produces sterile offspring or offspring that are less able to compete than either of their parent populations in a given ecological niche, or are more susceptible to infectious disease. A major reason for this is thought to be the incompatibility of groups of genes that have evolved to function together in different populations, and different species often have different numbers of chromosomes, which prevents viable hybrids being born. There is also evidence of sexual selection against hybrids. For example, in hybrids of collared and pied flycatchers, the female hybrids are sterile and the male hybrids are less likely to pair successfully. This lack of success seems to be mainly because their 'intermediate' plumage is less attractive to females.[6] There is therefore evidence that biology discourages hybridization and favours the boundaries between species by making animal hybrids an 'evolutionary dead-end'.

On the other hand, it is known that hybrids of some species can reproduce and survive in regions between the populations of the two parent species ('hybrid zones') or sometimes within them. Hybrids of the ring-necked dove (*Streptopelia capicola*) and the vinaceous dove (*Streptopelia vinacea*) found in Uganda have a call that is distinct from that of either parent species but is understood by them, enabling the hybrids to establish breeding territories.[7] Stable hybrid zones have developed between three closely related species of mussels when they are introduced by shipping or aquaculture, and hybrids between California tiger salamanders (*Ambystoma californiense*) and introduced barred tiger salamanders (*Ambystoma tigrinum mavortium*) appear to have greater fitness than the parent species.[8] (Hybrids have also been created in zoo breeding programmes, either unintentionally between subspecies not recognized as such or intentionally, such as the breeding of (sterile) lion–tiger hybrids as a novelty in China.[9])

Some scientists argue that 'static' ideas of species purity are 'anti-evolutionary' and that hybridization and gene flow are natural parts of the evolutionary process; they could even rescue small inbred populations of endangered species. It has been suggested that hybridization between species may have had a role in the creation of animal species by adaptive radiation, where there is rapid creation of species in a new environment; for example, the common ancestor of all wild goats may have acquired more efficient mitochondria through hybridization, enabling the species to live at high altitude.[10]

Hybrid populations today are often seen as a biological anomaly because their existence and their genes lack a clear evolutionary origin. They challenge genetic science because their gene combination is not a result of evolutionary adaptation – they have two different evolutionary histories. Taxonomy has no place for them, and unsurprisingly they are excluded from the provisions of the International Code of Zoological Nomenclature along with 'hypothetical concepts' and 'teratological [monstrous or abnormal] specimens'.[11]

Scientists tend to consider genetically 'pure' populations as 'the real thing' and hybrid populations or individuals as in some way lacking in validity. They are sometimes seen as a threat to the 'genetic integrity' of an animal population.[12] Wildcats (*Felis silvestris silvestris*) hybridize with domestic cats in Scotland and in Iberia (Spain and Portugal), where genetic analysis indicates that nearly 7 per cent of the wildcat population has hybrid ancestry. Hybridization could threaten the Iberian wildcat population partly because populations that lack 'genetic purity' are less likely to be considered worthy of conservation funding.[12] The North American recovery plan for the plains bison or buffalo (*Bison bison*), now numbering around 1 million on both public and private lands, has discovered considerable hybridization between bison and domestic cattle. Genetic analysis has found cattle genes in 8 out of 11 federal bison populations studied.[13] Some scientists consider these impure bison to be genetic fakes, while others believe that since these animals look like bison, behave like bison and fulfil the ecological role of bison, the recovery plan has achieved its goal despite the mixed genes.[13]

Pedigrees have a scientific function that is entirely separate from the non-scientific valuation of superiority that is generally given to the word when used to describe domesticated animals. A pedigree is simply a record of parentage and is useful in studying the inheritance of genes, the effects of inbreeding, and also the social structures and breeding strategies among wild animals. As well as written records, statistical analysis of microsatellite markers can be used to confirm, correct or, in some cases, construct pedigrees.[14] The analysis of parentage records is used to avoid inbreeding in domestic animals or maintaining genetic diversity in small populations of rare or minority livestock, or in captive populations of wild animals.[15] In the absence of gene analysis, pedigree information has been used historically as one of the main methods of selective breeding, based on the observation that offspring often resemble parents.

Pedigree, breed purity and genetic purity have come to have connotations of moral value that have little to do with science. While most modern scientists would be entirely aware of the difference between a scientific description and a moral evaluation, in the past scientists have undoubtedly had a hand in confusing the two.

## 10.2 Some historical examples of pedigree anxiety

### 10.2.1 Human pedigrees, hybrids and eugenics

A closed breeding policy began to be applied to most domestic animals towards the end of the 19th century, a time when both Darwinism and the Mendelian theory of inheritance were of great interest to scientists and the

---

### BOX 10.2 BRANDING

The pedigree of a domestic animal is essentially a marketable brand. While it is supposed to guarantee a particular type of commodity to consumers, it also serves to protect those who invest in the brand by breeding. Pedigree horses and cattle are still physically branded – that is, their distinctive breed logo approved by the breed societies is indelibly marked on their skin. Numerous official brands are registered with agricultural authorities and breed societies. Crowns, shields, crosses and other symbols of the animals' high-quality status abound on breed brands: the Bavarian Warmblood brand incorporates both a shield and a crown; the British Warmblood brand is a crown topped by a cross.[16] Today, freeze branding is mainly used for horses: a branding iron shaped with the required logo is chilled in liquid nitrogen (a temperature of $-196°C$) and held to the horse's skin for several seconds, burning and destroying the pigment cells in the skin so that the hair grows back white in the shape of the brand. On light-coloured horses, the brand is held on longer so that no hair grows back. Hot branding, more commonly used for cattle to identify ownership, is a cheaper but more painful method and involves burning through the upper layer of the skin to produce a permanent area of sufficiently wide scarring in the shape of the brand. American racing thoroughbreds are required to have an identification code tattooed in the inside of the lip. Cattle may be branded and castrated at the same time without anaesthesia.

---

public. In Europe and the US, there was also an increasing preoccupation with the classification of people and populations according to their perceived genetic value, which included defining human nationalities and races and their assumed hereditary national characteristics. It was a time when society policed class and racial boundaries rigorously.

In 1904 the biological statistician Francis Galton was involved in founding a Eugenics Record Office at University College London, with the aim of investigating the breeding records of 'able families' such as those of the scientist Fellows of the Royal Society. In the following years scientists aimed to investigate the inheritance of various specific abilities and also of diseases and abnormalities, as well as 'deficiencies', including 'feeblemindedness', 'shiftlessness' and 'pauperism'. Over the next decades, eugenics (the study of 'good breeding') became a popular creed (see also Chapter 13). The historian of science Daniel Kevles details how these ideas were based both on Darwinian ideas of evolutionary fitness as applied to human society and on frequently simplified versions of Mendel's theory of the inheritance of characteristic traits in discrete units, in ways similar to the inheritance of some coat colours in animal species.[17] The terms in which scientists at that period discussed human breeding are entirely familiar today in contemporary discussions of livestock, dog, cat or horse breeding.

Racial purity began to be seen as an important issue (as 'breed purity' still is today). As a result of the immigration to the US from non-'Nordic' regions of Europe (Nordics were assumed to be the premier white race), race 'mongrelization' was feared. It was expected that blood from Southern Europe would make the general population eventually 'darker in pigmentation, smaller in stature, more mercurial ... more given to crimes of larceny, kidnapping, assault, murder, rape, and sex-immorality'.[17]

The perceived success of animal breeding, especially Thoroughbred breeding, was quite frequently held up as a model for what the human race could aspire to if eugenic policies were followed. The American eugenics researcher and popularizer Charles Davenport received a research endowment from a racehorse-owning family who thought that the human species would also benefit from selective breeding. Davenport himself believed that a woman should no more accept a man 'without knowing his biologico-genealogical history' than a breeder of livestock would take 'a sire for his colts or calves ... without pedigree'. As contemporary breeders of livestock, cats and dogs often believe, Davenport's motivations were entirely for what he saw as the good of his 'breed'. He considered that if 'human matings could be placed upon the same high plane as that of horse breeding', this could achieve 'the most progressive revolution in [human] history'. Exhibits to explain the principles of good human breeding were often set up under the auspices of the American Eugenics Society at state fairs. One educational placard asked the public: 'How long are we Americans to be so careful for the pedigree of our pigs and chickens and cattle – and then leave the *ancestry of our children* to chance or to "blind" sentiment?' Eugenics field researchers were provided with a '*Trait Book*' to enable them to identify people whose families should be investigated.[17]

Comparisons between the desirable and undesirable characteristics of people and animals, and the desire to weed out 'off-types', were not unusual in the early 20th century, even from future Nobel Prize-winning scientists. Karl von Frisch concluded a popular biology book of 1936 with a section on race hygiene, worrying that natural selection was no longer operating to weed out undesirable 'variations' in human populations. In 1938 Erich Jaensch, a biologist and ardent Nazi, published a paper entitled 'The henhouse as a means of research and explanation in human race questions', comparing, with scientific gravitas, quantitative tables and photographs, the pecking styles of northern versus southern breeds of chicken. His studies showed him that southern chickens mirrored the less desirable behavioural characteristics of southern European humans as compared with the superior northern races; southern chickens pecked rapidly, but impulsively and inaccurately, while northern chickens pecked steadily and accurately.[18]

The confusion of science and valuation can still be found in some contemporary discussion of animal breeds. Visitors to Dartmoor National Park in south-west England, famous for its free-ranging ponies, are given a lesson in policing equine reproduction. An information leaflet explains that 'pure-bred' Dartmoor ponies with a pedigree ('more refined than the native breed') are too valuable to be left out where they might interbreed with non-registered ponies. The ordinary 'native' ponies live freely on the commons with 'mixed-breed' ponies and stallions, and so it is not possible to know their parentage. In contrast, the 'pure-bred' ponies have fathers 'chosen for their good breeding' who were 'introduced to the mare in a controlled environment'.[19]

## 10.2.2 Blood purity and thoroughbred racing success

The American horse Lexington (1850–1873) was a legend in the racing industry. A wonder of speed and endurance, Lexington was withdrawn from racing at the age of five because of blindness, probably inherited from his father who had also become blind, and was used as a stud for many years in Kentucky. Considered the most important sire of the US Thoroughbred industry in the second half of the 19th century, he appeared in the pedigrees of most of the American horses born during this period. At the turn of the 20th century, questions were being asked about the breed purity of American Thoroughbreds, and Lexington was one whose ancestry was suspect. Illustrative of the times, Lexington's original trainer was black and a former slave, and thus not permitted to race Lexington under his own name.[20,21]

As Peter Willett's history of the Thoroughbred details, the desire of Thoroughbred breeders in England to maintain what they saw as the blood purity was severely tested by events that proved that the 'purest' was not necessarily the best. At the turn of the 20th century, racehorse breeding in the US and Australia resulted in a flood of imported horses, which competed with British breeders and their export markets and also, in the British view, were of dubious ancestry. In response, volume XIX of the General Stud Book required that imported horses claimed to be Thoroughbreds must have proof of 'eight or nine crosses of pure blood, to trace back for at least a century, and to show such performances of its immediate family on the Turf as to warrant the belief in the purity of its blood'. The stable door was finally shut to impurity by the subsequent Jersey Act of 1913 (after Lord Jersey, the previous chief steward of the Jockey Club). Under this new rule, a horse could only be admitted to the Thoroughbred Stud Book if his or her pedigree could be 'traced without flaw' on both sides to horses and mares already in earlier volumes of the Stud Book. This disqualified Lexington. One of Lexington's descendants, Durbar II, similarly impure, won the Derby the next year, followed by a series of racing successes by 'half-breds' or horses of doubtful blood purity. Undeterred, the Jockey Club continued to maintain that purity of blood, not racing performance, was what mattered.[20]

By the time World War II ended, the 'purity of blood' argument was becoming untenable and in 1948 both the prestigious St Leger and the Two Thousand Guineas races were won by horses debarred from the Stud Book. The requirement that all new horses admitted should have ancestors already in the Stud Book was withdrawn. This climb-down came just in time to save the Jockey Club's rationale for existence, as within the next 15 years four Derby winners and four St Leger winners would previously have been debarred.[20] It may be relevant that this reformulation came at a period when the experience of Fascist racism had led to the scientific and political discrediting of 'theories' of innate superiority conferred by race or caste as applied to humans.

## 10.2.3 Defining blood purity of Arabian horses

A more recent controversy emerged over the definition of the 'pure-bred' Arabian breed of horse, and what was, or was not, blood purity of descent. The point at issue here was whether 'Arabian' horses required a pedigree leading specifically to the Arabian desert. According to equine legend, the Bedouin Arabs developed the 'Original' or 'Elite' Arab breed, used as a cavalry horse from the time when Arabs conquered the southern Mediterranean region, but not all horses originating in the Middle East could be considered pure Arabians.

In 1974 the World Arabian Horse Organization (WAHO), whose mission is to 'maintain throughout the world the purity of the blood of the horses of the Arabian breed', adopted a pragmatic definition of a purebred Arabian horse as 'one which appears in any purebred Arabian Stud Book or Register listed by WAHO as acceptable' and accredited stud books in nearly 60 countries.[22] This definition was made on the grounds that Arabian horses had never been a clearly defined breed either at their origin or during their global imports during the 19th century, meaning that disputes about ancient parentage were now fruitless. The Arabian Horse Registry of America (AHRA) refused to accept the purity of most South American horses claimed to be Arab and withdrew from WAHO. The AHRA considered that its own registration guaranteed that the horse's pedigree 'traces in all lines to the Arabian desert', a claim that WAHO saw as without scientific, historical or geographical foundation. WAHO claimed that 98 per cent of new horses registered by 1970 with the AHRA did not have the required 'desert' root of ancestry and carried out detailed investigations through the AHRA register to make its case against the 'desert-bred' claim. These disputed pedigrees went back to horses imported in the 19th century, including horses designated as 'high-caste Arab', 'original arab', some certified as born and mated in the deserts, but some whose pedigree had been lost or unproven in so far as deserts were concerned.[22]

Attempts to define Arabian blood purity also took place among Russian, Polish and Ukrainian breeders, and moves at the turn of the 20th century were made to compile a separate stud book for horses that had 'the slightest drop of non-Arabian blood' (these were the large majority). Horses were again distinguished by whether they were or were not imported from the desert 'without a drop of alien blood'. One proposal was that horses were sufficiently Arab for a reputable stud book if they had 66 per cent proven Arabian blood (interestingly, the use of local mares for breeding seems not to have been thought a problematic 'infusion of alien blood', possibly because the female was seen primarily as the receptacle rather than a genetic contributor). Many American horses originated from these studs, providing evidence to WAHO that the desert-root claim was often unhistorical.[22] Analysis of mitochondrial DNA has more recently been brought to bear on this issue in order to compare the pedigrees and genetics of Arabian horses recorded as having maternal ancestors bred in the desert. Studies of AHRA-registered Arabian horses in 2000 and of Polish Arabians in 2007 concluded that the pedigree was accurate for the majority of maternal lines, but not for all. The Polish study found common genetic markers in different pedigree lines, including between a line founded by a Polish mare of unknown origin and an imported 'desert-bred' mare.[23]

By 2008 the (American) Arabian Horse Association (the successor to the AHRA) required only that registered horses should be 'of pure Arabian blood, as verified by pedigree'. Alternatively, the horse may be registered in separate registries as a half-Arabian (although crosses with mules or 'any other animal' are not acceptable), or as Anglo-Arabians (a cross with a Thoroughbred, itself a breed created through crossing), which are required to have between 25 and 75 per cent of Arabian descent.[24]

## 10.2.4 Hybrids and degeneration

Biologists have sometimes been protective towards the purity of species in ways that mirror the animal breeders' concern with pedigree. One of the most famous zoologists of the 20th century, Konrad Lorenz, associated the purity of wild animal species with superior beauty and moral integrity compared to the degenerate behaviour of hybrid or domesticated animals (or humans). The account of his life by Richard Burkhardt Jr. shows that Lorenz's strongest statements on the subjects were made after the Nazi occupation of Austria in 1938, when he was probably attempting to improve his research funding by showing how modern views of animal biology supported Nazi racial ideology. But these statements were linked to his genuine beliefs as a biologist about the inherent beauty and nobility of the wild in contrast to the degeneration of the tame or domesticated. The tame included the 'domesticated' urban civilized human despised by the National Socialists.[18]

Lorenz's 1938 paper on 'Breakdowns in instinctive behaviour of domestic animals' contrasted the moral behaviour of the full-blooded 'respectable' greylag goose (*Anser anser*) with the 'degenerate' behaviour of crosses between greylag and domestic geese; these hybrids lacked the normal inhibitions inborn in the wild geese and could be induced to mate much more easily. Lorenz commented that 'man has an inborn abhorrence for humans who have degenerate instincts' and 'this abhorrence has also certainly a species-preserving value'. This was shown by the abhorrence of pure greylag geese for 'street-walkers'. The fact that pure-blooded wild geese reached sexual maturity much later than domestic or hybrids of wild and domestic geese and tended to be monogamous over many years showed their superior moral virtue. Hybrids and domestic geese lost their inborn aversion to mating with siblings and copulated without forming pair bonds, he found. He saw indiscriminate, promiscuous breed-polluting sexual behaviour as typical of domestication, even if a goose had only a fraction of 'domestic' blood. By cross-breeding and recording changes in behaviour, Lorenz concluded that even 1 part in 32 of domestic blood made a drake more likely to chase and rape females. He warned that only a small fraction of tainted blood could influence a pure-blooded race.[18]

Lorenz subsequently compared the physical changes he saw develop in domestic animals and in people living in cities (pot-bellied and wearing spectacles), changes that he claimed both animals and humans naturally judge to be 'ugly or base'. He collected paired photos and drawings to illustrate the degeneration of the domestic compared to the wild. These included examples of wild and domestic poultry and a Pekinese dog compared to a wolf (Lorenz had also considered using a pug or a bulldog, but decided that the Peke was the most degenerate).[18] Similar prejudices (or in Lorenz's terms, 'inborn schemata') against hybrid or domestic animals may still linger in the minds of some biologists.

## 10.3 The impact on animals

There are many ways in which an animal's genetic classification as 'pure' or 'mixed/impure' can affect perceptions of an animal's value and have an impact on the outcomes in the animal's life. These could include the amount of expenditure on veterinary care, the conditions in which animals are kept and transported, the likelihood of being kept alive or destroyed, and the willingness to protect a wild animal population and its habitat. At the extreme, it has been proposed by a veterinarian and politician in Denmark that the best way to ensure that dogs of 'dangerous breeds' can be identified would be to require all dogs to have pedigrees registered in breed stud books and to kill mongrel puppies at birth.[25] Objections to hybridization can even lead to the persecution of a species, as in the case of the ruddy duck extermination from the UK (see Box 10.3). From the point of the well-being of an individual animal, what counts is the animal's subjective experience. Individual animals can have no interest in human classifications of the breed or species they may belong to, except in so far as this affects their life experience.

An emphasis on pedigree can result in a breeding population being restricted deliberately, to the extent that parents are more likely to be closely related (as in pedigree dogs; see Chapter 6). Breeders of livestock and dogs have long known that inbreeding increases the risk of ill health and infertility, while often continuing to practise it. Harmful recessive genetic mutations are more likely to be expressed in inbred individuals because they are more likely to have inherited two copies of the recessive gene from a common ancestor of both their parents. There is also evidence from wild animal populations that inbreeding is related to increased susceptibility to disease. In studies of California sea lions (*Zalophus californianus*), the more inbred individuals were found to be more likely to suffer from gut parasites and cancer and take longer to recover from illness.[26] There is the tragic example of the very small isolated wolf population on Isle Royale, in Lake Superior, where the majority have been found to be suffering from painful deformities of the spine as a result of inbreeding over decades.[27] In wild populations, females often choose to avoid mating with closely related males.[28]

There are many understandable reasons why scientists and breeders need to classify animals according to genetic similarities or differences in the everyday use and exploitation of animal genetic resources by society. Genome analysis will probably bring us many surprises and paradoxes in future about the relationships between individuals, breeds and species; research in Sweden has suggested that there can be relatively greater genetic differences between individuals within a particular species of yeast than there are between the human and chimpanzee species.[29] But terms such as 'pure blood' or 'pedigree' to imply some superiority in the individual animals or animal group are not suitable for use in a scientific context ('purebred' dogs tend to be less healthy than mongrels). They have so many non-scientific connotations that it would be well to stop using them entirely in relation to sentient animals. It would be more accurate to refer to pedigree domestic animals as 'genetically restricted' or 'genetically limited'. But a dog show or cattle show for 'genetically restricted' animals somehow does not have the same ring about it.

---

### BOX 10.3 ENFORCING BREED PURITY: THE EXTERMINATION OF RUDDY DUCKS IN THE UK

One of the most controversial examples of the scientific approach to species purity is the European-wide campaign, backed by an international Conventions, against the hybridization of the two similar species of wild duck classified by scientists as the ruddy duck (*Oxyura jamaicensis*) and the white-headed duck (*Oxyura leucocephala*) that belong to the same family known as stifftailed ducks. It also highlights the potential divergence between a conservationist perspective and the interests of individual animals.

Ruddy ducks and white-headed ducks look strikingly similar except for their feather colour, ruddy ducks having a richer brown body feathering and a black cap to their heads, while the white has an almost entirely white head. Both have bright blue bills. The ruddy duck is native to North America where there is a population of hundreds of thousands. After being imported to England as an ornamental bird, ironically by a wildfowl conservation charity, some individuals escaped and bred successfully. Their population reached several thousand in the UK and spread into Europe, although 95 per cent of the European population was in the UK. The white-headed duck is described as Europe's rarest native duck. Its numbers fell from around 100,000 to around 10,000 over the 20th century as a result of hunting and habitat loss, and the species disappeared in Italy, Morocco, Hungary and other countries. In Spain, hunting and destruction of the ducks' marshy habitat due to human activity, such as agriculture, were the main reason that the species was endangered. Numbers were reduced to 22 birds during the 1970s, after which a ban on hunting and habitat conservation efforts raised numbers to 2600 by 2003.[30–34]

Ruddy ducks in Europe do not attack or transmit disease to white-headed ducks, but they do mate with them. Hybrids of the ruddy duck and the white-headed duck are fully fertile and breed with white-headed ducks, reducing the pure white-headed duck population. Hybridization came to be seen by conservationists as the main threat to the survival of the white-headed duck as a separate European native species, particularly in Spain. The decision was taken, supported by wildlife conservation organizations, that it was necessary to save the white-headed duck species by exterminating all members of the ruddy duck species in Europe, which meant mainly in the UK, where there were an estimated 6000 ruddy ducks in 2000.[30,32,34]

The white-headed duck is listed as a species to be protected by the Convention on International Trade in Endangered Species (CITES) and by the Bonn Convention (for the Conservation of Migratory Species of Wild Animals) and the Bern Convention (on the Conservation of European Wildlife and Natural Habitats). Conservation organizations, including the Royal Society for the Protection of Birds (RSPB), the Non-Native Species Secretariat, Scottish Natural Heritage, English Nature and others joined with the UK Department for Environment, Food and Rural Affairs (Defra) in a campaign to exterminate the ruddy duck, in spite of considerable public opposition. The UK government funded years of trial culls to confirm that eradication was feasible and the final five-year shooting campaign started in 2005, at a cost of over UK£900 per duck killed.[30,32,34] Over the first two years 3691 ruddy ducks were reported killed, out of an estimated starting population of 4400. Around 70 per cent were adults and 30 per cent were young birds, some of them unfledged[33] (additional young presumably died as a result of losing one or both parents). Birds of other species were inevitably sometimes shot by mistake and either killed or wounded.[35]

Critics of the ruddy duck extermination saw it as irrational and with worrying overtones of species fascism and national chauvinism (with the ruddy duck in the role of a pushy North American invader).[31,34] The RSPB and others responded that the cull was to save a globally endangered species (albeit most endangered by human hand), whereas the ruddy duck species was not in danger of extinction. To critics, the survival of the white-headed duck as a 'distinct species' rather than as a hybrid was a purely human preoccupation, irrelevant to the ducks themselves.

The ruddy duck cull looks less illogical if the European political ramifications are included. The RSPB admitted that the extermination campaign was in part a public relations exercise in order to maintain the profile of conservation efforts in Spain when they stated: 'The white-headed duck is a symbol of successful conservation in Spain, in the same way that the red kite is in the UK. If it was to disappear then a key argument used in achieving protection of wetland habitats and control of hunting would vanish. This could have serious consequences for these wetlands, their flora and fauna and for future conservation initiatives.'[32]

The ruddy ducks were caught in a political hunting net and doubtless to them there was no difference between being shot in the cause of species purity or in the cause of a good lunch. The ruddy duck extermination effort was one widely debated incident in the much larger attempt being made by conservation professionals worldwide to police the frontiers of species and of their countries against unwanted invasions, as discussed in Chapter 11.

## Notes

1  Sewell, A. (1877) *Black Beauty*, Wordsworth Editions, 1993, Chapter 1 and Chapter 48

2  British Pig Association 'British pig breeds', www.britishpigs.org.uk/trad7.htm, accessed July 2009

3  Shakespeare, W. (circa 1599) *Henry V*, Act III scene VII

4  Russell, N. (1986) *Like Engend'ring Like: Heredity and Animal Breeding in Early Modern England*, Cambridge University Press

5  Rieseberg, L. H., Wood, T. E. and Baack, E. J. (2006) 'The nature of plant species', *Nature*, vol 440, pp524–527; Bachmann, K. (1998) 'Species as units of diversity: An outdated concept', *Theory in Biosciences*, vol 117, no 3, pp213–230; Tudge, C. (1992) *Last Animals at the Zoo: How Mass Extinction Can Be Stopped*, Island

Press; see also Dawkins, R. (1993) 'Gaps in the mind', in P. Cavalieri and P. Singer (eds) *The Great Ape Project: Equality Beyond Humanity*, Fourth Estate, pp80–87

6   Svedin, N. et al (2008) 'Natural and sexual selection against hybrid flycatchers', *Proceedings of the Royal Society, B*, vol 275, pp735–744

7   Netherlands Organization for Scientific Research (2008) 'Turtle doves commit adultery', *ScienceDaily*, 22 October

8   Shields, J. L., Barnes, P. and Heath, D. D. (2008) 'Growth and survival differences among native, introduced and hybrid blue mussels (*Mytilus* spp): Genotype, environment and interaction effects', *Marine Biology*, vol 154, no 5, pp919–928; Fitzpatrick, B. M. and Shaffer, H. B. (2007) 'Hybrid vigor between native and introduced salamanders raises new challenges for conservation', *Proceedings of the National Academy of Sciences*, vol 104, no 40, pp15,793–15,798

9   Tudge, C. (1992) *Last Animals at the Zoo: How Mass Extinction Can Be Stopped*, Island Press, Washington, DC; Gao, J. (2007) 'Year of the tiger', *Nature*, vol 449, pp16–18

10  Vrijenhock, R. (1995) 'Natural processes, individuals, and units of conservation', in B. G. Norton et al (eds) *Ethics on the Ark: Zoos, Animal Welfare and Wildlife Conservation*, Smithsonian Institution Press, pp74–92; Seehausen, O. (2004) 'Hybridization and adaptive radiation', *Trends in Ecology and Evolution*, vol 19, no 4, pp198–207; Ropiquet, A. and Hassanin, A. (2006) 'Hybrid origin of the Pliocene ancestor of wild goats', *Molecular Phylogenetics and Evolution*, vol 41, no 2, pp395–404

11  International Commission on Zoological Nomenclature (2000) *International Code of Zoological Nomenclature*, fourth edition, para 1.3, 'Exclusions'

12  Oliveira, R. et al (2008) 'Hybridization versus conservation: Are domestic cats threatening the genetic integrity of wildcats (*Felis silvestris silvestris* ) in Iberian Peninsula?', *Philosophical Transactions of the Royal Society, B*, vol 363, pp2953–2961

13  Halbert, N. D. and Derr, J. N. (2007) 'A comprehensive evaluation of cattle introgression into US federal bison herds', *Journal of Heredity*, vol 98, pp1–12; Marris, E. (2009) 'The genome of the American west', *Nature*, vol 457, pp950–952

14  Pemberton, J. M. (2008) 'Wild pedigrees: The way forward', *Proceedings of the Royal Society, B*, vol 275, pp613–621

15  See, for example, discussions in Simm, G. et al (eds) (2004) *Farm Animal Genetic Resources*, BSAS Publication 30, Nottingham University Press; Holt, W. V. et al (eds) (2003) *Reproductive Science and Integrated Conservation*, Cambridge University Press

16  See, for example, the list given at www.horsedata.co.uk/horse_brands.htm; see also Spiegel, M. (1998) *The Dreaded Comparison: Human and Animal Slavery*, Preface by A. Walker, Heretic Books

17  Kevles, D. J. (1995) *In the Name of Eugenics: Genetics and the Uses of Human Heredity*, Harvard University Press

18  Burkhardt, R. W. Jr. (2005) *Patterns of Behavior: Konrad Lorenz, Niko Tinbergen, and the Founding of Ethology*, University of Chicago Press

19  Dartmoor National Park Authority (2004) *The Dartmoor Ponies Factsheet January 2004*, Dartmoor National Park Authority

20  Willett, P. (1966) *An Introduction to the Thoroughbred*, Stanley Paul

21  Horseracing.com, *Biography of Lexington*, www.horseracing.com/horses/lexington/, accessed July 2009

22  World Arabian Horse Organization (2007) *Arabian Horse Definition 2007*, www.waho.org/Definition.html, accessed July 2009; World Arabian Horse Organization (1998) *Is Purity the Issue?*, WAHO Publication 21, January 1998

23  Bowling, A. T., del Valle, A. and Bowling, M. (2000) 'A pedigree-based study of mitochondrial D-loop DNA sequence variation among Arabian horses', *Animal Genetics*, vol 31, no 1, pp1–7; Głażewska, I. et al (2007) 'A new view on dam lines in Polish Arabian horses based on mtDNA analysis', *Genetics Selection Evolution*, vol 39, pp609–619

24  Arabian Horse Association (2008) *Rules of Registration*, www.arabianhorses.org/

25  *The Economist* (2009) 'Shoot the puppy!', *The Economist*, 22 August, p31

26  Smith, K. F., Acevedo-Whitehouse, K. and Pedersen, A. B. (2009) 'The role of infectious diseases in biological conservation', *Animal Conservation*, vol 12, pp1–12; Acevedo-Whitehouse, K. et al (2003) 'Disease susceptibility in California sea lions', *Nature*, vol 422, p35; Acevedo-Whitehouse, K. (2009) 'Inbreeding and disease – a threat to wildlife populations?', in *Darwinian Selection, Selective Breeding and the Welfare of Animals*, Proceedings of the UFAW International Symposium, Bristol, 22–23 June 2009

27  Hadhazy, A. (2009) 'Gene pool jeopardy: Can Isle Royale's wolves be saved?', *Scientific American*, 7 April

28  Clutton-Brock, T. and McAuliffe, K. (2009) 'Female mate choice in mammals', *Quarterly Review of Biology*, vol 84, no 1, pp3–26

29  Svahn, K. (2009) 'The genetic differences between yeasts greater than those between humans and chimpanzees', University of Gothenburg, *News*, 11 February 2009; Liti, G. et al (2009) 'Population genomics of domestic and wild yeasts', *Nature*, vol 458, pp337–342

30  Henderson, I. (2002) *UK Ruddy Duck Control Trial Final Report*, Central Science Laboratory, York

31  Cox, D. (2003) 'Sex and the single duck', *New Statesman*, 30 June 2003; Fowler-Reeves, K. (2007) *With Extreme Prejudice: The Culling of British Wildlife*, Animal Aid

32  Royal Society for the Protection of Birds (2005, 2009) *RSPB Policy: Ruddy Ducks and White Headed Duck*, www.rspb.org.uk; Non-Native Species Secretariat, Eradication of Ruddy Ducks in the UK to Protect the White-Headed Duck, LIFE Project Number – LIFE05 NAT/UK/000142, 'Questions and answers'

33  Non-Native Species Secretariat (2007) *3rd Ruddy Duck Eradication Bulletin*, September 2007, Eradication of Ruddy Ducks in the UK to Protect the White-headed Duck, LIFE Project Number – LIFE05 NAT/UK/000142

34  BBC (2002) *The UK's Ruddy Duck Problem*, BBC online, 4 January, www.bbc.co.uk/dna/h2g2/A663004; BBC (2003) *RIP Ruddy Duck*, BBC News online, 3 March, http://news.bbc.co.uk

35  Non-Native Species Secretariat (2006) *1st Ruddy Duck Eradication Bulletin*, November 2006, Eradication of Ruddy Ducks in the UK to Protect the White-Headed Duck, LIFE Project Number – LIFE05 NAT/UK/000142

# 11

# Population Control:
# Pests, Aliens and Endangered Species

## 11.1 Background and context: Unwanted versus valued species

### 11.1.1 Defining a pest

The Great Leap Forward in China established a slogan 'Wipe Out the Four Pests' – rats, sparrows, flies and mosquitoes – and in May 1958 Mao Zedong urged the 'whole people, including five-year-old children' to mobilize against them. Sparrows ate grain. Villages, including entire schools, went out to knock down sparrow nests, break eggs and kill nestlings. Populations coordinated with military precision to beat gongs and cooking pots at every spot where sparrows were trying to roost in the evenings over several days, until the sparrows were exhausted. In some areas, sparrow populations were almost eliminated for years. After Chinese scientists pointed out that sparrows also eat insects and are themselves useful for pest control, sparrows were removed from the list.[1] The naturalist Flora Thompson, writing in the 1920s, described how villagers in England similarly used to gather under rookeries in spring, with guns, slings, beer and much conviviality, for a morning of population control and sport. They shot or stoned the fledglings who could not yet fly into a heap of mangled corpses under the trees while the parent rooks circled helplessly above.[2]

The control of unwanted populations of animals often involves us in quite large-scale killing, not always humanely. This chapter will investigate the problem of unwanted animal populations and whether, in the 21st century, society could be making much greater efforts to prevent the growth of unwanted animal populations by more humane means.

'Pest' originally referred to a plague. An animal 'pest', self-evidently, is a category determined by people rather than an inherent characteristic of the animal. Essentially 'pest' refers to an animal species or population that interferes with human activities, causes economic damage, particularly to livestock-keeping or crops, or changes ecosystems or the balance of species in ways that are considered undesirable. Pests are often, but not always, 'aliens' or 'non-native species'. Alien pests are animals that 'shouldn't be there' – in our view, they are living and reproducing in the wrong country or ecosystem and are also 'invasive'.

In Britain alone, the list of animal species that some sections of the human population consider a problem to be controlled or removed includes rats, mice, mink, moles, hedgehogs, pigeons (wild and feral), rabbits, grey squirrels, red foxes, badgers, wild boar, seals, gulls, starlings, sparrows, magpies, crows, rooks, red kites and other raptors, reintroduced white-tailed eagles, otters, reintroduced beavers, sika deer, muntjak deer, parakeets, harlequin ladybirds, American mitten-crabs, ruddy ducks, American bullfrogs, signal crayfish, catfish, cats (domestic and feral) and others.

In spite of our knowledge of evolution and taxonomy, we still distinguish between animal populations in terms of human needs, likes and dislikes. As science and society demarcate domestic species into more or less desirable breeds and strains, so we define wild species as more or less desirable too. Thus farmed pigs are desirable, but feral pigs are invasive aliens. This way of thinking follows an ancient tradition of classifying and valuing animals according to their relationship to humans, rather than according to their intrinsic characteristics; every animal was believed to be designed to fill some human purpose, whether practical, moral or aesthetic.[3] Some wild animal species (such as the wild rat) are still categorized as 'bad' by nature. Correspondingly, there is relatively little public or official concern about the humaneness of the methods we use to remove them from the environment.

---

### BOX 11.1 REMOVING 'ALIEN' POPULATIONS

- Between 2001 and 2005 the Ecuador National Park Service exterminated a population of around 80,000 feral goats, previously introduced by people, that had over-browsed the vegetation and competed with native animals on Santiago Island, Galapagos.[4]

- In 2008 the US Department of Agriculture Wildlife Services killed over 4.2 million pest birds, mostly non-native (European starlings and house sparrows, pigeons, blackbirds, cow-birds and grackles).[5]

- In the mid 1950s, 1.5 million North American grey squirrels were killed over five years under a bounty scheme in Britain. Populations of several thousands each of feral muskrats and coypu, both originating from fur farms, were exterminated from Britain by campaigns during the 1930s and the 1980s, respectively.[6]

---

## 11.1.2 The history of pests and invasions

Human activities, past and present, are the root cause of nearly all the animal pest problems that are with us today. The simplest way to reduce the reproductive success of an animal is to limit access to the resources needed for breeding – habitat and nutrition. Very often, human activities have greatly increased the supply of these resources. Pests are often animals that are able to take advantage of the food sources and shelter that humans provide through farming, with its concentrations of livestock and their dung and feed, large areas of food-crop monocultures, and through food storage and distribution, catering, refuse, wastage and street littering from fast food. The name of the house sparrow (*Passer domesticus*) and the house mouse (*Mus domesticus*) confirms that they often choose to live and breed close to people, including in the centre of towns.

Very often pests and aliens are species that we have transported to new habitats where their breeding is unconstrained by the ecological factors, such as pathogens and predators, that limited their population growth in the habitats they evolved in. We have taken them with us, often unintentionally in ships or on traded goods, or intentionally to farm or hunt for food or fur, to hunt for sport, as pets, ornaments and amusements in gardens and zoos, and even to control existing pests.[7] A certain number of individuals of any species deliberately introduced with the intention of keeping them captive in zoos, homes and farms are almost certain to escape or be released into to the wild. Many of the qualities that we admire and try to achieve in species we want to encourage, such as adaptability, robustness and fecundity, are often the (un-admired) characteristics of pests and invaders.

In the early 20th century, North American mink (*Mustela vison*) were imported to Britain to be kept in cages to breed and kill for their fur. Today the ancestors of those that escaped or were released are wild, resilient and fertile predators, viewed by conservationists as a major environmental problem. Grey squirrels (*Sciurus carolinensis*) were introduced as a novelty from North America to England, Scotland and Wales from the later 19th century up to 1930.[8] They are now established all over the UK except for parts of Scotland, the Isle of Wight and the island of Anglesey (Ynys Mon). European starlings (*Sturnus vulgaris*) were deliberately released in Central Park, New York, around 1890, as an English addition to the local fauna; their descendants took only 60 years to reach the West Coast and rapidly became seen as a pest.[7] In Australia, cane toads (*Bufo marinus*), native to South America, were deliberately introduced to Queensland during the early 20th century with the aim of using them as predators to control an existing sugar cane beetle (sugar cane was also introduced to Australia in the 19th century). Cane toads extended their range at up to 50km per year across northern and eastern Australia to inhabit over 500,000 square kilometres and are still expanding southwards. The cane toad is fatally poisonous to any wildlife that eats it, leading to 'frequent assertions of ecological catastrophe'; but by 2006 its overall impact on other species was still unclear.[9]

The role of human help in providing grasslands, croplands and protection to 'pest' species is illustrated by the story of the European rabbit (*Oryctolagus cuniculus*), which was intentionally introduced all around the world for its meat and fur. It took 700 years for European rabbits to spread throughout the British Isles after being introduced from Western Europe between 1000 and 2000 years ago. Rabbits became an agricultural pest in the 18th century when the expansion of crop farming and the reduction in predators such as foxes by hunting allowed their populations to increase.[10] Thomas Austin introduced a couple of dozen European rabbits to Australia in the mid 19th century and subsequently killed 20,000 rabbits on his land within six years of the introduction. Again, rabbits benefited from the efficiency of farmers in sowing grass, making ponds, killing off native animals that were the rabbits' competitors for food, such as kangaroos and possums, and predators such as dingoes and birds of prey.[7] Within ten years rabbits had become a pest species across the country and by 1926 the population had increased to an estimated 10 billion.[7,11] In South America, rabbits were introduced into Chile in the late 19th century and then crossed the Andes to settle in the grasslands of Argentina, advancing at 15km to 20km per year.[7] Rats are also attracted by livestock production. The Norway or brown rat (*Rattus norvegicus*) arrived in America in the 18th century and had settled in every state by 1926.[12] By the turn of the 21st century, there were estimated to be at least 1.8 billion rats on US poultry farms, one rat for every five chickens.[13]

But agricultural pests are not always invaders and invaders are not always pests. Kangaroos were in Australia before farmers but, like rabbits, they are pests to sheep and cattle farmers as they take advantage of grassland. In contrast, Australia's stocks of 86 million sheep and 28 million cattle, both introduced species, are not considered either pests or aliens.

## 11.1.3 Alien species and international Conventions

Globally and nationally, the distinction between alien and desirable species is set down in law. The United Nations Convention on Biological Diversity (CBD), agreed in 1992–1993, is legally binding and had been signed by 189 countries and by the European Union (EU) by 2007. The Contracting Parties agreed to 'prevent the introduction of, control or eradicate those alien species which threaten ecosystems, habitats or species'. The EU's 1979 Directive on Wild Birds gives protection to all wild birds 'naturally occurring' in the EU and states that the goal of conservation is 'the maintenance and adjustment of the natural balances between species as far as is reasonably possible', including controlling the introduction of non-native species. The 1979 European Convention on the Conservation of European Wildlife and Natural Habitats (the Berne Convention) creates an obligation to 'strictly control the introduction of non-native species' and its *Strategy on Invasive Alien Species* (2002) aimed for rapid 'detection' and 'eradication' of these species. The strategy states that 'Eradication is the most coherent solution in terms of biodiversity conservation and can be more effective, cost effective and ethical than other management alternatives (control, containment, do nothing).'[14] The theme of the United Nations International Day on Biological Diversity on 22 May 2009 was 'Invasive Alien Species – one of the greatest threats to biodiversity, and to the ecological and economic well-being of society and the planet'.[15]

### 11.1.4 What is a native, an alien and an invasive species?

A non-native species is usually defined as one that has not evolved with the other species in its environment, going back to some generally agreed point in time that is usually taken to be the end of the last ice age. Scientists and conservationists are aware that the distinction between a native and a non-native animal species can be unclear in terms of when the historical line is drawn and that some animals become 'naturalized' in their new environment or at least accepted by people over time.[16,17] Both the rat and the rabbit are non-native to Britain (as is the very popular brown hare *Lepus europaeus*) but they are generally seen today as simple pests rather than as non-native species. In Spain, on the other hand, the European rabbit is native and an essential part of ecosystems. The critically endangered Iberian lynx (*Lynx pardinus*) and the Spanish imperial eagle (*Aquila adalberti*), the most endangered raptor in Europe, are both specialist rabbit predators.[18]

An animal species typically comes to be seen as 'invasive' when:

- its population growth becomes much greater than would have been possible in the ecosystem in which it evolved;
- it unbalances the new ecosystem by eating or destroying vegetation that is needed by the existing native species;
- it directly preys on, attacks, outcompetes, hybridizes with or transmits disease to existing native species, threatening their survival as species.

In practice only a relatively small proportion of the species that are introduced to a non-native environment become 'invasive'; conservationists estimate that this is around 1 per cent (10 per cent of introduced species become established in the environment and, of these, 10 per cent become invasive).[16,17]

Invasive alien species (both plants and animals) are considered by many ecologists the second greatest threat to the world's endangered species;[19] but the primary threat is loss of habitat. Loss of habitat is almost always due to human activities such as farming, industry, transport and the expansion of cities and settlements. Human activity has substantially altered an estimated 77 per cent of the Earth's ice-free surface[20] and human-induced climate change is predicted to be a major driver of extinction in the 21st century.

### 11.1.5 Language: Angels and demons

In both popular and sometimes in scientific language, animals that are pests or invasive aliens are often presented as particularly unpleasant, aggressive or dangerous. The 2002 *Fauna Britannica* states that 'The introduction of grey squirrels has been an ecological disaster', while 'The red has been pushed out of its territories by the invading grey in most regions.'[10] The scientific journal *Nature* described greys as 'thieves, bullies and virus-ridden vectors of diseases'. In contrast, the native red squirrel has been described as a 'perfect little gentleman'.[21] The Royal Society for the Protection of Birds noted that the invasive ruddy duck's mating behaviour is 'promiscuous', while the native European white-headed duck is 'monogamous'[22] – hence threatening hybridization (see Box 10.3 in Chapter 10).

A BBC news story of 2008 warned of a 'time bomb' of a new generation of 'alien invaders' that could 'potentially cause devastation'.[23] Australian wildlife managers aim to 'protect lambs and other livestock from being mauled and killed by invasive predators', and accompany the statement by a gory photograph of a wild boar eating a small white lamb.[24] *The Adelaide Advertiser* warns of an imported aquarium fish, the Mozambique tilapia, 'an aggressive, fast-breeding, invasive fish species is muscling its way into the waterways of northern Australia'; from cane toads to foxes, aliens have been kicking out the locals.[25] The National Audubon Society, a US conservation organization, likewise urges vigilance to 'stop the "alien" attack' and warns that harmless-seeming aliens are 'taking over your community' and threatening native species.[26] The US National Invasive Species Council management plan is illustrated by a pair of sinister alien blue eyes staring out of the dark from behind foliage.[27] The Global Invasive Species Programme, a collaboration of scientists and policy-makers established in 1997 with the mission to reduce the spread and impact of invasive species, claims that they 'threaten our world'.[28] Scientists advocate an 'eradication ethic' in the face of invasive mammals.[4]

These statements evidently contain elements of truth, of sensationalism and of propaganda. But such statements may have important implications for animal welfare. The negative and sometimes emotive language applied to pests and aliens that are also sentient animals risks making us less concerned to ensure their humane treatment.

## 11.2 Practices, technologies and approaches

### 11.2.1 National and regional situation and programmes

The International Union for Conservation of Nature (IUCN) maintains a Global Invasive Species Database covering 22 bird species (including the house sparrow and starling), 34 mammal species (including black and brown rats, rabbits, foxes, grey squirrels, cats and dogs), 44 invasive fish species, 9 reptile species, 9 amphibian species (including the cane toad), and 58 insect species (including fire ants and the common mosquito).[29] Many countries now have specialized agencies to deal with aliens and invaders. In 2008, Delivering Alien Invasive Species Inventories for Europe (DAISIE) listed 11,000 alien species, of which 5 per cent were vertebrates. Among its '100 worst' are the grey squirrel, Norway (brown) rat and the coypu. It was estimated in 2009 that the monetary cost of invasive species (both plants and animals) in Europe is at least 10 billion euros annually.[30]

Australia, where European species unknown to the Australian ecosystems were intentionally released, is the country where aliens have had the most impact and where most effort is put into control methods. By 2004 the Invasive

**Table 11.1** *Costs of main invasive species in Australia, 2004*

| Invasive species | Total costs (AU$) 2004 | Main impact |
|---|---|---|
| European red foxes | 227.5 million | Mainly environmental (predation) |
| Feral cats | 146.0 million | Environmental (predation) |
| European rabbits | 113.1 million | Economic (agriculture) |
| Feral pigs | 106.5 million | Economic (agriculture) |

*Source:* McLeod (2004)[31]

Animals Cooperative Research Centre (CRC) estimated that the total economic impact of all alien invasions was nearly AU$720 million a year.[31] The CRC lists 56 invasive vertebrate animal species and the top nine species in terms of their cost impact are listed as the fox, feral cat, rabbit, feral pig, dog, mouse, carp, goat and cane toad, with wild horses in tenth place.[31] All these species were intentionally introduced to the Australian ecosystem by settlers: the European red fox (*Vulpes vulpes*) for sport hunting; the rabbit, pig, goat and carp for food and possibly their skin and fur; the cane toad for pest control. In 1999 it was estimated that red foxes, the number one invasive animal, were a known or 'perceived' threat to 34 endangered species of native Australian wild animals which had this new predator deliberately placed among them, including 7 bird species, 21 mammal species, 5 reptile species and 1 species of frog.[32] Feral pigs, the descendants of farmed pigs who escaped into the wild from the later 18th century onwards, were introduced across natural barriers such as deserts. Now Australia's number two agricultural pest, they are thought to number 23 million and are reported to prey on lambs.[24,33]

By 2007 it was estimated by the US Department of Agriculture (USDA) that 81 non-native species of mammals, 94 species of birds and 86 species of reptiles or amphibians had become established. As well as the common domestic livestock these include rats, mice, wild horses, mongooses, feral pigs, feral dogs and cats, starlings, sparrows, pigeons, bullfrogs (introduced from the eastern states where they are native), Burmese pythons that are reproducing in South Florida, and brown tree snakes that have decimated native species on Guam. Many of the birds and reptiles were introduced by the pet industry, exotic animal breeders and for hunting.[34] The introduction of alien reptiles and amphibians by pet owners and the pet industry in Florida was said to be reaching 'epidemic proportions'.[35]

The total costs of economic damage caused and efforts to control the populations of non-native species were estimated to be over US$46 million, of which US$27 billion was accounted for by rats and US$14 billion by feral cats.[13] The non-native and native pest animals killed ('lethally removed') by the USDA Wildlife Services in 2008 included over 89,000 coyotes, nearly 400 grey wolves that attacked livestock, and nearly 14,000 feral pigs, in addition to the 4.2 million starlings and blackbirds mentioned earlier.[5]

## 11.2.2 Population control methods: Overview

Population control involves either killing a proportion of the population or taking measures to reduce the breeding of the population. Table 11.2 summarizes some of the current methods used.

The result of efforts to reduce population size may be uncertain. If the population size is reduced but the resources of food, water and nest sites available remain the same, the result may be that the remaining breeding animals have better reproductive success or a longer lifespan as a result of reduced competition.[36] Animals may also change their breeding strategies and their sex ratios when they need to in order to oppose a breeding decline.[37] Farmers and cities that provide abundant resources of food and shelter typically carry out permanent programmes of poisoning rats and mice for years on end without making a long-term reduction in numbers. The city of Baltimore, with an estimated rat population of 50,000, failed to reduce the overall number of rats over the last 50 years.[38]

**Table 11.2** *Pest and alien population control methods: Actual and potential*

| Method | Current status | Result |
|---|---|---|
| Physical: shooting, trapping, snaring, electrocution, explosives in warrens | Common | Lethal |
| Poison: poisoned bait, poison gas, poison delivery devices | Common, especially for large populations, inaccessible or evasive populations, large areas of land | Lethal |
| Biological (disease) agents (myxoma and rabbit haemorrhagic disease viruses) | Common | Lethal |
| Wetting (degreasing) agent | Used to kill roosting starlings by hypothermia | Lethal |
| Relocation | Practical for smaller populations | Non-lethal removal |
| Scaring or repellent devices or chemicals | Common; not a population control method | Non-lethal deterrence |
| Limit access to resources such as crops, grain, food refuse, nest sites | Unclear; should be standard practice | Fertility reduction |
| Egg sterilization or removal (urban birds) | Practical, relatively rare | Fertility reduction |
| Contraceptive drugs (hormones, vaccines and others) | Research and development; limited use in field | Fertility reduction |
| Genetically modified (GM) infectious agents (such as viruses) for contraceptive vaccine delivery | Research, limited trials | Fertility reduction (may include lethal control) |
| 'Daughterless', sterile or 'Trojan gene' technology (GM) | Theoretical and research | Genetic extinction |

© League Against Cruel Sports

**Figure 11.1** *Snares are legal in the UK and risk injury and death of non-target animals and protected species, such as this dead snared badger*

## 11.2.3 Examples of lethal methods

The main considerations in the regulation of the control of pest populations up to now have been the safety of humans and non-target animals, rather than minimizing the suffering of the animal concerned. One exception is the EU ban on the leg-hold trap and the import of furs from animals trapped in this way; but snares (thin wire nooses) are still legal in the UK and glue traps (sticky boards) for rodents are readily available to the public. The Universities Federation for Animal Welfare has pointed out that individuals who buy traps or poisons would not necessarily have the expertise to kill humanely rodents that are live-trapped, accidentally trapped by a leg or a tail in kill-traps, or found poisoned but still alive.[39] The Rodenator is an explosive device for killing burrowing animals underground (or as a method of collapsing empty tunnels and burrows) using a combustible gas mixture. It has been described by the public agency Natural England as 'enormously cruel' and is illegal in England as a pest-killing method.[40]

Common poisons include sodium monofluoroacetate (known as Compound 1080), used to kill animals that predate livestock (foxes and feral pigs in Australia and coyotes in the US). It disrupts the production of energy in animal cells, causing heart and nervous system failure and, in foxes, 'hyper-excitability, vocalization, manic running and retching', breathing difficulties and convulsions.[41] The poison 3-chloro-4-methylbenzenamine hydrochloride (known as DRC 1339) is used in bait for killing birds that are agricultural pests in the US, and leads to a slow death from kidney failure. Sodium lauryl sulphate is a de-greasing compound that removes oil from pest birds' feathers, causing death from hypothermia.[42]

The commonest method of killing rat and mouse pests is by anticoagulant poisons such as warfarin, brodifacoum and diphacinone, which build up in the animal's bodies over days as they continue to eat the bait. The poison interferes with the metabolism of vitamin K in the body, which prevents platelets from forming an effective blood clot when blood vessels break, and causes death from internal bleeding into organs and tissues. Tested animals show laboured breathing, bloody eyes and nose, muscle weakness, agitation, irregular heart beat, bruising and bleeding into joints, bloody urine and stools, and spitting blood during the slow poisoning process, and 'severe discomfort, which can last for several days, occurs in a large proportion of all reported studies'.[43] Other poisons used for pests can include strychnine, phosphine gas and cyanide, depending on jurisdiction.[44] 'Biological control' by pathogens has been used to attempt to exterminate rabbits where they are pests, by releasing first the myxoma virus (from 1950) and then the rabbit haemorrhagic disease virus (RHD virus, or calici virus) in the 1990s.[11,18] Both these diseases cause an unpleasant death.

## 11.2.4 Fertility control

Fertility control is *prima facie* more logical than allowing animal pests to breed and then killing them, and it has the potential to be considerably more humane. It is more challenging from a technical, practical and also regulatory point of view than shooting, trapping or poisoning, and as yet has been used successfully in a limited number of cases. Because of the greater effort involved, fertility control so far has been applied to populations of animals that are more highly regarded by the public, such as wild horses, white-tailed deer, popular wild goats and urban birds, rather than the largest groups of pest species. One of the ironies of wild animal population control is that hunters may oppose fertility control in order to preserve populations for shooting.[45]

### 11.2.4.1 Urban birds: Removing or sterilizing eggs

Large populations of urban-breeding gulls are perceived as pests in towns and commercial sites, and lethal control has been common. An alternative is to oil the eggs to seal the shell and kill the early embryo shortly after laying, when the parents are out of the nest. The parent birds take some time to realize that the eggs are not developing and do not re-lay immediately. These methods can reduce gull populations by nearly one third per year, but they are labour intensive and involve operators to identify and access individual nests.[46]

Feral pigeons can be attracted to artificial central breeding sites, such as dovecotes, where the public can feed the birds and eggs can be more easily oiled or removed. Nottingham City Hospital in England suspended lethal control of pigeons in 2000–2001 in favour of creating dovecotes, reducing the pigeon population by 50 per cent in a year. These approaches clearly require commitment and some toleration of the birds.[46]

Egg oiling may be superseded by anti-hatching drugs in some countries. The drug nicarbazin, used as an antimicrobial in poultry production, can be fed to feral pigeons daily in bait at automated feeding stations. When the drug level has built up in the pigeon's body, it prevents the development of embryos in eggs subsequently laid. Registered in the US as OvoControl P™, it reduced the pigeon population at a bait site in San Diego by 53 per cent in the first year of use. These large reductions are possible because of the generally high mortality rate of feral pigeons.[47]

### 11.2.4.2 Contraceptive drugs and immunocontraception

A number of contraceptive drugs that interfere with different stages of the reproductive process in mammals or birds have been tested or used in wild animals. Since the 1980s, the most scientific interest and research has been directed to the possibility of immunocontraception, which involves vaccination against one of the molecules or compounds that are essential to reproduction. By 2009, successful vaccines had been made against the zona pellucida of the mammalian egg and against gonadotrophin-releasing hormone (GnRH).[45,48–51]

The zona pellucida (ZP) vaccine produces antibodies to some elements of the protein molecules on the transparent layer that forms the outside of the egg (the zona pellucida). The antibodies attach to the animal's own eggs, blocking the sperm and preventing fertilization of the eggs. The GnRH vaccine couples the small GnRH molecule to a large carrier protein so that it is recognized by the animal's immune system. The immune system produces antibodies that bind to GnRH, blocking or substantially decreasing the production of the sex hormones that control the oestrous cycle and the production of sperm.[48,51]

Both the ZP and GnRH vaccines have been delivered by injection (after capturing the animal), and the ZP vaccine has also been delivered remotely by dart.[45,50] A major difference between the effects of the ZP and the GnRH vaccines, from the point of view of the animal, is that the GnRH vaccine makes the animals non-reproductive and all sexual behaviour is reduced or stopped, males behaving as if they have been castrated. By 2008 it was possible to reduce conception significantly in mustang mares for a period of four years by using a single injection of either ZP or GnRH vaccine (the ZP being considerably more effective in the last two years).[51]

Contraceptive vaccines need to be delivered to the animal in an effective dose, in a way that stresses the animal minimally and reaches a sufficient number of animals. For animals that society values, it would also be a requirement that the drug delivery should cause no injury or other side effects, and that the contraceptive effect should be reversible. Drugs that are relatively easy to use for captive wild animals in zoos are obviously much harder to deliver in natural conditions. Baited food raises problems of delivering the correct dose and could potentially be eaten by other species. Remote darting has been used

**Table 11.3** *Examples of contraceptive drugs used or under development for wild living animals, as of 2009*

| | Hormones (steroids and GnRH agonists, e.g. Deslorelin implant) | ZP vaccine (e.g. SpayVac)[50,52] | GnRH vaccine (e.g. GonaCon™)[51] | Nicarbazin (e.g. OvoControl™)[47] | Cholesterol mimic (e.g. Diazacon)[53] |
|---|---|---|---|---|---|
| Method of action | Prevents production of sex hormones | Blocks fertilization of mammalian egg | Prevents production of sex hormones | Prevents embryo development in avian egg | Lowers cholesterol, inhibits sex hormone production |
| Examples of species | Horses, deer, wallabies, wild lionesses[54,55] | Horses, deer, elephants; trials on rabbit, house mouse, fox, coyote, possum | Deer, horses; possums, feral pigs, wallabies | Geese, pigeons; other birds | Birds;* trialled on rats, prairie dogs |
| Methods of delivery used or researched | Injection, implants | Injection, dart, GM virus or bacterium | Injection, GM bacterium (dual vaccine[56]) | Bait (species specific) | Bait |

*Note:* * Also registered for pigeons under the trade name Ornitrol

successfully as an alternative to capturing animals for injections;[45,50] but it requires a level of commitment, skill and the identification of individuals and would not be practical for rats, mice and rabbits.

One method researched since the 1980s, particularly in Australia, is to produce a self-disseminating vaccine. Contraceptive vaccines can in principle be delivered by using a carrier virus, a bacterium (such as *Salmonella*) or other infective agent that has been genetically engineered to express the reproductive protein that is being used as an antigen. In virally vectored immunocontraception (VVIC), a gene for the protein is inserted into the genome of a virus that the target species is known to be susceptible to, such as the myxoma virus for rabbits, the murine cytomegalovirus for the house mouse and the canine herpes virus for foxes. If the aim is to achieve a large and rapid reduction in the animal population, the virus would need to be highly transmissible. Lethal transmissible strains of the myxoma virus could be used to deliver contraceptive vaccines to rabbits, meaning that the rabbits that were not killed by the virus would be sterilized by it. By 2008 none of the research had produced a usable drug for field use, mainly because it had not been possible to achieve high transmission of laboratory strains of the viruses among the target animals or to achieve effective and permanent sterilization.[57,58]

A successful genetically engineered infective agent carrying a contraceptive vaccine would be designed to be highly transmissible between animals of the target species but not transmissible between species or with no contraceptive effect in other species. In either case, the potential for unintended consequences exists. If the virus were accidentally or intentionally exported, or unexpectedly infected another species, it would not be possible to recall it or foresee the long-term consequences. For example, Australia wants to reduce or eliminate the population of European rabbits, but in Spain the need is for a vaccine to protect native rabbits against the myxoma and RHD viruses that have already been released.[18] It seems questionable whether the present state of public opinion would allow the release of a highly transmissible genetically engineered contraceptive vaccine.

Other research is ongoing to find drugs with contraceptive effects, such as drugs that destroy oocytes or prevent follicular development in mammals.[52] This type of experimentation, while it could lead to humane contraception, is likely to cause considerable suffering and animal wastage during the research and development stage.

### 11.2.4.3 Extinction technologies

Scientists now have theoretical genetic 'nuclear options' for some pest species that do not involve disease or killing and are species specific because they work only through mating. Genetic techniques now exist to fit vertebrate animals with 'autocidal' modified genes that would be inherited by males and that would lead to the particular animal population breeding itself into extinction. One method would be to use a constructed 'daughterless' gene that converts carriers to functional males, or a gene that sterilizes or kills females at an early age. As the gene spread through the population, there would be fewer and fewer females capable of breeding until the population was essentially extinguished. The gene would need to be restocked regularly, and in the case of rats this would mean producing and releasing up to 2000 GM males and sterile females per month, considered feasible given the numbers routinely bred for biological research.[37] At realistic restocking rates, simulation studies in Australia of the breeding patterns of cane toads and brown rats have concluded that the use of a female-sterilizing gene could extinguish a typical city's rat population in under 20 years, although the daughterless, female-sterile or female-lethal genes would take 80 years to eliminate cane toads.[37,59]

A related breeding-to-extinction technology is known as the 'Trojan gene', in reference to the Trojan horse taken inside the walls of Troy, hiding Greek soldiers who subsequently emerged and destroyed the city. The Trojan gene essentially reverses the principle of Darwinian selection because it increases the likelihood that the least fit males have the greatest reproductive success. Fish genetically engineered to grow faster and larger than normal may be preferred by female fish, although their survival traits are less good than normal fish. Studies of GM and wild medaka fish (*Oryzias latipes*) show that the GM males are 83 per cent heavier and have a fourfold mating advantage compared to the normal males but their offspring have a reduced survival rate. According to computer models calculated on the basis of these results, extinction of the wild population could occur in around 50 generations.[60,61] Models suggest that the Trojan gene would not cause extinction in cane toads, even at high restocking rates.[37] Scientists investigating the 'daughterless' gene note that the spread of cane toads depends most critically on females, who can lay up to 30,000 eggs in one clutch.[59]

Genetic modification technologies will have costs to animal welfare because of the invasive animal experimentation involved. But the major uncertainty over all the genetic modification technologies, when they involve transmissible genes, is whether society would ever consider them safe to release into the wild. Nevertheless, previously, the deliberate release of species-specific transmissible myxoma and the rabbit haemorrhagic disease viruses went ahead with the approval of the farming community and the scientists involved in pest control.

---

## BOX 11.2 CAPTIVE BREEDING AND CONSERVATION

### The threat of extinction

While pest populations have spread globally, more than one in five of the world's mammal species, one in eight of the world's bird species and nearly one in three of the world's amphibian species are threatened with extinction. In 2008, 200 species of primate, nearly half of the total number of primate species, were classified as either critically endangered, endangered or vulnerable.[62]

The animals least likely to be able to survive in a human-dominated world are those whose needs for habitat and prey conflict with the needs of humans (especially in agriculture) or those whose meat and body parts are wanted by humans. Much of the rainforest habitat of the endangered Sumatran tiger has been lost to logging and palm oil production over the last 20 years.[63] The number of wild African elephants has been reduced from 10 million in the early 20th century to half a million in the early 21st century,[64] mainly due to poaching for ivory. Endangered species whose habitat is shrinking are more likely to come into conflict with people and be viewed as pests.

### Breeding and reintroduction

Can endangered populations be preserved by captive breeding? The accepted goal of zoo breeding programmes is to preserve at least 90 per cent of the genetic diversity of the breeding group for at least 100 years[65] – until such time as the human population may make it possible for them to survive again in their natural habitat. As a result of captive breeding, the black-footed ferret (*Mustela nigripes*) was reintroduced into the American prairies during the 1990s[66] and the species has been upgraded from 'extinct in wild' to 'endangered.' Ironically, the black-footed ferret had been driven to extinction partly by an official campaign in the early 20th century to exterminate the prairie dog. This burrowing rodent, considered a pest, was the ferret's source of food and shelter.[66] But captive breeding populations are often too small to preserve genetic diversity and fewer than 200 species of threatened mammals (out of a total of over 1000) are being bred sustainably in the world's zoos.[67] The promise of reintroduction is unrealistic for the majority of species (even 'a marketing tool'[68]), usually because their habitat has disappeared,[69] and many scientists conclude that the resources would be better spent on protecting wild animals and their habitats. Captive elephant populations in Europe and North

America are not self-sustaining because of breeding difficulties, partly attributed to stress; but wild elephants breed successfully if they are protected.[70]

### Species versus individuals

Captive breeding aims to benefit an animal species in the long term but it entails costs to individual animals. Animals have to be subjected to the constraints and stress of captivity, which can be severe for some species, and to breeding and contraception procedures that are sometimes invasive. The black-footed ferret breeding programme used both artificial insemination and experimental embryo transfer,[66] and some scientists envisage a need to extend reproductive technology to the management of endangered populations in the wild. Developing the technology involves experimentation, often using less valuable animals (such as domestic cats and livestock in experiments to clone endangered species[71]). An instrumental approach may develop that regards animals primarily as carriers of useful or less useful genes and captive breeding inevitably leaves zoos with surplus and unwanted animals. Reintroduction also raises ethical dilemmas; captive-bred animals reintroduced to the wild are faced with parasites, predators, hunger and injury from which they were protected during captivity, and it is normal that many fail to survive.[69,72]

## 11.3 The impact on animals

### 11.3.1 Second-class animals?

There is little historical tradition of concern to minimize or prevent the suffering of animals seen as pests or invasive aliens. Conservationists see an overriding need to remove them from ecosystems that they are damaging. Their activities can be damaging to human property, public health or safety. Many people fear, dislike or resent these animals. An overpopulation of rats can threaten the harvest or livelihood of a whole community, and eliminating them can be a matter of survival. Most methods of trapping or killing are relatively cheap and easy to carry out, compared with the investment and commitment that is needed to develop and carry out safe and effective fertility control. Probably most of the people in developed countries who use guns or dogs for killing pests see it in some respects as a sporting activity. For all these reasons, society has tolerated methods of reducing pest populations that in most cases would not be tolerated for killing other animals.[73]

In 1997 the UK's Pesticide Safety Directorate concluded that anticoagulant poisons for rodents, the most common method used by contractors and the public, are 'markedly inhumane'[43] A 2008 study for the Australian government of the relative humaneness of different pest-control methods concluded that 'many of the methods used to control pest animals in Australia are far from being humane'.[74]

## 11.3.2 Actual and potential impacts of population control methods

Methods of population control, lethal or non-lethal, can have a number of effects on the target animals themselves, their offspring, their group and non-target animals. Table 11.4 sets out some of the known and possible impacts. Many of these adverse impacts could also occur in natural conditions through disease, predation, injury, accident or weather events, such as drought or flood. However, impacts caused by human intervention have ethical implications that natural causes do not.[36] Animals may also suffer in the absence of population control if their numbers are higher than their limited habitat can carry.

**Table 11.4** *Actual and potential impacts on animals of population control methods, including the impact on the target animal, others of the same species or non-target species*

| Negative impact | Lethal methods: Trapping, shooting, explosives | Lethal methods: Poisoning (baits, gas, devices) and lethal pathogens | Fertility control (contraception or prevention of hatching) | Genetic extinction technology |
|---|---|---|---|---|
| Fear due to approach of humans or handling | Very likely in trapped animal or shooting at close range | Likely in rabbits blinded by myxomatosis | Avoided by darting and baits (likely if individuals caught for injection) | |
| Inability to get to food and water/ inability to eat and drink | Very likely in trapping | Very likely | | |
| Distress due to inability to move, defend self or get to cover | Very likely in trapping; probable when wounded | Very likely (blinded rabbits, weakness from poison) | | |
| Injury, wounds, other physical damage (including disease) | Very likely (either from bullets, explosives, trap or self-inflicted in effort to escape) | Very likely (internal bleeding due to anticoagulants, lesions due to lethal pathogens) | Possible as result of darting or injecting drugs, or side effects of contraceptive drugs | |
| Fear due to restraint or confinement | Certain in trapped animals | | Possible if handled | |
| Discomfort due to restraint or confinement | Very likely in trapping (or live trapping before shooting) | | Possible if handled | |
| Weakness, loss of body condition | Likely in prolonged trapping or wounding without killing | Very likely for slow poisons and lethal pathogens | | |

| Negative impact | Lethal methods: Trapping, shooting, explosives | Lethal methods: Poisoning (baits, gas, devices) and lethal pathogens | Fertility control (contraception or prevention of hatching) | Genetic extinction technology |
|---|---|---|---|---|
| Disorientation, agitation, panic | Very likely in trapped animals | Very likely | | |
| Pain over period of minutes, hours or days | Very likely, except in case of clean head-shot | Very likely | Possible (injection site lesions, side effects of contraceptive drugs) | |
| Death of dependent young from starvation, dehydration or lack of protection after parent killed | Very likely (unless offspring also located and killed) | Very likely (unless offspring also located and killed) | | |
| Distress due to loss of mate or parent (depending on species) | Very likely | Very likely | | |
| Distress due to loss of group members (social species) | Likely, but undocumented | Likely, but undocumented | | Possible as population declines |
| Social conflict due to disruption of group structure | Possible | Possible | Unlikely but possible | Possible as population declines |
| Social conflict due to failure of females to come into oestrus | | | Reported in elephants when no oestrus[75] Not observed if normal oestrus | Possible if males compete for remaining fertile females |
| Loss of body condition due to prolonged breeding season (failure to conceive) | | | Possible | Possible |
| Death or injury of non-target animals, including endangered species | Possible in shooting; very likely in trapping or explosives | Likely in poisoning (direct and secondary poisoning) Danger to 'native' rabbits from released rabbit viruses | Potential spread of transmissible GM vaccines | Potential spread of GM autodestruct gene |
| Suffering and wastage during animal experimentation and technology testing | Experimentation less likely for these methods* | Very likely (poisons and pathogens) | Very likely for contraceptive research and testing | Very likely (genetic engineering) |

*Note:* * Some invasive procedures can be used in culls, such as the use of sterilized females induced into permanent oestrus by sex hormone implants to attract males for killing.[4]
*Source:* Sharp and Saunders (2008)[74] used for some areas of impact

### 11.3.3 Impacts of fertility control drugs

Table 11.4 suggests that fertility control by contraception or by preventing eggs from hatching has the potential to provide a humane alternative to lethal control.[76] Contraception using ZP vaccine has been shown to have a positive impact on the overall health of an animal group, improving body condition and extending lifespans.[50] But as yet there are no animal contraceptive drugs for all species that are ideal in the sense of being harmless for long-term use, effective and reversible, if required.

Contraceptive drugs may not be harmless. Progesterone-like drugs such as melengestrol acetate (MGA) have serious side effects on some species. Some contraceptive vaccines have produced long-lasting inflammatory lesions at injection sites due to vaccine adjuvants that are designed to be highly irritant, and possibly other damage to body tissues. GnRH vaccines may not be fully reversible and may cause abnormalities in males.[77] Diazacon is only suitable for animals that have a short breeding season because it has been found to cause muscle tremors in pigeons with long-term use.[53] A double standard could develop in relation to the side effects considered acceptable, depending on whether the animal is long-lived or short-lived, and whether the animal is popular or whether it is merely or mainly a pest. Contraception can also potentially affect animals' behaviour and social structure, either by encouraging them to extend their breeding seasons or by eliminating sexual behaviour.[45,51] However, lethal control methods also affect social structure and behaviour, probably more profoundly than contraception.[45]

If safe and effective contraceptive drugs for wildlife already existed, as they do for people, they would be the obvious option in situations where the alternative is for the animals to be killed or where they are suffering due to overpopulation in a restricted habitat. Unfortunately, the development of those drugs inevitably requires animal experimentation, often on wild-born animals. This is likely to cause suffering, possibly without achieving a useful result. Australian scientists used several tens of red foxes in immunocontraception research between 1994 and 2007. Most of the foxes were wild-born and were difficult to house and handle in a laboratory setting. Procedures were a 'major source of stress' to the foxes, affecting their fertility. As outbred wild animals, their individual immune responses were highly variable. The scientists commented that large numbers of foxes would be required to obtain statistically significant results.[78]

## 11.4 The professionals, the public and the future

### 11.4.1 Levels of concern for pests and aliens

The lines that society, and some conservation scientists, draw between good and bad species has consequences for our treatment of animals. Some of the consequences are as follows:

---

### BOX 11.3 HUMANENESS OF METHODS FOR KILLING
### GREY SQUIRRELS

There are ongoing official campaigns in England and Scotland to kill grey squirrels in order to protect native red squirrels from competition and from infection with the squirrel pox carried by greys. In addition, squirrels of either species have been killed in the past to reduce their damage to forestry. In 2009 reviews for Natural England and Scottish Natural Heritage of the humaneness of grey squirrel killing stated that ideally methods 'should be painless, achieve rapid unconsciousness and death, require minimum restraint, avoid excitement, minimize fear and psychological stress to the animal', but that 'there is little or no information on how often suffering (both duration and severity) occurs in practice'. Natural England pointed out that 'the public will need reassurance that the most humane methods are being used competently, otherwise their support [for the cull] may not be forthcoming'.[79]

Squirrels often present a fast-moving target, making a clean head-shot difficult to achieve. Squirrels shot in the chest may remain conscious until they die from bleeding or inability to breath. Some shooters fire 'blind' into dreys. Squirrels caught in cage-traps try vigorously to escape and are inevitably subjected to stress, fear and panic. They are usually killed either by being shot in the cage-trap or by being tipped into a sack and hit on the head. This may require two or more shots or blows. Some are chased from the live-trap into a kill-trap.[79] These methods may, in the best circumstances, ensure a quick death; but they clearly risk error and suffering and the squirrel's last hours and minutes are certain to have been terrifying. Some squirrels are drowned, but this is not an approved method. In areas where there are no red squirrels or pine martens, grey squirrels are poisoned with warfarin, an inhumane poison,[43] for the protection of forestry.

---

- A lower level of concern exists for the suffering of pest or alien animals than for many other animals that people are in daily contact with.
- Pest or alien animals have little protection from animal welfare law in practice.
- Some legal methods of killing pests or aliens are inhumane.
- Private citizens are in practice (even if not in theory) free to kill animals of pest species by any method they see fit.
- Animal protection non-governmental organizations (NGOs), with some exceptions,[80] seem unwilling to campaign to change public attitudes and public policy in relation to less well-regarded pests.

It may even be felt by some that pest and alien animals deserve in some way to suffer, in revenge for the damage they do to property, ecosystems or valued species. While there is no ethical or scientific justification for allowing an animal to suffer because the species is disliked rather than liked, this may be a fairly common human approach. A commercial pest-control brand is appropriately named 'Strikeback'. Those using the Rodenator find it satisfying to use ('you got this guy') because pests are 'trying to take the money out of your pocket' and 'fighting you' and can be 'very enraging'.[40]

Other members of the public may see pest culls as cruel and arbitrary, and some pests and aliens are popular. People intentionally feed urban gulls, feral pigeons, grey squirrels, red foxes and badgers (but not rats). White-tailed deer in suburban America have been described as 'our beloved pests'.[81] For quite other reasons, the breeding of some nominally pest species, such as foxes and feral pigs, is sometimes deliberately encouraged by the hunting community.

Alternatively, one person's endangered species may be another person's pest. Conservation organizations continue to find large birds of prey, such as eagles, hen harriers, red kites and peregrine falcons, lying dead on the ground, sometimes near a poisoned bait that may have been put out by gamekeepers protecting gamebirds for sport shooting. The Royal Society for the Protection of Birds emphasizes that 'Hen harriers ... are not pests to be killed out of hand' and denotes this poisoning 'callous', 'cruel', 'merciless' and a 'persecution'.[82] It is doubtful, though, whether these highly valued birds suffer more than the thousands or millions of 'pest' animals that are routinely killed by similar methods without raising concern.

## 11.4.2 Conservation and alien species

Several species have their population controlled for both economic reasons (damage to agriculture) and conservation reasons (usually as invasive aliens). The conservationists' argument is that the evolved ecosystem is by definition the balanced and the 'right' ecosystem, with the maximum biological diversity; where humans have been responsible for unbalancing an ecosystem, then humans have the right and the duty to restore it to a pre-human condition. If non-native species become dominant in a new ecosystem so that they disrupt the balance and reduce the genetic diversity, then it is considered ethically and scientifically justified to remove them by killing. Some ecologists fear a globalization or 'McDonaldization' of ecosystems and find non-native species objectionable for cultural or aesthetic reasons, as well as for scientific ones.[16] In this view the lives of non-native animals have little value when they are in the 'wrong' ecosystem. Conservation is not intended to be the same thing as animal welfare.

From the perspective of animal protection NGOs, whose priority is to protect the interests of individual sentient animals, the well-being of the particular animal is important but the welfare of a 'species' (except as a collection of individual animals) cannot be said to have a real meaning. Therefore any human project that causes suffering to one type of animal, in order to fulfil a blueprint of how we believe an ecosystem should be, must raise serious questions.[83]

More recently, some conservation scientists have started to question the practicality or the theoretical need to restore a 'pre-human' or pristine state of nature. There may be 'novel ecosystems' arising that function well even though they have a mix of species originating from different continents. They point out that change is not necessarily the same thing as 'harm' and question the assumption that a 'native' species is inherently more desirable than a non-native one.[20,84] Other scientists have pointed out the uncertainties in trying to distinguish native from alien species, and the unpleasantly xenophobic and racist overtones in some of the scientific discussion that appears to demonize non-native animals.[12,13,84] The existing ranges of species are also likely to shift as a result of climate change and the ways in which plants and animals can or cannot adapt to it,[85] potentially challenging current thinking about which species should be where.

The debate about how and whether to intervene to control an unwanted species in an environment where it has no natural predators will never be an easy one. Should we allow rats to colonize an island and destroy the entire population of ground-nesting birds? Should we allow feral goats to eat vegetation down to the ground? Should we introduce once-native predators such as wolves to Scotland where they could change the browsing behaviour of the red deer in ways that benefit the environment, but could be seen as a threat by farmers?[86]

## 11.4.3 Case study: Red and grey squirrels in Britain

Eurasian red squirrels (*Sciurus vulgaris*) are a conservation priority in Britain. This was not always so and they were killed as pests of forest plantations when their numbers were high in the 19th century, when squirrel-killing clubs paid bounties for them.[8] There are estimated to be around 160,000 red squirrels left in Britain, mostly in Scotland.[8,87] Scottish Natural Heritage (SNH) believes that 'the main [threat] to our native red squirrel is competition with the more robust greys'.[88] Grey squirrels (*Sciurus carolinensis*) have been demonized as aggressive invaders, sometimes even in the language of conservation scientists.

There are two main reasons for the growth of the grey squirrel population and the decline of the reds. Greys can make better use of seeds in broadleaf habitats, whereas reds have a feeding advantage in conifer woods. In broadleaf areas, the greys have better body condition and greater reproductive success than reds. Past and present forestry policies that focus on planting native oaks have unintentionally favoured grey squirrels and disadvantaged reds.[8] A second cause is that grey squirrels carry and transmit the squirrel pox virus, which causes them no disease but is fatal to red squirrels and causes suffering.

One of the main features of the British red squirrel conservation campaign is the killing of several thousand grey squirrels per year, including during the breeding season when there may be dependent young, carried out by a number of governmental and voluntary organizations supported by taxpayer funding.[79] The number of greys killed per unit area in England, Wales and Scotland increased by 50 per cent between 1995 and 2006. The Red Squirrel Protection Partnership in Northumberland claimed to have killed 20,000 greys in a 20-month period in 2007 to 2008.[79] Conservation policy has designated 'stronghold sites'[89] in Scotland to be defended against the greys and 'buffer zones' around the areas where there are red squirrel populations, in which greys can be detected and killed.

Is it essential to maintain red squirrel populations in mainland Britain at this time? It may well not be. Red squirrels in Britain today are not uniquely British but originate from squirrels imported from various European sources such as Scandinavia over the last 150 years, after they became almost extinct in the 18th century as a result of deforestation. They now have a mixed genetic origin and there is no genetic difference between red squirrels in Britain and in continental Europe. This means that the disappearance of the Eurasian red squirrel from Britain would not endanger the species as a whole and that red squirrels could be reintroduced to Britain from Europe, where they are abundant, at any time in the future. According to biologists at the University of Bristol: 'Globally, red squirrel populations are not threatened and the conservation effort in Britain is of little importance.'[8]

Possibly the most important problems that conservationists could tackle are technical ones: most importantly, the development of a vaccine against squirrel pox (which causes suffering) and potentially a contraceptive drug for grey squirrels,[90,91] together with improving woodlands to advantage reds. Red squirrels populations could then be reintroduced from continental Europe, as they have been in the past.

## 11.4.4 Case study: The Uist hedgehogs

Differing points of view on non-native species were well illustrated by the case of the Uist hedgehogs. At the start of the 21st century, the governmental conservation body Scottish Natural Heritage (SNH) decided to exterminate hedgehogs that had been introduced without due thought to islands in the Outer Hebrides several decades earlier. Hedgehog populations were officially reported to have reached 5000 and the hedgehogs were eating the eggs of ground-nesting birds, such as dunlin, redshank, lapwing and oystercatcher, causing steep declines in their populations.[92]

SNH started to eradicate hedgehogs from the island of Uist by killing them as they emerged from winter hibernation prior to the breeding season. This met with public opposition, as hedgehogs are popular animals, and demands that the hedgehogs should be relocated rather than killed. Animal protection organizations and volunteers from all over Britain arrived in spring to collect and re-home hedgehogs on the mainland.[93]

SNH, in turn, deplored the relocation strategy, arguing that killing was kinder than relocation. Celebrities and hedgehog experts lined up against SNH and the killing policy. Finally, in 2007, SNH agreed to switch from killing to relocation, after an estimated 600 hedgehogs had been killed and another 756 had been relocated by the Uist Hedgehog Rescue coalition. Advocates for Animals (Edinburgh), a member of the coalition, hoped that 'conservation organizations will incorporate a respect for animals and their welfare into future policies'.[94]

## 11.4.5 The need for a different approach

Decisions about whether and how to deal with pest and alien species are difficult and unpleasant ones to make. The more we intervene, the more ethical conflicts seem to arise. Tolerance is not always possible when people's property, livelihood or safety is threatened. The more humane and tolerant options tend to have promise in the long term rather than immediately, and therefore tend to be put off in favour of killing to remove the problem. Often, killing is used as a substitute for prevention.

Nevertheless, it is time for perceptions and policies to change because current ones are out of step with modern animal protection standards for equivalent animals or even the same species in different circumstances (compare rats as pests and as pets). A 2008 assessment of population control methods for the Australian government concluded that 'There is a pressing need to improve the humaneness of control programs and to develop a process that enables the most humane methods to be identified.'[74] Some approaches that could prove useful in moving society towards more humane methods include the following:

- commitment to prevent the growth of large populations of problem animals, including:
  - preventing access to crops, food stores, animal feed, refuse or buildings;
  - preventing the trading, breeding or importing of exotic pets that could establish themselves in the environment;
  - control of accidental dispersal of animal species in shipping and other transport;
- commitment to develop fertility control products for free-living wild animal populations as an alternative to lethal control, including:
  - commitment by scientists and research funding agencies to achieve effective and non-harmful products, such as contraceptive vaccines and methods of drug delivery;
  - commitment to facilitating and implementing this control option, as an alternative to killing, by policy-makers, drug regulators and drug producers;
- prohibition of the most inhumane forms of population control, including:
  - leg-hold traps, snares, rodent glue traps, anticoagulant poisons and other poisons that cause substantial suffering;
  - killing of lactating females or killing during the breeding season, unless dependent young can be located and killed humanely;
- training and certification in humane methods, which should be required for all those involved in animal population control, specifically:
  - training and independent licensing of all operators of pest-control measures, including private individuals such as farmers and householders;

- prohibition of sale to the public of pest-control traps or poisons without a licence of competence in humane operation;
- assessment of the humaneness of the various existing control methods by independent animal welfare and veterinary scientists, followed by recommendations to policy-makers:
  - scientists, conservationists, policy-makers and the media could take more care in the language used to describe unwanted animal populations, to avoid sensationalism or terms that could encourage intolerance and hatred;
  - animal protection NGOs could campaign to ensure that sentient 'pests' and 'aliens' are legally protected from suffering at the same level as other animal populations;
  - society in developed countries could encourage greater tolerance towards minor damage or inconvenience caused by wild animals to businesses and households.

## Notes

1  Shapiro, J. ( 2001) *Mao's War against Nature*, Cambridge University Press
2  Thompson, F. (1986) *The Peverel Papers: A Yearbook of the Countryside*, J. Shuckburgh (ed), Century Hutchinson Ltd
3  Thomas, K. (1984) *Man and the Natural World: Changing Attitudes in England 1500–1800*, Penguin Books
4  Cruz, F. et al (2009) 'Bio-economics of large-scale eradication of feral goats from Santiago Island, Galápagos', *Journal of Wildlife Management*, vol 73, no 2, pp191–200
5  USDA (United States Department of Agriculture) (2008) *Wildlife Services' 2008 Annual Tables*, www.aphis.usda.gov/wildlife_damage/prog_data/prog_data_report_FY2008.shtml, last accessed July 2009
6  Parrott, D. et al (2009) *Review of Red Squirrel Conservation Activity in Northern England*, Report No NECR019, Natural England; Henderson, I. (2002) *UK Ruddy Duck Control Trial Final Report*, Central Science Laboratory, York
7  McNeill, J. R. (2000) *Something New Under the Sun: An Environmental History of the Twentieth-Century World*, Allen Lane, Penguin Press; Tenner, E. (1997) *Why Things Bite Back: Technology and the Revenge of Unintended Consequences*, Vintage Books
8  Harris, S., Soulsbury, C. D. and Iossa, G. (2006) *Is Culling of Grey Squirrels a Viable Tactic to Conserve Red Squirrel Populations?*, Advocates for Animals
9  Invasive Animals Cooperative Research Centre, *Cane Toads*, http://invasiveanimals.com/invasive-animals/cane-toads/index.html, last accessed July 2009; Kimberley Toad Busters (2008) *Kimberley Toad Busters Airlifted into Battle as Cane Toads Found 53kms from the WA/NT Border (and Where Is the NT Government?)*, Media release, 3 February 2008; Shine, R. et al (2006), 'The biology, impact and control of cane toads: An overview of the University of Sydney's research program', in K. Molloy and W. Henderson (eds) *Science of Cane Toad Invasion and Control*, Proceedings of the Invasive Animals CRC Cane Toad Workshop, 5–6 June 2006, Brisbane; see also other papers in same proceedings
10  Hart-Davis, D. (2002) *Fauna Britannica: The Practical Guide to Wild and Domestic Creatures of Britain*, Weidenfeld & Nicolson

11  Invasive Animals Cooperative Research Centre, *Rabbits*, www.invasiveanimals.com/invasive-animals/rabbits/index.html, last accessed July 2009

12  Barnett, S. A. (2001) *The Story of Rats: Their Impact on Us, and Our Impact on Them*, Allen & Unwin; Sullivan, R. (2004) *Rats: Observations on the History and Habitat of the City's Most Unwanted Inhabitants*, Bloomsbury

13  Pimentel, D. (2007) 'Environmental and economic costs of vertebrate species invasions into the United States', in G. W. Witmer, W. C. Pitt and K. A. Fagerstone (eds) *Proceedings of International Symposium: Managing Vertebrate Invasive Species*, USDA National Wildlife Research Center, Fort Collins, CO, 7–9 August 2007

14  United Nations Convention on Biological Diversity (1992); Council Directive 79/409/EEC of 2 April 1979 on the Conservation of Wild Birds, EU Lex 31979L0409; European Convention on the Conservation of European Wildlife and Natural Habitats (Berne Convention) and Strategy on Invasive Alien Species

15  Global Invasive Species Programme, www.gisp.org, accessed July 2009

16  Warren, C. R. (2007) 'Perspectives on the "alien" versus "native" species debate: A critique of concepts, language and practice', *Progress in Human Geography*, vol 31, no 4, pp427–446

17  Hettinger, N. (2001) 'Exotic species, naturalisation, and biological nativism', *Environmental Values*, vol 10, pp193–224; Woods, M. and Moriarty, P. V. (2001) 'Strangers in a strange land: The problem of exotic species', *Environmental Values*, vol 10, pp163–191

18  Angulo, E. and Bárcena, J. (2007) 'Towards a unique and transmissible vaccine against myxomatosis and rabbit haemorrhagic disease for rabbit populations', *Wildlife Research*, vol 34, pp567–577; Henderson, W. R. and Murphy, E. C. (2007) 'Pest or prized possession? Genetically modified biocontrol from an international perspective', *Wildlife Research*, vol 34, no 7, pp578–585

19  Global Invasive Species Programme, *Invasive Species Are 2nd only to Habitat Destruction as a Threat to Biodiversity*, www.gisp.org/publications/brochures/gispposters1.pdf, accessed August 2009

20  *Nature* (2009) 'Editorial: Beyond the pristine', *Nature*, vol 460, pp345–346

21  Gerwin, V. (2002) 'Grey squirrels nick reds' nuts', *Nature*, News online, www.nature.com, 7 February 2002; BBC (2009) *PM Programme*, Radio 4, 29 May

22  BBC (2009) *Nature*, Radio Four, 20 May

23  Morelle, R. (2008) 'Alien invaders: The next generation', BBC News online, http://news.bbc.co.uk, 16 October

24  Invasive Species Cooperative Research Centre, *Pigs*, http://invasiveanimals.com/view/14849/iacrc_sub/compound-1080.html; www.invasiveanimals.com/invasive-animals/pigs/index.html, both accessed November 2008

25  Osborne, D. (2008) 'Invasive fish calls northern waters home', *Adelaide Advertiser*, 19 February

26  Audubon (2009) *Invasive Species Campaigns*, www.audubon.org/campaign/invasives/index.shtm, accessed 15 January 2009

27  National Invasive Species Council (2008) *2008–2012 National Invasive Species Management Plan*, NISC

28  Global Invasive Species Programme: Mission Statement, www.gisp.org/about/mission.asp, last accessed July 2009

29  Global Invasive Species Database, www.issg.org/database/welcome/, accessed November 2008

30  DAISIE, www.daisie.ceh.ac.uk/; Hulme, P. E. et al (2009) 'Will the threat of biological invasions unite the European Union?', *Science*, vol 324, pp40–41

31  Invasive Animals Cooperative Research Centre, www.invasiveanimals.com/, last accessed July 2009; McLeod, R. (2004) *Counting the Cost: Impact of Invasive Animals in Australia 2004*, Cooperative Research Centre for Pest Animal Control, Canberra

32  Invasive Animals Cooperative Research Centre, *Foxes*, http://invasiveanimals.com/invasive-animals/foxes/index.html, accessed November 2008; Biodiversity Group Environment Australia (1999) *Threat Abatement Plan for Predation by the European Red Fox*, Environment Australia

33  Lapidge, S. J. (ed) (2003) *Proceedings of the Feral Pig Action Agenda*, James Cook University, Cairns, June 2003, Pest Animal Control Cooperative Research Centre, Canberra

34  Witmer, G. W. et al (2007) 'Management of invasive vertebrates in the United States: An overview', in G. W. Witmer, W. C. Pitt and K. A. Fagerstone (eds) *Managing Vertebrate Invasive Species: Proceedings of an International Symposium*, USDA National Wildlife Research Center, Fort Collins, CO, 7–9 August 2007

35  Campbell, T. S. (2007) 'The role of early detection and rapid response in thwarting amphibian and reptile introductions in Florida', in G. W. Witmer, W. C. Pitt and K. A. Fagerstone (eds) *Managing Vertebrate Invasive Species: Proceedings of an International Symposium*, USDA National Wildlife Research Center, Fort Collins, CO, 7–9 August 2007

36  Tuyttens, F. A. M. and Macdonald, D. W. (1998) 'Fertility control: An option for non-lethal control of wild carnivores?', *Animal Welfare*, vol 7, pp339–364

37  Thresher, R. E. (2007) 'Genetic options for the control of invasive vertebrate pests: Prospects and constraints', in G. W. Witmer, W. C. Pitt and K. A. Fagerstone (eds) *Managing Vertebrate Invasive Species: Proceedings of an International Symposium*, USDA National Wildlife Research Center, Fort Collins, CO, 7–9 August 2007

38  Wiley-Blackwell (2009) 'City rats are loyal to their neighborhoods', *ScienceDaily*, 27 May 2009; Garnder-Santana, L. C. et al (2009) 'Commensal ecology, urban landscapes, and their influence on the genetic characteristics of city-dwelling Norway rats (*Rattus norvegicus*)', *Molecular Ecology*, vol 18, no 13, pp2766–2778

39  Universities Federation for Animal Welfare (2009) *Guiding Principles in the Humane Control of Rats and Mice*, UFAW

40  Rodenator, www.rodenator.com/pests-controls-videos-rodenators, accessed November 2008; Bidewell, C. A. et al (2008) 'Deaths of wild rabbits associated with a novel method of pest control', *Veterinary Record*, vol 162, no 5, p163; Natural England (2008) *Natural England Calls on Rodenator Users to Heed the Law*, Wildlife Management and Licensing, February 2008

41  Sharp, T. and Saunders, G. (undated) *FOX002 Aerial Baiting of Foxes with 1080*, NSW Department of Primary Industries; Saunders, G. and McLeod, L. (2007) *Improving Fox Management Strategies in Australia*, Bureau of Rural Sciences, Canberra; Invasive Animals CRC (undated) *Feral Pigs and PIGOUT®*, Leaflet; National Wildlife Research Center (2008) *Vertebrate Control Products*, 2 October; Australian Pesticides and Veterinary Medicines Authority (2008) *Sodium Fluoroacetate Review Backgrounder*, January

42  APHIS (US Animal and Plant Health Inspection Service) Wildlife Services (2001) *DRC-1339 (Starlicide): Technical Note*, US; Spurr, E. B. (2007) 'Bird control chemicals', in D. Pimentel (ed) *Encyclopedia of Pest Management*, Taylor & Francis, pp52–55; APHIS (2008) *Sodium Lauryl Sulfate: European Starling and Blackbird Wetting Agent: Technical Note*

43  Pesticides Safety Directorate (1997) *Assessment of Humaneness of Vertebrate Control Agents*, Department for Environment, Food and Rural Affairs, UK; Mason, G. and Littiin, K. E. (2003) 'The humaneness of rodent pest control', *Animal Welfare*, vol 12, no 1, pp1–37; EXTOXNET (Extension Toxicology Network) (1996) *Diphacinone*, Oregon State University

44  APHIS (US Animal and Plant Health Inspection Service) (2008) *Vertebrate Control Products*, National Wildlife Research Center, US; EXTOXNET (Extension Toxicology Network) (1996) *Zinc Phosphide*, Oregon State University; APHIS (2001) *M-44 User Tips: Technical Note*

45  Kirkpatrick, J. F. (2005) 'The elusive promise of wildlife contraception: A personal perspective', in A. T. Rutberg (ed) *Humane Wildlife Solutions: The Role of Immunocontraception*, Humane Society of the United States, pp1–22

46  Rock, P. (2003) 'Joined up action: Some ways forward', presentation to the National Conference on Urban Gulls organized by Gloucester City Council, November 2003; Calladine, J. R. et al (2006) *Review of Urban Gulls and Their Management in Scotland: A Report to the Scottish Executive*; PiCAS UK (Pigeon Control Advisory Service) (2006) *Alternatives to Lethal Control*, www.picasuk.com/, last accessed November 2009

47  Avery, M. L. et al (2008) 'Nicarbazin bait reduces reproduction by pigeons (*Columba livia*)', *Wildlife Research*, vol 35, pp80–85; Innolytics LLC (2009) *The Efficacy of OvoControl® P (nicarbazin) in Feral Pigeons (Columba livia)*

48  Rhodes, L. and Moldavem K. (2002) *Contraception and Fertility Control in Animals*, AlcheraBio, for Alliance for Contraception in Cats and Dogs

49  Asa, C. S. and Porton, I. J. (eds) (2005) *Wildlife Contraception: Issue, Methods and Applications*, The Johns Hopkins University Press

50  Kirkpatrick, J. F. and Frank, K. M. (2005) 'Contraception in free-ranging wildlife', in C. S. Asa and I. J. Porton (eds) *Wildlife Contraception: Issues, Methods and Applications*, The Johns Hopkins University Press, pp195–221

51  APHIS National Wildlife Research Center (2008) *GonaCon™ Immunocontraceptive for Deer* and *GonaCon™–Birth Control for Deer: Questions and Answers*; Fagerstone, K. A. and Miller, L. A. (2008) 'Recent developments in wildlife contraception', in *Proceedings of the 14th Australasian Vertebrate Pest Conference*, Darwin, 10–13 June 2008, p108, www.invasiveanimals.com; Massei, G. et al (2008) 'Effect of the GnRH vaccine GonaCon on the fertility, physiology and behaviour of wild boar', *Wildlife Research*, vol 35, pp540–547; Killian, G. et al (2008) 'Four-year contraception rates of mares treated with single injection porcine zona pellucida and GnRH vaccines and intrauterine devices', *Wildlife Research*, vol 35, pp531–539

52  Mauldin, R. E. and Miller, L. A. (2007) 'Wildlife contraception: Targeting the oocyte', in G. W. Witmer, W. C. Pitt and K. A. Fagerstone (eds) *Managing Vertebrate Invasive Species: Proceedings of An International Symposium*, USDA National Wildlife Research Center, Fort Collins, CO, 7–9 August 2007

53  APHIS National Wildlife Research Center (2009) *Development of Reproductive Control Methods for Overabundant Birds and Mammals: Diazacon*

54  Hinds, L. A. et al (2008) 'Effect of a GnRH vaccine (GonaCon™) on the fertility of male and female wallabies', in *Proceedings of the 14th Australasian Vertebrate Pest Conference*, Darwin, 10–13 June 2008, p113, www.invasiveanimals.com

55  Bertschinger, H. J. et al (2008) 'The use of deslorelin implants for the long-term contraception of lionesses and tigers', *Wildlife Research*, vol 35, no 6, pp525–530

56  Kemp, J. M. and Miller, L. A. (2008) 'Oral vaccination and immunocontraception of feral swine using *Brucella suis* with multimeric GnRH protein expression', in R. M. Timm and M. B. Madon (eds) *Proceedings of 23rd Vertebrate: Pest Conference*, University of California, Davis, CA, pp250–252

57 Tyndale-Biscoe, H. and Hind, L. A. (2007) 'Introduction – virally vectored immunocontraception in Australia', *Wildlife Research*, vol 34, pp507–510

58 Cowan, D. P. and Hinds, L. A. (2008) 'Preface to Fertility control for wildlife', *Wildlife Research*, vol 35, no 6, ppiii–iv; see also other papers in *Wildlife Research*, vol 35, no 6; Hinds, A. L. (ed) (2007) 'Virally vectored immunocontraception', *Wildlife Research*, vol 34, no 7 (see all papers in this issue); Arthur, A. D. et al (2009) 'The transmission rate of MCMV in house mice in pens: Implications for virally vectored immunocontraception', *Wildlife Research*, vol 36, no 5, pp386–393

59 Invasive Animals CRC (2007) *Daughterless Toads*, www.invasiveanimals.com/research/terrestrial_products_and_strategies/5.t.3-daughterless-toads-project/index.html, accessed November 2009; Koopman, P. (2006) 'Daughterless cane toads' in K. L. Molloy and W. R. Henderson (eds) *Science of Cane Toad Invasion and Control*, Proceedings of the Invasive Animals CRC Cane Toad Workshop, June 2006, pp111–116

60 Muir, W. M. and Howard, R. D. (1999) 'Possible ecological risks of transgenic organism release when transgenes affect mating success: Sexual selection and the Trojan gene hypothesis', *Proceedings of the National Academy of Sciences*, vol 96, no 24, pp13,853–13,856

61 Howard, R. D., DeWoody, J. A. and Muir, W. M. (2004) 'Transgenic male mating advantage provides opportunity for Trojan gene effect in a fish', *Proceedings of the National Academy of Sciences*, vol 101, no 9, pp2934–2938

62 Hilton-Taylor, C. et al (2009) 'State of the world's species', in J.-C. Vié, C. Hilton-Taylor and S. N. Stuart (eds) (2009) *Wildlife in a Changing World: An Analysis of the 2008 IUCN Red List of Threatened Species*, IUCN, Gland, Switzerland, pp15–42; IUCN Red List 2008, Table 4a, 'Red List category summary for all animal classes and orders'

63 BBC (2009) 'Tiger attacks trigger expert plea', BBC News online, http://news.bbc.co.uk, 25 February; ZSL (2009) 'Tiger conservation in Sumatra', www.zsl.org/conservation/regions/asia/tiger/the-jambi-tiger-project,43,AR.html, accessed August 2009

64 Bradshaw, G. A. et al (2005) 'Elephant breakdown', *Nature*, vol 433, p807

65 Hosey, G., Melfi, V. and Pankhurst, S. (2009) *Zoo Animals: Behaviour, Management, and Welfare*, Oxford University Press

66 Howard, J., Marinari, P. E. and Wildt, D. E. (2003) 'Black-footed ferret: Model for assisted reproductive technologies contributing to in situ conservation', in W. V. Holt et al (eds) *Reproductive Science and Integrated Conservation*, Cambridge University Press, pp250–266

67 Conway, W. (2007) 'Entering the 21st century', in A. Zimmerman et al (eds) *Zoos in the 21st Century: Catalysts for Conservation?*, Zoological Society of London, pp12–21

68 West, C. and Dickie, L. A. (2007) 'Introduction: Is there a conservation role for zoos in a natural world under fire?', in A. Zimmerman et al (eds) *Zoos in the 21st Century: Catalysts for Conservation?*, Zoological Society of London

69 Loftin, R. (1995) 'Captive breeding of endangered species', in B. G. Norton et al (eds) *Ethics on the Ark: Zoos, Animal Welfare and Wildlife Conservation*, Smithsonian Institution Press, pp164–180

70 Clubb, R. et al (2009) 'Fecundity and population viability in female zoo elephants: Problems and possible solutions', *Animal Welfare*, vol 18, pp237–247

71 Gómez, M. C. et al (2009) 'Cloning endangered felids using heterospecific oocytes and interspecies embryo transfer', *Reproduction, Fertility and Development*, vol 21, no 1, pp76–82; Lanza, R. P. (2000) 'Cloning Noah's Ark', *Scientific American*, November 2000

72 Beck, B. (1995) 'Reintroduction, zoos, conservation and animal welfare', in B. G. Norton et al (eds) *Ethics on the Ark: Zoos, Animal Welfare and Wildlife Conservation*, Smithsonian Institution Press, pp155–163

73 Mason, G. and Littin, K. E. (2003) 'The humaneness of rodent pest control', *Animal Welfare*, vol 12, no 1, pp1–37

74 Sharp, T. and Saunders, G. (2008) *A Model for Assessing the Relative Humaneness of Pest Animal Control Methods*, Australian Government Department of Agriculture, Fisheries and Forestry, ACT, Canberra

75 Delsink, A., Grobler, D. and van Altena, J. J. (2005) 'The Makalali Elephant Immunocontraception Program', in A. T. Rutberg (ed) *Humane Wildlife Solutions: The Role of Immunocontraception*, HSUS, pp43–52

76 See discussion in Oogjes, G. (1997) 'Ethical aspects and dilemmas of fertility control of unwanted wildlife: an animal welfarist's perspective', *Reproduction, Fertility and Development*, vol 9, no 1, pp163–168

77 Curtis, P. D. et al (2008) 'Physiological effects of gonadotropin releasing hormone immunocontraception on white-tailed deer', *Human–Wildlife Conflicts*, vol 2, no 1, pp68–79

78 Strive, T., Hardy, C. M. and Reubel, G. H. (2007) 'Prospects for immunocontraception in the European Red Fox (*Vulpes vulpes*)', *Wildlife Research*, vol 34, no 7, pp523–529

79 Parrott, D. et al (2009) *Review of Red Squirrel Conservation Activity in Northern England*, report no NECR019, Natural England (Appendix 8 reviews killing methods); Central Science Laboratory (2009) *Review of Methods of Humane Destruction of Grey Squirrels (*Sciurus carolinensis*)*, Scottish Natural Heritage Commissioned Report no 317

80 See, for example, Advocates for Animals (2008) *Parliamentary Briefing: Action to Protect the Red Squirrel*, www.advocatesforanimals.org.uk; Advocates for Animals. (2009) '"We love all squirrels, whatever their colour" – SQUIRRELS UNITED!', news release, 9 February, http://advocatesforanimals.org.uk/images/ stories/pressrelease/090209-squirrels-united-pr.pdf, accessed April 2010; Fowler-Reeves, K. (2007) *With Extreme Prejudice: The Culling of British Wildlife*, Animal Aid, www.animalaid.org.uk

81 Rutberg, A. T. (2005) 'Deer contraception: What we know and what we don't', in A. T. Rutberg (ed) *Humane Wildlife Solutions: The Role of Immunocontraception*, HSUS, pp23–42

82 RSPB (2007) *Poisoning*, www.rspb.org.uk/ourwork/policy/wildbirdslaw/ wildbirdcrime/poisoning.asp; RSPB (2008) *Enough is Enough*, www.rspb.org.uk/ news/details.asp?id=tcm:9-206625; RSPB (2008) *The Killing Has to Stop*, www.rspb.org.uk/supporting/campaigns/birdsofprey/why.asp, accessed August 2009; McCarthy, M. and Johnston, I. (2008) 'Gamekeepers "kill off" the last of the hen harriers', *Independent*, 22 December

83 See, for example, discussion in Jamieson, D. (1995) 'Wildlife conservation and individual animal welfare', in Norton, B. G. et al (eds) *Ethics on the Ark: Zoos, Animal Welfare and Wildlife Conservation*, Smithsonian Institution Press, pp69–73; Jamieson, D. (2008) *Ethics and the Environment: An Introduction*, Cambridge University Press

84 Marris, E. (2009) 'Ragamuffin earth', *Nature*, vol 460, pp450–453; Davis, M. (2009) 'Immigrant species aren't all bad', *New Scientist*, 25 September, pp26–27; Davis, M. (2009) *Invasion Biology*, Oxford University Press

85 Walther, G.-R. et al (2002) 'Ecological responses to recent climate change', *Nature*, vol 416, pp389–395

86 Manning, A. D., Gordon, I. J. and Ripple, W. J. (2009) 'Restoring landscapes of fear with wolves in the Scottish Highlands', *Biological Conservation*, vol 142, no 10, pp2314–2321

87    Non-Native Species Secretariat (undated) *Grey Squirrel, Scirius carolinesis: Factsheet*
88    Scottish Natural Heritage (2008) 'Confirmation of first non-native grey squirrel in Inverness', News release, 25 April
89    Species Action Framework (Scotland) (undated) *Red Squirrel, Sciurus vulgaris: Five-Year Implementation Plan 2007–2012*
90    Sainsbury, A. W. et al (2008) 'Poxviral disease in red squirrels Sciurus vulgaris in the UK: Spatial and temporal trends of an emerging threat', *EcoHealth*, vol 5, no 3, pp305–316
91    Forestry Commission (2002) 'Grey squirrel contraception research put on hold', News release, www.forestry.gov.uk, 30 October; BBC (2007) 'Birth control for grey squirrels', BBC News online, http://news.bbc.co.uk, 3 October
92    Defra (Department for Environment, Food and Rural Affairs) (2003) *Review of Non-Native Species Policy: Report of Working Group*, Defra
93    Uist Hedgehog Rescue (2004) 'Animal groups mount Uist hedgehog rescue and slam taxpayer-funded "unethical killing policy"', News release, 3 April
94    Advocates for Animals (2003) 'Scottish Parliament committee backs rescue of Uist hedgehogs', News release, 25 March; Press Association (2007) 'Uist hedgehog cull scrapped', *Guardian* online, www.guardian.co.uk, 20 February

12

# Laboratory Animal Breeding: Designed for Science

## 12.1 Background and context: Laboratory animals

### 12.1.1 Breeding for disease

The use of dogs by the medieval European aristocracy in times of political intrigue to test whether their food had been poisoned is one example of the very ancient practice of animal experimentation. Small dogs are depicted walking among the dishes in a famous painting of the banqueting table of the Duc de Berry in the early 15th century. This may reflect the Duke's known enthusiasm for dogs, but they may have been tasting dogs (*chiens-goûteurs*) used to check the Duke's food in an early form of toxicity testing.[1]

There must have been so many spare dogs around the courts of the time that it was not necessary to breed tasting dogs deliberately for the purpose. In the earlier years of animal experimentation in medical research, during the 19th century, scientists likewise used stray or unwanted domestic or farm animals (and the use of dogs in vivisection without anaesthesia led to the first antivivisection movement across society in Britain and America[2]). Today, when animal experimentation is the basis of much of the global research effort in genetics and medicine, and animal testing is required for regulatory approval of nearly every product sold for use, more than 100 million experimental animals of vertebrate species are bred for the purpose annually. The large majority of the animals are mice (with rats and fish in second place) and an increasing proportion of them are bred to have some form of genetic mutation.

Specialized strains of mouse and rat were first bred for use in medical and genetic research at the beginning of the 20th century.[3–5] By the turn of the 21st century, mice and rats designed as 'models' for human diseases had become commercial purpose-bred commodities and some of them were patented. By 2009 one of the major American commercial suppliers had a catalogue of over 4000 mutant mouse strains,[6] kept either as live animals or as frozen embryos or sperm, with precise specifications of their genotype and phenotype.

Laboratory animal breeding presents a contrast to every other area of human breeding of animals. Laboratory animals are often designed to be models of disease, not models of health. While several of the previous chapters have shown that human breeding of animals has led to ill health in animals in several cases, ill health is not the objective. In the case of laboratory animals, it often is. Inbreeding and disease susceptibility are considered something to avoid in most other areas of animal breeding but they are often an explicit part of the laboratory animal breeder's programme.

For experimental results to be statistically reliable and repeatable, scientists want to reduce the genetic sources of variation between the animals that they use for any particular test. Genetic uniformity – to produce something close to a clone – has been the explicit aim of breeding laboratory mice and rats since the first inbred laboratory mouse strains were developed. In much of the fast-growing area of genetics research that uses mice as 'models' for human disease, the mice are often deliberately bred to be diseased or to be abnormally suscep-tible to disease. When breeders of farmed animals or companion animals discover that they have inadvertently produced a damaging mutation in their animals, they are expected to reject those animals for breeding in order to avoid perpetuating the defect. Laboratory animal breeders, in contrast, create and perpetuate damaging genetic mutations so that they can be studied as aspects of basic biology or in medical research. In this sense, laboratory animals can justifiably be said to be designed and bred to suffer (albeit with the stated aim of reducing human suffering). This chapter looks at aspects of how animals are bred and supplied for laboratory use, focusing mainly on mice as the majority species.

## 12.1.2 From fancy to laboratory

The production of inbred mice on a large scale, tailor made for scientific research in relation to their genotype and phenotype, began in the early 20th century. The development arose from two areas of research: cancer studies and the study of Mendelian genetics in animals. The breeding of fancy mouse strains from the later 19th century onward turned out to have an important role in the development of today's laboratory mice. Fancy mouse breeders, as they still do today, concentrated on obtaining different coat and eye colours, sometimes starting from fancy mouse strains obtained from Japan, where mouse breeding had started earlier. Several of the main recognized fancy mouse strains of today, such as the black, silver and white, date from the end of the 19th century.[7] The first published demonstration of the Mendelian inheritance of coat colour in mice was in 1903.[8]

From the early stages of the mouse fancy, some mouse strains developed harmful mutations. One of the earliest defective strains used was the 'waltzing mouse', which may have contributed the pink-eye gene. The mutation that caused the waltzing mouse had apparently been perpetuated intentionally in Japan to produce novelty pets before it was imported and used in mouse breed-ing in Britain and the US. This strain was believed to have an inner ear defect and possibly epilepsy, which made the animal permanently unbalanced. According to a 1933 news article, the mouse began to 'dance' at about one week old and its life thereafter was a permanent battle to find its balance, causing it to run in circles and perform other amusing behaviour – this included whirling on a hind leg, running a figure of eight and continually twitching, jerking and swaying its head.[9]

By the early years of the 20th century American scientists, including Clarence Cook Little at Harvard University, started to breed genetically uniform strains of mice for studies of genetics and disease, particularly cancer. It was observed that some strains of waltzing mouse tended to develop mammary tumours and did not reject tumours transplanted into them. Abbie Lathrop, a fancy mouse breeder who supplied the laboratory, had stocks of 10,000 mice and Little himself recorded the birth of over 10,500 mouse pups between 1909 and 1912. By 1916, at the Jackson Laboratory, Little had produced the first inbred laboratory mouse strain, the dilute brown non-agouti (DBA), after generations of brother–sister matings. He went on to produce the C57Black, the most commonly used mouse strain today.[5,8] These inbred mice were intended to be homozygous for almost every gene so that their offspring, too, would be almost genetically identical.

The Jackson Laboratory developed into a mass production enterprise and from the 1930s was primarily 'a mouse factory, not a research factory'.[5] Today it is one of the world's largest breeders of laboratory mice. The 450 standard inbred laboratory mouse strains of today are believed to derive 68 per cent of their genetics from Western European domestic mice, but also include genes derived from mouse subspecies ranging from Eastern Europe to Russia, Western Europe, South-East Asia, China and Japan. These were combined in the European 'fancy' mouse, the origin of today's laboratory strains.[10]

## 12.1.3 Overview of laboratory animal numbers and main uses

### 12.1.3.1 Estimates of numbers

An analysis of global reporting figures made in 2008 estimated that a total of 127 million vertebrates were used in scientific procedures in 2005,[11] but the total number of experimental animals bred and used globally may be more than this because not all countries have a comprehensive reporting system and the criteria for reporting differ. The large majority of the animals are mice, followed by rats and fish. The number of any invertebrate species, such as lobsters and crabs, that are not covered by regulations is not included in the official statistics.

In Great Britain, mice and rats account for nearly 80 per cent of the total animals used.[12,13] The number of animals used is increasing, largely because of the explosion in the use of mutant and genetically engineered animals in research (a worldwide phenomenon). The increase in animal use in Britain between 2000 and 2008 was 35 per cent, 'with the rise in breeding procedures accounting for a significant part of this increase,' according to the Home Office.[13]

In the US, mice, rats and birds used for research are excluded from the scope of the Animal Welfare Act and therefore from reporting requirements.

**Table 12.1** *Use of experimental animals in Great Britain in 2008*

| | Number of procedures using the species | Percentage of total procedures (rounded) |
|---|---|---|
| *Main species used* | | |
| Mice | 2,418,604 | 66% |
| Rats | 355,370 | 10% |
| Fish | 605,155 | 17% |
| Birds | 123,259 | 3% |
| Sheep | 35,820 | 1% |
| Reptiles and amphibians | 32,783 | 1% |
| Guinea pigs | 29,293 | 0.8% |
| Rabbits | 17,060 | 0.5% |
| | | 99.3% |
| *Selected other species used* | | |
| Horses and other equines | 9365 | |
| Pigs | 6824 | |
| Dogs (Beagle breed) | 6074 | |
| Dogs (other breeds) | 31 | |
| Macaque monkey | 4230 | |
| Cattle | 2302 | |
| Marmosets | 368 | |
| Cats | 360 | |
| *Total (all species)* | *3,656,080* | |

*Source:* Home Office (2009)[13]

Thus the US reported usage in the year to September 2007 was only 1 million animals, but this may represent only 20 per cent of the total, or less, if the mice and rats used in all research institutions were included. Among the 1 million animals were 72,037 dogs, 69,990 primates, 22,687 cats, 65,615 pigs, 236,511 rabbits and 207,257 guinea pigs (an increase on 2006 for all these species except rabbits).[14]

In the European Union (EU) and Great Britain, most of the experiments are categorized as medical and fundamental biological research, followed by various forms of toxicity and safety testing for medical, industrial and consumer products.[13,15] In Great Britain in 2008, rabbits were used for nearly 500 procedures involving toxicity for eyes, nearly 750 procedures for testing skin irritation and 6750 pyrogenicity tests (where rabbits have substances injected into the bloodstream to test whether they induce fever).[13]

The EU25 recorded the use of 12.1 million laboratory animals in 2005. (This figure is not directly comparable with UK statistics since the criteria for reporting are different, and exclude breeding colonies of mutant and genetically modified (GM) animals recorded in the UK.) Of these, 6.4 million (53 per cent) were mice, 2.3 million (19 per cent) were rats and 1.8 million (15 per cent) were fish, amphibians and reptiles. No great apes such as chimpanzees were used. Nearly half of all the experiments were carried out in three countries: France, Germany and the UK.[15] Canada recorded the use of 2.1 million animals 2007, a 19 per cent reduction on 2006, and Australia recorded the use of 5.3 million laboratory animals in 2005.[16]

## 12.1.3.2 Breeding for purpose

The large majority of laboratory animals are bred for the purpose either by commercial suppliers or by laboratories or teaching institutions themselves, but this is not always the case. The EU Directive of 1986 on the protection of laboratory animals states that purpose-bred animals from designated suppliers should be used whenever possible and proposals in 2008 for a revised Directive would require that only the offspring of animals born in captivity could be used.[17,18] In Canada, only 26 per cent of the cats and around half of the dogs used in 2007 were purpose bred and thousands of cats and dogs were 'obtained from random sources'.[16] In Great Britain, 99 per cent of the procedures in 2008 used animals from 'designated sources'. The large majority of the animals brought in to the UK from outside the EU were rats and mice, most of them genetically modified.[13]

Since the 1980s, the revolution in genetic technology has meant that the hundreds of existing standard strains of laboratory mice have been increased to thousands by the creation of genetically mutated animals, designed for a specific scientific use. In Great Britain, the generation and maintenance of breeding colonies accounted for 68 per cent of all uses of GM animals in 2003.[19] By 2008, the breeding of mutant and genetically modified animals accounted for an astonishing 38 per cent of all scientific procedures. Table 12.2 shows that the number of procedures using genetically abnormal animals is increasing much faster than the number using normal animals, and accounted for nearly half of all procedures. By 2008, the use of GM animals had increased more than sixfold since 1995[13] in a continuing trend.

**Table 12.2** *Increase in procedures using transgenic or mutant animals in Great Britain*

|  | Using genetically normal animals | Using animals with harmful genetic mutation | Using genetically engineered/ modified (GM) animals | Total using animals not genetically normal | Total |
|---|---|---|---|---|---|
| Number of procedures in 2008 | 1.9 million | 0.43 million | 1.3 million | 1.73 million | 3.7 million |
| Percentage of total procedures | 51% normal | 12% mutant* | 35% GM** | 47% | |
| Increase on 2007 | +9% | +35% | +16% | Breeding of mutant and GM +19% | |

*Note:* * Mostly rodents, fish and amphibians; ** mostly mice and fish.
*Source:* Home Office (2009)[13]

## 12.2 Practices and technologies

### 12.2.1 Genetically engineered mice

Mice are fast breeding and cheap enough to be disposable, and their small size makes them easy to house and maintain in large numbers and easy to handle. Probably more than 100 million laboratory mice are bred in the world's animal laboratories annually, and the main reasons driving the increase in their numbers are the research possibilities offered by genetic mutations. Genetically altered mouse strains can be derived from naturally occurring mutations, or from chemically or virally produced mutations, or from genetic engineering to insert a modified gene or to disable a specific gene in the mouse genome.

The first transgenic mouse was created in 1982 and the first 'knockout' mouse (that is, with a particular gene disabled) in the late 1980s.[20] In 1996 Lexington Genetics, a commercial company, reportedly aimed to produce 500,000 new mutant strains within five years[21] (this did not happen but it shows the scale of ambition), and mutant mice rapidly became an essential tool of genetic and medical research, enabling scientists to study the effect of gene mutations involved in human disease. 'Knockout' mice promise to reveal the function of each and every gene. By 2004 several thousand mutant mouse strains had been created and the International Mouse Knockout Consortium estimated that nearly 4000 targeted gene 'knockouts' has been made in mice by 2007.[19,22]

The genome of the C57 Black strain was sequenced in 2002 and indicated that mice have around 30,000 genes.[4] The number of mutant strains of mice that could be produced, in principle, is therefore enormous. By 2004, scientists had the ambition of creating at least ten mutations for each of these genes, which could produce 300,000 mutant mouse lines over the next couple of decades.[23] In addition, the International Mouse Knockout Consortium, set up in 2007, aimed to knock out all the protein-coding genes in the mouse genome

---

**BOX 12.1 GENE-TARGETED AND KNOCKOUT MICE**

Specific genes in mammalian cells in culture can be modified by introduced DNA through homologous recombination, the process by which DNA sequences are exchanged between chromosome pairs. Research during the 1980s succeeded in gene targeting mouse embryonic stem cells (ES cells). ES cells are 'undifferentiated' cells from early embryos and have the potential to develop into all types of body cell (skin, muscle, etc.). Gene-targeted ES cells are then injected into mouse embryos and the embryos that carry the mutation are transferred into live female mice for gestation and birth. An important application of gene targeting was that it allowed specific genes to be disabled ('knockout mice') and the method was awarded the Nobel Prize in Physiology or Medicine in 2007. Subsequent research made it possible to control when the targeted genes are switched off, important because many of the knockout mutations would be lethal to the embryo. The Nobel Assembly termed the knockout mouse 'the beginning of a new era in genetics'.[24]

by 2010.[25] By 2009, the Knockout Mouse Project, run by the National Institutes of Health in the US, was offering researchers a choice of 2500 knockout mouse strains available from Mutant Mouse Regional Resource Centres and from commercial companies such as Lexicon and JAX. In 2009, Taconic had a database of 3200 'readily available' mouse lines from its Knockout Repository.[26] In addition, the Complex Trait Consortium, involving hundreds of scientists globally, aimed to breed crosses of different standard strains and thus produce 1000 new mouse strains in addition to the 450 standard laboratory strains already in existence.[27]

Standard laboratory strains or mutant strains of mice are now supplied as laboratory reagents like any other, and detailed in catalogues from supply companies. The Jackson Laboratory offers a catalogue of around 60 'Most Popular JAX® Mice Strains', both standard and genetically mutated, with details of their genotype and phenotype, 'key features', common medical uses and any genetic defects. Like the food animal production companies, JAX maintains pedigree 'foundation stocks', expansion stocks and production stocks of mice, and has procedures to limit 'genetic contamination' of any lines by accidental cross-mating and the slow change in the genetics of a population, known as genetic drift.[28] The company offers a speed-breeding service to transfer a mutation or knockout from one strain of mouse to another on demand. Commercial breeders can also supply rats and mice already surgically fitted with cannula (flexible tubes with needles) before shipping, and they supply female mice who have been hormonally superovulated and recently mated as a source of very early embryos.[29] The large number of mouse strains in existence means that not all can be kept in live form and many are kept in the form of frozen genetic material that can be reanimated when required.

## 12.2.2 Examples of mutant mice and their uses

Some of the earliest mutant mice were the nude mice, discovered in the 1960s, that lack a functioning thymus gland and do not produce T cells, a type of lymphocyte essential to effective immune function. These mice do not reject human tumours transplanted into them and the lack of hair makes the tumours easy to see and monitor. The SCID mouse strains, suffering from severe combined immune deficiency, have hair but are even more immune deficient than the nude mouse, lacking several different components of the immune system.

Many mice strains have been bred to be highly susceptible to cancer. One strain survives for 200 days and develops an 'extensive tumour burden', especially in the lungs; another survives for five months with a high frequency of soft tissue sarcomas; another develops a number of malignant tumours, particularly bone, lung and liver tumours; another develops testicular cancer by six months of age; another survives 16 months with a 'broad spectrum' of cancers.[30]

**Table 12.3** *Examples of biological investigations using genetically mutated mice*

| Area of research | Characteristics of mutant mice used to study |
|---|---|
| Maternal and social behaviour | Females with the oxytocin receptor gene disabled failed to nurture their pups and males lacked social behaviour[31] |
| 'Itch gene' | Mice bred without this gene scratched less when exposed to irritants, but were normally responsive to painful stimuli[32] |
| Skin cancer | Mutant mouse had persistent wound-like skin condition and developed skin cancers[33] |
| Parkinson's disease | Mutant mice produced many of the non-motor symptoms of Parkinson's disease, such as depression and sleep problems[34] |
| Memory and learning | Mutant mouse had 'severe memory deficit' and did not remember events just occurred[35] |
| Sleep needs | Mutant mice with a gene found in people who need little sleep were less tired than normal mice when subjected to sleep deprivation[36] |
| Neurological disorders | Mice with a mutated gene that causes the death of brain cells walked backwards when they tried to walk forwards ('moon-walking') for study of neurological disorders[37] |

Other strains of mice are available that either carry or lack genes leading to such conditions as impaired movement, diabetes, inflammatory disease and chronic enterocolitis, reduced pain response, retinal degeneration, muscular dystrophy and vertebral deformation, among many others.[30] A transgenic mouse strain with enhanced energy metabolism can run for 6km without stopping.[38] 'Mouse models' of neurodegenerative diseases may exhibit tremors, loss of control of bodily movements, confusion and disorientation. A 'mouse model' of cleft palate may develop severe deformities of the skull, face and teeth.[39] A mutant mouse has been bred as a model for prion disease and shows symptoms similar to people suffering from vCJD (Creutzfeldt-Jakob disease), the human equivalent of mad cow disease.[40] Mice and rat strains have also been bred to have differences in behaviour – for example, in their degree of fear, anxiety or boldness in an unfamiliar environment. Some mice strains show 'depressive'-like behaviour, tested by measuring the length of time the mice attempt to keep swimming in a beaker of water from which they cannot escape. Some of the many strains of mice engineered to have enhanced learning and memory have side effects such as increased pain response or stress (an inability to forget).[41]

## 12.2.3 Methods of producing mutant mice and rats

### 12.2.3.1 Random mutations

Mutations in mice can be created either randomly, such as by radiation or chemical treatment of the parent, or by genetic engineering. Mice exposed to X-rays produce a rate of gene mutation that is 20 to 100 times greater than the normal mutation rate in mice. During the Cold War period the T-stock mouse strain, carrying seven known recessive mutations, was developed at Oak Ridge laboratory for testing radiation-induced mutations, and a single paper in 1951 reported testing 85,875 offspring.[42] Chemicals can produce a faster rate of genetic mutation even than radiation and in the 1970s the chemical N-ethyl-N-nitrosourea (ENU), injected into mice, was found to cause point mutations in the male's spermatagonial stem cells. By 2005 there were 13 research centres screening thousands of offspring mice for gene mutations caused by ENU in the US, UK, Japan, Australia and Canada, looking for genes associated with a wide range of medical, developmental and behavioural research areas.[42,43]

### 12.2.3.2 Genetic engineering and knockout mice

The main method for genetic engineering of mice has been the use of gene targeting of mouse embryonic stem (ES) cells (see Box 12.1). If the procedure is successful, the first generation of mice born from the embryos containing genetically modified ES cells are 'mosaic' and carry the genetic modification in some body cells but not in others (these mice are usually identified by coat colour). Because some of the modified cells have developed into sperm cells, some of the mosaic offspring can transmit the mutation to their own offspring (germ-line transmission). The mosaic mice are mated with normal mice, resulting in some genetically modified offspring and some normal offspring.[24] In practice, many litters may be required to get the required gene targeting established on the required genetic background strain of mouse (see section 12.3.5).

Depending on the method of causing the mutation, it takes from 50 to several hundred mice to establish a particular mutant strain.[19] A Japanese immunologist credited with running one of the world's most successful knockout 'mouse factories' used 6000 mice in one six-month period.[44] Other research developments, such as the production of mice from induced stem cells (meaning ordinary body cells that are reprogrammed to be 'pluripotent' and capable of developing into a number of different tissue types) may also increase the future use of mice in breeding experiments.[45]

### 12.2.3.3 Knockout rats

Large-scale production of knockout rats is becoming possible. SCID rats have been produced by knocking out genes necessary for immune system functioning. By 2009, the biotech company Transposagen was aiming to knock out each of the 30,000 genes in the rat genome and to create a frozen repository of the sperm of each knockout strain.[46] Zinc-finger nuclease technology has been used to knock out rat genes and produce live offspring capable of transmitting the mutation, the first successful use of zinc finger technology for gene targeting in a mammal (zinc finger nucleases are proteins that allow DNA to be cut at a specific point, thus allowing precise modifications to genes). EURATRANS, a multimillion euro collaboration involving researchers in Europe, the US and Japan, aims to make a 'major assault on the rat' genome, including the use of ES cells to create knockout rats.[47]

## 12.2.4 Mutant and knockout zebrafish

Zebrafish are the animal species where the number of mutant strains has been increasing most rapidly, apart from mice. Zebrafish are popular with scientists because their embryos are transparent, allowing development and abnormalities to be observed. Mutant and transgenic strains are created from chemically induced mutations or by genetic engineering (injecting DNA into zebrafish embryos). A EU project covering seven countries, funded in 2004 to over 12 million euros, planned to create 180 knockout zebrafish strains and to screen 6000 mutant genomes.[48] Zinc-finger nuclease technology has been used for gene targeting in zebrafish, potentially allowing knockout versions to be created for every zebrafish gene, and there is also ongoing research on methods to clone zebrafish.[49]

## 12.2.5 Transgenic monkeys and pigs

The first transgenic monkeys (marmosets) capable of transmitting an introduced gene to offspring were reported in 2009 by scientists in Japan.[50] This development may open the way to large-scale production of transgenic strains of monkeys in the future and the scientific journal *Nature* believes that 'The study of human diseases will require engineered marmosets that are born with and live their entire lives with a genetic defect that they pass on to their progeny.'[51] These experiments were also heavy on animal use, requiring 80 embryos in 50 surrogate mothers to produce five transgenic offspring, two of which survived to breeding age.[50,52]

Around 130,000 pigs are used annually for experiments and surgical procedures in the US and the EU together (often these are 'miniature' pigs, suitable for keeping in laboratory conditions).[14,15] Transgenic pigs have been bred for at least a decade, with the aim of providing suitable organs for transplant that avoid hyperacute rejection of the organ by the human recipients.

---

**BOX 12.2 CAT BREEDING FOR RESEARCH**

The contrast between public expectations for an animal that is bred to be used in experiments and an animal normally bred as a companion is most marked in the case of cats and dogs. In the late 1990s it was brought to public attention in England that a 'family farm' not far from Oxford University was breeding cats in a factory-style operation, producing several litters per week and supplying research institutes and universities with hundreds of kittens per year. Two years of public protests, some violent, led to the cat farm closing in 1999. Parentage records of the breeding cats showed a number of caesarean births, possibly for specific pathogen-free status, and litter production records showed a number of cases of kittens being eaten by their mothers, possibly as a result of stress. When the farm closed, the Royal Society for the Prevention of Cruelty to Animals (RSPCA) removed 800 breeding cats and kittens from the site for re-homing.[53] Cats have often been used for eye research. Colonies of Abyssinian cats carrying a recessive mutation that causes degenerative disease of the retina, leading to blindness in early adulthood, have been bred since the 1980s in order to study the related condition in humans.[54]

Transgenic pig organs were transplanted into monkeys during experiments in the UK during the late 1990s (during which some of the monkeys died a slow and unpleasant death).[55] One approach to gene targeting in pigs is cloning by nuclear transfer, which allows the manipulation of genes in the DNA of the donor cell before inserting it into an 'empty' egg cell to create a reconstructed embryo (see also section 2.3.3 in Chapter 2). Research developments in producing pigs from induced pluripotent stem cells may prove another route to the production of lines of genetically engineered pigs.[56]

## 12.2.6 Procedures involved in mouse breeding

Although most laboratory animals are produced by natural breeding, the process of creating mutant mice via embryonic stem cells involves the hormonal superovulation of females, the removal of early embryos after mating, and embryo transfer. Embryos, sperm and oocytes may also be collected in order to freeze-store and later recover GM strains. In most cases embryos, sperm and oocytes are collected after killing the mice by cervical (neck) dislocation. Establishing strains of mutant mice or of other laboratory animals, such as pigs or cats, that are specific pathogen free (SPF) also requires either embryo transfer to a pathogen-free surrogate mother or birth by hysterectomy or caesarean section. Pregnant females or embryo donors belonging to less valuable species are likely to be killed during this process.

In the creation of genetically altered strains, young mice generally have the ends of their tails amputated, cutting through nerves and bone, to confirm whether they carry the desired mutation (if not, they will probably be killed). The amputation is painful at the time and may lead to the formation of neuromas and permanent sensitivity of the tail-tip.[19,57] Further interventions used in the production and typing of mutant mice include needle-tattooing newborn mice on the skin of their paw-pads, immobilizing newborns or pregnant mice by anaesthetic for imaging purposes, or immobilizing newborns by hypothermia. Tests for behavioural phenotyping can include frightening the mice to assess their anxiety levels and tests of their pain perception.[58]

## 12.3 The impact on animals

### 12.3.1 The impact of genetic mutations

The legislation that defines the permitted use of laboratory animals in the EU (broadly typical of legislation in all developed countries) characterizes that use as procedures that may cause 'pain, suffering, distress or lasting harm', including breeding procedures.[17,59] Harm caused by breeding genetically altered mice potentially affects two groups of animals: the parent animals used in breeding procedures and the offspring born with damaging conditions or mutations. As the examples in section 12.2.2 indicate, mutant mice have been designed to suffer from a wide range of physical and psychological conditions that are known to be painful or distressing in humans.

## 12.3.2 The impact of restrictive laboratory housing

Laboratory animals are inevitably bred and kept in conditions that are more restrictive than the natural environment of their species. It is difficult, if not impossible, for laboratories to house them in conditions that genuinely meet their behavioural needs. Many laboratory mice are housed in factory style in tiered racks of small transparent plastic boxes ('cages'), each resembling a shoe-storage box and incorporating a food rack and water bottle (see Figure 12.1). There may be nothing else in the box but the animals and some floor litter. Mouse cage racks can be supplied with 12 tiers of cages, allowing the housing of hundreds of mice in one room and tens of thousands in a single research institution.

Official guidelines recommend that mouse cages should be 'enriched' by providing nesting material (such as paper tissues) and some shelter (such as pieces of plastic or cardboard) and that group housing should be used whenever possible, rather than caging mice in isolation. Surveys of National Institutes of Health facilities in the US and of British facilities suggest that most animal units now provide this level of 'enrichment' at least.[60] But even the 'enriched' cages would be much less complex and interesting than either a natural environment or the life of a companion animal allowed out of the cage regularly for exercise and exploration. Being kept in standard cages and being kept alone are both associated with increased anxiety, to the extent that laboratory rats and mice may be 'severely abnormal' as a result of chronic stress.[61,62] Rats anticipate transfer to an enriched cage as something 'highly rewarding'.[62] Various studies have shown that providing rats and mice with greater environmental complexity and group housing can improve brain function and memory.[61,63]

Genetic alterations may restrict the way in which animals can be housed. Some of the strains that lack a normal immune system need to be bred and housed in sterile conditions to be viable and fertile. If exposed to a normal laboratory environment they develop inflammatory conditions such as inflammatory bowel disease. Some strains of mice or rats may be unable to take advantage of a more complex environment, such as those that have seizures when startled or handled and those that have been bred, intentionally or as a side effect, to be nervous.[64] The maintenance of specific pathogen-free colonies of cats and pigs may also require that the breeding animals are kept with very limited furnishing and without bedding.

Mice in standard laboratory housing engage in stereotypic behaviour such as repetitive bar-biting, jumping, twirling and somersaulting, thought to result from thwarting their strong motivations to escape and to search for shelter, and they pluck patterns of fur from other mice or from themselves. In two common laboratory strains, 80 to 98 per cent of the mice perform stereotypies in standard housing conditions, indicative of psychological distress, negative internal experiences and frustration of natural behaviour.[61,65,66]

**Figure 12.1** *Rack of laboratory mouse cages in the animal wing of a pharmacology department*

Studies at Purdue University showed that laboratory mice provided with materials such as found in natural conditions built elaborate and complex nests very similar to those of wild mice. The scientists suggested that nest-building acted as a form of stress relief as well as providing a better environment.[67] An experiment at Oxford University Zoology Department showed that a group of standard laboratory rats rapidly returned to the natural behaviour of their species when they were released as adults into an enclosed farmland habitat, after 200 generations of laboratory breeding. Within hours they had adopted the bounding gait characteristic of wild rats, started digging and found shelter and water. They rapidly developed a social system, foraged for natural food, climbed, competed vigorously for mates, and showed instinctive avoidance of cats, demonstrating that captivity has not 'taken the wild out of the rat'.[68] Studies that demonstrate how rats enjoy playing and the capacity of rodents for causal reasoning and for using tools underline the extent of deprivation that captivity in a typical laboratory setting implies.[69]

**Table 12.4** *Actual and potential impact of breeding animals for laboratory use*

| Area of breeding: Use and management | Actual or potential impact |
|---|---|
| Creating or breeding of animals with harmful genetic mutations | • 'Pain, distress, suffering and lasting harm' either physical or psychological)[17]<br>• Invasive procedures<br>• Wastage of animals used for breeding<br>• Surplus offspring having no scientific value |
| Housing | • Restriction of natural behaviour (such as exploratory behaviour, nesting, sheltering, exercise, social behaviour)<br>• Unnatural social groups<br>• Isolation<br>• Stress<br>• Fighting within cages<br>• Psychological distress, sometimes severe (abnormal behaviour patterns)<br>• May encourage perception that animals are disposable (large numbers, housed in tiers) |
| Early weaning and separation from mother or social group | • Disruption of emotional bonds between mother and offspring, between littermates or between group members<br>• Psychological and physiological effects on offspring |
| Artificial breeding methods | • Invasive procedures<br>• Potential for 'pain, distress, suffering and lasting harm'<br>• Wastage of animals |
| Creation and maintenance of breeding colonies | • Production and disposal of low-value surplus animals<br>• Breeding animals intensively used and then discarded<br>• Use of wild-caught primates for breeding |

## 12.3.3 Bonds between mothers and offspring

The Nuffield Council report on the ethics of experimental animal use noted in 2005 that laboratory conditions mean that 'many natural behaviours are probably thwarted in relation to reproduction, early weaning age and maintaining a relationship with mother and siblings up to a natural dispersal age'.[19] Separation from the mother – for example, to produce uniform numbers in litters – is quite common in commercial breeding of mice and rats. It can have a number of lasting effects on offspring, including a greater susceptibility to infection, changes in pain perception, changes in maternal and social behaviour, and decreased ability to cope with stress when adult.[70,71] The hormonal basis of bonding between mothers and young in mice is similar to that in other mammals, including humans.[31,72]

## 12.3.4 Over-breeding and surplus animals

Over-breeding and the need to dispose of surplus animals is likely in any breeding programme that has target numbers to fulfil. Research protocols call for a specific number of animals of a specific age, type and sex. The proportion of animals surplus to requirements may be a substantial proportion of all the animals bred but animals that are born and killed without being used may not appear in official statistics. Bred in conditions that are far from ideal from the point of view of animal well-being, in some cases they have been born for no purpose at all.

In the mid 1990s the National Anti-Vivisection Society (NAVS) conducted an undercover investigation at a British medical school and found that the number of surplus rodents bred, never used and destroyed was greater than the number of animals bred and used in experiments. Based on laboratory records, overall 29 per cent of the rats and mice bred were used in experiments, 7 per cent died before weaning and 64 per cent were gassed as unwanted. For the main mouse strains, 53 per cent of those born were killed as surplus to requirements and a further 24 per cent died before being weaned. For some strains, such as the nude rats and SCID mice, the estimate was that 86 per cent of those weaned were killed as surplus to requirements. In another laboratory, the NAVS investigator witnessed 2500 surplus animals being killed or removed for killing over a period of eight months.[73]

## 12.3.5 Usage and wastage in breeding mutant mice

The establishment of a strain of mutated mice can generate large numbers of unwanted offspring.[19,74] With their high rate of breeding, female mice are put into continuous pup production for a period of a few months and then discarded. The first stage of creating a genetically engineered strain of mice is to produce mice that carry the required gene or knockout in some, but not all, of their body cells (mosaic mice). The success rate may be high or low. Establishing the strain also entails producing mice that are not 'mosaic' and 'mosaic' mice that cannot transmit the required gene. Their ability to transmit the gene can only be discovered by breeding, and even those that do transmit the gene may only transmit to a small proportion their offspring.[75]

An additional cause of wastage is that transgenic or knockout mice of a particular strain may be created by one group of scientists when another group of scientists has already made the same strain. The intense competition between different research groups and accompanying secrecy in some research programmes almost certainly makes this more likely to happen.

---

### BOX 12.3 BREEDING AND SUPPLY OF PRIMATES FOR RESEARCH

Primates used for research in the EU are typically bred in captivity, some of them in breeding and supply centres in their countries of origin, such as China, the Philippines, Vietnam, Indonesia and Mauritius, with China now the largest breeder. In 2008 Great Britain used 1850 primates acquired from sources outside the EU.[13] One British drug testing company imported at least 476 juvenile cynomolgus macaques from Vietnam over the 12 months to May 2008, a journey of 30 hours in a small crate. Investigations by animal protection organizations have found that some breeding operations keep monkeys in small, bare and sometimes squalid cages, house them in isolation (to accustom them to conditions during transport), breed from the same females frequently, and wean offspring too early.[76]

Macaques, baboons and capuchins need to remain in contact with their mothers for one year to 18 months from birth. Those reared in peer groups without mothers are more likely to show abnormal fear and to clasp each other.[65,77] Undercover investigations by the Humane Society of the United States (HSUS) in a large laboratory in the US have shown young primates removed, apparently terrified, from their mothers for various procedures, such as forcible 'tubing' to introduce a test substance into their mouths or for apparently painful injections.[78]

The breeding and use of chimpanzees in invasive experiments continues in the US. In spite of a breeding moratorium agreed by the National Institutes of Health,[79] investigations in 2008 by the HSUS found that at least 110 chimpanzees were bred in one US research institution between 2002 and 2008, and were shipped as infants (18 months old) to other laboratories for medical experiments.[78] One 21-year-old chimpanzee observed by HSUS was kept in permanent isolation in a small, bare metal cage because of 'mental problems', manifested by bouts of attacking himself and screaming.[78] Many chimpanzees in captivity are probably suffering from the equivalent of human psychiatric illness.[80]

Chimpanzees live for up to 50 years. In 2008 the Great Ape Protection Act was introduced to the US Congress, which aimed to end invasive experiments on all chimpanzees (estimated to number around 1200) in US laboratories and to retire 500 chimpanzees owned by the federal government to sanctuaries.

---

## 12.4 The professionals, the public and the future

### 12.4.1 Debates over the use of experimental animals

The number of animals born, used and killed globally for scientific experiments and toxicity testing annually is a small fraction of the number of animals reared and killed for food production. Around 500 times the number of chickens are reared and slaughtered for meat annually (the majority in factory-farmed conditions) than the number of animals used in experiments. And yet the production and use of animals for experiments remains an equally, or even more, controversial issue. Possibly this is because large-scale use of experimental animals is only about a century old. But the main reason seems to be that animal experimentation is a legalized form of deliberate harm to animals, conducted in the full knowledge that the animals are likely to suffer.

Because of the inevitable harm, there has emerged a general consensus among the public, policy-makers and many scientists that animals should only be used when it is judged to be scientifically essential and that, in the long term, the use of animals should be discontinued. Disagreement remains over what we mean by 'essential' and 'long term'. Over the years, many committees of scientists and ethicists have considered the ethics of animal experimentation, and tried to weigh the balance of harm to the animals against the benefit to people. So far, all of these have endorsed animal experimentation where it is considered essential for the development of human medicine and where no non-animal methods can provide the information required. Most of them urge that the number of animals used and the severity of the experiments should be reduced. In 2005 the Nuffield Council on Bioethics expressed the aspiration that 'A world in which the important benefits of ... research could be achieved without causing pain, suffering, distress, lasting harm or death to animals involved in research must be the ultimate goal.'[19] But in reality the number of animals used has steadily increased since the end of the 20th century.

The question of the necessity and usefulness of animal 'models' of human disease is fundamental, as this medical justification underlies the large majority of experiments using mice and other laboratory animals. This is too large an area for discussion in this chapter; but it is fair to question whether there is an adequate scientific justification for each and every of the animal models of human disease and the strains of mutant animals that are created. For many medical scientists the breeding and use of genetically mutated animals is the key to the future of medicine. A minority of scientists have questioned the medical necessity for the production of so many different transgenic lines, arguing that there are numerous examples where a disease in humans is too complex to be satisfactorily studied in a transgenic or knockout mouse, or where the mouse 'model' does not reproduce all the relevant features of the human disease.[39] The highly competitive nature of research exerts pressure to get results into print fast and first. Researchers may jump to make a mutant 'mouse model' of a neurological disease that turns out not to respond to drugs in the same way as humans do.[81] But the current climate of scientific opinion and the major scientific, professional and funding opportunities strongly favour a continued and rapid expansion in the application of genetic technology to laboratory animal breeding.

## 12.4.2 National regulations and the 3Rs

Most of the developed countries have some regulatory framework, guidelines or legislation that applies to breeding and use of laboratory animals. Most of these, including the EU, Australia and Canada, explicitly aim to implement the '3Rs'.[82] The 3Rs (replacement, reduction and refinement in relation to animal experiments) require that, wherever possible:

- Animal use should be replaced by methods that do not use animals.
- The number of animals used in any procedure should be reduced.
- Procedures should be refined to reduce the suffering of animals.

The countries of the EU have national legislation implementing the 1986 Directive on 'the protection of animals used for experimental or other scientific purposes', and a proposal for a revised Directive was published in late 2008. The Directive is intended to provide 'a solid basis for a full implementation of the principles of the 3Rs – Replacement, Reduction and Refinement of animals in experiments'. According to the European Commission: 'All efforts should be made to reduce the numbers of animals used in experiments to a minimum', although 'with current scientific knowledge, a complete phase-out of animal experimentation is not yet achievable'.[18]

Canada has self-regulation through Institutional Animal Care Committees, under the Canadian Council on Animal Care, one of whose stated aims is to promote the 3Rs, including a specific website devoted to the subject. Guidelines require not only that 'unnecessary pain and distress is avoided' but also that scientific projects provide a scientific justification for why sentient animals need to be used, and their numbers.[83] In Australia, institutional Animal Ethics Committees operate under a Code of Practice for the Care and Use of Animals for Scientific Purposes. This Code also subscribes to the aim of replacement, refinement methods to avoid pain and distress, and methods to reduce the use of animals.[84]

As a result of the strong expression of public concern and years of lobbying by animal protection organizations, some positive changes in the regulation and practice of animal use have occurred, including the following.

*Great apes.* The European Commission has proposed to end the use of great apes throughout the EU. Japan, Britain, Australia, New Zealand and several European countries have already restricted or ended experiments using great apes.[79] Thus society in most developed countries (with the current exception of the US) appears to have decided that the invasive experimental use of great apes is no longer ethically acceptable.

*Changes in practice.* Some painful or wasteful procedures have become less common. The live animal (ascites) method of producing monoclonal antibodies in the abdominal fluid of mice is now widely regarded as unacceptable and is being replaced by cell culture. The EU has (from March 2009) prohibited the testing of cosmetic or toiletry products on animals and the sale of such products that have been tested elsewhere (with an extension to 2013 for some tests). The EU has funded the European Centre for the Validation of Alternative Methods (ECVAM), which promotes, researches and validates alternatives to animal tests such as the notorious Draize tests on the skin and eyes of rabbits, and lethal toxicity testing.[85] The UK no longer uses animals to test tobacco and alcohol products. Apparently running counter to this progress, the EU may use between 54 million and 141 million animals, mostly rats, in toxicity testing under chemical safety regulations (REACH) by 2018. Most of this use will be in breeding two generations of offspring from rats exposed to the chemicals, a toxicology method that is now considered outdated.[86]

As any other industry, the animal research industry tends to resist regulation. In 2008 the European Biomedical Research Association lobbied against proposals for a revised European Directive that were intended to increase oversight (for example, in the definition of the severity of procedures), ethical evaluations and transparency.[87]

### 12.4.3 How effective is regulation?

Can research always be 'careful' and 'meticulously regulated'?[88] Well-publicized exposures of animal suffering in laboratories over the years have typically been made by animal protection organizations, whistle-blowers or journalists, rather than by regulatory authorities. All the evidence suggests that it is extremely difficult to translate the aspirations of guidelines into consistent everyday practice. Some countries that are major users of laboratory animals have almost no animal protection law at all.

The 2008 investigation of a large primate research centre by the Humane Society of the United States documented and filmed treatment of monkeys and chimpanzees that would shock most observers, given that the treatment was not for the benefit of the animals concerned. Footage showed white-coated staff members manhandling, subduing and forcibly treating a single huge but helpless adult chimpanzee, reminiscent of scenes from a horror movie. Monkeys were filmed being dragged struggling and screaming from their small metal cages on the end of restraint poles and locked into restraint jackets for treatments. Many of the animals were apparently suffering from psychological distress or extreme fear of the procedures they were subjected to, including frequent darting for sedation. A whistle-blower had previously recorded the deliberate harming of chimpanzees for amusement, unrelated to experiments.[78]

It would be hard to argue that regulation has given mice, rats, monkeys, cats and dogs kept in laboratories a good quality of life. Some aspirations published in guidelines look frankly unrealistic. The UK's Medical Research Council has recommended that: 'Primates must be provided with a complex and stimulating environment that promotes good health and psychological well-being and provides full opportunity for social interactions, exercise and to express a range of behaviours appropriate to the species.'[89] This seems improbable within the normal management, research schedules and resources of most laboratories – it is not even possible in many zoos.

Apart from inadequate regulation, there are wide variations between, and sometimes within, countries in many areas of experimental use, which could include the:

- severity of harmful genetic mutations that are considered acceptable to produce;
- level of justification required to produce animals with harmful genetic mutations;
- length of time that animals are kept alive in pain, incapacity or illness before being humanely destroyed;
- likelihood of animals being given pain relief;
- use of painful methods for convenience or cost reasons;
- effort or encouragement to reduce the number of animals used for all procedures;
- quality of animal housing, breeding conditions and care;
- regulation of methods of supply (use of wild-caught animals or unwanted or stolen domestic animals);
- species of animal that are covered by regulations.

---

### BOX 12.4 LABORATORY DOGS AND THE PUBLIC

The UK Kennel Club's breed standard for the Beagle describes the dog's temperament as 'amiable', 'equable', 'benign' and without either aggression or timidity – possibly a reason why the breed is favoured for laboratory experiments – making the dog 'the essence of quality' and 'a first-class family pet'.[90]

More than 6000 Beagle dogs were used in experiments in the UK in 2008, most of them in the category of medical research. At least two exposés of the experimental use of Beagles have caused public outrage in the UK. In 1975, the *Sunday People* newspaper published photographs of dogs confined in small boxes and forced to breathe tobacco smoke through pipes attached to their noses. In 1997 the British public was shocked again by a television programme (*It's a Dog's Life*) showing undercover film of a large contract animal testing laboratory.[19] Beagles used in drug toxicity testing were shown being subjected to frequent blood collections by needle from veins (sometimes incompetently carried out) and rough handling, including hitting and shouting, while they were slowly poisoned close to death by the test substance and then destroyed.

In the US an undercover investigation by an animal protection organization of a 'Class B' dog dealer, shown to the public in HBO's *Dealing Dogs* in 2006, became a major news story. Dealers are licensed to buy dogs from breeders, dog pounds and shelters and sell them on to research laboratories and veterinary schools. The investigations during 2001–2002 found dogs kept in appalling conditions in a large dealership in Arkansas: in dirty cages, some dogs severely emaciated, wounded and bleeding from fights, with multiple infections, including heartworm, and some of them already dead. The programme-makers estimated that 42,000 dogs were supplied by dealers to laboratories annually and some of the dogs filmed were pets, either stolen or unknowingly given up to a 'good home'.[91]

Invertebrates are excluded from the regulations in most countries,[92] although this is changing in the light of scientific evidence of sentience in some invertebrate species.[93] The proposed revision of the EU Directive on animal experiments would be updated to include certain invertebrates and also late embryos on the grounds that all of these animals may be capable of 'experiencing pain, suffering, distress and lasting harm'.[18]

There is therefore a global and regional 'postcode lottery' for laboratory animals, and globalization of the research enterprise means that scientists who wish to undertake a particular procedure may be able to move to, or collaborate with, a laboratory operating under a different set of rules. It also means that scientists who feel that they are being undercut by looser regulation in other countries can put pressure on their own authorities not to regulate experiments too much, on the grounds that this would advantage rivals in the highly lucrative and competitive global biotechnology industry.

## 12.4.4 Targets for ending the experimental use of animals

Whatever view we take about the ethics, scientific justification and benefit to humans of animal experimentation – and experimentation shades untidily into many aspects of the breeding of farmed animals, sports animals, companion animals and wild animals – the fact remains that society is uneasy about it when the impact on the animals is brought to public attention. Our dislike of experimentation on animals is counteracted by the hope for new medical treatments, encouraged by those scientists who claim that medical advances are impossible without animal experiments.

Few people today take the view that the suffering of animals is of no importance when weighed against a possible benefit to people. There is something disturbing to most people about breeding sentient animals with genetic defects or disease conditions, keeping them in small barren cages, carrying out procedures on them that cause distress or suffering, and disposing of them when they have served their use. Likewise, many scientists engaged in animal research say that they look forward to the day when it will not be necessary to use animals. In practice, the number of experimental animals used is increasing, making the efforts of regulators look ineffective at best. Although predictions are dangerous, it seems likely that the number will continue to increase with the genomic revolution of this century unless there is a much stronger commitment to change.

To make more rapid progress towards the end of invasive animal experimentation will require us to introduce reduction targets, as is the way forward to achieve change in any other industry. Reduction targets could apply to the number of animals bred and used and to the severity of impacts on them. As greenhouse gas emission targets in the car industry have shown, mandatory targets are the mothers of invention, of industry investment and of new options for the public. It is hard to believe that a scientific community that is capable of carrying out spectroscopy by remote control on planet Mars[94] is incapable of inventing non-animal methods of medical research. While the globalized nature of animal experimentation may be a factor inhibiting reform, a large regional grouping such as the EU could take the lead in setting reduction targets. Some of the advantages of target-setting would be the following:

- Targets would lead to funding and investment in non-animal research methods.
- Funding opportunities would attract high-quality scientists into the area of non-animal research methods.
- Targets and progress reports would reassure the public that consistent progress was being made.
- Proof of consistent progress would counteract the arguments of some activists that 'direct action' against animal experimentation is the only way to bring change.

Some of the targets that would encourage research without the large-scale breeding and use of sentient live animals could include the following:

- an immediate end to both the breeding of chimpanzees and of invasive experiments on chimpanzees and the retirement to sanctuaries of existing chimpanzees captive in laboratories (in line with the proposed Great Ape Protection Act of 2008 in the US);
- an immediate end to the use of wild-caught primates for breeding or research;
- phased reduction targets to end the breeding of all other primates for research and of invasive experiments on all other primates;
- an immediate end to the creation and breeding of genetically mutated strains of monkeys, cats or other domestic animals such as pigs;
- phased reduction targets and maximum quotas for creating and breeding genetically mutated strains of the most commonly used sentient animals, such as mice, rats and fish;
- phased reduction targets for the breeding and invasive use of all other sentient species.

## Notes

1  'January' in the Calendar section of the *Très Riches Heures du Duc de Berry*, painted around 1412; see Macdonogh, K. (1999) *Reigning Cat and Dogs: A History of Pets at Court since the Renaissance*, Fourth Estate

2  Kean, H. (1998) *Animal Rights: Political and Social Change in Britain since 1800*, Reaktion Books; Turner, J. (1980) *Reckoning with the Beast: Animals' Pain, and Humanity in the Victorian Mind*, Johns Hopkins University Press; Mason, P. (1997) *The Brown Dog Affair: The Story of a Monument that Divided the Nation*, Two Sevens Publishing, London; Turner, E. S. (1992) *All Heaven in a Rage*, Centaur Press; Lederer, S. E. (1995) *Subjected to Science: Human Experimentation in America before the Second World War*, The Johns Hopkins University Press

3    Rat Genome Sequencing Consortium (2004) 'Genome sequence of the Brown Norway rat yields insights into mammalian evolution', *Nature*, vol 428, pp493–521

4    Mouse Genome Sequencing Consortium (2002) 'Initial sequencing and comparative analysis of the mouse genome', *Nature*, vol 420, pp520–562

5    Rader, K. (2004) *Making Mice: Standardizing Animals for American Biomedical Research, 1900–1955*, Princeton University Press

6    *Nature* (2009) 'News: Mouse patent sparks uncivil "spat"', *Nature*, vol 459, p620

7    National Mouse Club (2009) *History*, www.nationalmouseclub.co.uk/, accessed 17 March 2009

8    Cardiff, R. D. and Kenney, N. (2007) 'Mouse mammary tumour research', in G. F. Vande Woude and G. Klein (eds) *Advances in Cancer Research, Vol 98*, Academic Press, pp54–117

9    *Time Magazine* (1933) 'Animals: Dancing mice', *Time Magazine*, 27 March 1933

10   Frazer, K. A. et al (2007) 'A sequence-based variation map of 8.27 million SNPs in inbred mouse strains', *Nature*, vol 448, pp1050–1053

11   Knight, A. (2008) 'Estimates of worldwide laboratory animal use', *Alternatives to Laboratory Animals (ATLA)*, vol 36, pp494–496

12   Home Office (2008) *Statistics of Scientific Procedures on Living Animals 2007*, Home Office

13   Home Office (2009) *Statistics of Scientific Procedures on Living Animals 2008*, UK

14   USDA (US Department of Agriculture) (2008) *Animal Care Annual Report of Activities, Fiscal Year 2007*; USDA (2007) *FY2006 AWA Inspections*, www.animalexperiments.info/studies/animal_use_us_2006.htm, accessed August 2009

15   European Commission (2007) *Annex to the Report from the Commission to the Council and the European Parliament Fifth Report on the Statistics on the Number of Animals used for Experimental and other Scientific Purposes in the Member States of the European Union, COM (2007) 675 Final*; European Commission (2007) *Fifth Report on the Statistics on the Number of Animals Used for Experimental and other Scientific Purposes in the Member States of the European Union*

16   Canadian Council on Animal Care (2008) *2007 CCAC Survey of Animal Use*, CCAC; Australian Society for Humane Research Inc (undated) *Animal Experimentation Statistics*, www.animalexperiments.info/assets/studies/Animal%20use%20Australia%202005.pdf, accessed November 2009

17   European Commission (1986) *Council Directive of 24 November 1986 on the Approximation of Laws, Regulations and Administrative Provisions of the Member States regarding the Protection of Animals Used for Experimental and other Scientific Purposes (86/609/EEC)*

18   European Commission (2008) *Proposal for a Directive of the European Parliament and of the Council on the Protection of Animals Used for Scientific Purposes, COM(2008) 543 Final*

19   Nuffield Council on Bioethics (2005) *The Ethics of Research Involving Animals*, Nuffield Council on Bioethics

20   *Nature* (2002) 'The life history of the mouse in genetics', *Nature*, vol 420, pp510–511

21   Coghlan, A. (1996) 'Gene trap catches "knockout" mouse', *New Scientist*, 19 October, p22

22   International Mouse Knockout Consortium (2007) 'A mouse for all reasons', *Cell*, vol 128, pp9–13

23   Abbott, A. (2004) 'Geneticists prepare for deluge of mutant mice', *Nature*, vol 432, p541

24  The Nobel Assembly at Karolinska Institutet (2007) 'The Nobel Assembly at Karolinska Institutet has today decided to award the Nobel Prize in Physiology or Medicine 2007 jointly to Mario R. Capecchi, Martin J. Evans and Oliver Smithies for their discoveries of "Principles for introducing specific gene modifications in mice by the use of embryonic stem cells"', press release, 8 October 2007

25  Flint, J. and Mott, R. (2008) 'Applying mouse complex-trait resources to behavioural genetics', *Nature*, vol 456, pp724–727

26  National Human Genome Research Project (2009) The Knockout Mouse Project, www.genome.gov/17515708#4, accessed August 2009; Taconic Knockout Repository, www.taconic.com/wmspage.cfm?parm1=1647, accessed August 2009

27  Callaway, E. (2007) 'The mouse map gets a lot more signposts', *Nature*, vol 448, pp516–517

28  The Jackson Laboratory (2008) *Most Popular JAX® Mice Strains June 2008–May 2009*, sales brochure

29  'Tacona superovulated mice for blastocyst retrieval', www.taconic.com/wmspage.cfm?parm1=620, accessed August 2009; Tacona, 'Surgical modifications', www.taconic.com/wmspage.cfm?parm1=667, accessed August 2009

30  See examples in the Jackson Laboratory database: http://jaxmice.jax.org/findmice/index.html, accessed March 2009

31  Takayanagi, Y. et al (2005) 'Pervasive social deficits, but normal parturition, in oxytocin receptor-deficient mice', *PNAS*, vol 102, no 44, pp16,096–16,101

32  Sun, Y. G. et al (2009) 'Cellular basis of itch sensation', *Science*, vol 325, no 5947, pp1531–1534; Sun, Y. G. and Chen, Z. F. (2007) 'A gastrin-releasing peptide receptor mediates the itch sensation in the spinal cord', *Nature*, vol 448, pp700–703; Washington University School of Medicine (2009) 'Itch-specific neurons identified in mice offers hope for better treatments', *ScienceDaily*, 8 August

33  Demehri, S., Turkoz, A. and Kopan, R. (2009) 'Epidermal Notch1 loss promotes skin tumorigenesis by impacting the stromal microenvironment', *Cancer Cell*, vol 16, no 1, pp55–66; Washington University School of Medicine (2009) 'Mice with skin condition help scientists understand tumor growth', *ScienceDaily*, 9 July

34  Taylor, T. et al (2009) 'Non-motor symptoms of Parkinson's disease revealed in an animal model with reduced monoamine storage capacity', *Journal of Neuroscience*, vol 29, no 25, pp8103–8113; Emory University (2009) 'Mouse model of Parkinson's reproduces nonmotor symptoms', *ScienceDaily*, 30 June

35  National Institute for Physiological Sciences (2009) 'Severely memory-deficit mutant mouse created', *ScienceDaily*, 20 June

36  He, Y. et al (2009) 'The transcriptional repressor DEC2 regulates sleep length in mammals', *Science*, vol 325, pp866–870; University of Utah Health Sciences (2009) 'Gene variation that lets people get by on less sleep transferred to create insomniac mice', *ScienceDaily*, 17 September

37  'Mutated gene gets mice "moonwalking"', *New Scientist*, 6 April 2009, p13; Becker, E. B. E. et al (2009) 'A point mutation in TRPC3 causes abnormal Purkinje cell development and cerebellar ataxia in moonwalker mice, *PNAS*, vol 106, no 16, pp6706–6711

38  Hakimi, P. et al (2007) 'Overexpression of the cytosolic form of phosphoenolpyruvate carboxykinase (GTP) in skeletal muscle repatterns energy metabolism in the mouse', *Journal of Biological Chemistry*, vol 282, no 45, pp32,844–32,855

39  Bhogal, N. and Combes, R. (2006) 'The relevance of genetically altered mouse models of human disease', *ATLA*, vol 34, pp429–454

40  Cell Press (2008) 'Mouse model of prion disease mimics diverse symptoms of human disorder', *ScienceDaily*, 28 November 2008

41  Abbott, A. (2007) 'Model behaviour', *Nature*, vol 450, pp6–7; Heurteaux, C. et al (2006) 'Deletion of the background potassium channel TREK-1 results in a depression-resistant phenotype', *Nature Neuroscience*, vol 9, pp1134–1141; '"Happy mice" to pave way for depression cure', *The Vancouver Sun*, 24 August 2006; Lehrer, J. (2009) 'Small, furry ... and smart', *Nature*, vol 461, pp862–864

42  Davis, A. P. and Justic, M. J. (1998) 'An Oak Ridge legacy: The specific locus test and its role in mouse mutagenesis', *Genetics*, vol 148, pp7–12

43  Cordes, S. P. (2005) 'N-ethyl-n-nitrosourea mutagenesis: Boarding the mouse mutant express', *Microbiology and Molecular Biology Reviews*, vol 69, no 3, pp426–439

44  Cyranoski, D. (2007) 'Innate ability', *Nature*, vol 450, pp475–477

45  Cyranoski, D. (2008) '5 things to know before jumping on the iPS bandwagon', *Nature*, vol 452, pp406–408; Boland, M. J. et al (2009) 'Adult mice generated from induced pluripotent stem cells', *Nature*, vol 461, pp91–94

46  'Transposagen creates a rat model of the human immune system', *Reuters*, 6 August 2009

47  Abbott, A. (2009) 'The return of the rat', *Nature*, vol 460, p788; Geurts, A. M. et al (2009) 'Knockout rats via embryo microinjection of zinc-finger nucleases', *Science*, vol 325, p433

48  Bradbury, J. (2004) 'Small fish, big science', *PLoS Biology*, vol 2, no 5, pe148

49  Ekker, S. C. (2008) 'Zinc finger-based knockout punches for zebrafish genes', *Zebrafish*, vol 5, no 2, pp121–123; Meng, X. et al (2008) 'Targeted gene inactivation in zebrafish using engineered zinc finger nucleases', *Nature Biotechnology*, vol 26, no 6, pp695–701; Siripattarapravat, K. et al (2009) 'Somatic cell nuclear transfer in zebra fish', *Nature Methods*, vol 6, no 10, pp733–736

50  Sasaki, E. et al (2009) 'Generation of transgenic non-human primates with germline transmission', *Nature*, vol 459, pp523–527

51  *Nature* (2009) 'Editorial: Time to connect', *Nature*, vol 459, p483

52  Cyranoski, D. (2009) 'Marmoset model takes centre stage', *Nature*, vol 459, p492; Schatten, G. and Mitalipov, S. (2009) 'Transgenic primate offspring', *Nature*, vol 459, pp515–516

53  BBC (1999) 'Controversial cat farm closes', BBC online news, news.bbc.co.uk, 13 August; Malle, A. (ed) (2002) *A Cat in Hell's Chance: The Story of the Campaign against Hill Grove Cat Farm*, Slingshot Publications

54  Menotti-Raymond, M. et al (2007) 'Mutation in CEP290 discovered for cat model of human retinal degeneration', *Journal of Heredity*, vol 98, no 3, pp211–220

55  Uncaged Campaigns (2009) *The Diaries of Despair Report*, Overview and links to the reports, www.xenodiaries.org/overview.htm, accessed August 2009

56  Oxford University Press (2009) 'World first: Chinese scientists create pluripotent stem cells from pigs', *ScienceDaily*, 3 June

57  Sorensen, D. B. (2007) 'The impact of tail tip amputation and ink tattoo on C57BL/6JBomTac mice', *Laboratory Animals*, vol 41, no 1, pp19–29; Arras, M. et al (2007) 'Should laboratory mice be anaesthetized for tail biopsy?', *Laboratory Animals*, vol 41, no 1, pp30–45

58  Bhogal, N. and Scrivens, M. (2008) 'Welfare implications of standardised protocols for phenotyping and genotyping genetically altered mice', *ATLA*, vol 36, no 5, pp599–612

59  Guidance on the Operation of the Animals (Scientific Procedures) Act 1986, ordered to be printed by the House of Commons, 23 March 2000, www.archive.official-documents.co.uk/document/hoc/321/321-02.htm#gen45, accessed August 2009

60  Balcombe, J. P. (2006) 'Laboratory environments and rodents' behavioural needs: A review', *Laboratory Animals*, vol 40, pp217–235

61  Knight, J. (2001) 'Animal data jeopardised by life behind bars', *Nature*, vol 412, p669

62  van der Harst, J. E. et al (2003) 'Access to enriched housing is rewarding to rats as reflected by their anticipatory behaviour', *Animal Behaviour*, vol 66, no 3, pp493–504; Nakayasu, T. and Ishii, K. (2008) 'Effects of pair-housing after social defeat experience on elevated plus-maze behavior in rats', *Behavioural Processes*, vol 78, no 3, pp477–480

63  Arai, J. A. et al (2009) 'Transgenerational rescue of a genetic defect in long-term potentiation and memory formation by juvenile enrichment', *Journal of Neuroscience*, vol 29, no 5, pp1496–1502

64  Nicol, C. J. et al (2008) 'A targeted approach to developing environmental enrichment for two strains of laboratory mice', *Applied Animal Behaviour Science*, vol 110, no 3/4, pp341–353; Perry, S. et al (2008) 'Dietary supplementation with S-adenosyl methionine was associated with protracted reduction of seizures in a line of transgenic mice', *Comparative Medicine*, vol 58, no 6, pp604–606

65  Mason, G. and Rushen, J. (eds) (2006) *Stereotypic Animal Behaviour: Fundamentals and Applications to Welfare*, second edition, CABI; for images and video clips of laboratory mice and primates, see the book's website, www.aps.uoguelph.ca/~gmason/StereotypicAnimalBehaviour/library.shtml, accessed August 2009

66  Garner, J. P. and Mason, G. J. (2002) 'Evidence for a relationship between cage stereotypies and behavioural disinhibition in laboratory rodents', *Behavioural Brain Research*, vol 136, no 1, pp83–92

67  Purdue University (2008) 'Stress relief: Lab mice that exercise control may be more normal', *ScienceDaily*, 9 December

68  Ratlife, www.ratlife.org/Home/0Main-frameset/Mainframeset.htm, accessed August 2009

69  Panksepp, J. and Burgdort, J. (2003) '"Laughing" rats and the evolutionary antecedents of human joy?', *Physiology and Behavior*, vol 79, pp533–547; Blaisdell, A. P. et al (2006) 'Causal reasoning in rats', *Science*, vol 311, pp1020–1022; Okanoya, K. et al (2008) 'Tool-use training in a species of rodent: The emergence of an optimal motor strategy and functional understanding', *PLoS ONE*, vol 3, no 3, pe1860 (includes links to movie clips of tool use)

70  Dickinson, A. L., Leach, M. C. and Flecknell, P. A. (2009) 'Influence of early neonatal experience on nociceptive responses and analgesic effects in rats', *Laboratory Animals*, vol 43, no 1, pp11–16; *Nature* (2009) 'Neuroscience: Early stress marks genes', *Nature*, vol 462, 12 November, p140

71  Melo, A. I. et al (2006) 'Maternal and littermate deprivation disrupts maternal behavior and social-learning of food preference in adulthood: Tactile stimulation, nest odor, and social rearing prevent these effects', *Developmental Psychobiology*, vol 48, no 3, pp209–219

72  Latham, N. R. and Mason, G. J. (2008) 'Maternal deprivation and the development of stereotypic behaviour', *Applied Animal Behaviour Science*, vol 110, no 1/2, pp84–108; Jin, D. et al (2007) 'CD38 is critical for social behaviour by regulating oxytocin secretion', *Nature*, vol 446, pp41–45

73  Bingham, B. et al (1996) *Access Denied: A Report on Animal Experiments in Two British Laboratories*, 'Section 2: Animal care, housing and supply', National Anti-Vivisection Society (NAVS), www.navs.org.uk/publications/reports/c=1, accessed August 2009

74  Animal Welfare Committee (2006) *Guidelines for the Generation, Breeding, Care and Use of Genetically Modified and Cloned Animals for Scientific Purposes*, National Health and Medical Research Council, Australian Government

75   Robinson, V. et al (2003) 'Refinement and reduction in production of genetically modified mice: Sixth report of the BVAAWF/FRAME/RSPCA/UFAW Joint Working Group on Refinement', *Laboratory Animals*, vol 37 (supplement 1), ppS1:1–51

76   Langley, G. (2006) *Next of Kin: A Report on the Use of Primates in Experiments*, British Union for the Abolition of Vivisection (BUAV) and European Coalition to End Animal Experiments, UK; RSPCA (2002) *Caged and Cruel*, RSPCA; Prescott, M. J. (2001) *Counting the Cost: Welfare Implications of the Acquisition and Transport of Non-Human Primates for Use in Research and Testing*, RSPCA; Animal Defenders International (2009) *Primate Testing in Europe*, ADI

77   Scientific Committee on Animal Health and Animal Welfare (2002) *The Welfare of Non-Human Primates Used in Research*, European Commission

78   Humane Society of the United States (2009) *The HSUS Investigates Primate Use at the New Iberia Research Center (NIRC) New Iberia, Louisiana*, www.hsus.org/animals_in_research/animals_in_research_news/undercover_investigation_reveals_chimpanzee_abuse.html, accessed March 2009

79   Knight, A. (2008) 'The beginning of the end for chimpanzee experiments?', *Philosophy, Ethics, and Humanities in Medicine*, vol 3, p16, www.peh-med.com/content/3/1/16

80   Bradshaw, G. A. et al (2008) 'Building an inner sanctuary: Complex PTSD in chimpanzees', *Journal of Trauma and Dissociation*, vol 9, no 1, pp9–34; Brüne, M. et al (2006) 'Psychopathology in great apes: Concepts, treatment options and possible homologies to human psychiatric disorders', *Neuroscience and Biobehavioral Reviews*, vol 30, pp1246–1259

81   Schnabel, J. (2008) 'Standard model', *Nature*, vol 454, pp682–685

82   Russell, W. M. and Burch, R. L. (1959) *The Principles of Humane Experimental Technique*, Methuen

83   Canadian Council on Animal Care (2006) *Terms of Reference for Animal Care Committees*, www.ccac.ca/en/CCAC_Programs/Guidelines_Policies/PDFs/TOR_2006_en.pdf; Canadian Council on Animal Care, CCAC 3Rs Microsite, www.ccac.ca/en/alternatives/index.html, accessed March 2009

84   National Health and Medical Research Council, Australian Government (2004) *Australian Code of Practice for the Care and Use of Animals for Scientific Purposes*, seventh edition, www.nhmrc.gov.au/publications/synopses/_files/ea16.pdf, accessed March 2009

85   ECVAM (European Centre for the Validation of Alternative Methods), http://ecvam.jrc.it/

86   Hartung, T. and Rovida, C. (2009) 'Chemical regulators have overreached', *Nature*, vol 460, pp1080–1081; Gilbert, N. (2009) 'Chemical-safety costs uncertain', *Nature*, vol 460, p1065

87   European Biomedical Research Association (2008) *Bulletin December 2008*, www.ebra.org/ebrabulletin-the-proposed-new-directive-is-published_188.htm, accessed August 2009

88   Academy of Medical Sciences, Medical Research Council, The Royal Society and Wellcome Trust *The Use of Non-Human Primates in Research*, Working group report chaired by Sir David Weatherall (2006); Academy of Medical Sciences (2006) 'Independent group announces recommendations on the use of non-human primates in research', Media release, 12 December

89   Cited in Langley, G. (2006) *Next of Kin: A Report on the Use of Primates in Experiments*, British Union for the Abolition of Vivisection (BUAV) and European Coalition to End Animal Experiments

90   Kennel Club (2003) *The Kennel Club's Illustrated Breed Standards: The Official Guide to Registered Breeds*, Ebury Press

91  Crews, C. (2006) 'HBO's "dogs": A gnawing portrait of despair', *Washington Post*, 21 February; *Last Chance for Animals, The Pet Safety and Protection Act*, www.lcanimal.org/cmpgn/cmpgn_dog_pspa.htm, accessed September 2009
92  FRAME (Fund for the Replacement of Animals in Medical Experiments) (2009) 'The law and animal experiments', www.frame.org.uk/page.php?pg_id=65, accessed September 2009
93  European Food Safety Authority, AHAW Panel (2005) '*Report on Aspects of the Biology and Welfare of Animals Used for Experimental and Other Scientific Purposes*', *Annex to the EFSA Journal*, vol 292, pp1–136
94  Mars Rover Mission (2009) *Overview*, http://marsrover.nasa.gov/overview/, accessed August 2009

# 13

# Eugenics, Commerce and Control in Human and Animal Reproduction

## 13.1 Background and context: Good breeding

### 13.1.1 The eugenic view of people and animals

The fairy tale of *The Princess and the Pea* by Hans Christian Andersen (1805–1875) illustrates how, historically, people have wanted to think that 'well-born' individuals are physiologically and psychologically different from ordinary people, with heightened and more refined sensibilities. Only a 'real' princess would do for a prince to marry. Only a real princess would have a sleepless night because she could feel that there was a pea underneath the pile of 20 mattresses and 20 feather quilts on the bed she was lying on. We still make somewhat similar evaluations in relation to the species and breeds of animals whose reproduction we control. The perception lingers today that pedigree dogs have heightened and refined sensibilities in comparison to mongrels, and many people would probably take it for granted that dogs have heightened and refined sensibilities in comparison to rats.

Pedigrees and eugenics – the application of selective breeding to people – are thoroughly out of fashion in contemporary thinking about human populations. The determinism of 'blood' in creating worth is discredited. Diversity, individuality, consent and choice are accepted as pre-eminent values in human society and in choices about families and relationships. Unscientific and hierarchical concepts such as 'old families', 'old blood' or 'good blood' that were the norm in discussions of human populations up to the mid 20th century are now almost entirely rejected (genetically, all human families are equally old). But this thinking is still the norm in relation to human control of animal breeding. Animal owners still take the same pride in controlling the breeding of their 'stock' as the heads of human households used to take in choosing suitable marriage partners for their offspring.

When Aldous Huxley wrote his famous novel *Brave New World* (1932) the idea of improving the human species by applying science to human reproduction was fashionable among many scientists and social reformers. The prominent biologist J. B. S. Haldane had speculated in his futuristic book *Daedalus* (1923) that breeding from the best human genes could be accomplished by separating reproduction (done in laboratories using scientific selection) from family life and sexual relationships. In *Brave New World* people are bred in laboratories where human eggs and sperm are stored and combined by Fertilizers, using Incubators, Hatcheries, Conditioning Centres and Predestinators to produce different strains of people from Alpha to Epsilon. The aim was to produce 'standard' people in 'uniform batches', suited to their work and role in society.[1] A reproduction system similar to this had indeed been developed by the end of the 20th century, but it was used for breeding animals, not people. (Something that is notably lacking in the factory farm is the contentment that was bred into the inhabitants of the authoritarian society described by Huxley.)

Animal breeding is still about pedigree, differential valuation, uniformity and control. The values of the 19th century have survived in surprising detail. Here is the aristocracy of bloodlines, thoroughbreds, purebreds, breed standards. And there are the millions of undifferentiated working masses of food production animals, computer-selected by analysis of their attributes for a particular purpose, whose names and faces are unknown and whose achievements are mainly visible in supermarkets and fast food outlets rather than in the UK's Crufts, Aintree or the Royal Show. Human valuations of course only matter to animals if they influence the way we treat them. But we do differentiate animal populations into hierarchies of moral concern. The hierarchy is possibly headed by the favoured companion animals, through charismatic wild animals and sports animals, down to low-value food production animals, surplus and cull breeding animals, and ending with the pests slated for eradication.

This chapter looks at parallels and differences between the aims and the methods of the control of both human reproduction and animal breeding, and at how the paths of human and animal reproduction may converge or diverge in the future. While the human control of animal breeding has tightened over the last 50 years, the reproductive choices that people can make have expanded radically, both socially and technologically: artificial insemination and *in vitro* fertilization became relatively routine procedures, as they are in animals, and genetic technology started to raise the possibility again of genetic selection of babies, but more effectively than the early 20th-century eugenicists could aim for. The future will tell whether human reproduction follows animal reproduction down the route of breeds and strains and what choices people will make in a consumer market for reproductive technologies.

## 13.1.2 Animal breeding as a model for human reproductive decisions

Eugenicists of the later 19th and early 20th century drew their inspiration from Darwinian understanding of the inheritance of 'fitness' traits due to natural selection and from experiments that had shown the Mendelian inheritance of traits such as coat colour or disease in experiments in animal breeding. Some believed that traits in humans such as 'feeble-mindedness', drunkenness, 'fecklessness' and criminality were inherited in the same way as coat colour might be inherited by guinea pigs.[2] What was required, they believed, was control over human breeding in the same way as the stock breeder controls his animals. Francis Galton, an originator of the scientific study of human heredity and the originator of the term 'eugenics', constantly compared human and animal breeding. Writing in *Macmillan's Magazine* during 1865 he compared the men and women of his time as so far from what they could be under eugenic control as the 'pariah dogs of an Eastern town are to our own highly bred [dog] varieties'. With eugenics, he believed we could produce a 'highly bred human race, with no more tendency to revert to meaner ancestral types than is shown by our long-established breeds of race-horses and foxhounds'.[3]

Eugenicists bemoaned the fact that people were selected for mating much less carefully than were prize cattle. Francis Galton explained in his book *Hereditary Genius* of 1869 that in the same way as 'It is easy ... to obtain by careful selection a permanent breed of dogs or horses gifted with peculiar powers of running, or doing anything else, so it would be quite practicable to produce a highly-gifted race of men by judicious marriages during consecutive generations.'[4] Enthusiasts for eugenics tended to use the term 'stocks' to refer to the human breeding population, as they did for livestock, horses and dogs. Some contemporary critics accused eugenicists of wanting to introduce 'the methods of the stud farm' to human reproduction.[3]

Other intellectual influences of the 19th century emphasized the struggle for existence within and between human societies in the same way as animals struggle to survive and, by implication, the need to select the best. In 1798 the economist Thomas Malthus published his *Essay on the Principle of Population* arguing that human population always tends to grow faster than the growth in the means of subsistence. Herbert Spencer's book *A Theory of Population, Deduced from the General Law of Animal Fertility* (1852) coined the phrase 'Survival of the fittest', later also used by Darwin.[5] Even Darwin considered that 'excepting in the case of man himself, hardly anyone is so ignorant as to allow his worst animals to breed'.[6] While there is much evidence that Darwin abhorred slavery,[7] he also seems to have believed in a hierarchy among human races, from the 'civilised' to the 'savage'. In his *Descent of Man* (1871), Darwin predicted that the 'civilised' races would exterminate or replace the 'savage' races and exterminate the great apes.[6,8]

### 13.1.3 Improving the human species

Some of the more politically radical geneticists of the early 20th century ridiculed the eugenicists' belief in family and racial pedigrees as the carriers of the good traits that the human population needed. The biologist Lancelot Hogben (1895–1975), a professor of social biology at the London School of Economics, linked mainstream eugenics with 'ancestor-worship, anti-Semitism, colour prejudice, anti-feminism, snobbery, and obstruction to educational progress'.[2] But mainstream eugenicists enthusiastically used pedigrees to prove their point that desirable and undesirable human characteristics were inherited in different families or different races. Some were equally enthusiastic about removing poor specimens of humanity from the breeding stock and promoting the breeding of the most 'fit'. The inventor Alexander Graham Bell (1847–1922) explained in a popular article in 1908 that the genetic qualities of 'men and women who are thoroughbred' would be 'prepotent' and would lead to 'an increase in the proportion of superior offspring produced from the average or inferior with whom they have mated'.[2]

For many of the intellectuals of the time the aim of eugenics was the betterment of the human race and the abolition of poverty, rather than to target people considered 'inferior'. Eugenics seemed to offer a scientifically validated and socially progressive method of solving social problems, increasing equality, improving the human species and human welfare, as well as dealing with the challenge of unwelcome human populations.[2,3,9]

But some in the eugenics movement believed that the human species must be subjected to the same harsh processes of natural selection as described by Darwinians, including removing the least desirable people from the breeding population. The more extreme ideas put forward in the eugenicists' publications of the period, such as *Birth Control News* and *Eugenic Review*, make startling reading today but some aspects of these views were held by people who were prominent intellectuals and scientists of their time. In 1923 *Birth Control News* reported that the objectives of the Eugenics Committee of the US included 'Selective immigration, sterilization of defectives and control of everything having to do with the reproduction of human beings'. Opponents of eugenics who pointed out its inherently authoritarian bent, such as the writer G. K. Chesterton (1874–1936), were seen as unscientific and backward-looking.[3]

### 13.1.4 Preventing bad breeding

Eugenics became increasingly associated with those who wanted to restrict the population of undesirables. A meeting of the Church Congress held in Cambridge in 1910 on the subject of heredity and social responsibility discussed preventing undesirables from breeding by segregating them in work colonies, and agreed that 'the reproduction of the feeble-minded must be prevented by legislative action'.[10] Several American states and governments in Sweden, Denmark and Finland enacted various eugenic sterilization measures in the early 20th century. Such measures were strongly criticized at the time, but even H. G. Wells thought about whether the human stock might be improved by 'the sterilization of failures'.[2]

People believed that selection and rejection of people for breeding was essential for the good of human society as a whole, echoing our modern views about the importance of animal breed 'improvement'. In the sterilization of undesirables, the good of society took precedence over the wants of the individual. In 1912 Leonard Darwin, a son of Charles Darwin, suggested that a proper examination of family histories enables 'many strains [to] be discovered which no one could deny ought to be made to die out in the interest of the nation'.[3] In the US by the end of the 1920s, around 24 states had laws that restricted the marriage or permitted compulsory sterilization of people considered 'unfit for propagation', such as people who were mentally deficient, insane, suffered from epilepsy, had committed sexual offences, or were habitual criminals, among other reasons.[2,3] The 1924 Immigration Act in effect restricted the immigration of people other than north-western Europeans (assumed to be the premier human breed). Calvin Coolidge as vice-president had written in *Good Housekeeping* in 1921: 'Biological laws show ... that Nordics deteriorate when mixed with other races.'[2]

By the beginning of the 20th century, some offenders in state institutions were being sterilized in the US by castration or vasectomy. Vasectomy was not thought to need anaesthetic. In a parallel with some contemporary attitudes to animal castration without pain relief, the doctor who pioneered this method reported that 'the subject returns to work immediately and suffers no inconvenience'. By 1941 over 30,000 legal sterilizations had been carried out in the US. These laws were often opposed as unconstitutional or unscientific, and in the mid 1920s the case of Carrie Buck, a young woman who the Virginia Colony institution wanted to sterilize, went as far as the US Supreme Court.[2]

In Germany under the National Socialist regime the Eugenic Sterilization Law of 1933 applied to all people who suffered perceived hereditary disabilities, including blindness and epilepsy, and aimed to prevent 'poisoning the entire bloodstream of the race' in the interests of 'future generations'. Up to 225,000 people were sterilized within three years. Eugenicists outside Germany did not necessarily disapprove of the sterilization law, which did not at that time have specifically anti-Jewish provisions. In 1939 the Nazi regime moved on to kill tens of thousands of patients in mental institutions by either shooting or gassing, referred to as 'euthanasia'. In order to spread good genes, subsidies were paid to couples considered biologically sound to encourage fertility. Members of the Nazi SS were urged to father children with suitable women, and homes were established for the care of the SS mothers.[2]

### 13.1.5 Human rights and reproductive freedom

Scientific and political thinking about human genetics and race performed a U-turn in the second half of the 20th century. After 1945 the use of biological science as a tool of racial discrimination became increasingly discredited and the United Nations (UN) declarations in the following years strongly rejected eugenics and state control of human reproduction. Declarations on race by the United Nations Educational, Scientific and Cultural Organization (UNESCO) in 1950–1951 started from the position that 'Scientists are generally agreed that all men living today belong to a single species, *Homo sapiens*, and are derived from a common stock' and denied any scientific basis for distinctions between races, because 'mankind is one'.[11] The UN Universal Declaration of Human Rights (1948) also affirmed the reproductive freedom of all people. By Article 16, men and women of 'full age' have the right to marry and 'found a family', but only if free and full consent is given by both.[12]

The Universal Declaration did not prevent the existence of anti-'miscegenation' laws forbidding people of different races from marrying in apartheid South Africa (passed by the National Party government in 1949) and in a number of American states. In 1967 all such laws were declared unconstitutional by the US Supreme Court in its ruling that marriage was 'one of the basic civil rights of man', which 'cannot be infringed by the state'.[13]

By the 150th anniversary of Darwin's *Origin of Species* in 2009, scientists were emphasizing both the genetic unity and overlap between human populations. Current scientific thinking is that the whole world population is genetically related and that the more the genomes of individuals are studied, the more this leads to 'the blurring of our concept of discrete human populations' and to the conclusion that 'we are all multiracial'.[14]

A parallel development to the understanding of the essential genetic unity of the human species is the search to find what separates the human species from all others and, in our own eyes, makes us different and special. Scientists hoped that comparative analysis of the human, the chimpanzee and the mouse genome would reveal the secret of what it is to be human. This has not yet happened. Studies of animals' behaviour, cognitive abilities and brain function in many ways point in the opposite direction as increasing parallels continue to be found between the cognition and emotions of humans and other animals. This may have profound ethical implications for how people treat animals in the future. As the Farm Animal Welfare Council, a UK government advisory body, has pointed out: 'It is not clear that a radical distinction between human and non-human animal is now defensible, either biologically or ethically, nor that any such disjunction is sufficient to warrant the treatment of other living creatures merely as means.'[15]

## 13.2 Reproductive technologies and genetic selection in humans and animals

### 13.2.1 The development of artificial reproductive methods

Animal and human reproductive technologies developed from the same research base, often in animal experimentation, and share many features. By the last decades of the 20th century, both animal and human reproductive technology made use of the same basic elements: semen, eggs, reproductive hormones, *in vitro* fertilization, embryo transfer, cryogenic technology, DNA analysis and surrogacy. Animal and human reproductive technologies are both now large-scale industries. An estimate from research at the Harvard Business School is that infertility products and services used in 2004 in the US had a value of US$2.9 billion.[16] By 2000 1.2 million US women, or around 2 per cent of women of reproductive age, had some form of fertility treatment or investigation annually.[17] Some of the features of human fertility services that most resemble the development of the animal breeding industry are its growing market orientation, its global expansion and the potential for pre-birth genetic selection.

Artificial insemination with donor sperm is the simplest reproductive technology for both animals and people, the first recorded successful use for animals and humans being at the end of the 18th century. Cattle and human sperm could be successfully frozen and thawed by the 1950s, enabling the development of sperm banks and large-scale use. Artificial insemination for people became routine in the 1970s and led to over 1 million births worldwide within a couple of decades. Embryo transfer was first successfully carried out on rabbits in 1890, and during the 1940s and 1950s live offspring were born after embryo transfer in sheep, goats, pigs and calves. In 1971 the first commercial company offering cattle embryos, Alberta Livestock, was formed. The technology of freezing and thawing embryos of cattle and mice developed by the 1970s, enabling long-distance trading and long-term storage.[18,19]

By the early 1940s attempts were being made in the US and the UK to fertilize eggs in laboratory dishes and successfully transfer them back into a female recipient, using eggs from mice, rabbits and humans. The first human births using *in vitro* fertilization (IVF) were of Louise Brown in 1978 in England and of Elizabeth Carr in 1981 in the US. In 1997 came the birth of Dolly, the lamb cloned from the mammary cell of a six-year-old sheep, which opened the way in principle to cloning any chosen animal or human. The use of intracytoplasmic sperm injection (ICSI) with IVF, where sperm is injected directly into the egg, has reduced the need to use donor sperm by about 85 per cent in the UK since the early 1990s.[20]

In the US, 57,564 babies were born as a result of IVF cycles reported to the Centers for Disease Control database in 2007, and nearly 16,000 embryo transfers used donor eggs (11 per cent of all treatment cycles).[17] In the UK 12,596 babies were born from IVF treatment in 2006 (1.7 per cent of all births).[20] In 2009 the replacement of mitochrondrial DNA in monkey eggs opened the way for using the technique in humans, using eggs from both the genetic mother and another woman in order to prevent the inheritance of diseases known to be inherited by mutations in the mother's mitochondrial DNA.[21]

## 13.2.2 Selecting and using donor services

In countries where centralized legal regulation of human reproductive technology is relatively light, such as the US, a consumer market in reproductive products and fertility services has developed. Some commercial sperm banks offer information on their donors' religion, physique and temperament, occupation, education and family health history, sometimes with photographs and audiotapes.[16] In 2009 California Cryobank offered 'the largest and most diverse donor selection in the industry' and provided lifestyle profiles of selected 'donors of the month' with photos of the men's previous offspring. Potential customers could select hair colour, eye colour and ethnic origin before browsing the website for available donors.[16,22]

**Table 13.1** *Parallels and differences in the development of animal and human reproductive technologies*

| Technology or application | Application in animals | Application in people |
|---|---|---|
| Artificial insemination (AI) | • Circa 1780: AI of bitch, birth of puppies<br>• Early 20th century: births from horses, sheep and cattle, commercial use for cattle<br>• Mid 20th century: frozen-thawed cattle sperm<br>• Late 20th century: routine method for inseminating dairy cattle and pigs; ongoing research on freeze-thawing pig sperm<br>• From 1970s: oestrus control by intra-vaginal progesterone release devices[18,19] | • 1790s: impregnation via syringe, occasional use in 19th and early 20th century<br>• 1950s: human sperm frozen and thawed<br>• From 1970s: AI from donor sperm widely available[18] |
| Embryo transfer (ET) using superovulation and AI (multiple ovulation and embryo transfer, or MOET) | • 1890: in rabbits<br>• Late 1940s and 1950s: sheep, goats, pigs and cattle<br>• 1970s commercial ET in cattle<br>• 1970s: frozen-thawed embryos of mice, rabbits, and cattle<br>• Current ET use: cows, horses, sheep, goats, deer, pigs[18,19,23] | |
| Egg extraction, *in vitro* fertilization (IVF) and embryo transfer | • From1960s: mice<br>• 1982: IVF calf<br>• Current: cows, sheep, goats, deer, pigs<br>• Experimental uses[18,19] | • From 1978: IVF<br>• From 1990s: intracytoplasmic sperm injection (ICSI) |
| Surrogacy | • Yes, used with all ET and cloning procedures | • Yes, either gestational surrogacy or genetic surrogacy using AI |
| Sex determination | • Cattle (sperm sorting)<br>• Ongoing sperm-sorting research in pigs | • Yes, using IVF plus pre-implantation genetic diagnosis (PGD)<br>• Sperm sorting in development |
| Genetic selection | • Selective breeding by performance records and pedigree<br>• Statistical analysis to calculate breeding values<br>• Genetic testing of potential breeding animals (genetic diseases, relatedness, quantitative trait loci (QTL) for production or other traits)<br>• Mitochondrial DNA replacement[21] | • Choice of egg and sperm donors (phenotype)<br>• IVF (using PGD):<br>  – for genetic diseases<br>  – for gender selection<br>  – potentially for traits (eye colour prediction?) |

| Technology or application | Application in animals | Application in people |
|---|---|---|
| Genetic engineering | • From1980s–1990s: mutant and transgenic fish, sheep, pigs, rats, mice, rabbits; gene-targeted and knockout mice; transgenic cattle<br>• 2000s: gene-targeted and knockout pigs and rats; transgenic monkeys; other experimental applications[24] | • Likely in future research, including human transgenic embryos and human stem cells in animals[25] |
| Reproductive cloning by nuclear transfer (live offspring) | • 1950s: frogs<br>• 1980s: sheep and cattle cloned from embryonic cells<br>• 1997: Dolly – sheep cloned from adult cell<br>• 1990s–2000s: cattle, sheep, pigs, horses, cats, dogs, 'endangered' guar and wildcats<br>• Other experimental applications[18,19,26] | • No: research on production of cloned human embryos only |
| Inter-species gestational surrogacy | • Yes, for cloning 'endangered species'[26] | • No |
| Inter-species hybrid embryos or embryo production using egg of another species | • Yes[27] | • Yes[27] |

For those women (or male couples) who are not able to use their own eggs in IVF treatment, the market for eggs has become differentiated as some customers pay more for what they perceive as the best genes. At the top end of the market, eggs may cost US$50,000 (an 'Ivy League egg'[4]) although prices are more likely to be a few thousand dollars. Buyers can specify a donor with a prescribed minimum height, SAT score, hair and eye colour or athletic ability. Commercial providers list their potential egg donors with information on parents' ethnicity, skin, eye and hair colour, hair texture, height, weight, education (such as 'pre-med'), sports activities ('tennis') and interests ('painting').[16,28]

The market for eggs has apparently expanded even though the process of egg donation is unpleasant. The woman donating (or selling) eggs requires weeks of hormone treatment with different drugs to control the timing of her oestrous cycle and then induce superovulation. (Superovulation is the standard treatment, but it can be avoided in some cases by removing immature eggs and maturing them in the laboratory.) In the typical treatment, the egg donor undergoes daily injections and multiple medical appointments for blood testing and ultrasound examination. Side effects commonly include mood swings, abdominal swelling, pressure in the ovarian area and bruising at injection sites, and can include temporary menopause-like symptoms and, occasionally, the serious condition of 'ovarian hyperstimulation syndrome' where fluid leaks into the abdomen.[16,28–30] Egg harvesting from the ovary is a surgical procedure causing 'mild to moderate discomfort' in which a needle is guided by ultrasound through the vaginal wall to reach the ovary. This may need additional drugs to control nausea and antibiotics to prevent infection. Egg harvesting is not without risks and in rare cases leads to serious damage to nearby organs.[29] This method of egg retrieval from women uses the same surgical technique as is used routinely to remove eggs from cows for *in vitro* production of bovine embryos.[19]

### 13.2.3 Using gestational surrogates

Gestational surrogacy, where the surrogate mother has no genetic relationship to the embryo that is implanted in her uterus, has raised a different type of concern – that of 'renting wombs'.[16] In this case the genetic or social characteristics of the surrogate may be of no interest to the person who uses her services, providing she is healthy and avoids damaging the unborn baby. Payments to a surrogate in the US are of the order of US$20,000, which can be very many times the minimum wage in some developing countries. US providers of fertility services may charge between US$50,000 and $70,000 in total for a surrogate pregnancy, depending on whether a donor egg is required.[16,31]

Some have concluded that in the US a surrogacy structure developed where embryos were typically the offspring of relatively wealthy (often white) couples, and were gestated by relatively poor non-white women.[16] In the UK, a market developed for British Asian couples to use surrogacy services in India, partly because of the lower cost and partly because Asian egg donors and surrogates are very rare in the UK. Fertility clinics in India are reported to maintain houses where several surrogates can live, some clinics having 20 surrogate pregnancies ongoing at any one time. The women serving as surrogates can earn ten times what their normal salary would be.[32] As at 2009, commercial surrogacy was not permitted in the UK.

### 13.2.4 Embryo screening and designer babies

Technology is moving in the direction that will allow increasing genetic selection of humans before birth. Pre-implantation genetic diagnosis (PGD) is a procedure where embryos are screened before implantation by removing one cell for testing, and was originally intended to identify embryos carrying known genetic diseases. In 2009 the UK's Human Fertilisation and Embryology Authority (HFEA) operated a list of over 60 inherited genetic disorders that could be tested for in pre-implantation embryos, including thalassaemia, cystic fibrosis, the BRAC 1 breast cancer gene, Duchenne muscular dystrophy, haemophilia, Huntingdon's disease and sickle cell anaemia, among others. In 2006 42 babies were born after PGD for genetic conditions, and the procedure was used in 1 in every 240 IVF cycles in the UK.[33]

PGD can also be used for gender selection of embryos and is almost 100 per cent reliable. Sperm-sorting methods, similar to those used to produce sexed semen in cattle, are also being developed for humans (known as the Microsort technology), but to date produced less reliable sex selection. As a result, PGD for gender selection is in high demand globally from those countries where it is legally and freely available. In the UK, the HFEA has authorized gender selection only when a sex-linked genetic defect is being screened for, and no licensed clinics may offer gender selection for social reasons, such as 'family balancing'. In a case taken to the UK High Court, PGD was finally allowed in order to produce a tissue match for stem therapy for an existing child in the family because this procedure would also mean screening the embryo for the same genetic disorder. PGD of IVF embryos can already potentially offer further genetic selection services, such as prediction of eye colour.[34–36]

## 13.2.5 Surplus embryos

Laboratory production of embryos, whether animal or human, often involves producing more embryos than are implanted. In IVF treatment for women, typically around ten eggs are retrieved in each cycle of superovulation. After the eggs have been fertilized, usually one or two embryos are selected for implantation (although international reports of the transfer of multiple embryos continue). This often leaves a surplus of viable embryos for frozen storage, either to be used in a subsequent treatment cycle or for long-term storage or for disposal. Future screening techniques to select only the 'best' eggs may reduce the number of embryos produced but, in the past, tens of thousands of surplus embryos have been built up.

By the early 2000s the US was estimated to have 400,000 stored frozen embryos.[37] In Britain half of the 2 million embryos recorded as created between 1991 and 2005 were not used, and regulations specify that embryos can only be stored for up to five years, with an extension to ten years on request, before they are destroyed.[38] To some, the creation and destruction of surplus human embryos is unethical. Others in the scientific community would rather see the surplus embryos used for research, possibly reimbursing couples or health providers some of their large costs for fertility drugs. The UK allows the use of surplus IVF embryos in approved research programmes, under licence, if the use of human embryos is 'necessary' and 'justified'.[16,39]

## 13.2.6 Hybrids and transgenics

There is a long history of the scientific mixing of animal and human DNA and mixing the DNA of different animals. In 'pharming', human DNA has been put into animal embryos to produce various human pharmaceutical proteins in the milk or blood of animals. As long ago as the 1980s pig embryos were genetically engineered to carry human and bovine growth hormone genes.[40] Early-stage embryos have been created by transferring DNA from the horse, antelope, buffalo, and yak into cow eggs, DNA from monkeys, the panda and the cat into rabbit eggs, and DNA from the dog into yak eggs. Embryonic cells from sheep and goats have been combined to produce a live chimeric goat-sheep ('geep').[27]

More recently, scientists working on human embryonic stem cells have seen a need to use animal eggs to produce human embryos because human eggs are in short supply. Animal eggs taken from superovulated rabbits or from cow ovaries obtained from slaughterhouses can in principle be used to produce human embryos by the process of nuclear transfer. These embryos contain a small contribution from the mitochondrial DNA of the animal from which the egg was taken, but their nuclear DNA is human. These are referred to as 'cytoplasmic hybrids', rather than real genetic hybrids that contain nuclear DNA from two species. Human nuclear DNA has in the past been put into eggs taken from rabbits and cows, with variable success.[27,41]

In 2008 the UK's HFEA licensed research projects that would combine human DNA with eggs from animals such as rabbits, pigs, cows, sheep and goats. The UK Parliament went further and voted in favour of the creation of not only 'cytoplasmic' hybrids but true genetic animal–human hybrid embryos for research purposes. The 2008 Human Fertilization and Embryology Act thus enables research on human–animal hybrid ('human-admixed') embryos up to 14 days of development. Most countries now accept research on surplus human embryos and the creation of (at least) cytoplasmic hybrids for stem-cell research under licence. The production of animal–human hybrids for gestation is seen, at present, as beyond the bounds of public acceptability in most jurisdictions.[27,42] The Academy of Medical Sciences envisages that scientists may need to make both 'human–human' transgenic embryos, where human DNA is manipulated without inserting animal genes, and also real genetic hybrid embryos by mixing human and animal sperm and eggs, as well as creating more research animals that contain human DNA and cells.[23]

## 13.2.7 Consent and welfare

The services of egg donation and surrogacy for payment, sometimes considerable, have raised questions about choice and welfare. Both egg donation and surrogacy can entail medical risks. The long-term effects of taking fertility drugs are unknown and some scientists have suggested that hormones given to 'hyperstimulate' the ovaries may increase the risk of developing cancer.[43] Unlike blood or sperm donation, donating eggs through hyperstimulation is a potentially 'life-threatening risk'.[30]

Stem-cell research, seen as one of the most important areas of human medical science, needs human embryos. This need has put pressure on scientists to obtain human eggs and in turn raised the possibility of pressure on women to produce them. Typical guidelines insist that 'it is imperative that embryos (or gametes donated to produce embryos) for research are freely given and that people donating them have made an informed choice'.[44] In the past, scientists have not been able to compete with commercial fertility clinics in the market for eggs because paying women to produce eggs for research has been forbidden by law in most countries. Some scientists now believe that it should be allowed, and in 2009 the state of New York became the first jurisdiction to allow payment for eggs intended for research.[44] Scientists working at Seoul National University are reported to have used over 2200 eggs from 119 donors, some from women members of the research team, in their attempts to create human cloned embryos. In 2006 two Korean women involved in this programme took legal action, claiming that they had not been informed of all the risks and the side effects of producing the eggs.[45]

In the UK, explicit payment for reproductive goods and services is not permitted, and the state takes a paternalistic view of the decisions that people should be allowed to make about the use of reproductive technology. The globalization of the reproduction market may make regulation harder in future, and has already started to do so as British couples use IVF and surrogacy services internationally.

The essential difference between reproductive technology in animals and in people is not in the technology that is available, but in the aims and values that it serves. The application of human reproductive technology is primarily to assist the fertility of the person being treated and to ensure the health of the unborn baby. In the case of animals, the technology is used for the benefit of the animals' owners, not the animals. Maintaining and optimizing family relationships and protecting the bond between mother and offspring are some of the most important human social values. In animal reproduction, the breaking of social bonds and maternal deprivation are routine.

Animal breeding may provide a vision – or perhaps a warning – about how consumer choice in genetic selection of babies could develop. When people have the power to create a creature to a specification, whether to reflect a value, to make a statement or to turn a profit, they have often put the best interests of the potential offspring to one side.

## 13.3 Animal breeding, human interests and animals' interests

We are very concerned, rightly, that our approaches to human reproduction should never come to resemble the ways in which we breed animals. But, in reverse, animals would greatly benefit from some of the consideration for the interests of every individual that is still a fundamental part of society's approach to human reproduction.

As the understanding of what animals need for physical and psychological well-being expands globally,[46] it has become clear that human wishes or technical possibilities may have to be limited to meet the requirements of animal welfare. For example, selective breeding of excessively fast-growing animals for meat is often incompatible with the interests of the animals in not suffering from painful lameness and from heart disease. Fast-growing meat animals are not a necessity for human society. In these cases, it would be reasonable for the interests of those animals in avoiding pain to take precedence over the wishes of the people who own or use them.

Several examples exist where the law has already put the interest of animals in health and well-being before human freedom of action in animal breeding. These include ending the use of barren battery cages for laying hens (eggs are a reproductive product), of sow stalls (gestation crates) for pregnant pigs, and veal crates for young calves, already agreed in the European Union and in some states and by some food-producing companies in the US. Restrictions are also placed on the use of bitches in licensed dog breeding. It may happen in future that the recommendations of the 1995 resolution of the Council of Europe on dog and cat breeding,[47] to end exaggerated head or body shapes, distorted eye shapes, hairlessness or taillessness, are translated into national laws. Legal or voluntary decisions may end the breeding of dairy cows genetically capable of producing excessive quantities of milk, of sows genetically capable of producing excessively large litters of piglets, and of meat chickens genetically capable of growing excessively fast, on the grounds of the damage to the health of these animals that results. The EU's Scientific Panel on Animal Health and Welfare was scheduled to review the welfare implications of broiler chicken genetics during 2010. Medical scientists may, in future, make determined efforts to find alternatives to breeding animals as 'models' for disease.

Changing existing practices would not always be easy. There are some areas of animal breeding or population control, such as the control of pest animals and the conservation of endangered wild species, where the problems are intractable and entirely acceptable solutions are still to be found. But there are other areas, such as the breeding of farmed, companion and sports animals, where we could take immediate action to improve the life experience of the animals without any loss to society as a whole. In the case of farmed animals (by far the numerically largest category), changes would be in the interest of our own species. A move to dual-purpose and lower-yielding breeds and to more extensive and humane husbandry methods would entail a reduction in the production and consumption of animal-based foods in the most developed countries of the world at least. This would be highly beneficial for both the local and the global environment and for human health.

## Notes

1   Huxley, A. (1932, 1969) *Brave New World*, Penguin Books; Haldane, J. B. S. (1923) *Daedalus, or Science in the Future*, Kegan Paul

2   Kevles, D. J. (1995) *In the Name of Eugenics: Genetics and the Uses of Human Heredity*, Harvard University Press

3   Chesterton, G. K. (1922, 2000) *Eugenics and Other Evils*, M. J. Perry (ed), Inkling Books

4   Cited in Spar, D. L. (2006) *The Baby Business: How Money, Science and Politics Drive the Commerce of Conception*, Harvard Business School Press

5   Summaries of contemporary views are given in Oldroyd, D. R. (1983) *Darwinian Impacts: An Introduction to the Darwinian Revolution*, The Open University Press

6    Darwin, C. (1871, 2004) *The Descent of Man, and Selection in Relation to Sex*, Introduction by J. Moore and A. Desmond, Penguin Books
7    Bynum, W. F. (2009) 'A vision of humanity united', *Nature*, vol 457, pp792–793
8    See also Clark, S. R. L. (2000) 'Deconstructing Darwin', in N. Thompson (ed) *Instilling Ethics*, Rowman & Littlefield, pp119–140
9    Kline, W. (2001) *Building a Better Race: Gender, Sexuality, and Eugenics from the Turn of the Century to the Baby Boom*, University of California Press
10   *Nature* (1910) 'Heredity at the Church Congress', *Nature*, vol 84, 6 October, p431
11   UNESCO (1950) *The Race Question*, 18 July 1950; UNESCO (1951) *Statement on the Nature of Race and Race Differences*, L. C. Dunn, rapporteur, June 1951
12   United Nations General Assembly (1948) *The Universal Declaration of Human Rights*
13   *Economist* (2008) 'Mildred Loving, law-changer, died on May 2nd, aged 68', *Economist*, 15 May 2008
14   Chakravarti, A. (2009) 'Kinship: Race relations', *Nature*, vol 457, pp380–381
15   Farm Animal Welfare Council (1998) *Report on the Implications of Cloning for the Welfare of Farmed Livestock*, FAWC; the evolutionary and cognitive parallels between great apes and humans are discussed in Cavalieri, P. and Singer P. (eds) (1993) *The Great Ape Project*, Fourth Estate
16   Spar, D. L. (2006) *The Baby Business: How Money, Science and Politics Drive the Commerce of Conception*, Harvard Business School Press
17   CDC (Centers for Disease Control) (2009) *Assisted Reproductive Technology: Home*, www.cdc.gov/ART/; National Summary Table, 2007, apps.nccd.cdc.gov/ART/NSR.aspx?SelectedYear=2007, accessed August 2009; data for 2007 are preliminary
18   Wilmut, I., Campbell, K. and Tudge, C. (2000) *The Second Creation: The Age of Biological Control, by the Scientists Who Cloned Dolly*, Headline
19   Gordon, I. (2004) *Reproductive Technologies in Farm Animals*, CABI Publishing
20   Human Fertilisation and Embryology Authority (2009) *Donor Conception – Treatments: Treatments and Patients Using Donated Eggs or Donated Embryos 1992–2007*, www.hfea.gov.uk/3414.html, accessed August 2009; HFEA (2008) *Facts and Figures 2006: Fertility Problems and Treatment*, HFEA
21   Tachibana, M. et al (2009) 'Mitochondrial gene replacement in primate offspring and embryonic stem cells', *Nature*, vol 461, pp367–372; Cyranoski, D. (2009) 'DNA swap could avoid inherited diseases', *Nature*, Online news, 26 August, www.nature.com
22   California Cryobank, www.cryobank.com/, accessed March 2009
23   Thibier, M. (2006) *Data retrieval committee annual report*, International Embryo Transfer Society (IETS), www.iets.org/pdf/data_retrieval/december2006.pdf
24   Niemann, H. and Keus, W. A. (2007) 'Transgenic farm animals: an update', *Reproduction, Fertility and Development*, vol 19, pp762–770
25   The Academy of Medical Sciences (2007) *Inter-Species Embryos*, AMS; The Academy of Medical Sciences (2007) 'Inter-species embryo research vital for understanding and treating human disease', Media release, 17 June; The Academy of Medical Sciences (2009) 'Academy launches study on the use of animals containing human material', Media release, 10 November
26   *Nature* (2001) 'News in brief: Gaur's death a setback for cloning hopes', *Nature*, vol 409, 18 Janaury, p277; Goméz, M. C. et al (2003) 'Nuclear transfer of synchronized African wild cat somatic cells into enucleated domestic cat oocytes', *Biology of Reproduction*, vol 69, pp1032–1041
27   Human Fertilisation and Embryology Authority (2007) *Hybrids and Chimeras: A Report on the Findings of the Consultation*, HFEA

28  Surrogacy Solutions, 'Egg donors', www.surrogacysolutions.net/donors.htm, accessed August 2009; The Fertility Institutes, 'Egg donors and procedures, Partial list of egg donor profiles', www.fertility-docs.com/egg_donors.phtml, accessed August 2009

29  Egg Donor Information Project (2002) *The Medical Procedure of Egg Donation*, Stanford University, www.stanford.edu/class/siw198q/ websites/eggdonor/procedures.html, accessed August 2009

30  Mundy, L. (2007) *Everything Conceivable: How Assisted Reproduction is Changing Men, Women and the World*, Penguin Books

31  The Fertility Institutes, 'Fertility evaluation and procedures: Procedure fees', www.fertility-docs.com/news_events.phtml?ID=23, accessed 26 March 2009

32  BBC Radio Asian Network (2008) *Asian Network Report: Baby Tourism*, 13 October

33  Human Fertilisation and Embryology Authority (2009) *Latest UK Pre-Implantation Genetic Diagnosis (PGD) Figures – 2006*, www.hfea.gov.uk/1271.html, accessed August 2009

34  Kalb, C., Nadeua, B. and Schafer, S. (2004) 'Science: Brave new babies – parents now have the power to choose the sex of their children', *Newsweek*, 2 February

35  Public Health Genetics Unit, Wellcome Trust (2003) 'Appeal Court decides to allow Hashmi family to use PGD with tissue typing', News release, 10 April

36  The Fertility Institutes (2008) *Microsort Limited Availability (and Alternative Gender Selection Offer via PGD)*, 8 May, www.fertility-docs.com/ news_events.phtml, accessed March 2009; The Fertility Institutes (2008) *News: Eye and Hair Color Program Suspension – New!*, 2 March, www.fertility-docs.com/ news_events.phtml, accessed March 2009

37  *Living on Earth* (2006) 'The baby business: Interview with Debora Spar', *Living on Earth*, 1 September 2006

38  Woolf, M. (2007) 'IVF clinics destroy 1m "waste" embryos', *Sunday Times*, 30 December

39  Hen, B. C. and Cao, T. (2006) 'Refund fertility-treatment costs for donated embryos', *Nature*, vol 443, p26; Human Fertilisation and Embryology Authority (2006/2007) *Human Embryo Research in the UK*, HFEA

40  Pursel, V. G. et al (1989) 'Genetic engineering of livestock', *Science*, vol 244, pp1281–1288; Pursel, V. G. et al (1990) 'Integration, expression and germ-line transmission of growth-related genes in pigs', *Journal of Reproduction and Fertility, Supplement*, vol 41, pp77–87

41  Chen, Y. et al (2003) 'Embryonic stem cells generated by nuclear transfer of human somatic nuclei into rabbit oocytes', *Cell Research*, vol 13, pp251–263; Chung, Y. et al (2009) 'Reprogramming of human somatic cells using human and animal oocytes', *Cloning and Stem Cells*, vol 11, no 2, pp213–223; Coghlan, A. (2009) 'Fatal blow for stem cells from human-animal hybrids?', *New Scientist*, 4 February 2009, p11

42  Human Fertilisation and Embryology Authority (2008) *Statement on Licensing of Applications to Carry Out Research Using Human–Animal Cytoplasmic Hybrid Embryos*, 17 January, HFEA; *Nature* (2008) 'British Parliament backs hybrid embryos', *Nature*, vol 453, p441; Human Fertilisation and Embryology Act 2008, Part 1, Section 4, 'Prohibitions in connection with genetic material not of human origin'

43  Calderon-Margalit, R. et al (2009) 'Cancer risk after exposure to treatments for ovulation induction', *American Journal of Epidemiology*, vol 169, no 3, pp365–375

44  Human Fertilisation and Embryology Authority (2007) *Human Embryo Research in the UK*, HFEA; New Scientist (2009) 'New York researchers can pay for human eggs', *New Scientist*, 27 June 2009, p6; Maher, B. (2009) 'Egg shortage hits race to clone human stem cells', *Nature*, vol 453, pp828–829; *Nature* (2009) 'The ethics of egg manipulation', *Nature*, vol 460, p1057

45  *Nature* (2006) 'Korean women launch lawsuit over egg donation', *Nature*, vol 440, p1102; BBC (2005) 'S. Korea cloning pioneer disgraced', BBC News online, 24 November, http://news.bbc.co.uk

46  OIE Global Conference on Animal Welfare (2004) *Context Paper: Applying Science to Animal Welfare*, www.oie.int/eng/Welfare_2004/context%20paper.htm; conference papers downloadable at www.oie.int/eng/Welfare_2004/speakers.htm, accessed August 2009

47  Report of the Meeting of the Multilateral Consultation on the European Convention for the Protection of Pet Animals (ETS 125), Strasbourg, 7–10 March 1995

# Index